$39.00

**W9-ANA-592**

# The ATHENE Series

**An International Collection of Feminist Books**

General Editors
**Gloria Bowles**
**Renate Klein**
**Janice Raymond**

Consulting Editor
**Dale Spender**

The Athene Series assumes that all those who are concerned with formulating explanations of the way the world works need to know and appreciate the significance of basic feminist principles.

The growth of feminist research has challenged almost all aspects of social organization in our culture. The Athene Series focuses on the construction of knowledge and the exclusion of women from the process—both as theorists and subjects of study—and offers innovative studies that challenge established theories and research.

On Athene—When Metis, goddess of wisdom who presided over all knowledge was pregnant with Athene, she was swallowed up by Zeus who then gave birth to Athene from his head. The original Athene is thus the parthenogenetic daughter of a strong mother and as the feminist myth goes, at the "third birth" of Athene she stops being Zeus' obedient mouthpiece and returns to her real source: the science and wisdom of womankind.

MEN'S STUDIES MODIFIED The Impact of Feminism on the Academic Disciplines
*Dale Spender*, editor

WOMAN'S NATURE Rationalizations of Inequality
*Marian Lowe* and *Ruth Hubbard*, editors

MACHINA EX DEA Feminist Perspectives on Technology
*Joan Rothschild*, editor

SCIENCE AND GENDER A Critique of Biology and Its Theories on Women
*Ruth Bleier*

WOMAN IN THE MUSLIM UNCONSCIOUS
*Fatna A. Sabbah*

MEN'S IDEAS/WOMEN'S REALITIES *Popular Science*, 1870-1915
*Louise Michele Newman*, editor

BLACK FEMINIST CRITICISM Perspectives on Black Women Writers
*Barbara Christian*

THE SISTER BOND A Feminist View of a Timeless Connection
*Toni A.H. McNaron*, editor

EDUCATING FOR PEACE A Feminist Perspective
*Birgit Brock Utne*

STOPPING RAPE Successful Survival Strategies
*Pauline B. Bart* and *Patricia H. O'Brien*

TEACHING SCIENCE AND HEALTH FROM A FEMINIST PERSPECTIVE
A Practical Guide
*Sue V. Rosser, editor*

FEMINIST APPROACHES TO SCIENCE
*Ruth Bleier, editor*

INSPIRING WOMEN  Reimagining the Muse
*Mary K. DeShazer*

MADE TO ORDER  The Myth of Reproductive and Genetic Progress
*Patricia Spallone* and *Deborah Lynn Steinberg, editors*

TEACHING TECHNOLOGY FROM A FEMINIST PERSPECTIVE
A Practical Guide
*Joan Rothschild*

FEMINISM WITHIN THE SCIENCE AND HEALTH CARE PROFESSIONS
Overcoming Resistance
*Sue V. Rosser, editor*

RUSSIAN WOMEN'S STUDIES  Essays on Sexism in Soviet Culture
*Tatyana Mamonova*

TAKING OUR TIME  Feminist Perspectives on Temporality
*Frieda Johles Forman, editor, with Caoran Sowton*

RADICAL VOICES  A Decade of Feminist Resistance from *Women's Studies
International Forum*
*Renate D. Klein* and *Deborah Lynn Steinberg, editors*

THE RECURRING SILENT SPRING
*H. Patricia Hynes*

EXPOSING NUCLEAR PHALLACIES
*Diana E.H. Russell, editor*

THE WRITING OR THE SEX?  or why you don't have to read women's writing to
know it's no good
*Dale Spender*

FEMINIST PERSPECTIVES ON PEACE AND PEACE EDUCATION
*Birgit Brock-Utne*

THE SEXUAL LIBERALS AND THE ATTACK ON FEMINISM
*Dorchen Leidholdt* and *Janice G. Raymond, editors*

WHENCE THE GODDESSES  A Source Book
*Miriam Robbins Dexter*

NARODNIKI WOMEN  Russian Women Who Sacrificed Themselves for the
Dream of Freedom
*Margaret Maxwell*

FEMALE-FRIENDLY SCIENCE  Applying Women's Studies Methods and Theories to
Attract Students
*Sue V. Rosser*

SPEAKING FREELY  Unlearning the Lies of the Fathers' Tongues
*Julia Penelope*

BETWEEN WORLDS  Women Writers of Chinese Ancestry
*Amy Ling*

THE REFLOWERING OF THE GODDESS
*Gloria Feman Orenstein*

ALL SIDES OF THE SUBJECT  Women and Biography
*Teresa Iles, editor*

CALLING THE EQUALITY BLUFF  Women in Israel
*Barbara Swirski* and *Marilyn P. Safir, editors*

LIVING BY THE PEN  Early British Women Writers
*Dale Spender, editor*

# Living By The Pen

## Early British Women Writers

EDITED BY

## Dale Spender

TEACHERS COLLEGE PRESS
Teachers College Press, Columbia University
New York and London

Published by Teachers College Press, 1234 Amsterdam Avenue, New York, New York

*Library of Congress Cataloging-in-Publication Data*
Living by the Pen : early British women writers / edited by Dale
    Spender. — 1st ed.
        p.   cm. — (The Athene series)
    Includes index.
    ISBN 0-8077-6260-1 (alk. paper). — ISBN 0-8077-6259-8 (pbk. :
alk. paper)
        1. English fiction — 18th century — History and criticism.   2. Women
and literature — Great Britain — History — 18th century.   3. English
fiction — Women authors — History and criticism   4. Sex role in
literature.   I. Spender, Dale.   II. Series.
PR858.W6L58   1992
823′.5099287 — dc20                                          90-49804

Printed on acid-free paper

Manufactured in the United States of America

99  98  97  96  95  94  93  92      8  7  6  5  4  3  2  1

For **Faith Bandler,**
another initiator of women's literary traditions

# Contents

# Acknowledgments

I would like to thank the convenor of the first University of London Women's Studies Summer Institute, Diana Leonard, without whom this book would not have been realized. I would also like to thank the participants in the Early British Women Writers course at the Institute, many of whom have contributed to this volume. Ros Ballaster and Jane Spencer, both of whom presented state-of-the-art and excellent lectures, were inspirational in terms of the course and the construction of this volume.

I would also like to thank Janet Todd for sharing so much of her knowledge of the period with me, and I am grateful to the Athene editors for their support and enthusiasm for this project. I have a particular debt to Phyllis Hall, whose personal commitment to feminist publishing has made it possible for many women's voices to be heard.

I am indebted to my sister, Lynne Spender, for her editing (and culinary) skills and to Robyn Daniels for reading between the lines; and I owe Cheris Kramarae—the best possible colleague—so many apologies for leaving her to deal with some of our joint responsibilities while I have been busy—reading novels.

# Living By The Pen

# Introduction

## A Vindication of the Writing Woman

===== Dale Spender =====

While many changes took place in the eighteenth century, two are of primary concern here; they are:

the emergence of the novel, and
the establishment of the professional woman writer.

But these two major developments of the eighteenth century are not in themselves the sole concern. That the two occurrences are not normally linked together, that the possible correlations between the success of women *and* the genre have not been a focal point in literary history, is also a matter which calls for attention. In drawing together these two great events—the birth of the novel and the growth of the professional woman writer—and in looking at some of the reasons behind their apparent separation and suppression, new issues are raised and new connections are made.

The following questions help to suggest the scope of this fascinating literary area:

Who were these eighteenth-century women writers,
what did they write, and
what was their relationship to the novel?

Why did they write,
what did they write about, and
what was the response to their writing?

What were the conditions under which they wrote,
what was their creative and professional achievement and

Why is their emergence and contribution not part of the readily acknowledged cultural heritage?

1

Although it is not possible in this introduction to address all these questions at length, it is possible to give some idea of the extent and diversity of this heritage and to posit some of the research priorities of the future.

Because of the increasing interest being shown in early British women writers, the picture is constantly changing. Already these questions have lost some of the shock-force they had when asked in 1985; that was the year the University of London Institute of Education planned a summer school at which the course Early British Women Writers was to be offered. When taught in 1987, the course not only proved to be very popular (with many of the participants providing contributions for this volume), but it also prompted a particular line of discussion: How could it be that there were so many early women writers, that they had overcome so many obstacles and written so many books, when in contemporary times so few of them were in print, so few of them were known, there were so few courses (were there any others?), so few publications on them. (One exception was Fidelis Morgan's excellent publication on the women playwrights, *The Female Wits: Women Playwrights of the Restoration,* 1981.) There are questions here about the nature of knowledge as well as those about the women and their work. (Many of these issues are discussed in Cheris Kramarae and Dale Spender, in press.)

Since 1985 some of the more pressing problems have been remedied. For example, many of these early British women writers are now much better known thanks to the availability of such excellent publications as *Fetter'd or Free? British Women Novelists 1670–1815,* edited by Mary Anne Schofield and Cecilia Macheski (1986); *The Rise of the Woman Novelist; From Aphra Behn to Jane Austen* by Jane Spencer (1986); and the considerable contributions of Janet Todd—*Sensibility; An Introduction* (1986) and *A Dictionary of British and American Women Writers 1660–1800* (1987); to name but a few.

Some of these early women writers have been brought back into print, partly because of the efforts of women's publishing houses and presses (see particularly *Mothers of the Novel Reprint Series* [a list of reprint titles is included at the end of this article] and Virago Classics). Internationally, in English departments and Women's Studies courses, more interest is being shown—perhaps even as a product of feminist interest and pressure—in the contributions of these women writers in both their own times and in contemporary terms. But still, many issues remain unresolved and many questions unanswered: issues about professional women writers and about the transmission of knowledge from one generation to the next.

Then too, the area is so vast that it is difficult to survey and itemize all that it contains. It is located so far in the past (and has been so shamefully neglected) that much of the material and many of the records have been lost, buried, or mislaid, so that it is a demanding task to find all the women and their publications, let alone to read and assess them. Currently, the information which has become available has done little else than whet the appetite.

A door may have been opened and a rich resource glimpsed, but impatience to explore and document the find is not the only response; there is a measure of frustration as well. Why was the door ever closed? Why does it seem so difficult now to keep it open? And is this concealment of women's creativity but an unfortunate accident of the past, or does it have contemporary implications? What is the position of the woman writer, the place of her work, past, present, and future?

These are some of the topics that are the substance of this collection. Not that any claim is being made for comprehensiveness; quite the contrary. As might be expected with a relatively recently unearthed research area, the gaps in knowledge are extensive. But in opening the door just a little further, in noting what *is* there, as well as what remains to be examined, this book plays a part in recovering and reconstituting women's participation in the literary heritage.

Because the articles in this collection cannot attempt to cover the many concerns that emerge, this overview is provided. Once the broad outlines have been sketched, it can be much easier to place in context the individual writers and works, as well as their collective achievement and the response it gave rise to. Where possible, further reading will be referenced, and where practicable, future research directions will be recommended.

## WHO WERE THE EIGHTEENTH-CENTURY WOMEN WRITERS AND WHAT DID THEY WRITE?

The number of women writers of the period and the range of their publications are readily demonstrated by the list of entries in *A Dictionary of British and American Women Writers 1669–1800*. And while the table now requires modification (with more entries added and some of the existing ones clarified), the inventory which is published in *Mothers of the Novel* (Dale Spender, 1986: pp 119–137) and which includes 106 writers and their 568 novels, serves to emphasize the astonishing extent of the achievement. Not that women's literary output was confined to novels, of course.

Women wrote across every existing genre and played an innovative role in the evolution of new forms as well. The following summary provides some of the basic information in terms of who these women were and what they wrote.

### Letters and Journals

The primary source of women's writing was letters and journals. As so many female critics have suggested, Virginia Woolf among them, letter writing has been one of the literary forms actively encouraged in women. It has also been

suggested that it is a mark of women's creative achievement that they should
have been able to transform this genre into the epistolary novel and, in the
process, provide themselves with a profession (see Perry, 1980, for further
discussion).

This was the pattern that evolved: allowed to excel at the art of letter writing, women expanded the form to meet some of their own needs for information, self-realization, and wider communication. They created for
themselves a public voice and the potential to influence values, views, events,
not just among their own sex but throughout the whole society. Women made
a crucial contribution to the transition of the private letter into the pub-
lic/published epistolary novel and the development of fiction.

What has to be noted is that in the seventeenth and eighteenth centuries,
the only communication, apart from direct contact, had to be through letters;
with the establishment of the Post Office in 1660 and the introduction of the
"penny post" twenty years later, letter writing really came into vogue during
this period—And not just letters which maintained family relationships and
for which women could be expected to assume responsibility. Letters then
were very different from the displaced form they have generally become today:

> Educated people were expected to know how to write graceful letters, how to
> compose their thoughts on paper. Schools trained this skill—letter writing was
> a standard composition assignment and students read and copied from classi-
> cal examples. Londoners must have been accustomed to writing them, for **The
> Spectator** reports a steady stream of letters addressed to the editor; "I have Com-
> plaints from Lovers, Schemes for Projectors, Scandal from Ladies, Congratula-
> tions, Compliments and Advice in Abundance"[1]—testimony to the readiness with
> which readers took pen in hand to scribble off their reactions to even so imper-
> sonal a target as that popular daily. (Ruth Perry, 1980 p. 64)

Women, however, were not likely to have enjoyed such a range of letter
writing opportunities; not normally "educated," nor encouraged to go "public," their choices were considerably curtailed. (At a time when newspapers
did not usually find their way into many homes but were confined to coffee
houses and such places on the grounds that their content was inappropriate
for females, women probably comprised very few of the writers to the editor
or writers of travel reports, dispatches, business letters, etc.) But the letter certainly became a significant form of communication (and self-expression) in
the seventeenth and eighteenth centuries, and the boundaries of women's literary possibilities were extended as a result.

As Ruth Perry (1980) has commented, "Letters were the one sort of writing
women were supposed to be able to do well" (p. 68) and in the expansive
climate of the time, it is not surprising that women should have extended
their horizons beyond the members of their own family and the intimate
communications of the private sphere. That extraordinary and prolific writer,
Margaret Cavendish, Duchess of Newcastle (1623–73)—whose literary con-

tribution cries out for critical evaluation—published her *Sociable Letters* in 1664, and it is clear from their contents that they were never intended as personal correspondence with a friend but as advice and counsel to a much wider circle. One of the early women writers who sought professional status for her sex, Margaret Cavendish's efforts afford a good example of Ruth Perry's assessment that letter writing "was the mode of expression appropriated by women writers *en route,* so to speak, to professional authorship" (p. 68).

This was Virginia Woolf's thesis as well. In *A Room of One's Own* and "Women and Fiction," where she accounts for the emergence of the professional woman writer, Virginia Woolf also starts with the remarkable contribution of Margaret Cavendish and then moves on to the oft-quoted and illuminating letters which Dorothy Osborne (1627–1695) wrote to her lover, William Temple:

> "Had she been born in 1827, Dorothy Osborne would have written novels;" says Woolf, "had she been born in 1527 she would never have written at all. But she was born in 1627, and at that date though writing books was 'ridiculous for a women' [as Dorothy Osborne said of the Duchess of Newcastle when she dared to write and publish her *CCXI Sociable Letters*] there was nothing unseemly in writing a letter."[2]
> Furthermore, letter writing could be made to fit in with the scope and expectations of a woman's life. "It was an art that could be carried on at odd moments, by a father's sick-bed among a thousand interruptions, without exciting comments, anonymously as it were, and often with the pretense that it served some useful purpose"[3](Ruth Perry, 1980 pp. 68–69)

No doubt there were times when letter writing was an onerous obligation, but there would have been times too when for women, letter writing (and journal keeping) were eagerly embraced activities. Given the isolated circumstances which were the limits of many women's lives, a letter could be one of the few means of communicating with the world outside, and a journal entry one of the few means for creating a friend or confidante (see Fanny Burney, in Joyce Hemlow, 1958: p. 26; and the introduction to *The Diary of Elizabeth Pepys* for further discussion on the role of journals).

Men had much more freedom of movement; the mobility of women was restricted, either because they belonged to a class which could not *afford* travel, or else to a class which would not *allow* women to move about independently. In this context, the letter could be a vital link to experience beyond the "here and now."

Apart from providing access to information and experience outside one's own four walls, the letter was also a primary means of maintaining relationships. "Correspondence became the medium for weaving the social fabric of family and friendships in letters of invitation, acceptance, news, condolence and congratulations," comments Ruth Perry (p. 69).

Then too there was the opportunity that the letter provided for the author to create a "self," and one which was positive, exciting, entertaining—worthy of esteem. "Letters were the perfect vehicle for women's highly developed art of pleasing, for in writing letters it is possible to tailor a self on paper to suit the expectations and desires of the audience" (Ruth Perry, 1980, p. 69).

The capacity of letters to forge and foster relationships and to provide a forum for the self-actualization of the author became even more significant during the period of British expansion, when letters to and from the far-flung colonies were the only fragile life lines among families and friends. And when from strange continents women wrote home, aware that their audience could be the entire assembled family who waited on every word, it is not difficult to detect yet another influence working to transform the letter into the epistolary novel. Rare was the women who wanted to worry those back home, so some of the most serious and stressful experiences were recorded between the lines or commented on only **after** the danger or despair had passed. More common was the woman correspondent who composed the entertaining episode—in virtually serial form—in which she figured as the "heroine" confronting challenges in an exotic climate. For example, Rachel Henning wrote some of the most entertaining "stories" about Australia between 1853 and 1882 and without any background information, it simply would not be possible to determine whether her letters were indeed real or works of fiction. (For further discussion of this aspect of Australian women writers, see Dale Spender, 1988.)

That women used letters (and diaries) to explore and explain so many aspects of their personal lives was another contributory factor in the development of the epistolary novel, according to Perry: "Because so many private relationships came to be conducted in letters, especially for home-bound women, these exchanges came to be understood as the repository for emotions usually enclosed by convention, the place to look for records of a person's secret doings" (p. 70). Not surprisingly, there was a growing market for such disclosures. During the eighteenth century, the literary distinction between public and private became blurred when real private letters were sometimes seized for publication (though even here, as in the case of Delariviere Manley's and Katherine Philips' poems, there is some debate as to whether the material was truly seized or whether it was a ruse), and where fictional letters were sometimes presented as the real thing (as with some of Aphra Behn's publications). What can be said with confidence is that the boundaries between letters and fiction collapsed, and that women played a critical role in the process.

But if letters were at the center of literary innovation in the seventeenth and eighteenth centuries, they have no such significance today. Many are those who regret their passing; although the concern that biographers might be deprived of sources with the displacement of the letter by the telephone is not now quite so serious given the appearance of the fax machine. Another matter for regret, however, is that this literary form of the past, with all its strengths, complexities, and nuances, is so little studied. Far from being a "popular" or prestigious research area (a status well warranted), women's letters are rarely included in the valued literary tradition; and this can have no correlation with the quantity—or quality—of the contribution (see Dorothy van Doren, 1929, for some indication of the art of the area). There have been so many women letter writers whose accounts provide a fascinating documentation of self-examination, of interpersonal networks and friendships, as well as an illuminating record of their time *and* a satisfying example of literary skill and accomplishment. The suggestion that it is because they are the work of women that women's letters have not become part of the legitimated "world of letters" is one which deserves serious attention.

Lady Mary Wortley Montagu (1689–1762) is one woman writer whose letters have enjoyed a measure of public acclaim; but still more could be known—and more could gainfully know—of her witty *Embassy Letters* (written in Turkey in 1716) which are a remarkable "anthropological" study of period and place. An inveterate traveler and letter writer (who recorded her own part in the popularization of smallpox vaccination, for example), Lady Mary's letters inform, entertain, and present much of the inner life of a perceptive woman and her relationships with daughter, granddaughter, with love, marriage, and women's education!

Apart from the correspondence of individuals such as the remarkable Elizabeth Montagu (1720–1800), older sister of the equally remarkable novelist, Sarah Scott (1723–1795), there are the many letters of groups of women, such as the Bluestockings. To be able to study the extensive correspondence between Elizabeth Carter (1717–1806) and Catherine Talbot (1721–1770)— not to mention that of Hester Thrale Piozzi (1741–1821) and Mary Delaney (1700–1788)—with all their contemporary references to literary women and their influences, would be an exciting, even inspirational prospect. The letters of so many "literary ladies" (particularly those written to each other) could be another source of enormous interest, and because of the position they occupied at the center of literary innovations, their correspondence could cast further light on the shift from personal letters to public ones.

There are letters between women and letters between women and men; Mary Hays's love letters (literally used as part of the text in *The Memoirs of Emma Courtney*, 1796–1987) and Mary Wollstonecraft's Letters to Gilbert Imlay (1798), as well as her travel *Letters Written During a Short Residence in Sweden, Norway and Denmark* (1796), can only begin to suggest the range of women's epistolary writing during the seventeenth and eighteenth centuries.

And of course, diaries and journals began to come into their own during this period; dependent upon a notion of individual identity and worth, the seventeenth and eighteenth centuries witnessed women's move away from the devotional record (such as that of Lady Margaret Hoby's *Diary*, 1599–1605) to the focus on self-examination and character development—all very consistent with the evolution of fiction. And very useful too as a form of literary apprenticeship, as Fanny Burney's diary demonstrates.

## Autobiographies and Biographies

Margaret Cavendish—again—was a pioneer in the area of autobiography and biography; "A True Relation of My Birth, Breeding and Life" (which occurred at the end of Nature's Pictures Drawn By Fancy's Pencil to the Life, 1656) is, in the words of Nancy Cotton (1987), "the first autobiography published by a woman in England," and The Life of the Thrice Noble, High and Puissant Prince, William Cavendish, Duke, Marquess and Earl of Newcastle" (1667) "is considered the first biography of a husband to be published by an Englishwoman" (p. 232)

Charlotte Charke (1713–1760), novelist, playwright and autobiographer, wrote a scintillating account of her life with an ulterior motive, that of "persuading" her father to leave her a legacy (which he did not), and published in serial form in the Gentleman's Magazine in 1755. Laetita Pilkington (1712–1750) published her three volumes of Memoirs (the first in 1748) in the attempt to realize her self and define her life. There was no literary area into which women did not venture in the seventeenth and eighteenth centuries and no form on which they did not leave their mark.

In relation to biographies, it was not uncommon for women to write "testimonials" for their husbands; Lucy Hutchinson (1620–?) wanted to record her husband's part in the Civil War (The Memoirs of Colonel Hutchinson—not published until 1806) and Anne Fanshawe (1625–1680) wrote an account of her husband's life, after his death, so that their son would be aware of his father's qualities and worth.

In taking these pioneering literary steps, in providing an account of one person's life, in telling a story, and developing a character, these women were also making a contribution to the novel in its present form. Currently there is a revival of interest in biography as the bridge between "fact" and "fiction" (with many suggestions that the increasing popularity of the genre with women writers and readers is precisely because of the way in which it can reveal the private life behind the public figure). To return to the origin of contemporary biography and the contribution of women is to construct an enriching continuity. Though not for long did women confine themselves to biographies of husbands; Hester Thrale Piozzi's account of Samuel Johnson (Anecdotes of the Late Samuel Johnson, 1786) extended the scope of women's literary efforts and revealed the way the figure of a great man can appear very different when portrayed through the eyes of a gifted women.

## Poetry

The seventeenth and eighteenth centuries marked the transition from the high-culture poetry, written by aristocratic women (such as Katherine Philips, 1631–1664) to the published poems of milkmaids; and while many privileged women might have continued to write classical poetry for their own private purposes and many milkmaids might not have turned to verse, the published efforts of women poets during this period are quite extraordinary. Anne Finch, Countess of Winchilsea (1661–1720) deserves sustained critical study, and there are so many more whose contributions should be represented in the literary heritage (see Germaine Greer, Jeslyn Hedoff, Melinda Sansone, Susan Hastings, 1988, for an indication of the range, diversity, and excellence of women's achievements during this period).

That no poets per se have have been included in this volume is a matter for regret; for with the contributions of such women as Elizabeth Rowe, Mary Robinson, Helen Maria Williams, Anna Seward, not to mention that of Charlotte Smith, there is sufficient justification for numerous volumes on early women poets alone. In such a context, the contribution of women working class poets could also be explored. Ann Yearsley (1752–1806), who was referred to as *Lactilla*, the poetical milkwoman, was assisted in her efforts by another celebrated woman writer, Hannah More, and published *Poems on Several Occasions* in 1784. Janet Little (1759–1813) was the author of *Poetical Works of Janet Little, The Scotch Milkmaid* (in 1792), and Elizabeth Bentley, (1767–1839), the daughter of a cordwainer, published *Genuine Poetical Compositions on Various Subjects* in 1791.

## Plays

Apart from the contribution of Fidelis Morgan (*The Female Wits*) and that of Kendall (*Love and Thunder; Plays by Women in the Age of Queen Anne*), very little attention has been given to the outstanding achievement of women playwrights during this period. Indeed, despite the overwhelming evidence to the contrary, (now *and* then) the assertion that women have not excelled as dramatists can still persist.

Many of the early women writers wrote plays, and many of them were marvelous successes. During the Restoration era, it is likely that women of the caliber of Aphra Behn, Catherine Trotter, Delarivière Manley, Mary Pix, and Susanna Centilivre, were in the ascendancy, and much more research could be undertaken on them and their individual and collective contributions to the theatre. More too should be known about some of the popular playwrights such as Anna Wharton, Jane Wiseman, Mary Davys, and Sophia Lee, as well as of the highly influential playwright, poet, and religious writer,

Hannah More (1745–1833). In the eighteenth century there was Frances Boothby, Elizabeth Powhele, Elizabeth Cooper, Catherine Clive, Frances Brooke, and Elizabeth Griffith who all deserve attention in their own right, not to mention playwright and novelist Frances Sheridan (1724–1766), whose satirical *The Discovery* (staged in 1763) and *The Dupe* (also 1763) were highly successful. Frances Sheridan's *A Journey to Bath* (published but not staged) contains a colorful character, Mrs. Tryfort, "the prototype for Mrs. Malaprop in her son's play, *The Rivals*" (David Meredith, 1987: p. 283).

Eliza Haywood wrote plays, as did Fanny Burney, and Elizabeth Inchbald not only acted and authored numerous plays, she also wrote the critical prefaces to Longman's 25-volume *British Theatre*—thereby becoming one of the first drama critics in the English language.

Joanna Baillie, whose contribution is treated briefly in this collection, was another whose achievement should have permanently laid to rest the myth that women could not be dramatists; poet and playwright, she made a classic contribution to the development of drama, and she was acclaimed as *the* woman playwright of her day.

And still, there were more. These are only the broad outlines of women's part in the drama; it is clear that the whole area of the history of women and theater needs more detailed attention and evaluation.

## Criticism

During this period, women also started to write as literary critics. With the shift from aristocratic patronage and a commitment to high culture, to more popular forms (a shift which Alexander Pope of course deplored and decreed to be the end of the world of letters), women were not so disadvantaged by their exclusion from formal education and were more confident about their ability to appraise the literary output of the period. So Elizabeth Inchbald became the drama critic and Anna Laetitia Barbauld (1743–1825) edited *The British Novelists* (1810) in fifty volumes. Novelist and critic Clara Reeve (1729–1807) wrote *The Progress of Romance* (1785), one of the first evaluations of fiction (in which a distinction is made between novels and romance, a distinction which is discussed in this volume in Ros Ballaster's provocative article "Romancing the Novel; Gender and Genre in Early Theories of Narrative" p. 188) Maria Edgeworth was another who "defended" fiction and its form; *Letters for Literary Ladies* (1795; reprinted in part in Dale Spender & Janet Todd, 1989, pp. 355–371) is a critical text in any appreciation of the role that literature has played in women's lives.

There is no accessible history of women's literary criticism but such a compilation would not only make exciting reading, it could change fundamentally some of the received wisdom about the literary tradition and the process of its construction.

## Guidebooks

During the seventeenth and eighteenth centuries, there was a great demand for books on the education of young women. Not necessarily interested in expanding intellectual horizons, the bulk of these publications was concerned with the cultivation of good manners and refinement, and the conduct books were turned out by male and female authors alike. Perhaps because—as Mary Wollstonecraft was to assert so authoritatively—it was that women were made, not born, it was necessary to produce so much material on the desirability of gracious dependence and the necessity of meek subservience. Many of the women who earned their living by their pens wrote such guide books, often from the paradoxical position of trying to persuade their readers to follow the path NOT "of what I do, but of what I say."

## Politics

Then there were the political treatises; *A Serious Proposal to the Ladies* (1694) and *Some Reflections on Marriage* (1700) made clear the position of Mary Astell (1666–1731). Her critique of women's education and channeling for the self-denial of marriage is still relevant today, as is the protest of Mary Wollstonecraft *(Vindication of the Rights of Woman)*. Mary Hays (1760–1843) wrote *Appeal to the Men of Great Britain in Behalf of Women* (1798), as well as *Female Biography: or Memoirs of Illustrious and Celebrated Women, of All Ages and Countries,* 1802, and she was in good company with other Rights' philosophers such as Mary Anne Radcliffe (1745?–1810?, who wrote *The Female Advocate; or, An Attempt to Recover the Rights of Women from Male Usurpation,* 1799). As Janet Todd has said, "Almost every female author [of this time] considered the state of her sex, and, however conservative, in some way disturbed patriarchal assumptions—necessarily so since her very existence as a writing subject challenged the prevailing ideology of female marginality" (1987, p. 23).

## Travel, History, and Translation

Lady Mary Wortley Montagu (as has been mentioned) wrote of Turkey; Mary Wollstonecraft wrote of Scandinavia; and many were the women who "went abroad" (including Celia Fiennes [1662–1741] who wrote *Through England on a Side Saddle in the Time of William and Mary,* 1881) and wrote "letters" and other accounts of their travels. Helen Maria Williams not only reported on Switzerland in turmoil, she chronicled the course of the French Revolution, while Catherine Macaulay (1731–1791) wrote her six volume *History of England from the Accession of James I to that of the Brunswick Line* (published between 1762–1783).

When it came to translations, women's work was ubiquitous. Despite the educational disadvantages, there were women who translated from the classic (Sarah Fielding and Elizabeth Carter among them); more common, however, were translations from contemporary European sources with Mary Wollstonecraft for example, teaching herself German from a dictionary in order to work as a paid translator.

## Magazines

While women's magazines then were not as popular as they have become today, some of the seeds of the contemporary product were planted in the eighteenth century. Eliza Haywood, who was not only the author of plays, novels, and conduct books but of translations as well, also played a pioneering role on women's magazine publications; from 1744 to 1747 she brought out *The Female Spectator*. And there is some suggestion that this was not her first venture; an earlier publication, *The Parrot* (1728), was edited by one, Mrs. Penelope Prattle, often taken to be Eliza Haywood.

*The Female Spectator* was also preceded by *The Female Tatler* (1709), under the editorship of Mrs. Crackenthorpe, widely assumed to be Delarivière Manley—if not indeed the editor, there is some evidence that Delarivière Manley wrote for *The Female Tatler* (see Janet Todd, 1987, p. 211).

While these publications had their share of scandal sheets (and advice columns!), they also contained political items, pleas for education, and some short fiction (which requires further examination, particularly in relation to the first short story writers, Harriet and Sophia Lee (see Dale Spender, in press). But *The Female Tatler* and *The Female Spectator* did not reach the same standard as Charlotte Lennox's monthly periodical, *The Lady's Museum* (which was also one of the first publications to include serialized fiction, in this case Charlotte Lennox's own novel, *Sophia*).

Then too there was Lady Mary Wortley Montagu's political periodical, *The Nonsense of Commonsense* (published every Tuesday, it ran to nine issues from December 16, 1737 and was intended to refute the Whig opposition paper, *Commonsense*). And Frances Moore Brooke (1724–1789) published *The Old Maid* under the pseudonym of "Mary Singleton, Spinster"; this periodical ran from November 15, 1755 until April 10, 1756, and while the title remains something of a mystery (Frances Moore became the wife of John Brooke in 1756), there can be no doubt about its contents. Frances Brooke wrote "with lively wit on subjects ranging from courtship to current events, from religion to theater," comments Leo Manglaviti (1987, p. 61).

## CONCLUSION

While this survey suggests some of the major innovations, lists some of the outstanding writers, and gives some idea of the dynamism of the time, it cannot begin to document in detail the number of women writers and the

individual significance of their works. That specific articles on Mary Wollstonecraft, Ann Radcliffe (1764–1823), Sarah Scott and Harriet and Sophia
Lee are not included in this collection is a regrettable omission; while many
attempts were made to find people who could comment on the achievements
of these writers, they were, unfortunately, not successful. (For further discussion of Mary Wollstonecraft and Ann Radcliffe, see Dale Spender, 1986. There
is also an illuminating introduction by Jane Spencer to Sara Scott [1723–1795]
and her friend, Lady Barbara Montagu, in the Virago edition of *Millenium
Hall* [1762 and 1986], an account of an utopian female community. Harriet
[1757–1851] and Sophia [1750–1824] Lee also call for further examination;
Harriet for her contribution to the short story [see *Canterbury Tales*,
1799–1805]; and Sophia for her rewriting of women's history in fictional form
in *The Recess* [1783–85]—where the heroines are the twin daughters of Mary,
Queen of Scots, and it is their version of history the reader is provided with.
The information is supposed to have come from an old manuscript, and in
summarizing the author's intention, Jane Spencer [1986] says that Sophia Lee
promises to disinter some of the buried truths of women's history, "through
the story of these two sisters, revealed in their own writings, which were
preserved for posterity by being entrusted to a female friend" [p. 195]. Such
a significant novel deserves a collection concerned with its own contribution
to the genre and the tradition of women's writing.)

Perhaps the most important point that can be made in relation to all these
early women writers and their contributions is that this was a critical period
in women's history; it marks the beginning of the development of women's
literary culture, which, with all its associated characteristics, continues to this
day and nourishes concepts of education, self-realization, and women's rights.

Deprived of formal education, denied professional occupation, and increasingly confined to the domestic sphere in the seventeenth and eighteenth centuries, many females sought knowledge of the world and intellectual
stimulation—and they frequently taught themselves to read and write. Then
they turned their talents towards communicating with others; and so a literary community came into being. This was an age when there was a dramatic
increase in the size of the female reading public and in the number of female
writers. The two were closely interrelated. The more women readers there
were, the more women writers were required; the more women writers who
emerged, the more women readers they won. Each helped to mold and shape
the other, and both created an environment conducive to the development
of a literary culture and the success of the novel.

## WHAT WAS WOMEN'S
## RELATIONSHIP TO THE NOVEL?

Any discussion of women's relationship to the novel must encompass some
of the issues involved in the difference between the novel and the romance!

Basically, romances were a known genre at the beginning of this period; the term customarily referred to the "romance literature" of the classical or courtly love tradition (particularly of France; see Madeleine de Scudery for example). A romance consisted of fantastical acts performed by fantasy figures in far away and idyllic pastures, in different times. And the new form, the novel, was distinguished from this rarified plane by its social and domestic realism. "Romances" happened to princely people in distant places, but novels could be about ordinary people leading ordinary lives in the place next door. Clara Reeve (1785) made this distinction in her critical work when she declared that "The Romance is a heroic fable which treats of fabulous persons and things—The Novel is a picture of real life and manners and of the times in which it was written" (*The Progress of Romance, I,* 1785, p. 111).

Which is all very neat and orderly, and it would have been convenient if fiction writers and literary critics had continued to preserve this distinction; but, unfortunately, most of them didn't.

Romance and novel, as Ros Ballaster makes clear in this volume, became a gender distinction as well; and almost invariably, women are associated with romances, and men with novels. And this may have little or nothing to do with the content of their contribution. While on the one hand there is ample evidence—now and then—that women could be just as concerned with social and domestic realism, on the other hand they were (and still are) likely to be branded with the pejorative term romance.

Eliza Haywood, for example, made an explicit and courageously creative comment about her commitment to realism in the introduction to *The Disguised Prince, or the Beautiful Parisian:*

> Those who undertake to write Romances are always careful to give a high Extraction to their *Heroes* and *Heroines;* because it is certain we are apt to take a greater Interest in the Destiny of a Prince than a *private person.* We frequently find, however, among those of a middle State, some, who have Souls as elevated, and Sentiments equally noble with those of the most illustrious Birth; Nor do I see any reason to the Contrary; *Nature* confines her blessings not to the *Great* alone. . . . As the following Sheets, therefore, contain only real Matters of Fact, and have, indeed, something so very surprising in themselves, that they stand not in need of any Embellishments from Fiction: I shall take my *Heroine* just as I find her, and believe the reader will easily pass by the Meanness of her Birth, in favour of a thousand other good Qualities she was possessed of. (1728, pp. 1–2)

But no matter her protestations about an ordinary heroine and "Matters of Fact," Eliza Haywood is labeled as a romantic writer. In one sense, this is not surprising; virtually *all* women novelists from Jane Austen to Mary Gordon, from Elizabeth Gaskell to Margaret Drabble, Alice Walker—*and Barbara Cartland*—are broadly categorized as writers of romance in contemporary literary circles. Which says more about the nature of literary judgments than the nature of women's writing (see Dale Spender, 1989, for clarification).

In the circumstances it is tempting to suggest that—one woman's realism is another man's romance.

This is certainly consistent with some of the conventional evaluations of women's writing. As Candida Lacey (1986) pointed out in her perceptive appraisal of proletarian writers of the thirties, in the United States, when women writers introduced the added—*and realistic dimensions*—of the conflict between working for the union or becoming a wife, the verdict was invariably that these novels were flawed. Rather than recognize that for women it can be common place to have to choose between career and marriage—between being the union organizer and being the *wife* of the union organizer—female proletarian writers were criticized and condemned for their inclusion of "romantic interests" which distracted from the centrality of the class struggle.

(Interestingly, however, the same standard does not seem to apply in general to male writers who include—or even concentrate on—relationships in their fiction. D. H. Lawrence, for example, is not ordinarily devalued as a writer of romances, and the question arises as to whether *his* treatment of relationships is qualitatively different from that of the women who are consigned to the category. It could be revealing to undertake "blind" studies of some of his work; if placed between the typical covers of a popular romantic press's publication, would his novels pass as romance?)

Of course, one of the characteristics of most women's novels is that they focus on relationships, frequently on relationships between the sexes. And it could be that this is the salient feature which attracts the derogatory label—*romance*.

The primary reason that relationships are central to women's fiction is that they are central to women's lives; whether this fascination with human relationships is born of necessity (because women are so frequently on the receiving end in male-dominated society and must know which way the wind blows, managing their lives indirectly by managing relationships) or whether it is born of desire (the proper and most profitable study of humankind, *is* humankind) is impossible to determine. Certainly the combination of women, novels, and relationships is a complex and enduring one. It was at the heart of women's literary culture when it came into existence, and it still characterizes the reality of many literate women today. That the area is so under-researched, under-reported and under-recognized, however, is more an indication of traditional literary priorities than of women's realities.

Why women read novels, what they read, what they get from them, who they share their experiences with, what communities and networks they create from this common cultural exposure, how they are changed by the process—*and why women write novels for other women to read*—are among some of the most elementary and enlightening issues which could be addressed, particularly in contemporary times, when the very existence of the book and the novel is being questioned. The study of women's relationship to the novel in every century since the seventeenth and including the twenty-first, has much to recommend it in the interest of establishing the scope and nature of women's literary traditions and contemporary community.

What began as a trickle of women's novels at the beginning of the eighteenth century became a proverbial flood by the end, with women writers such as Fanny Burney, Maria Edgeworth, and Ann Radcliffe commanding respect as the leading literary figures of their day. While, as has been indicated, women still wrote in every other genre, it was the novel which was recognized as "women's form."

Perhaps this was because—as Virginia Woolf suggested—it was that the novel was *the* new form and was, therefore, sufficiently malleable to be bent to women's purposes. But perhaps the novel now has its recognizable form precisely because it was shaped by women and reflects the reality of their lives. Either way, it can be stated with conviction that in the eighteenth century women became avid writers and readers of the novel and to this form they brought the experiences of their own particular circumstances.

As it was within women's experience to write letters, the shift to the epistolary novel was accomplished relatively easily. As it was within women's experience to construct and maintain relationships—which meant that women were required to be sensitive to responses—writing the replies as well as the original letters was no great departure into the unknown. As Ruth Perry (1980) has commented, the epistolary novel called for "two or more people, separated by an obstruction which can take a number of forms, (who) are forced to maintain their relationship through letters" (p. 93). Such a format did not even demand an imaginative leap on the part of many women writers.

And once women realized the opportunity to write *in* the familiar style which they cultivated in their letters and to write *about* the domestic realities of women's lives, there was no stopping them. Women wrote about their own position, about relationships, about love and marriage, and, even in the eighteenth century, they wrote novels about ideas, politics, and the nature of reality (see Helen Thomson's fine article on Charlotte Lennox in this volume, pp. 113–125), although this did not prevent their novels from being labeled and belittled as romances.

Women's relationship to the novel as writer, reader, and critic is a story yet to be told in full; some of the contributions in this volume provide the outline for what promises to be a stimulating and fascinating narrative of the future.

## WHY DID WOMEN WRITE?

Women wrote for business, and women wrote for pleasure; women wrote for many of the reasons that men wrote—because they needed occupation, and remuneration, and writing was something they were able to do, and which provided them with certain satisfactions. And the women who are included for discussion in this volume typify women's reasons for writing.

If Aphra Behn had not been paid for her writing, she surely would have spent more than one short period in debtors' prison. For Eliza Haywood, who left her husband, the choice was simple; she needed to earn her living and she preferred to sell her literary labors than to sell her self. Delarivière Manley also appears to have had a choice between working at the oldest profession for women or the newest; for all these women who had neither privilege nor patron the way was clear—if they didn't write, they didn't eat.

Sarah Fielding welcomed every penny she earned (although she was never wholly financially independent, and it probably isn't a coincidence that she was concerned with the construction of utopian societies and the principles of sharing). And while Elizabeth Inchbald was known for her parsimonious practices, the fact that she spent some time as a penniless actress (reduced even to stealing and eating raw turnips in a field) no doubt helped her to seek decent payment for her work and to protect her financial interests.

Charlotte Smith wrote desperately to keep the wolf at bay and to support her many children, as well as her granddaughter! And Charlotte Lennox's adult life seems to have been one long battle with poverty—which she lost, dying destitute; like Charlotte Smith, she too left her husband who was a terrible financial burden.

Fanny Burney's *first* novel, *Evelina* (1778), may have been written for pleasure, but *Camilla* (1796) was written to support husband and family.

Joanna Baillie earned her living by her pen, and of the women discussed in this anthology, it was probably only Maria Edgeworth and Mary Brunton who were supported by men and who wrote more for the pleasure than the profit. So much for the old allegation that women were dilettante writers, who had no need to earn their bread. As Jane Spencer has wryly commented: "Well born or not, most women novelists needed the money" (1986: p. 7).

Women also wrote because the opportunity to write was available; "Writing for publication, especially fiction," comments Janet Todd (1987), "was one of the few growth industries at a time when more traditional female occupations from millinery to midwifery were being appropriated by men" (p. 1).

But these are just the basic reasons for women seeking employment; why women should turn to writing as their particular profession has its psychological and aesthetic rationales as well.

Women wrote because they needed to find a form of self-expression, because they needed to consciously construct their reality, realize their potential, and define their own lives. Women wrote too because they needed a voice; they needed to feel that they had agency, that they were participants on the human stage and could affect some of the events of their domestic circumstances and their own society. Sometimes they even wrote to vindicate themselves and their writing.

And women wrote because they needed to make contact with other women and to create a community, a sense of solidarity; so a clergyman's daughter in one country town (Jane Austen) could communicate with a clergyman's daughter in another country town (Charlotte Brontë). So Maria Edgeworth subscribed to Jane Austen's novels and offered the highest praise to Elizabeth Inchbald in relation to *A Simple Story:* "I never read *any* novel—I except *none*—I never read any novel that affected me so strongly, or that so completely possessed me with the belief in the real existence of all the persons it represents" (in Anne Elwood, 1843, p. 325). So Jane Austen was intimidated by Mary Brunton's *Self Control,* and then included reference to so many of her sister writers in *Northanger Abbey;* by such means is a community created, isolation overcome, and a cultural milieu generated.

When Delarivière Manley published her novels, Lady Mary Wortley Montagu protested in her letters that she couldn't obtain a copy of the "key" to work out who the scandalous representations applied to; when Fanny Burney published *Evelina,* conversations, letters, and diaries of the day concentrated on speculations about the author and her heroine and whether either should or should not have indulged in certain activities.

And instead of being condemned to routine and monotonous lives, women readers became privy to a wide range of marvelous characters and witness to any number of exciting events—which is why there is no mystery about their enthusiasm for the novel and the demand for women writers.

These conversations, which can bring characters alive, continue to this day; whether they are about Evelina, Emma, Mrs. Ramsay, or the likely eventuality of *The Handmaid's Tale,* members of this literary community have a shared experience which can cross national boundaries and which addresses some of the central issues of women's lives.

Many of the early women writers were aware of the contribution they were making to this "conversation" (though it is unlikely that they knew how long it would continue or how extensive it might become); and many of them took their role very seriously. In the absence of an educational curriculum for women, women's novels frequently served as women readers' connection with the wider world. It was from novels such as *Evelina or Adeline Mowbray* or *Emmeline* or even *Emma* that women readers could become acquainted with the pitfalls that threatened innocent women in society and with the tragic consequences of "going wrong."

Discussions as to whether Adeline Mowbray was noble or a fool when she went to live with her lover were no mere titillations; they represented the genuine moral dilemmas of the day (and indeed, in this case, were meant to reflect the realities of Mary Wollstonecraft's life; see Dale Spender, 1986, p. 318–323). The questions of whether a woman should marry, or marry for love, or money, whether she should follow the dictates of her heart or elect to provide security for her mother and brother (as is the case in Frances

Sheridan's *The Memoirs of Miss Sidney Bidulph*), were not self-indulgent speculations but real conflicts of interest in many women's lives. And deprived of direct experience of the world, of education, and tutoring in the exercise of moral judgment, novels were the best means available for trying to determine why people behave as they do and whether there are other viable options.

Few are the issues that novels did not raise or the lessons they did not teach. It is no exaggeration to suggest that novels can (and have) covered the gamut of human experience that can be articulated; even today, it would be possible to use women's novels as a basis for an excellent education. To construct such a curriculum would be a rewarding challenge and a refreshing experience.

## WHAT DID THEY WRITE ABOUT?

Heroines, in the main, were the subject of early women's writing. But to choose to write convincingly about ordinary women's lives was not without its difficulties—And not just because the events of ordinary women's lives may not have been the best raw material for the making of an exciting or edifying narrative, but because to provide a women with adventures was to make her unfit to be a heroine of her time. "In the eighteenth century," comments Jane Spencer (1986) wryly, "the very word *adventure* in connection with a woman implies a loss of virtue. . . . (The) ideal woman in eighteenth century society is the woman about whom there is nothing to say. . . . Any woman whose life is eventful enough to be the subject of romance has compromised feminine virtue" (Spencer, 1986, p. 190). No properly brought up or supervised young lady would ever be in a dramatic or discreditable predicament (hence the abundance of orphans in early fiction writing), and no respectable, responsible married woman would do anything which attracted attention to her person. So certain "devices" had to be developed which allowed authors to create heroines who clearly retained their virtue, but who also had their share of risk taking in their lives. And as Katharine Rogers has revealed in this volume, Elizabeth Inchbald excelled in her efforts to overcome this contradiction.

Motherless daughters afforded considerable potential; like Evelina, their lack of information about the world could leave them open to a number of dramatic possibilities without necessarily calling their virtue into question. Then too, there were the daughters of inadequate mothers (a category into which Amelia Opie's heroine, Adeline Mowbray, falls) which presented similar authorial opportunities; these heroines were given poor or improper advice by their mothers and could not be blamed completely for their ignorance or mistakes (as Jane Spencer explains, this volume, pp. 201–211).

Both the motherless daughter and the inadequately reared one allowed the authors to show their heroines engaged in a learning process, involved in self-examination and personal insight, and this also conveniently provided a context in which a case could be made for better education for women and for a more just and equitable society.

Eliza Haywood exploited a new vein when she presented a reformed heroine in the shape of Betsy Thoughtless—a poor but honest heroine—and made it very difficult for her audience to condemn such a likable young woman who, admittedly, behaved very foolishly (though not at all wickedly) and who soon saw the "error of her ways." And limitless were the opportunities for adventure that such a format provided. The heroine could get into all manner of scrapes—some very dangerous, some very comic—but while even she recognized that she had done the wrong thing and was prepared to make amends (even if only in the last chapter), she could pass as an acceptable leading lady.

The reformed heroine was also put in the position of being a "learner"; she too could lament her own inadequate preparation for the world (including the absence of an education), and she too could call for the end of a sexual double standard. By the end of the eighteenth century, the young women who had "learned" from being exposed to temptation were quite popular characters in women's novels. In some respects the association of *didacticism* with women's fiction has its origins in this particular configuration. But if the heroine learned a lesson, the writers learned as well; there was more than one way for women to know something of the world and to preserve their good name and standing.

For many reasons Charlotte Smith created an entirely different sort of heroine; no flighty young women who is sobered and matured by the lessons of the world provides the focus of her fiction. Rather, she starts with the women who have tasted some of the bitter fruits of experience, who have suffered the fate of "women's lot." As Pat Elliott points out in her appraisal of Charlotte Smith (see page 91), many of the author's characters reflect the circumstances and conclusions of her own life. And as Charlotte Smith herself was a victim of marriage, husband, and an unjust society, so too do some of her "heroines" deal with debt, dissolute husbands, and the desire for a better life. While it may have presented the author with many more problems to write a captivating account of these trials (and to arrive at a happy ending), there can be no doubt of Charlotte Smith's ability to hold her audience's attention, even if it was to issue a warning or to remind readers of the awful penalties that could be paid for an error of judgment. Dire consequences could await the woman who chose "the wrong man."

That the choice of a husband should be a primary concern in the novel is perfectly understandable, given that this was often the biggest event in a woman's life. And it was a choice on which so much rested; the happiness of the heroine, the happiness of her husband. Should a woman marry to obey her father or please her mother? Or should she too treat marriage as a career and look for promotion and the best financial prospects? Or was this a marriage market to which she had vehement objections?

(That women writers of the time might have been most concerned with this issue in fiction and in life is a point made by Janet Todd, [1987]: "Writing women, especially professional ones, no doubt represented a higher incidence of failed marriages than the population as a whole; otherwise marriage could almost be said to have broken down" [p. 7].)

How *not* to choose a man is part of the moral of Charlotte Lennox's amazing tale, *The Female Quixote: the Adventures of Arabella;* in this satire the author introduces a heroine who has no proper parental guidance (her mother is dead, and her father keeps her isolated). Arabella has been reared on a diet of romance literature to the extent that she believes the world works on the principles of courtly love and high sentiment—and of course the author makes the point that only by keeping the heroine from the real world could such a false construction of reality have been possible. The novel, which is extremely entertaining as well as intellectually provocative, is structured around many of Arabella's misapprehensions; given her romance-reality, she sees the gardener as a young nobleman in disguise (and after her hand), a gentleman out riding as someone trying to abduct her, and the Thames as a refuge, inviting her into its welcoming depths when she believes she is being pursued by ravishers. Always center stage and convinced of her great courtly powers and capacity to command, Arabella calmly contemplates the death of the suitors she rejects, and orders Glanville (later her husband) to go, to stay, and when ill, to survive!

It's all very heady, and highly amusing stuff. We are confronted with a heroine who holds power. But of course, the power is only an "illusion." This is a point which Charlotte Lennox makes with persuasive clarity. For Arabella to let go of romance and join the world of mere mortals is for her to give up power; it is for her to give up her adventures:

> To retain her virtue, Arabella must relinquish her adventures; but as we can see from the subtitle of the novel, *The Adventures of Arabella,* this means giving up the story of her life and her identity as heroine. (Jane Spencer, 1986, p. 190)

While Arabella persists in thinking she is a romantic heroine who holds power over men, she is not a virtuous woman and cannot become Glanville's wife; but to become the virtuous woman, to recognize the realities of everyday life, is to abandon her concept of self and the romantic society. It's not much of a choice.

Charlotte Lennox has written a novel which works at many levels, and—as Helen Thomson argues—should stand at the starting point of any appreciation of women and fiction. It is a novel about the nature of romance and reality, of emotion and reason, of subjectivity and objectivity, and as Glan-ville tries to lead Arabella from feminine "error" to masculine "truth," (Jane Spencer, 1986, p. 189), the echoes of gender division are again loud and clear.

What does emerge from *The Female Quixote* is that the focus on romance, courtship, and marriage is not necessarily a narrow one. Rather, it can serve as a microcosm for the discussion of the range of human values. Issues of truth, objectivity, the nature of knowledge and reality—all issues of profound importance in this postmodern world—are treated perceptively by Charlotte Lennox and many other women writers as well. Indeed, some of the fundamental philosophical questions of why human beings behave as they do and whether they can behave differently provide the framework for much of women's fiction.

Do women (and men) behave as they do as a result of nature or nurture? Will they behave differently given a decent education? What is the proper form of expression for female power and influence? And would society have to be structured differently if women were to realize their full potential? All of these issues are consistent with the discussion of love and marriage and the role these institutions play in women's lives.

Early women writers wrote about the world, but they did so from women's perspective; the objects and events of the world pass through a different filter when women are in charge of the reality, which is why there are different priorities, perceptions, protests in the work of women. So, for example, while men may have been critical of their own educational provision, they were not obliged to question whether or not education was a good thing. But for women—who were excluded, for whom educational opportunities were actually limited after Henry VIII's dissolution of the religious houses, and who were routinely informed that, for women, education could be physically and psychologically damaging—the entire educational debate assumes very different dimensions (including those of: "Who says that women's uteruses would burst and their brains atrophy if exposed to education?").

Early women writers used fiction to explore their own world and to remedy some of the deficiencies of their exclusion and isolation:

> When asked why she does not read history, Catherine Morland, [the heroine of Jane Austen's novel, *Northanger Abbey*] replies, "history, real, solemn history, I never could be interested in . . . the men all so good for nothing, and hardly any women at all." (Jane Austen, 1969, p. 108)

But Catherine Morland reads novels, particularly Gothic novels where women are at the center of the action and where women's view of the world prevails:

> [Catherine Morland's] reason for preferring Gothic fiction is the same as Arabella's for preferring the versions of history that she gets in the French romances: women

are acknowledged there as they are not in history books. Women's fiction has always been concerned with redressing the balance and restoring women to the record. . . . (Jane Spencer, 1986, p. 192)

This is one of the main reasons that women have written fiction.

## WHAT WAS THE RESPONSE TO THEIR WRITING?

Readers, reviewers, and critics in the eighteenth century knew something not always widely known in the twentieth; namely, that the novel was "the woman's form." It was the genre which bore their imprint, and men could learn much from paying attention to the creative efforts of the women writer. So accepted was the premise that this was the area where women predominated, that there were males who adopted female pseudonyms in order to increase their ratings as authors.

"Among other literary frauds it has long been common for authors to affect the stile [sic] and character of Ladies," wrote a reviewer in the *Gentleman's Magazine* (June 1770, p. 273), and readers were assured that every attempt would be made to detect these great deceivers of the reading public. The *Critical Review* also contributed to reader awareness and exposed any likely false practices. "We suspect," wrote their reviewer in April 1778, "that Madame la Comtesse may be found in some British garret, without breeches, perhaps, but not yet in petticoats."

So on the one hand the response was positive; women were acknowledged as *the* writers of the novel. But on the other hand, the novel did not enjoy the highest status as a literary genre.

There could have been many reasons for this; the first, that it was primarily because women were associated with it that the novel was not accorded high status (see Spender, 1989, for a discussion of gender and status in the world of letters). Or an explanation could have been that the novel was a new—and lesser—form, and that, unlike poetry and drama, (it was argued) its production did not demand a classical education or understanding on the part of the author.

Alternatively, it could have been because it was popular that the novel was devalued. Popularity and prestige have not always been compatible within the literary canon, and while there was no doubt about the *quantity* of women's output in the eighteenth century (with F.G. Black, 1940, estimating that women wrote between two-thirds and three-quarters of the novels in the period 1760–1790), their very success could have been used to challenge their *quality*. (Such popularity could also have been a factor in the gender-based division of fiction into men's novel and women's romance.)

This would help to account for a literary heritage in which it is exclusively male authors who are held up as the originators of the novel, while so many of the works of female writers have been consigned to virtual oblivion; why all women's fiction can be classified as romance and treated as an inferior achievement.

If, however, there was a double standard in relation to the novel, it was not confined to the differential status of the sexes. There was a whole set of different expectations which related to female and male authors and which played an influential role in determining the critical response to individual women writers.

It might have been all right for a man to write bawdy, to present a tale about the sexual exploits of a hero; but it was a very different matter for a woman to write bawdy, to write about a young man's amorous adventures and escapades (young women, of course, not being allowed to have them). The response to the woman writer would be outrage; for her to know such things was to be condemned as a woman and, hence, as a writer.

Some of the women even took this issue up in their writing, Aphra Behn among them. Many of her prologues and prefaces contain protests about the unfair treatment of women writers who wanted to write—realistically—about the world outside the narrow sphere a woman was supposed to be confined to. (One reason that has since been given for Aphra Behn's "fade from fame," is that she was such an indecent writer; it has to be said that men who wrote bawdy do not seem to have suffered a similar fate, but rather, have been relished for their colorful and robust contributions to the literary heritage.)

A woman writer was supposed to be virtuous; she was enjoined to write about the virtuous and to recommend the blameless life. Which meant that many female authors were obliged to extol the virtues of an existence that was very much at odds with the way they lived their own lives. Admonishing young women to do their duty, to be subservient, obedient, and deferential, was not all that consistent with the survival strategies employed by many of the early women writers. Jane Spencer (1986) comments on the contradictions and the pressure this placed on women writers, and she provides an illustration with the life and work of Frances Brooke. In *The Excursion* (1779) Frances Brooke "produced an impeccably 'moral' work by criticizing the kind of independent and ambitious behaviour she showed in her own life," Jane Spencer states dryly (p. 20).

Trying to appear virtuous and trying to write about the virtuous, in a gripping and memorable style, were additional obstacles which confronted the woman writer. And if there were penalties for failure, there were also penalties for success.

Eliza Haywood was one of the most prolific and popular of the early women writers. She was also the target of some of the worst verbal attacks of the day. It was precisely because she was so successful that Alexander Pope, for example, tried so hard to discredit her; and because she was a woman, his attack centered on her sexuality. So he offers her sexual favors as a prize in a urinating competition between two publishers and portrays her in the most appalling, sexist terms. And while Pope's attack on popular writers who were "lowering the standards" was not confined to females, in "his attack on Haywood he could draw on an existing stereotype of the woman writer, according to which she was unclean, untidy, disgustingly sexual and a whore" (Jane Spencer, 1986, p. 5).

Today we could label Pope's actions as sexual harassment. There is considerable contemporary literature available on the way in which some men use sexual harassment as a device for keeping women out of territory they have defined as their own particular preserve (see MacKinnon, 1979). And certainly in the eighteenth century many men had defined the world of letters as their world and were prepared to go to great lengths to keep women out. (The extent to which authorship is seen as a male prerogative is discussed at length in Gilbert and Gubar, 1980.)

There is also some evidence that this strategy worked. For many years after the attack on her in *The Dunciad*, Eliza Haywood did not publish (at least, not under her own name). Whether this was because she was intimidated, or whether it was because publishers were influenced by Pope's treatment of her (and did not want to publish her work) is a matter for conjecture. Either way, it can be stated that when women did well, there were men who tried to prevent them from continuing to work in the area; women writers could be damned if they did well and damned if they did not. To some extent this is the salient feature of the reponse to women's writing.

## WHAT WERE THE CONDITIONS UNDER WHICH THEY WROTE?

The more general conditions under which women wrote were those of a society moving towards industrialization, where the economic position of women was deteriorating.[5] In defiance of the traditional historical theory of "steady progress," women found their opportunities persistently eroded during this period. "The disappearance of the convents at the time of the Reformation had deprived girls not only of convenient local places of learning, but also of a pool of women teachers in the shape of the nuns themselves," states Antonia Fraser (1984, pp. 123–124). And with men's appropriation of some of women's traditional occupations (such as midwifery), along with the adoption of the increasingly fashionable concept of bourgeois femininity (which had as its ideal the seclusion of women and the servicing of men) the result was "that by the eighteenth century women had been forced to withdraw from many public activities" (Spencer, 1986: p. 14).

But paradoxically, the very forces that were pushing women out of paid work and public influence were the same ones that were helping to make possible the emergence of the novel and women's expanded opportunities for authorship.

At the simplest level there had to be some sense of isolation and privacy before the realistic novel—in the domestic setting—could have a rationale for existence. It's probably not an accident that "novels" have not developed in small communities where little distinction is made between **public** and **private** and where the members of the community are reasonably familiar with the details of each other's lives. This changed with industrialization and urbanization, and the entrenchment of the private sphere; a curiosity began to surface as to what was happening behind other people's closed doors. It was the desire to know the intimate details of other people's lives (as well as the emergence of concepts of **individual** and **choice**) which established the context for the novel.

But before the novel could become the popular medium, certain conditions had to be fulfilled; there had to be the technological means of producing and distributing the books, and there had to be sufficient literate members of the population with time to read, and money to purchase the works of fiction.

To deal with the finances first. Of course the fact that men purchased more novels—and figured more prominently on subscription lists—cannot necessarily be taken as an indication of their commitment to literature, or as a mark of their reading habits; it is more a measure of their relative purchasing power and their ability to decide how money should be spent. Perhaps women readers did not have access to the same number of titles until the advent of the circulating library, which provided novels (in abundance) to those who could not afford to buy them. But book sales and library circulation constituted a huge demand (and an audience of both sexes) and generated at one level a positive climate for the development of the woman writer.

This was a period in which the reading public expanded (though there is something of the chicken-and-egg debate in trying to determine whether such expansion facilitated the growth of the novel, or whether it was a response to it, or both). During the seventeenth and eighteenth centuries writing and reading ceased to be the prerogative of the aristocracy (or the product of patronage) and became much more part of the repertoire of the urban middle classes. Tradesmen, "shopkeepers, clerks and their families—and also to some extent servants" were all members of this new community, which was ripe for the evolution of fiction (Jane Spencer, 1986, pp. 6–7).

That writing and reading were theoretically the only skills that women required to be the writers and readers was particularly fortunate; for at this time (in contrast to contemporary wisdom), it was considered quite normal for girls who had the opportunity in terms of books, light, and leisure, to teach themselves these skills. While there were privileged females who had access to some tuition—through parents, governesses, or brothers' tutors, etc.—if school attendance had been a necessary condition of authorship, there would have been many women writers who were disqualified.

So many women taught themselves to read and write, and took to it with such a vengeance; and so many made the "art" of both seem so effortless that many are the dismissive comments that have been made about women's facility for writing (and reading!) fiction. (This has been true even in the twentieth century; the Australian novelist, Vance Palmer, trying to illustrate how easy it was for women to write novels, in contrast to the creative struggle it meant for men, stated that "Writing a novel seems as easy to almost any literate woman as making a dress," (*Bulletin 3,* July 29, 1926).

So popular did writing and reading become with women (which supports the thesis of the creation of a continuing literary community) that grave fears were expressed that soon every woman would be doing it, even the servants. And with what disruptive consequences:

> . . . the number of *Authoresses* hath of late so considerably increased, that we are somewhat apprehensive lest our very Cook-wenches should be infected with *Cacoethes Scribendi,* and think themselves above the vulgar employment of mixing a puddings, or rolling a pye-crust. (*Monthly Review, 27,* 1762: p. 472)

Of course it wasn't just the writing that was questioned; in the eighteenth century and into the nineteenth grave fears were also expressed about the dangers of fiction for young women. (The fact that reading novels might have provided women with a world of their own, one that men did not directly have access to, and that it also made them "unavailable" to attend to men, could also have had something to do with the objections to women's novel reading. My discussions with women readers reveal that many men can still find it threatening when women are engrossed in novels, and they can even report that men will use disruptive strategies to prevent women from reading and to obtain their attention. This is apart from the fact that women can "get ideas" and become "awkward" as a result of reading.)

But while novel reading was often viewed with disapprobation, it was writing and the power of agency that it afforded which was reserved for the greatest condemnation.

> When a farmer's daughter sits down to *read* a novel, she certainly mispends [sic] her time, because she may employ it in such a manner as to be of real service to her family; when she sits down to *write* one, her friends can have no hope of her. (*Critical Review, 33* 1772, p. 327)

Women's efforts were rarely welcomed by the literary establishment. It wasn't just that women were considered to be without artistic merit, that they had their works rendered apolitical and "trivial" by being labeled as romance, but their very presence in the literary marketplace was deplored by many men as a "lowering of standards";

So long as our British Ladies continue to encourage our hackney Scribblers, by
reading every Romance that appears, we need not wonder that the Press should
swarm with such poor insignificant productions. (*Monthly Review, 28* 1760,
p. 523)

And there are contemporary echoes (see Spender, 1989).

The resistance to the idea that women's writing and reading represent skill
still persists (even among women themselves, unfortunately).[6] And this climate of devaluation characterizes the conditions under which women have
routinely written. Mary Wollstonecraft insisted that one of the last male bastions to fall would be that which appropriated for men intellectuality and
creativity. While enormous material and legal gains have been made in the
two hundred years since she presented her case in *Vindication of the Rights
of Woman* (1792), it could be argued that when it comes to the accreditation of women's authority as intellectual and creative beings, few, if any,
changes have been made.

Women became writers in the seventeenth and eighteenth centuries for
the very good reason that it was not possible to prevent them from doing so.
They were, of course, often discouraged; denied education, informed that they
were inferior, ridiculed at times for their literary efforts, and cautioned against
the corrupting influence of novels. It took enormous faith and confidence for
women to declare that they possessed— and could use well—creative and
intellectual faculties.

What they did not normally do in this period, however, was assert that
they wrote because they were ambitious and sought artistic fulfillment, financial independence, or **visibility and recognition of their work.** While the
pretexts for venturing into the literary work place are discussed at more length
in the final chapter, what must be stated here in relation to the writing woman's
working conditions, is that she had to collude in the making of the myth that
women were NOT autonomous beings who could occupy space in the public sphere and have a political agenda:

. . . Let a woman write to amuse her leisure hours, to instruct her sex, to provide blameless reading for the young, or to boil the pot; moral zeal was an accepted justification and poverty an accepted excuse; but there was one motive
which could be neither justified nor excused—ambition, the "boast" of conscious
power, craving to perform its task and receive its reward. The proper attitude
for a female talent was diffidence; the proper field for its exercise, the narrow
circle of her intimate friends; and if for any of the permitted reasons she stepped
outside the circle, let her at least sedulously avoid the disgraceful imputation
of assurance. (J. M. S. Tompkins, 1969, p. 116)

It was an offense for women to be confident, visible.

Many women wrote in the seventeenth and eighteenth centuries in psychological circumstances that would not now be considered conducive to
writing; many women wrote without "a room of their own" or "five hundred

pounds a year," the very basics advocated by Virginia Woolf as the conditions for the writing of fiction. Despite these "limitations," they played a crucial part in shaping and extending and securing the viability of a literary community, and their contribution deserves to be much better appreciated and more widely known.

## WHAT WERE THE CREATIVE AND PROFESSIONAL ACHIEVEMENTS OF THESE WRITING WOMEN?

The professional achievement of women is treated in more detail in the concluding chapter, and the underlying purpose of this overview has been to establish the extent of the early women writers' creative achievement. While they wrote across every genre and could be studied for their contribution to everything from drama to letters, from history to poetry, the part they played in the development of the novel is remarkable, and the full implications of their achievements will only be realized when even further research is undertaken on their lives, their work, and the traditions they helped to forge. And this is where the final question is relevant; *why is it that these women have not been at the center of the valued literary tradition which resources the views and values of the entire culture and which is transmitted from one generation to another?*

Why women are **not** at the center of the literary tradition—why they are not equally represented in the production of legitimated literary culture—is a question which invites numerous alternative explanations. If the full range of possibilities is to be canvassed, then one which must be entertained is that women have no central presence in the heritage for the very simple reason that their writing is not up to standard; that what they write, and how they write does not warrant praise, prestige, accreditation, or emulation. The identification of such a deficiency would then serve to account for women's relative absence from the the canon and exclusion from the curriculum and their relative invisibility in the cultural and educational heritage (for further discussion, see Dale Spender, 1989, and Joanna Russ, 1983).

But to discount the contribution of women in this manner is not to put an end to the problematic matter of women's lack of representation. On the contrary, to devalue women writers on the basis of their gender is to raise yet more awkward questions—not the least of which would be that there is no study within literary criticism which establishes the inferior nature of women's authorship. Despite the implicit assumptions and explicit assertions that women's writing is not as good as men's, there is no evidence which would support such a thesis.

However, the absence of a definitive study on the deficiencies of the writing woman has not always pre-empted the devaluation of her contribution;

in some respects the history of literary criticism is the history of the dismissal of women's achievement, as so much of feminist literary criticism makes clear. But if women have been—and still are—being judged as inferior when there is no conclusive evidence about the *standard* of their contribution, then this in itself becomes the overriding issue; **who decides?** Who is determining that women's writing is not of the same order as men's and not worthy of equal representation in the literary tradition?

Literary criticism is not immune from some of the epistemological questions which have challenged many of the disciplines in the social sciences and humanities:

- who are the knowledge makers?
- what is the nature of the knowledge they generate?
- whose interests are served by such knowledge construction? and
- how are the benefits of vested interests justified/rationalized?

Although issues about authority, validity—and vested interest—may not have been addressed in any systematic way in the past, they are, nonetheless, proper areas of investigation within the literary criticism paradigm. And they can give rise to some disturbing considerations.

The striking fact is that it has been literally the "men of letters" who have been primarily the knowledge makers; it has been mainly men—and a **particular** group of white, educated, privileged (able-bodied, and heterosexual) **men**—who have determined that the work of white, middle-class men is the best that can be written and deserves pride of place in the canon.

Such a value judgment and coincidence does not necessarily imply any insidious or conspiratorial strategy on the part of male literary critics of past generations. Rather, their preferences are understandable; for the very same reasons that women readers—and critics—may find the work of women more meaningful, relevant, more enriched with detail, nuance, and delineation, and hence a *greater artistic achievement,* so too may men place greater value on the offerings of their own sex. It is not male preference *per se* which has been responsible for women's eclipse (for women writers may have been the choice of women readers and critics, but this in itself has not resulted in the disappearance of the work of the men); it is that the preferences of men have prevailed. Men have been in a position to insist on the rightness (and the impartiality!) of their own assessments.

It is not difficult to establish that when it comes to the construction of the literary heritage and to the classification of good and great writers and their inclusion in a tradition which is transmitted from one generation to the next, it is men who almost exclusively have been the knowledge makers. They have constructed a tradition which has favored the contributions of their own sex (and class and ethnicity); they have provided a rationale which serves their own interests; and they have made their own case for their own supremacy in the area. The history of the novel constitutes a critical example.

As is argued in *Mothers of the Novel; 100 Good Women Writers Before Jane Austen* (Spender, 1986), the men of letters have rewritten literary history so that the greater contributions of women—in terms of number of titles, number of sales, payment for manuscripts, innovative and artistic developments—have been denied in favor of achievements of five males who are deemed to have been the originators of the novel.

Since the seventeenth and eighteenth centuries, women have written; some would go so far as to suggest that they may have even written more fiction than men. So it has been no mean feat to exclude this mammoth amount of work from the literary heritage. In the case of the fiction, extraordinary "revisions" were necessary to remove "the majority of eighteenth century novels" from the heritage. As Joanna Russ has indicated, extraordinary denials of women's achievements were required for these revisions to be rationalized:

She didn't write it.
She wrote it, but she shouldn't have.
She wrote it, but look what she wrote about.
She wrote it, but "she" isn't really an artist and "it" isn't really serious, of the right "genre"—i.e. really art.
She wrote it, but she wrote only one of it.
She wrote it, but it's only interesting/included in the canon for one, limited reason.
She wrote it, but there are very few of her.

(Joanna Russ, 1983, p. 76)

Such a challenge to the conventions of literary judgment is indicative of the increasing emphasis in feminist criticism on the sexual double standard and the role it has played in the exclusion of women. And the criticism has been leveled not so much at past social arrangements which accorded privileges to males so that they occupied the position of literary critics, nor at their preference for the writing of their own sex; for, while not excusable, such patterns of the past are understandable. What is of concern in the contemporary climate is the reluctance of the literary establishment to put its own house in order and to "revise its revisions"; it is the failure of many institutions and individuals to treat the nature of critical judgment as a serious issue and to seek to remedy some of the past omissions by reinstating women as equal representatives as writers and critics. What is of concern is the *continued* practice of the exclusion of women and the refusal of too many agencies—from course programmers to schools of criticism, from anthology compilers to research supervisors—to make the process of canon construction and value judgments (including those related to class and ethnicity) the subject of constant scrutiny and assessment. At the center of literary evaluation should be the premise that it is not just the study of those who are good and great (if these are to be the desired categories) but *who says so,* which is the range of reference for the discipline. Then questions of *why women have been*—and continue to be—*excluded* would become fundamental rather than marginalized issues.

Currently women are far from being equally represented in the tradition that is transmitted to the next generation in English speaking communities; while there is some difficulty in obtaining figures, the consensus seems to be that in college English courses fewer than seven percent of the writers studied are women.[7] And despite the perceived gains of the last decades, this could actually constitute a decrease in women's representation.

And it is not the case that the work of women has been systematically studied, that quantitative and qualitative analyses have been undertaken and have revealed women's writing to be below standard. Quite the reverse; it is not that women have been given a fair hearing and found wanting, but that women are found wanting, and are not given a fair hearing (and this is the thesis of *The Writing or the Sex? or, why you don't have to read women's writing to know it's no good*).

Prejudice against the writing woman still persists, and it works against women in a variety of ways. Just as in the seventeenth and eighteenth centuries it was not possible to prevent women from taking up their pens and enjoying considerable success in print, so too it has not been possible to prevent women writers from enjoying enormous success over the last decades. And yet just as the early women writers were kept out of the mainstream, so too are many contemporary writers precluded from representation in the establishment. For while the last twenty-five years have witnessed a virtual explosion in the publication of women's books, the reality is that *there has been no significant change in the canon or the curriculum*. When less than seven percent of the writers taught are women, it is obvious that female authors, past and present, continue to be silenced, suppressed, excluded.

In the seventeenth and eighteenth centuries, when women were denied access to formal education, women's novels were a welcome substitute; they were a means of communication which gave shape and substance to women's lives, which promoted an exchange of information and the encouragement of growth and learning. Perhaps in the current context they continue to provide a comparable service. For it is not uncommon to find the bookshop on the college campus stocked with a vast range of women's books which will sell widely to students—but which are not taken up and set as texts in the halls of learning. So women continue to write for each other and to generate an informal but shared literary culture. Which, while it may have its advantages, places the continuity of women's contribution in jeopardy. It's not just that women's writing from the past has not been incorporated into the cultural heritage; it is also that women's writing in the present could suffer a similar fate.

*Living by the Pen; Early British Women Writers* is both an attempt to reclaim a heritage and to ensure that it becomes a permanent and prized part of the literary repository for future generations. And while the women who have worked to contribute to these pages have made a significant start, much more remains to be done before women are assured of their rightful place and there is a Vindication of the Writing Woman.

## NOTES

[1]See *The Spectator, 581,* August 16, 1714.

[2]From *The Second Common Readers,* 1984, p. 151.

[3]p. 52

[4]Charlotte Brontë was subjected to the same double standard; with the publication of *Jane Eyre* (under the pseudonym of Curer Bell), the critical response was that if written by a man it was excellent but if by woman it was scandalous (see Spender, 1989, for further discussion).

[5]There are quite a few informative surveys of women's economic status in the seventeenth and eighteenth centuries, including Alice Clark, (1919 1982), Antonia Fraser (1984), and Ruth Perry (1980, pp 27–62).

[6]Eva Cox's current research on the assessment of women's skills, reveals how reluctant women are to perceive themselves as skilled; they can be gifted, but are often very resistant to the idea of having a range of skills (private communication, 1990, on ongoing research).

[7]Such a figure does not include Women's Studies courses where women writers are included; see Dale Spender, 1989, for further clarification.

## REFERENCES

Adburgham, Alison. (1972). *Women in print: Writing women and women's magazines from the Restoration to the accession of Victoria.* London: Allen & Unwin.

Austen, Jane (1969). *Northanger Abbey.* In Robert William Chapman (Ed.), *The novels of Jane Austen, Volume V.* Oxford: Oxford University Press.

Black, F.G. (1940). *The epistolary novel in the late eighteenth century: A descriptive and bibliographical study.* Eugene, OR: University of Oregon. *Bulletin.* (1926, July 29). 3, 3.

Chapman, Robert William, Ed. (1969). *The novels of Jane Austen.* Oxford: Oxford University Press.

Clark, Alice. (1919/1982). *Working life of women in the seventeenth century.* London: Routledge and Kegan Paul.

*Critical Review.* (1772). 33, 327.

Cotton, Nancy. (1987). In Janet Todd (Ed.), *A dictionary of British and American women writers 1660–1800.* London: Methuen.

Dorr, Priscilla. (1988). Joanna Baillie. In Paul Schlueter and June Schlueter (Eds.), *An encyclopedia of British women writers.* New York: Garland Publishing.

Elwood, Anne. (1843). *Memoirs of the literary ladies of England.* 2 Volumes. London: Henry Colburn.

Fraser, Antonia. (1984). *The Weaker Vessel: Woman's lot in seventeenth century England.* London: Weidenfeld & Nicolson.

Gilbert, Sandra M. and Gubar, Susan. (1980). *The madwoman in the attic; The woman writer and the nineteenth century literary imagination.* New Haven: Yale University Press.

Greer, Germaine; Medoff, Jeslyn; Sansone, Melinda; and Hastings, Susan (Eds.). (1988). *Kissing the rod: An anthology of seventeenth century women's verse.* London: Virago.

Haywood, Eliza. (1728). *The disguised prince, or the beautiful Parisian.* Ln. Publ.

Hemlow, Joyce. (1958). *The history of Fanny Burney.* Oxford: Clarendon Press.

Henning, Rachel. (1985) *The letters of Rachel Henning.* Melbourne: Penguin.

Kramarae, Cheris and Spender, Dale (Eds.). (in press). *The knowledge explosion: Generations of feminist scholarship.* Elmsford, NY: Pergamon Press.

Kendall, (Ed.). (1988). *Love and thunder: Plays by women in the age of Queen Anne.* London: Methuen.

Lacey, Candida. (1986). Striking fictions: women writers and the making of a proletarian realism. *Women's Studies International Forum, 9*(4), 373–384. In Candida Lacey (Ed.), *Political Fiction.*

MacKinnon, Catharine, A. (1979). *Sexual harassment of working women.* New Haven: Yale University Press.

Meads, Dorothy M. (1930). *The diary of Lady Margaret Hoby, 1599–1605.* London: Routledge.

Meredith, David W. (1987). In Janet Todd (Ed.), *A dictionary of British and American women writers 1660–1800.* London: Methuen.

*Monthly Review.* (1760). *28,* 523.

*Monthly Review.* (1762). *27,* 472.

Morgan, Fidelis. (1981). *The female wits: Women playwrights of the Restoration.* London: Virago.

Morgan, Fidelis. (1986). *A woman of no character: An autobiography of Mrs. Manley.* London: Faber & Faber.

Perry, Ruth. (1980). *Women, letters and the novel.* New York: AMS Press.

Piozzi, Hester Thrale. (1786). *Anecdotes of the late Samuel Johnson.*

Reeve, Clara. (1785). *The progress of romance.* 2 Volumes. Colchester: W. Keyymer. (Reprinted in 1970 by Garland Publishing, New York.)

Russ, Joanna. (1983). *How to suppress women's writing.* London: The Women's Press.

Russell, Rosalind. (1987). The "immortal" who fell from literary grace. *Scotsman,* February 2, 1987.

Schnorrenberg, Barbara Brandon. (1984). Joanna Baillie. In Janet Todd (Ed.) *A dictionary of British and American women writers.* London: Methuen.

Schofield, Mary Anne. (1990). *Masking and unmasking the female mind: disguising romances in feminine fiction 1713–1799.* New Jersey: Associated University Presses.

Schofield, Mary Anne and Macheski, Cecilia, (Eds.). (1986). *Fetter'd or free? British women novelists, 1670–1815.* Athens, OH: Ohio University Press.

Spencer, Jane. (1986). *The rise of the woman novelist: From Aphra Behn to Jane Austen.* Oxford: Basil Blackwell Ltd.

Spender, Dale. (1986). *Mothers of the novel: 100 good women writers before Jane Austen.* London: Pandora Press.

Spender, Dale. (1988). *Writing a new world: Two centuries of Australian women writers.* London: Pandora Press.

Spender, Dale. (1989) *The writing or the sex? or why you don't have to read women's writing to know it's no good.* Elmsford, NY: Pergamon Press.

Spender, Dale. (Ed.). (in press). *The diary of Elizabeth Pepys.* London: Grafton Books.

Spender, Dale. (Ed.). (in press). *Anthology of women's short stories.* London: Pandora Press.

Spender, Dale and Todd, Janet (Eds.). (1989). *Anthology of British women writers.* London: Pandora Press.

Todd, Janet (Ed.). (1987). *A dictionary of British and American women writers 1660–1800.* London: Methuen.

Todd, Janet. (1986). *Sensibility: An introduction.* London: Methuen.

Tompkins, J.M.S. (1932, 1969). *The popular novel in England 1770–1800.* London: Methuen.

van Doren, Dorothy. (1929). *The lost art: Letters of seven famous women.* New York: Coward-McCann.

White, Cynthia. (1970). *Women's magazines 1693–1968.* London: Michael Joseph.

Wollstonecraft, Mary. (1792). *Vindication of the rights of woman.* London: Joseph Johson.

Woolf, Virginia. (1928, 1974). *A room of one's own.* Harmondsworth: Penguin.

Woolf, Virginia. (1984). *The common reader.* London: Hogarth Press.

# MOTHERS OF THE NOVEL
## Reprint Series

Brunton, Mary. (1988). *Self-Control*. Introduced by Sara Maitland. London: Pandora Press. (Originally published in 1810–1811.)

Brunton, Mary. (1986). *Discipline*. Introduced by Fay Weldon. London: Pandora Press. (Originally published in 1814.)

Burney, Fanny. (1988). *The wanderer, or, female difficulties*. Introduced by Margaret Drabble. London: Pandora Press. (Originally published in 1814.)

Edgeworth, Maria. (1986). *Belinda*. Introduced by Eva Figes. London: Pandora Press. (Originally published in 1801.)

Edgeworth, Maria. (1986). *Patronage*. Introduced by Eva Figes. London: Pandora Press. (Originally published in 1814.)

Edgeworth, Maria. (1987). *Helen*. Introduced by Maggie Gee. London: Pandora Press. (Originally published in 1834.)

Fenwick, Eliza. (1988). *Secresy, or, the ruin on the rock*. Introduced by Janet Todd. London: Pandora Press. (Originally published in 1795.)

Fielding, Sarah. (1987). *The governess, or, little female academy*. Introduced by Mary Cadogan. London: Pandora Press. (Originally published in 1749.)

Hamilton, Mary. (1987). *Munster village*. Introduced by Sarah Baylis. London: Pandora Press. (Originally published in 1778.)

Hays, Mary. (1987). *The memoirs of Emma Courtney*. Introduced by Sally Cline. London: Pandora Press. (Originally published in 1796.)

Haywood, Eliza. (1986). *The history of Miss Betsy Thoughtless*. Introduced by Dale Spender. London: Pandora Press. (Originally published in 1751.)

Inchbald, Elizabeth. (1987). *A simple story*. Introduced by Jeanette Winterson. London: Pandora Press. (Originally published in 1791.)

Lee, Harriet and Lee, Sophia. (1988). *The Canterbury tales*. Introduced by Harriet Gilbert. London: Pandora Press. (Originally published in 1797/99.)

Lennox, Charlotte. (1988). *The female quixote*. Introduced by Sandra Shulman. London: Pandora Press. (Originally published in 1752.)

Morgan, Lady. (1986). *The wild Irish girl*. Introduced by Brigid Brophy. London: Pandora Press. (Originally published in 1806.)

Morgan, Lady. (1988). *The O'Briens and the O'Flahertys*. Introduced by Mary Campbell. London: Pandora Press. (Originally published in 1827.)

Opie, Amelia. (1988). *Adeline Mowbray*. Introduced by Jeanette Winterson. London: Pandora Press. (Originally published in 1804.)

Sheridan, Frances. (1987). *Memoirs of Miss Sidney Bidulph*. Introduced by Sue Townsend. London: Pandora Press. (Originally published in 1761.)

Smith, Charlotte. (1988). *Emmeline*. Introduced by Zoë Fairbairns. London: Pandora Press. (Originally published in 1788.)

Smith, Charlotte. (1987). *The old manor house*. Introduced by Janet Todd. London: Pandora Press. (Originally published in 1794.)

# Part One
# The Women

# Aphra Behn's *Oroonoko:*

## The Politics of Gender, Race, and Class

Heidi Hutner

Aphra Behn was the first professional, self-supporting British woman writer. She laid the foundation for the eighteenth-century women writers who followed her—against all odds. As Virginia Woolf (1928) claims, "All women together ought to let the flowers fall upon the tomb of Aphra Behn . . . for it was she who earned them the right to speak their minds" (pp. 113–114). In her own time Behn was as famous as William Wycherley or John Dryden, but until recent years she has not been treated by literary critics as a serious artist. Behn was a prolific and historically significant writer of plays, novels, translations, and poems; she also made "remarkable contributions to the rise of the novel" (Ferguson, 1985: p. 284). In the 200 years after her death most traces of Behn's life disappeared; what we know of her has been pieced together by various historians, critics, and biographers. ("History of the Life", 1696, Frederick M. Link, 1968, Angeline Goreau, 1980, George Woodcock, 1948, Maureen Duffy, 1977, Vita Sackville-West, 1927.) Many of these critics discredit her "historical" novel *Oroonoko* for not being based on her *real* experience; others assail her writing and life as too bawdy and indecent to merit study.[1] Angeline Goreau (1980) argues that from the beginning, the manner in which "critics and historians [have] talked about [Behn] . . . suggested that it was precisely because she was a woman and a writer and the first to venture into what was seen as male preserve that she was for so long dismissed and ignored" (p. 13). Angeline Goreau aptly links the absence of Behn's works from the canon of literature that is reprinted, read, and taught to the antifeminist biases of her male critics. For reasons of brevity, I will not plow through the various arguments and claims made about Behn. A study of the critics' and historians' resistance to Behn's work would require the length of one essay—at least. In this paper I shall suggest something of Behn's literary and historical significance as a critic of her culture by analyzing in her novel *Oroonoko* how she connects the oppression of women and black slaves in the late-seventeenth century to emerging economic forces, particularly those of imperialism and colonial expansionism. The significance of Behn's most famous novel can only be fully understood, however, within the historical and political context of her life and career. These socio-political and historical contexts are precisely those which are ignored by the traditional critics who dismiss her.

In 1640, the year Aphra Behn was born, eighty percent of the female population in England was illiterate. The mid-seventeenth-century ideological union of education and future occupation kept women out of the universities and the educational training for law and business; women of the seventeenth century were prepared solely for domestic work. Hilda L. Smith (1982) asserts that, "Puritan values encouraged 'the elegant, accomplished woman of the world who might have a pretty wit but was often empty-headed'" (p. 24). Modesty, self-containment, and chastity were the absolute social prescriptions for a woman's acceptable role.

If Behn's case is an example of seventeenth-century standards, to be a working female writer was often accounted little better than being a prostitute. The usurpation of traditional masculine roles threatened stereotypes of the domestic and objectified woman, thus threatening male power. By law, men held women as their property. The female body was her husband's or, if she was unmarried, her father's. When a female child was twelve years old, her father could legally marry her off or put her into servitude. The "normal" choices available to a young woman in the seventeenth century, therefore, were either to marry, to become a domestic servant, or to work and support herself—and the pay for the work available to women would hardly buy enough to eat. Of course these choices did not necessarily apply to women of fortune or women who had male protectors, but Aphra Behn had neither of these. Despite the limited education she received and the limited support from male writers, Behn wrote formidably *and* successfully. The factors which led her to the choice of a writing career are complicated; Behn needed the money, and she was exposed to unusual circumstances which may have diverted her from adopting a traditional female role.

Despite the recent renewed interest in her work, a number of contemporary feminist critics warn against painting Behn as a proto-feminist. Behn was a Tory propagandist; in the early 1680s she supported the succession of James III, a Catholic, to the English throne when the Protestant Parliament was dead set against it. Deborah C. Payne (1989) suggests that perhaps because Behn constantly fought against the criticism of being regarded (and disregarded) as merely a female writer, the role of the "devoted Tory" may have provided her with "just the necessary camouflage" to permit the author "to lay aside in print the issue of her sex once and for all" (p. 12). Whatever we may speculate about Behn's political loyalties, the dialectical relationship between her feminism and Tory allegiance to the King and Father remains unresolved.

Catherine Gallagher (1988) argues that Behn's libertine stance problematically perpetuates the misogynist sign of woman writer as prostitute (p. 42).

But Behn had no self-supporting female authors to emulate. She had to pave the way for her younger "sisters," making the mistakes and achievements only the next generations could look back upon and learn from. As Deborah C. Payne argues, "Behn could only constitute herself through available cultural discourses," and the only cultural discourses available to the professional writer of the seventeenth century existed within "patriarchal models" of language (p. 13). In order for a work to be published in the Restoration, it had to be approved by the licensing offices of both the Church and State; this de facto censorship profoundly affected what was printed and "[w]riters opposed to the status quo were invariably forced either to keep silent or to argue against establishment policies from within the rhetorical framework defined by their adversaries" (Robert Markley, 1988: p. 39). Behn literally wrote for her bread— she was acutely aware of her audience: what they would allow in print and what they would pay for in the theater. Bawdy was popular in the Restoration, so bawdy she wrote. What is significant about Behn's plays, however, is that she turns masculinist conventions of plot and character to new and potentially subversive purposes.

Behn's versions of sexual scandal and libertine values were markedly different from those of her male contemporaries: The female viewpoint is persistently the reference point in her writing (Dale Spender, 1986: p. 53). Through Behn's portrayal of her female characters, and in her prologues, epilogues, and poems, she sets forth the female condition in seventeenth-century culture, showing how painful, difficult, and powerless the role of the "other" was. Behn was among the first women writers of her time to cross socio-political and gender boundaries, to raise the private female word into the public sphere. Behn's career in itself was a political act—an assertion of female rights and power.

Aphra Behn lived a highly unusual and adventurous life for a woman of any period in history. If we assume that *Oroonoko* represents at least a rough approximation of Behn's experiences in the colonies, we can construct the following narrative about a crucial period in the author's life: in 1663, in her early twenties, Behn traveled with her family to Surinam, a British colony where apparently her father was to hold a post as Lieutenant General of Surinam. However, he died at sea, leaving Behn's status in the colony ambiguous. Her relationship with slaves and involvement with Indians was unusual for the white colonists, particularly for a white "lady" (Angeline Goreau, p. 48). Recent historians assert that Behn's portrayal of the colony of Surinam, the slave trade, and the African customs practiced by the slaves are all reasonably accurate (Goreau, p. 56). After the period described in *Oroonoko*, when Behn returned to England less then a year later (1664), she presumably married Mr. Behn, of whom nothing is known; he apparently died, leaving her no inheritance. In addition, she had been left no dowry by her father. By 1666 Aphra Behn *had* to work, and, oddly enough, she became a spy for the King,

Charles II. At this time there were virtually no women "working " for the King or involved in state matters of any kind; Behn may have secured her position through family connections to the Royalists in the Court. In 1666 Behn sailed to Antwerp at the time of the Second Dutch War, expecting to be paid for her work, but she was not. Although she wrote many letters from Holland, pleading for money she was owed, she received no satisfactory replies. Behn resorted to borrowing in order to pay for her spying efforts; when she returned to England, she was imprisoned in 1668 for the debts acquired while working for Charles II. The length of her imprisonment is uncertain.

At nearly thirty, Behn began to write for her living. Her first play, *The Forc'd Marriage*, was published in 1670. During the next twenty years, she wrote more than seventeen plays (and saw most of them produced), thirteen novels (at least six were published), and several collections of poems and translations. After supporting herself by writing plays for over ten years, she turned to the new genre of the novel. Behn may, in fact, be the initiator of "the novel" in British literature.[2] She had always been a prolific correspondent, and the new genre may have offered an artistic venue which was a natural extension of her letter writing. Further, the political discord in the 1680s—which included the turbulent rule of James II who was forced from the throne by the bloodless Revolution of 1688 and the subsequent ascension of William and Mary—had drained the finances of England's treasury and the theater companies were especially hard hit. Behn, as well as her contemporaries like Dryden and Shadwell, could no longer support themselves solely by having their plays produced. Many friends and peers from Behn's circle died during this time, as did Charles II.

In *Oroonoko*, as in most of her written works, Behn attacks the degrading intrusion of greed into human relationships. In the mid to late-seventeenth century, the English had just begun to earn visible profit from the slave trade, and its inhumanity had not yet been generally questioned (Goreau, p. 57). Behn's radical protest against slavery in the novel illustrates the evil of utilizing human beings—blacks and white women—as property to be bought and sold. The treatment of Oroonoko and the other slaves in the novel can be extended, in Behn's vision, to the treatment of white women as slaves in the seventeenth century. In *Some Reflections upon Marriage*, Mary Astell (1706) asks, "*If all men are born free*, how is it Women are born slaves? as they must be, if the being subjected to the *inconstant, unknown, arbitrary* will of Men be the *perfect Condition of Slavery?*" (p. 76). *Oroonoko* demonstrates that true freedom cannot exist in a world in which more than half the human population on the earth is subordinated to the financial interests of a chosen few. Behn's attack on slavery and her defense of human rights was "the first important abolitionist statement in the history of English literature" (Goreau, p. 289). The relationship between the six million black people who were shipped against their will to foreign shores, chained and forced to forget their native tongues, and the seventeenth-century white women who were also bound by emotional, intellectual, physical, and legal chains is established in *Oroonoko*. As William Spengemann (1984) asserts, "[a]s a slave, [Oroonoko] shares the plight of women" (p. 401). *Oroonoko* marks the beginning of the alliance between feminism and abolitionism (Goreau, p. 289).

The plot of *Oroonoko* reveals Behn's interest in the political issues of the slave trade and ideological conflicts between aristocratic and middle-class definitions of human nature. Oroonoko is an African prince and a fierce warrior, whose grandfather is the King of his land. Oroonoko falls in love with Imoinda and she with him. But the King calls on Imoinda to be his wife, and Imoinda is legally bound, as the law of their country dictates, to submit to the King. Both Imoinda and Oroonoko are heartbroken but eventually find a way to sleep together. When the King discovers they are lovers, he sells Imoinda to slave traders. Fearing Oroonoko's anger, the King tells Oroonoko that he has killed Imoinda. Oroonoko is distraught by his loss but maintains his loyalty to the King.

Oroonoko is later falsely befriended by one of the duplicitous captains of the slave trade ships, the same captain to whom Oroonoko had sold men he captured in battle. The captain lures Oroonoko and his fellow soldiers onto the ship for a feast, and they are trapped and made slaves. The ship is headed for Surinam, where, unbeknown to Oroonoko, Imoinda now resides. Oroonoko is sold to the owner of the same plantation where the narrator and Imoinda live. Oroonoko's natural royalty is apparent to most of the British plantation owners, and he is promised his future freedom. The lovers are married, and Imoinda becomes pregnant, but the couple are unhappy because they realize they will never be freed as promised; they are victims of political conflicts within the colony between honest Tories and duplicitous Whigs. Oroonoko leads a rebellion for all of the slaves, but they desert him in battle. Oroonoko finally surrenders, because he is promised his freedom, but he is again betrayed. Whipped mercilessly as an example to the other slaves, Oroonoko decides to take revenge upon his oppressors—which means his own death. Before taking his revenge, Oroonoko kills Imoinda and their unborn child, so that they will not be left alone and unprotected. She willingly dies. Oroonoko is caught in the forest after having killed her, and he is tortured to death in a horrific public display.

*Oroonoko* raises important questions concerning the powerlessness of the "other"—whether black slaves, native Indians, or white or black women. Although, as Laura Brown (1987) points out, Aphra Behn's Tory narrator may not be on equal footing with the black slaves; nonetheless, the novel serves as "a model for the mutual interaction of the positions of the oppressed in the literary discourse of its own age" (p. 43). While Behn's narrator does champion aristocratic ideology in her depiction of Oroonoko, the novel simultaneously questions imperialist and colonialist discourses which are oppressive to women and black slaves. *Oroonoko* subverts traditional notions of the "other" as weak, unintelligent, untrustworthy, and, in women, lacking sexual desire. Behn marks the potential for female self-possession and assertiveness through the female narrator's claiming authority and through her political and symbolic alliance with Oroonoko.

Behn's novel interlocks economies of class, race and, gender in part by contrasting images of the modern and prelapsarian worlds. Behn portrays the natives of Surinam as living in an Edenic paradise; as the narrator states, "these People represented to me an absolute *Idea* of the first State of Innocence, before *Man* knew how to sin" (p. 3). Oroonoko represents the "new man" who is the embodiment of "the best principles of progressive ideology more [successful] than most of his fellow moderns" (Michael McKeon, 1987: p. 250). In her portrait of Oroonoko, Behn creates an idealized aristocrat of prelapsarian vision and modern European nobility—a black man who is not culturally "other," a slave who is royal. Oroonoko's treatment of Imoinda is exceptional as well, for "contrary to the custom of his Country, he made her Vows, she shou'd be the only Woman he wou'd possess while he liv'd; that no Age or Wrinkles shou'd encline him to change; for her Soul wou'd be always fine, and always young" (p. 11). Oroonoko's unusual regard for Imoinda clearly surpasses that of men and women from *any* race or class in the seventeenth century. Oroonoko is depicted as "an archaic remnant of the world before its fall into modern depravity, the vestige of a time when noble birth justly signified inner virtue" (McKeon, p. 250). Constructed to be of the highest class, Oroonoko is simultaneously (and unrealistically) classless. In contrast, money grubbing, hypocritical European Whigs are portrayed as the real savages—the white male Tories, such as Trefry, befriend and support Oroonoko—and the lower-class black slaves desert Oroonoko during the rebellion.

Yet there are no easy set of oppositions in *Oroonoko* of class and race: within each group there are infinitely more divisions. Oppressive hierarchical relationships exist also among the Africans; for example, Imoinda is possessed against her will by a King, and Oroonoko sells slaves to white traders. Further, Oroonoko is ultimately destroyed by the aristocratic principles he initially embodies: his interest in learning more about Western culture draws him onto the ship, and as a slave his inherent nobility makes him more vulnerable than the other slaves, because it threatens the authority of his oppressors. Despite these apparent contradictions, Behn's novel demonstrates that it is always the matter of acquiring profit through dishonest and self-interested means which leads to the oppression of the *other* sex, race, or class. Finally, one of Behn's strategies for subverting white male repression of women and slaves is to demonstrate the political divisions, particularly between Tories and Whigs, within patriarchy.

The prologues and epilogues to her plays often reveal the difficulties Behn suffered as a published woman writer; they also articulate her great strength and outspokenness, as well as her concern for the oppression of women. In the prologue to her first play, *The Forc'd Marriage* (1670), Behn openly declares and defends her gender. In *Oroonoko*, Behn *never* lets her audience forget the author is a woman and what that means. She foregrounds her female identity, her female subjectivity, and her female authority in the novel *Oroonoko*. Her self-assertion is evident in *Oroonoko* in the use of the first person narrative—she creates a female "I" or "eye" who observes and comments upon the action she describes. At the beginning of the novel, the narrator states, "I was myself an Eyewitness to a great part of what You will find here set down; and what I cou'd not be witness of, I reciev'd from the Mouth of the chief Actor in this History, the Hero himself" (p. 1). The narrational use of the "I" was a new literary technique, a radical departure from traditional narrational forms (Goreau, 281). It seems even more radical if we consider that Behn's narrator in *Oroonoko* is a woman. The female narrator is the teller of her own history, the teller of the history of slavery, and a major actor in the plot (William Spengemann, p. 399). The narrator's authority is further constituted by telling her tale as a "true story" (Spengemann, p. 390). Behn's novel incorporates female truth-telling into traditional masculine notions of authority.

In Western literature the reader or spectator is constructed as male. And even more typically, the male spectator gazes upon a female *object* of desire. His gaze renders the female powerless: she is vapid, inhuman, a sexual object—it is *his* actions towards and responses to her which are important. As readers, we are ideologically indoctrinated into this game. We adopt the male gaze, because we are culturally induced to see through his eyes. Laura Mulvey (1975) explains how Woman is displayed as an "icon" for "the gaze and enjoyment of men, the active controllers of the look" (p. 13). Thus, identification with the male gaze is inescapable:

> In their traditional exhibitionist role women are simultaneously looked at and displayed, with their appearance coded for strong visual and erotic impact so that they can be said to connote *to-be-looked-at-ness*. Woman displayed as sexual object is the leit-motif of erotic spectacle. (Mulvey, 1975, p. II)

If we accept Laura Mulvey's argument concerning the female "other," we may extend the notion of the male gaze to include the category of race. Let us say we have a "white male gaze" in Western culture, which renders all who are not possessors of the white male phallus powerless, depleted, and subject to *"to-be-looked-at-ness."* The white male gaze resembles what Michel Foucault (1975) calls, "a great white eye that unties the knot of life" (p. 144). According to Foucault, the gaze, as we now recognize it, emerged from the eighteenth-century (male) medical study of the human body—not only the female body, but specifically the bodies of the poor who were experimented upon and were made spectacles for the benefit of the rich (p. 84). The gaze was the possession of the white wealthy patriarch who endowed the clinical white (male) doctor with a calculating power: "no longer a living eye, but the gaze of an eye that has seen death" (p. 144). The gaze represents the exercise of dominance and the fiction that the power relations it constructs are "natural" and inevitable.

What Behn does with the concept of the gaze is complex. While she does present a potentially subversive position in the use of the female narrator, it is always the white male gaze which is ideologically unmasked through her vision. As Behn demonstrates, the one looked at is made vulnerable by his or her becoming a spectacle. The person who is gazed upon becomes a commodity, a thing to be *had*, possessed, and consumed by the onlooker. Typically, it is women who are looked at as objects of desire, but Behn extends this assumption in *Oroonoko* to include all "others" who do not possess the white male phallus. Behn keeps shifting the direction of the gaze in *Oroonoko*—first it is aimed at Imoinda, then at Oroonoko, and, at times, at the narrator herself. In the novel, Behn describes a world in which the white male gaze is problematic; its coercive power relations are more or less visible, and the body is potentially freed from the seventeenth-century patriarchal eye of control.

Oppressive ideological discourses of gender and race conspire to construct Imoinda as a sex object and commodity. It is her forced role as an object of male desire which causes her to be enslaved. The King offers Imoinda the "Royal Veil" which means "she is cover'd, and secur'd for the King's Use; and 'tis Death to disobey; besides, held a most impious Disobedience" (p. 12). Imoinda's "Youth and Beauty" make her "liable to [the] cruel Promotion" of becoming the King's wife (p. 24). Later when she dances before the King and an audience which includes Oroonoko, Imoinda moves closer and closer to her lover and literally falls from the stage into his arms. Her prelapsarian bond with Oroonoko, unlike her relationship with the King, is mutual rather than hierarchical; between the lovers there exists a "powerful Language alone that in an instant convey'd all the Thoughts of their Souls to *each other*; that they *both* found there wanted but Opportunity to make them *both* entirely happy" (p. 17, italics added). Neither lover is exclusively the object of the other's desire. With the King, however, Imoinda "bemoan'd her own miserable Captivity," for she was a "trembling Victim" of his will (p. 17). When Imoinda acts on her own desires and sleeps with Oroonoko, the King sells her to the slave traders.

The economy of the gaze functions to enslave Oroonoko as well. Like Imoinda, who is initially made a slave because she is beautiful and female, Oroonoko is made captive because he can be sold for a great deal of money. They are both made objects of desire in order that slave traders and male colonialists may gain pleasure and profit at their expense. When Oroonoko is brought to the West Indies, the narrator is struck by his physical beauty; she describes him in much the same way a male narrator would depict the female object. After offering a litany of Oroonoko's honorable qualities which have been described to her, the narrator says she has a "Curiosity to *see him*" (p. 7, italics added). Critics have argued that Oroonoko is given qualities and physical characteristics which sound strangely like a white person's, such as his roman nose and "[fine] shaped" mouth, "far from those great turn'd Lips, which are so natural to the rest of the Negroes" (p. 8). Oroonoko is constructed as an idealized example of an aristocrat rather than a typical member of his race. He is depicted as a part of the white "us," rather that the monstrous "other."

Laura Brown argues that Oroonoko's physical description is racially and ideologically problematic; Behn adopts an absurd conflation of disparate cultural values and backgrounds in her picture of the hero (p. 48). Significantly, Oroonoko is explicitly compared to Charles I, the royal martyr who had been deposed and executed in 1649. The beheading of the King represented a subversive historical moment in the relationship of the individual to authority, and loyalty to the King and Father. The narrator tellingly paints Oroonoko as a Royalist object of her female desire:

> The whole Proportion and Air of his Face was so nobly and exactly form'd, that bating his Colour, there could be nothing in Nature more beautiful, agreeable and handsome. There was no one Grace wanting, that bears the Standard of true Beauty. His Hair came down to his Shoulders, by the Aids of Art, which was by pulling it out with a Quill, and keeping it comb'd; of which he took particular care. (p. 8)

But Oroonoko's inherently noble looks, like Imoinda's female beauty, make him susceptible to the male white gaze. Trefry, who purchases Oroonoko, is also struck by his physical appearance: "he fix'd his Eyes on him; and finding something so extraordinary in his Face, his Shape and Mein, a greatness of Look . . .,Trefry soon found he [Oroonoko] was yet something greater than he confessed" (p. 38). When Trefry takes Oroonoko down the river to the plantation, "numbers of People would flock to behold this Man. . . . The Fame of *Oroonoko* was gone before him." Oroonoko's royalty cannot be masked: "[t]he Royal Youth appear'd in spight of the Slave" (p. 39).

Once a slave, Oroonoko is made an object of desire which the public flocks to see and ultimately destroy. The Tories admire Oroonoko and recognize his inherent nobility, but the Whigs keep him enslaved and eventually execute him. In effect, Aphra Behn is asking her readers to judge the political morality of the colonists on the basis of how they respond to Oroonoko. Oroonoko's death is the heightened moment of public performance in the novel; he is made to suffer in the grips of the white male gaze and the power it represents. First he is publicly whipped, and later, at the same spot, his body cut to pieces—quarters to be exact—and the "frightful Spectacles of a mangled King" are parceled out to the plantations (p. 77). Oroonoko is finally multiplied into many objects owned by many white men—symbolically, the slave trader's dream.

Behn's narrator presents, on the other hand, a dialectical prelapsarian vision of Surinam in the Indian culture. Both aristocratic and imperialist discourses are temporarily turned on their heads. Through the portrait of the Indians, the dominant ideology of the white male gaze is potentially undermined:

> And though they are all thus naked, if one lives for ever among 'em, there is not to be seen an undecent Action, or Glance: and being continually us'd to see one another so unadorn'd, so like our first Parents before the Fall, it seems as if they had no Wishes, there being nothing to heighten Curiosity; but all you can see, you see at once, and every moment see; and where there is no Novelty there can be no Curiosity. (p. 3)

The natives are liberated by their nakedness and earthly connections; they "have a native justice, which knows no Fraud" (p. 4). The natives of Surinam represent, therefore, a preclass society, repressed by neither sexual nor political tyranny. When the narrator and her white company go into the forest to meet the Indians, traditional hierarchical roles are reversed; white people turn into the "other." The Westerners become the spectacle of the gaze, for they are dressed "very glittering and rich," and the natives are not (p. 55). Commodities, therefore, breed distance. In this scene Behn demonstrates that the objects of trade and profit—their costly clothes— are what make the white people vulnerable to the power of the gaze. Thus the Indians paw the colonialists, as the narrator describes, "feeling our Breasts and Arms, taking up one Petticoat, then wondering to see another. . . . In time, we suffer'd 'em to survey us as they pleas'd, and we thought they would never have done admiring us" (p. 55). The narrator notes that the Indians' lack of garments and ignorance of the Christian religion and Western law are, in fact, honorable, for "they understand no Vice, or Cunning, but when they are taught by *White Men*" (p. 4). Notably, the "Vice" the Indians are taught, as shown earlier in the novel, is to trade buffalo skins "paraketoes," or feathers with the white colonialists. In this respect, "Vice" and "Cunning" are by-products of the commodification and exploitation of their environment and their culture.

At the beginning of the novel, Oroonoko is complicit in the mercantile aspect of white culture; he sells the black soldiers he captures to the slave traders. He has also adopted Western customs in his language and style, which the narrator at first admires. But as the novel progresses, Oroonoko appropriates some of the prelapsarian qualities of the natives which represent his only hope of freedom from the white male gaze and the political repression it symbolizes. As the narrator notes, when Imoinda and Oroonoko look into each other's eyes—"*Ceasar* [Oroonoko's slave name] swore he disdained the Empire of the World, while he could behold his *Imoinda*; and she could gaze on *Oroonoko*" (p. 44). The freeing gaze between Oroonoko and Imoinda demonstrates that only when objects of profit do not come before equality in relationships can hierarchical and oppressive bonds be abolished.

When Oroonoko runs into the forest with Imoinda, with his plan to kill her, then his oppressors, and finally himself, he is both enacting an aristocratic ideal of noble virtue and imitating the warrior Indians he has met who cut off the pieces of their own faces and bodies to prove their valor (p. 58). While at first a horrific vision to the narrator, the Indians are soon regarded as "very humane and noble" (p. 57). In this respect, the definition of nobility shifts within the novel to include the natives of Surinam. Thus Oroonoko behaves more and more like the Indians and less like a European or African prince when he finally resists his enslavement. He has retreated to the forest, to Indian territory. Oroonoko cuts a piece of his own flesh from his throat and belly, as he has seen the Indian warriors do, and he smells strongly of the earth (p. 75). Rather than leave his wife, future child, and himself to lives of slavery, he takes all of their flesh and makes them one with nature—burying Imoinda beneath leaves and ripping at his own body in a display of self empowerment.

No matter how contradictory Behn's political allegiances may be to aristocratic ideology, native culture, and antislavery sentiment, *Oroonoko* finally suggests that only when money is no longer the primary object of human exchange can truly free and humane relationships exist. While Behn does not appear to be conscious of these contradictions, the diffuse sexual, racial, and social politics in the novel potentially subvert the repressive discourses of the late seventeenth and early eighteenth centuries. The eyes of the female narrator are undoubtedly conditioned by her patriarchal, white-dominated culture, which in part explains the problematic relationship of the sexual and racial politics in *Oroonoko*. The narrator's view of the native Indians and Oroonoko is never free of Tory propagandism, and thus the depiction of them is never entirely liberating by twentieth-century standards. However, just as the narrator is physically powerless to prevent the crimes done to Oroonoko (she is notably never present when the violence occurs to him), Behn may be similarly powerless in uncovering a language to describe her characters which is not bound by the prejudices, values, and assumptions of her age.

Why Behn supported Royalist principles which left all power to the King and Father, while she simultaneously bemoaned the fate of the oppressed throughout her work, remains, therefore, a problematic question. But to say point blank that Behn was racist and not a feminist is too simple. One of the first works to cry out openly against slavery, *Oroonoko* remains an important feminist and abolitionist novel. In *A Serious Proposal To The Ladies* (1696), Mary Astell proposes that we look

above the Vulgar by something more truly illustrious, than a sounding Title or a great Estate. . . . [And] [n]ot take up with the low thought of distinguishing . . . [ourselves] by any thing that is not truly valuable, and procure [us] such Ornaments as all the Treasures of the Indies are not able to purchase. (Astell, 1696, p. 139)

Like Astell, Behn asks her readers to look beyond the "fleeting and fickle" (Astell, p. 189) economic gain which was achieved, as *Oroonoko* so keenly demonstrates, at the great expense of black slaves in the colonies. The trinkets found in the "Profitable Adventures" (Astell, 1696, p. 139) of the British imperialists, like the South African jewels we wear today, are symbols of the interlocking economic forces by which women and black people were, and still are enslaved. So, above all else, Aphra Behn's novel tellingly describes the relationship between the oppression of black slaves and women of the seventeenth century with colonial expansionism and white male profit. The productive tensions in *Oroonoko* dramatize the contradictory ideological forces at work in her time.

## NOTES

[1]Edmund Gosse (1884) asserts in "Mrs. Behn" that Behn was the daughter of a barber and not a gentlewoman, as previously believed. This information was later found to be untrue. In 1913, Ernest Bernbaum argued in "Mrs. Behn's Biography, a Fiction," that Behn was not female, she never went to Surinam, she never warned the king of the Dutch attack, and there was no Mr. Behn. Behn's contemporary biographers obviously disagree.

[2]Michael McKeon (1987) suggests there is no "first" novel in British Literature (p. 267), but a number of feminist critics, including Angeline Goreau (1980, p. 284), Judith Kegan Gardiner (1989, p. 1), Moira Ferguson (1985, p. 143), and Maureen Duffy (1987, p. viii), consider Behn to be the first British novelist. The *Love Letters Between a Nobleman and His Sister* (published in three volumes: 1684–1687) was her first novel.

## REFERENCES

Astell, Mary. (1760 and 1986). Reflections upon Marriage, In Bridget Hill (Ed.), *The first English feminist: Reflections upon marriage and other writings by Mary Astell* (pp. 69–132). New York: St. Martin's Press.

Astell, Mary. (1696 and 1986). A serious proposal to the ladies. In Bridget Hill (Ed.), *The first English feminist: Reflections upon marriage and other writings by Mary Astell* (pp. 135–172). New York: St. Martin's Press.

Behn, Aphra. (1668 and 1973). *Oroonoko or, The royal slave.* New York, London: W. W. Norton.

Bernbaum, Ernest. (1913). Mrs. Behn's biography, a fiction. *PMLA, 28,* 432–453.

Brown, Laura. (1987). The romance of empire: *Oroonoko* and the trade in slaves. In Felicity Nussbaum & Laura Brown (Eds.), *The new eighteenth-century: Theory * Politics * English literature* (pp. 39–61). New York: Methuen.

Duffy, Maureen. (1977). *The passionate shepherdess: Aphra Behn 1640–89.* London: Jonathan Cape.

Duffy, Maureen. (1684 and 1987). Introduction. In Aphra Behn, *Love letters between a nobleman and his sister* (p. viii). London: Penguin-Virago.

Ferguson, Moira. (1985). *First Feminists: British Women Writers 1578–1799.* Bloomington, IN: Indiana University Press.

Foucault, Michel. (1975). *The birth of the clinic: An archeology of medical perception.* New York: Vintage Books. (Original work published 1973.)

Gallagher, Catherine. (1988). Who was that masked woman? The prostitute and the playwright in the comedies of Aphra Behn. *Women Studies, 15,* 23–42.

Gardiner, Judith Kegan. (1989). The first English novel: Aphra Behn, the canon, and women's tastes. *Tulsa Studies, 8*(2), 201–222.

Goreau, Angeline. (1980). *Reconstructing Aphra: A social biography of Aphra Behn.* New York: Dial Press.

Gosse, Edmund. (1884). Mrs. Behn. *Athenaeum, 2,* 304.

History of the life and memoirs of Mrs. Behn, by one of the fair sex (1696 and 1751). In Charles Gildon (Pub), *All the histories and novels written by the late ingenious Mrs. Behn* (pp. 1–2). London: T. Longman.

Markley, Robert. (1988). *Two-edg'd weapons: style and ideology in the comedies of Etherege, Wycherly and Congreve.* Oxford: Clarendon Press.

McKeon, Michael. (1987). *The origins of the novel, 1600–1740.* Baltimore: Johns Hopkins University Press.

Mulvey, Laura. (1975). Visual pleasure and narrative cinema. *Screen, 16,* 6–18.

Link, Frederick M. (1968). *Aphra Behn.* New York: Twayne.

Payne, Deborah C. (1991). "Poets shall by patron-poets live": Aphra Behn and patronage. In Mary Anne Schofield and Cynthia Macheski (Eds.), *Curtain calls: British and American women and the theater.*

Sackville-West, Vita. (1927). *Aphra Behn: The incomparable Astrea.* London: G. Howe.

Smith, Hilda L. (1982). *Reason's disciples: Seventeenth-century English feminists.* Urbana: University of Illinois Press.

Spender, Dale. (1986). *Mothers of the novel: 100 good women writers before Jane Austen.* London: Pandora.

Spengemann, William C. (1984). The earliest American novel: Aphra Behn's *Oroonoko. Nineteenth-century Fiction, 38,* 384–414.

Woodcock, George. (1948). *The incomparable Aphra.* London: T.V. Boardman.

Woolf, Virginia. (1928 and 1929). *A room of one's own.* New York: Harcourt, Brace.

# Preparatives to Love:

## Seduction as Fiction in the Works of Eliza Haywood

Ros Ballaster

Over a period of roughly forty years, Eliza Haywood pursued a relentless "career in love," establishing her place as the undisputed Queen of Romance in early-eighteenth-century British culture.[1] The dominance of this position is indicated by her position as one of the few women writers who "merited" a direct mention in Alexander Pope's *Dunciad* of 1728. Eliza Haywood is the prize for which the two publishers, Chetwood and Curll, compete in the goddess Dulness' "Olympic" games:

> See in the circle next, *Eliza* placed;
> Two babes of love close clinging to her waste;
> Fair as before her works she stands confess'd
> In flow'rd brocade by bounteous *Kirkall* dress'd,
> Pearls on her neck, and roses in her hair,
> And her fore buttocks to the navel bare.
>
> (Pope, 1963, 119–120)

The footnote continues to equate Eliza Haywood's writing with prostitution, where Pope tells us that Eliza is "the authoress of those most scandalous books call'd *The Court of Carimania* and *The New Utopia*" (p. 119) and that:

> In this game is expos'd in the most contemptuous manner, the profligate licentiousness of those shameless Scribblers, (for the most part of that Sex, which ought least to be capable of such malice or impudence) who in libellious Memoirs and Novels, reveal the faults and misfortunes of both sexes, to the ruin or disturbance, of publick fame or private happiness. (p. 119)

Haywood's "two babes of love" then are the two scandal novels that Pope refers to; they are her two illegitimate (that is, subliterary) children, spawned from a licentious and corrupted imagination. Throughout her lifetime, Haywood's works were transparently equated with her supposed sexual practices. More interestingly perhaps—since this is by no means an uncommon manner in which to denigrate women's writing—Haywood happily exploited this equation for personal profit and celebrity in her own writing, presenting herself as an expert amateur philosopher of love, eager to impart her worldly wisdom to her young and innocent female readers.

Haywood's career in love was a deeply checkered one. Part of a literary circle that included Aaron Hill, Susannah Centilevre, Richard Savage, and probably Daniel Defoe, her allies appear to have been anything but secure. Richard Savage, previously an admirer, turned on her viciously in his *An Author to be Lett* in 1729. Savage's polemic against marketplace practices in literary production centers Haywood as a symbol of the degenerate hack from its very title page, echoing the title of one of Haywood's earliest works, *A Wife to be Lett* (a play she wrote and in which she acted in 1723). As with Pope, it seems to have been her scandal novels that roused his indignation.[2] Savage presents her as a populist tout and bemoans her choice to waste her female talents on writing for a subsistence, rather than washing:

> She might have . . . considered the sullied Linen growing white in her pretty red Hands, as an Emblem of her Soul, were it well-*scoured* by Repentance for the Sins of her Youth: But she rather chuses starving by writing Novels of Intrigue, to teach young heiresses the Art of running away with Fortune-hunters, and scandalizing Persons of the highest Worth and Distinction. (n. p.)

Haywood's use of her femaleness to sell her works—her creation of a specifically feminine authorial persona with a direct address to female readers—is seen both as a form of scandalous prostitution and a seduction of other women. Haywood, in other words, chose to flaunt the sexuality that eighteenth-century patriarchy sought to regiment and police.[3] Not only were her works sold on the open market, they also entered the sacred heart of the social order, the middle-class home.

We know very little about Eliza Haywood's personal history. Her vast literary output is virtually the sole testament to the woman and a very unreliable witness, at that. She was probably born in 1693 and was the daughter of a shopkeeper named Fowler. When she was around thirty years old, she published her first novel, *Love in Excess,* over the years 1719–1720. On January 7th, 1721 *The Post Boy* carried a statement from the Reverend Valentine Haywood refusing to pay his wife's debts following her elopement from him in November, 1720. She died in 1757, presumably with pen in hand, because three more books (*The Wife, The Husband, in Answer to the Wife,* and *The Young Lady*) were published in the same year. These amount to the verifiable facts about her life, apart from at least 67 publications over the period of 1719 to 1770 which are directly attributable to her authorship (George Frisbie Whicher, 1915; Janet Todd, 1984), one of which, *Love in Excess,* was one of the three best-selling works of fiction before the publication of Richardson's *Pamela* in 1740 (John Richetti, 1969). Its illustrious companions were Jonathan Swift's *Gulliver's Travels* (1726) and Defoe's *Robinson Crusoe* (1719).

Haywood was an extraordinarily versatile writer, producing drama (both comedy and tragedy), romance, domestic and epistolary fiction, periodicals, scandal novels, poetry, empirical "philosophy," and seven "translations" from French. Her massive literary output is best explained by the small payment an individual work of fiction could command. Authors of novels usually received a lump sum from the publisher of between one and ten guineas (Robert Adams Day, 1966, p. 79). A woman supporting herself, possibly with children, would need to steadily turn out a large amount of fiction in order to provide herself with a living wage.

An unaccountable publishing silence (or rather retreat into the use of pseudonyms or anonymous publication) on Haywood's part, between the years 1728 and 1744, has generated a series of myths about her literary and personal career—inextricably linked as they seem to be. There is a distinctive shift in Haywood's style and moral perspective in this second period, when she reappeared on the literary stage with her periodical *The Female Spectator* and a novel entitled *The Fortunate Foundlings*. The salacious and exotic stories, peopled with characters at least nominally linked to the French romance, are replaced by moral speculation upon London society and British domestic arrangements. A typical erotic-pathetic scene of seduction from Haywood's earlier period is Philecta's seduction by Dorimenus in *The Masqueraders* (Part II, 1725) (Haywood, 1732, 1–45). Philecta, out of curiosity and revenge at her own ill-treatment at the hands of a previous lover, endeavors to steal the affection of Dorimenus from her closest friend, Dalinda. Having succeeded, she panics and determines not to see him again, realizing she has fallen passionately in love with him. He, however, searching to clarify her feelings, makes his way into her bedroom as she wakes, and "at last, amidst Delight and Pain, a Rack of Extasy on both sides, she more faintly denying, he more vigorously pressing, half yielding, half reluctant, she was wholly lost" (p. 41).

By the 1740s, however, Eliza Haywood appears to be attacking the very language and style of romance that she had previously employed to such effect. In the *Female Spectator* she criticizes the authors of romances, novels, and plays, who:

> dress their Cupid up in Roses, call him the God of soft Desires and ever-springing Joys, yet at the same time give him the vindicative Fury and the Rage of Mars—show him impatient of Control and trampling over all the Ties of Duty, Friendship, or natural Affection, yet make the Motive sanctify the Crime. . . . The Beauty of the Expression, steals upon the Senses, and every Mischief, every Woe that Love occasions, appears a Charm. (in Alison Adburgham, 1972, p. 97)

This mysterious change of heart is commonly explained in two ways, depending on the charity the critic exhibits towards Eliza Haywood. Bridget MacCarthy sees it as a shrewd marketing move on Haywood's part, following a change in reading tastes in the mid-eighteenth century. Richardson's *Pamela* in this view is interpreted as transforming a seemingly unquenchable desire for erotic titillation and voyeuristic indulgence in sexual fantasy on the part of eighteenth-century readers into an interest in the moral realism of the domestic, sentimental novel. Bridget MacCarthy describes Haywood as "gritting her teeth at the contradictions of her lifetime. In her young days, bawdy writers were sure of bread; now they were sure only of stones" (MacCarthy, 1944, p. 241).

The more charitable view is the one that Haywood herself sought to propagate, that of a sincere moral conversion. In her introduction to the first number of the *Female Spectator,* Haywood admits woefully, "My life, for some years, was a continued round of what I then called pleasure, and my whole time engrossed by a hurry of promiscuous diversions" (Haywood, 1744–46; p. 2). She quickly adds, however, that this experience had one advantage—it may have been of service to her public:

> [It] enabled me, when the too great vivacity of my nature became tempered with reflection, to see into the secret springs which give rise to the actions I had either heard or been witness of, to judge of the various passions of the human mind and distinguish those imperceptible degrees by which they become matters of the heart, and attain the dominion over reason. (p. 2)

This is the version that Clara Reeve accepts in *The Progress of Romance* (1785), where Haywood's associations with early libertine fiction are forgiven since "she repented of her faults, and employed the latter part of her life in expiating the offences of the former, (Reeve, 1785, p. 120) Here Haywood comes to sound suspiciously like her own romance heroines who retire in droves to convents or distant climes to expiate their sins of the flesh, providing they succeed in avoiding a miserable death as punishment.

Debate over the question of whether or not Haywood was a smart operator or the literary equivalent of St. Paul has obscured the fact that throughout her work there is a remarkable consistency in her presentation of sexual desire and in her view of fiction's role in the stimulation or repression of sexual passion in female readers. Haywood's fiction is underscored by a profound and gloomy cynicism about heterosexual love relations and their possibilities for longevity. At the same time as she lays the blame for this state of affairs squarely on the rapacious selfishness of male desire, she sees the only opportunity for redemption in female love. In this respect, she is indeed remarkably close to romantic fiction writers of the present day, who shore up patriarchal ideology by their idealized representations of male-female love relations, but also provide women readers with a sense of their instrumentality and power, by representing this stasis as being achieved only by the tender and loving influence of the woman upon the brutal but fatally attractive male.[4] Virginia Woolf, reviewing George Whicher's "biography" of Haywood in 1916, recognized the links between this early women's fiction and formula romance, and he despised her work because of it. Woolf writes: "There is the same desire to escape from the familiar look of life by the easiest way, and the difference is really that we find our romance in accumulated motorcars and marquises rather than in foreign parts and strange-sounding names" (Woolf, 1916, p. 95). Yet, the consolatory power of the romance formula is all too frequently refused by Eliza Haywood for a far bleaker picture of women's existence under male power.

Haywood's treatise on love, published in 1726, baldly states the gulf between male and female desire, which is acted out in her fiction. In her usual extravagant prose, she describes the "Winter of Indifference and Neglect, which rarely, if ever, fails to succeed the sultry Summer of too fierce Desire in Man's unconstant Heart" (1726: p. 53). Of female desire she writes:

> The other may love with Vehemence, but then it is neither so tender nor so lasting a Flame; and seldom does it carry them further than a Self-Gratification. . . . A Woman, where she loves, has no Reserve; she profusely gives her all, has no Regard to any Thing, but obliging the Person she affects and lavishes her whole Soul. (pp. 11–12)

Male sexual passion is exploitative, end-directed, and short-lived in Haywood's fiction. Possession of the love object almost inevitably breeds contempt. Her pages are littered with deserted heroines, cast aside in boredom, once the man has seduced them, in favor of a new object.

In *The Rash Resolve*, Emilius—persuaded that his mistress Emanuella has been unfaithful to him—sets out in pursuit of a new woman, Julia. Haywood, in one of her frequent asides, comments:

> O the Enchantments of *Novelty*, the Delights there are in having something to subdue—the pleasing Fears—the sweet hopes, the tender Anxieties—the thousand nameless, soft Perplexities which fill the roving Soul of Man when in pursuit of a *new* Conquest; but after *Possession* are no more remembered—Then *cold* Civility succeeds *tumultuous* Transport—when absent, curs'd *Indifference*, that of *impatient Longings*—and *dull insipid Gratitude* is all the *yielding Fair* can hope for, even from the best of Men. (pp. 80–81)

This is an equally common complaint in Haywood's later fiction, although the same dire moral warnings are now presented without the ameliorating representation of female sexual pleasure, in those short weeks of pursuit, and male fidelity. Even the most honorable of her later heroes, Mr. Trueworth in *Betsy Thoughtless*, is not above exploiting the female heart for personal pleasure when he finds Betsy's false friend, Flora Mellasin, is infatuated with him. While Haywood criticizes her heroine for her indiscretion and lack of thought about the hazards she is running to her reputation, Mr. Trueworth's honor seems to remain intact, despite his engagement in a full-blown sexual affair with a woman of quality. Trueworth uses Flora Mellasin to expel Betsy, whom he thinks unworthy of marriage, from his affections: "The amour with this fond girl afforded him a pleasing amusement for a time; and, without filling his heart with a new passion, cleared it of those remains of his former one . . ." (p. 283). Male fidelity is always the exception and never the rule. *The Surprise: Or, Constancy Rewarded* (1732, vol III, pp. 168–202) provides one of Haywood's rare comic resolutions, entailing reunited lovers and a double marrige. Euphemia, who thinks herself deserted by her lover, Bellamant, discovers that he was forced to leave her since neither his, nor her, fortune was sufficient to support them both. He then proceeds to court her wealthy cousin, Alinda. Alinda agrees to refuse him and accepts her other lover, Ellmour. When Bellamant is imprisoned for debt, Euphemia, who has now inherited a large fortune, secures his release and, disguised in a veil, asks him to marry her. He agrees out of gratitude, but she succeeds in forcing him to an admission that he loves "another" woman (Euphemia herself). She then reveals herself, and all four lovers are happily married. Haywood's "happily-ever-after" platitudes on this occasion are, however, tempered by her habitual vein of cynicism about the norms of heterosexual love:

> Thus was *Constancy* on all Sides *rewarded;* and by the continu'd Tenderness they had for each other after Marriage, gave a proof that Possession does not always extinguish Desire, and surpris'd the World with an Example, which I am afraid more will *admire* than *imitate.* (1732, III, p. 202)

The tragic obverse of this resolution is the more common one in Haywood's early fiction. Her *Idalia: Or, the Unfortunate Mistress* (1732, III, pp. 3–166) consists of a series of rapes, seductions, and betrayals inflicted upon the heroine whose "Beauty, like a fatal Comet, was destructive to all on whom it had any influence" (p. 39). To no one is it more destructive than to Idalia herself. From her first rape and abduction by a young nobleman to the tragic mistake of identity which leads her to murder her "true" lover, Myrtano, to her own suicide, Idalia is a victim. Reunited with Myrtano after a long separation engineered by his present wife, Idalia recommences their affair. Haywood prophetically warns that "guilty Pleasures are never of any long Continuance; the inconsiderate Heart, which quitting Virtue places its whole Felicity in *Love,* sooner or later, must confess the Error, and curse in unavailing Penitence the luscious Crime which lured them on to Ruin" (pp. 143–44).

It is not merely criminal or adulterous love that is fatal for women in Haywood's fictions, but love itself—unless they can learn to control and manipulate "that Tyrant Passion [which] lords it o'er the Mind, fills every faculty, and leaves no Room for any other Thought" (*The Rash Resolve,* p. 40). Women, Haywood argues, are less able to temper their passion, because they are offered no other form of social power or diversion. In *Reflections* she comments:

> . . . wanting the Avocatives of Business, or those Amusements which a Variety of Company affords the other Sex, they have more leisure as well as more

Desire to indulge their Thoughts and sooth deluded Fancy: Thus do the self-
decieved, supply Fuel to the unceasing Fire which consumes their Peace, and
rarely is extinguish'd but by Death. (Haywood, 1726: pp. 55–56)

Haywood's heroines are faced with what amounts to a conspiracy to love,
surrounded by romance fiction, beleaguered with impassioned letters from
their lovers, and finally seduced by Nature itself. In *The British Recluse*, two
women tell their stories of seduction and betrayal at the hands of the same
man. Belinda describes her lover's attempt to seduce her in a wood:

Never was a Night more delectable, more aiding to a Lover's Wishes! the arch-
ing Trees form'd a Canopy over our Heads, while through the gently shaking
Boughs soft Breezes play'd in willing Murmurings, and fann'd us with delicious
Gales! a thousand Nightingales sang amorous Ditties, and the billing Doves coo'd
out their tender Transports! . . . The very Soul of Love seem'd to inform the Place,
and reign throughout the Whole. (Haywood, 1725b, II, p. 93)

Trapped within this eroticized landscape, the female body gives up the unequal struggle, and Belinda reports that her "trembling Limbs refus'd to oppose
the Lovely Tyrant's Will!" (p. 93). So too in *Betsy Thoughtless*, Betsy's old
schoolfriend, Miss Forward, describes her inability to resist the power of Nature in her seduction by a Mr. Wildly. As she describes meeting her lover
at the gates to the school garden she recalls the "gentle zephyrs" and "thousand odours from the neighbouring plants," adding that "Nature herself seemed
to conspire my ruin" (p. 82). Haywood develops an effective strategy for reliev-
ing female guilt about sexual desire by insisting that the women are not responsible. Her female readers can thus indulge the pleasures of sexual fantasy,
while the author vindicates them. As Patricia Meyer Spacks points out, Haywood's heroines are frequently in a dream-state during her seduction scenes.
Haywood thus offers her female readers "a vision of irresponsibility, expressing female sexuality, without being subject to judgement" (Spacks, 1974–1975,
p. 33).

Romance emerges then in Haywood's fiction as a delusion which women
inhabit whether they will or no. Intelligence is no protection from the all-
embracing power of desire. Indeed, it only exacerbates female misery because
the woman can see her doom while being unable to avoid it. The preface
to her epistolary novel, *Letters from a Lady of Quality to a Chevalier* (1720),
one of many early-eighteenth-century derivatives of the massively popular *Portuguese Letters*,[5] comments that:

The happy *Idiot*, blest in Security, postpones not her Misfortune, and perhaps
for many Years, enjoys a State of Tranquillity; while the *Woman of Wit*, with
aking heart, perceives from far, the Ruin she is sure to meet, and fain would
fly, but cannot. (Haywood, 1724, p. 5)

Haywood's fiction offers a series of strategies for women to deal with the
oppressive power of romantic delusion and the abusive nature of male desire

in the shape of her heroines as moral exempla. As Mary Anne Schofield writes, "Haywood's novels and romances as a whole present the pattern of a group of typically obedient, chaste and passive heroines pitted against a large number of disobedient, unchaste and active women," (Schofield, 1982: p. 18). These are not in the full sense of the term "escape-routes" for women, because more often than not, whether passive or active, obedient or disobedient, Haywood's heroines come to a sticky end, ruined by the force of their own sexual passion and their believing attitudes toward the male sex. Female sexuality is thus both indulged and suitably punished in her novels. As Ann Barr Snitow points out in her essay on twentieth-century romantic fiction, "all our culture's rich myths of individualism are essentially closed to [women]. Their one socially acceptable moment of transcendence is romance" (Snitow, 1984: p. 265). Haywood simultaneously recognizes this fact about the power of romance and pulls the ground out from under her women readers' feet by revealing that the seeming pleasures of romance are in fact nothing more than a delusive *fiction* and a dangerous one at that.

Perhaps the most effective means of conquering the delusions of romance in Haywood, lies in a strategy she proffers which links back to her own role as a fiction writer. Her writing can be seen as a way for a woman "to make a profit" from the subjection of romance. In her novels, those heroines who, like their author, learn to manipulate the fiction of romance seem to offer a tentative way out of the endless resituation of the woman as victim. Instead of being subjected by the romance, they make themselves the subject of their own romances, witholding their "true" identities from their lovers and playing with the different feminine roles available to them within the game of seduction. These heroines to some extent "write their own scripts," refusing to be trapped in the closure of the repetitious seduction and betrayal motif that male desire sets in motion. I am referring in particular here to two short novels that appeared in *Secret Histories, Fantomina: Or, Love in a Maze* (1724) (Haywood, 1732, III, pp. 259–292) and *The Masqueraders* (1724–1725) (1732, IV, 1–45).

*Fantomina* is the story of a resourceful young woman whose real name, significantly, is never revealed to us. Curious to see how men behave toward the courtesans in the theater pit, she disguises herself as one, and is pursued by Beauplaisir. She takes lodgings near the theater to entertain him, calling herself Fantomina, and an affair begins between the two. Fantomina thus manages to preserve her virtuous reputation in society and indulge her sexual appetites in private. Although Haywood condemns her morally for being "wholly blind to . . . the Ruin of her *Virtue*," (Haywood, 1732, III, p. 267), she grudgingly admits that "she preserved an Oeconomy in the Management of this Intrigue, beyond what almost any Woman ever did (p. 268).

Eventually of course Beauplaisir proves not to vary "so much from his Sex, as to be able to prolong Desire, to any great Length after Possession" (p. 269).

When he leaves for Bath and will not let her accompany him, she realizes she has lost his affections. She is desperate to relive those early pleasures of first courtship—the one stage of a woman's restricted life when she is accorded total power and sway. "Her Design was once more to engage him, to hear him sigh, to see him languish . . ." (p. 270). To this end, she travels to Bath and gets herself engaged as the serving-maid, Celia, at his lodging house. Once again, he falls for her and this affair continues a month. Her next disguise is that of the young widow, Bloomer, who asks to travel in his coach to London with him and succumbs to his charms. She congratulates herself on the success of her schemes, reveling in the knowledge that she "has out-witted even the most subtle of the deceiving Kind, and while he thinks to fool me, is himself the only beguiled Person" (p. 279). Her final disguise is that of the fair Incognita, a wealthy woman in London, who will only entertain her lover in the dark or with a veil over her face.

Fantomina continues to congratulate herself on the ever-renewed pleasure she ensures with her lover. Here the roles are reversed; the male lover is the one who is deceived and reduced to slavery before his love object, while the woman gratifies her own needs under a series of disguises:

> . . . by these Arts of passing on him as a new Mistress, whenever the Ardour, which alone makes Love a Blessing, begins to diminish, for the former one, I have him always raving, wild, impatient, longing, dying. (p. 285)

Fantomina is the female equivalent to Haywood's male rakes, who assume a series of different identities to court their mistresses and avert the possibility of discovery. She takes her pleasure, however, not through the novelty of a new object of pursuit, but through the narcissistic display of herself as a constantly new mistress. By the end of the novel, her pleasure seems to lie as much in the adopting of new identities as in the sexual encounters themselves. Even pregnancy does not bring a full end to her series of disguises: "By eating little, lacing prodigious stout, and the Advantage of a great Hoop-Petticoat, . . . her Bigness was not taken notice of . . ." (p. 299). Only when her daughter's labor pains start at a ball, does her mother discover the truth. Fantomina, following the birth of a girl, is summarily packed off to a French monastery. Once again, lack of virtue is suitably punished without undermining the eroticism of sexual pursuit.

Fantomina, we are told, "had the Power of putting on almost what Face she pleas'd" (p. 276). Philecta too in *The Masqueraders,* assumes a different "face" to try and win the philanderer, Dorimenus, from her best friend's side. Philecta's interest is stirred by her friend Dalinda's compulsive narration of her sexual encounters with Dorimenus. After her nights with Dorimenus, Dalinda runs to Philecta and, Haywood tells us, "felt in the delicious Representation, a Pleasure, not much inferiour to that which the Reality afforded" (*S.H.,* IV, 1732: p. 12). As in *Fantomina,* acting out the romance, repeating it, affords a particular kind of pleasure for the woman narrator or reader. Dalinda's pleasure in Dorimenus is heightened, and her reader's (Philecta's) interest in romance, following a previous disastrous love affair, is restored. Philecta goes to a masquerade dressed in a replica of Dalinda's costume and enjoys Dorimenus' flattery under the disguise of her friend. She then counterfeits Dalinda's handwriting to secure an interview with him. Philecta, waiting for Dorimenus, practices her acting techniques to determine which "face" will appeal to him most:

> a thousand and a thousand times were the Patches plac'd alter'd and replac'd — the position of the Curls as often chang'd — now this — anon that Fashion she thought most becoming — sometimes one Glance, then its contrary seem'd the likeliest to attract. (p. 22)

Philecta, however, overestimates her own power to resist falling in love. Unlike Fantomina, she does not educate herself out of love by degrees to transform herself into a consummate female rake. The playacting stops once Dorimenus has "won her heart." Like Fantomina, she finally finds herself alone and pregnant, and "Undone in all which ought to be valuable, she curses the undoing Transport she so lately blest" (p. 45).

Despite the moral resolutions to these novels, Haywood does seem to come close to a viable alternative, a realization that women must learn to read the romance with cynicism, place themselves in the fiction and play within it, rather than fall victim to its idealism and its traps. In her first published novel, *Love in Excess* (Haywood, 1725, I), Haywood has her heroine, Melliora, criticize the reading of texts of love, in particular Ovid's epistles and romances, stating that "Books were, as it were, Preparatives to Love, and by their softening Influence, melted the Soul, and made it fit for amorous Impressions" (p. 84). In her fiction Haywood both exploits this effect of the book upon the reader and presents her own work as a pleasurable substitute for the real-life disappointments of the romance. Fiction comes to substitute for reality as a means of education and seduction, without the ruination attendant upon the "real thing." Haywood presents her romances as a means of protecting women, providing them with the worldly knowledge they need, while warning them against the dangers of the practice. Her *Female Spectator* dedicates much of its time to the importance of educating women in the artifices of the romance, which men practice upon innocent women. Rather than advocating total retreat for women, she warns that it only makes women more vulnerable:

> A girl, who is continually hearing fine things said to her, regards them but as words of course; they may be flattering to her vanity for the present, but will leave no impression behind them in her mind: but she, who is a stranger to the gallant manner with which polite persons treat our sex, greedily swallows the first civil thing said to her, takes perhaps what is meant as a mere compliment, for a declaration of love, and replies to it in terms which either expose

her to the designs of him who speaks, if he happens to have any in reality, or
if he has not, to his ridicule in all company where he comes into. (p. 101)

Her own fiction is thus presented as a harmless way of seducing women, who
might otherwise learn the hard way—through first hand experience.

In this way, Haywood manages to vindicate her writing and present herself as ultimately the heroine of her own text. She does not deny the seductive power of fiction upon the female reader. Rather, she insists upon its *moral*
uses. She stands as a moral icon, the woman who has managed to survive
through, rather than in spite of, romance and finally makes a profit out of
it. References to her own "wild youth," whether real or imaginary, are a necessary part of this self-representation. Whicher's ambiguous title for his biography, *The Life and Romances of Mrs. Eliza Haywood* signifies the potency of
Haywood's fictions about herself. Haywood's romances—her books—are only
possible because of her supposed "romances"—the string of lovers she reput-
edly enjoyed. Fiction then, in Haywood's novels, is in and of itself an escape
from and an education into the brutal realities of heterosexual love relations
in eighteenth-century society. Women, writing and reading their own "fictions" of romance, can resist being duped by the fiction of true love men propagate in order to ravish, seduce, and ruin them.

Haywood's fictions are without doubt voyeuristic, seductive, and salacious.
The female desire they represent is deeply masochistic, if not a form of extended rape fantasy. Her heroines long "to be sweetly forc'd to what [they
wish] with equal Ardour" (*Fantomina*, Haywood, 1732, III, p. 270). Rather
than using moral encomiums to educate her female readers into the dangers
of romance, she chooses to indulge their sexual fantasy and then expiate their
guilt by her punitive resolutions. As the authors of *Rewriting English* point
out, however, romance, although it appears to be the opposite of the real,
seeks to simultaneously deal with the realities of female desire and the realities of female existence:

> Romance works with the basic conflicts in women's lives. This is what makes
> it a popular form and allows the same stories to be told over and over again.
> Fundamental changes in the genre are likely only when the contradictions that
> shape women's lives are altered or resolved. (Janet Batsleer, Tony Davies, Re-
> becca O'Rourke, and Chris Weedon, 1985: p. 105)

That Haywood's fictions present such a depressing picture of both female desire and existence under patriarchy, may thus be an accurate register of female possibilities in the early eighteenth century. Yet, the texts themselves
are presented as a way out of "that Fate which all Women must expect, when
to gratify their Passion they make a Sacrifice of their Honour, that of being
slighted and forsaken" (*Reflections*, 1726: p. 18). The eroticism of her own
romance fiction, the release from guilt, and the indulgence of sexual fantasy
which they enable are offered to the female reader as a means of gratifying

passion without sacrificing honor. Fiction thus both compensates for and challenges the limits of reality—no mean achievement for the woman Jonathan Swift chose to dismiss as a "stupid, infamous, scribbling woman" (in Janet Todd, 1984: p. 159).

## NOTES

[1]For a discussion of the commodification of romantic fiction and the importance of the romance authoress' persona in 20th-century mass-market publishing for women, see Rosalind Brunt, 1984.

[2]Haywood's scandal novels are deeply indebted to the work of Mary Delarivière Manley, with whom she is frequently associated. Manley's most famous scandal novel was a satire of the Whig party, *The New Atalantis* (1709), which presented prominent Whig politicians as sexually voracious libertines preying on innocent maidens (Patricia Koster, 1971). Haywood's very titles echo Manley's, and she clearly meant her work to be associated with Manley's in the public mind.

[3]See Marlene Legates, 1977, on the 18th-century use of concepts of "chaste womanhood" to embody traditional values threatened by a new morality.

[4]For a somewhat bleaker picture of the power accorded to femininity and the fatal attractions of the brutal male in twentieth-century romantic fiction, see Mariana Valverde, 1985.

[5]The influence of the *Portuguese Letters,* translated into English by Sir Roger L'Estrange in 1678 as *Five Love-letters from a Nun to a Cavalier* on early-eighteenth-century romantic prose fiction cannot be overestimated. These letters, ostensibly by a Portuguese nun to her French lover who had deserted her, were taken to be the epitome of a natural rhetoric of passion. Aphra Behn (1987) took them as a model but used them for political satire. A series of "answers" from the cavalier and "continuations" from the nun were spawned, among them Haywood's book.

## REFERENCES

Adburgham, Alison. (1972). *Women in print: Writing women and women's magazines from the restoration to the accession of Victoria.* London: George Allen and Unwin Ltd.

Batsleer, Janet, Davies, Tony, O'Rourke, Rebecca, Weedon, Chris. (1985). *Rewriting English: Cultural politics of gender and class.* London: Methuen.

Behn, Aphra. (1987). *Love-letters from a nobleman to his sister (1683–1687).* London: Virago Press. (Original version published 1687.)

Brunt, Rosalind. (1984). A career in love: The romantic world of Barbara Cartland. In Christopher Pawling (Ed.), *Popular fiction and social change.* London: Macmillan.

Day, Robert Adams. (1966). *Told in letters: Epistolary fiction before Richardson.* Michigan: Ann Arbor University of Michigan Press.

Haywood, Eliza. (1724a). *Letters from a lady of quality to a chevalier.* 2nd Ed. D. London: Browne and Chapman.

Haywood, Eliza. (1724b). *The rash resolve: Or, the untimely discovery.* London: Browne and Chapman.

Haywood, Eliza. (1725a). *Memoirs of a certain island adjacent to the Kingdom of Utopia.* London: Booksellers of London and Westminster.

Haywood, Eliza. (1725b). *Secret histories, novels and poems.* 2nd Ed. Vol. I. and II. London: Browne and Chapman.

Haywood, Eliza. (1726). *Reflections on the various effects of love.* London: N. Dobb.

Haywood, Eliza. (1727a). *The fruitless enquiry.* London: J. Stephens.

Haywood, Eliza. (1727b). *Secret history of the present intrigues of the court of Caramania.* London: Booksellers of London and Westminster.

Haywood, Eliza. (1732). *Secret histories, novels and poems.* 3rd Ed. Vol. III and IV. London: Bettesworth, Hitch, Browne and Greene.

Haywood, Eliza. (1744–1746). *The female spectator.* Selections in Priestley, Mary (Ed.) (1929). *The female spectator: Being selections from Mrs. Haywood's periodical (1744–46).* London: John Lane, The Bodley Head Ltd.

Haywood, Eliza. (1751, 1986). *The history of Miss Betsy Thoughtless.* London: Pandora Press.

Koon, Helene. (1978–79). Eliza Haywood and the *Female Spectator. Huntington Library Quarterly, 42,* no.1: 43–57.

Koster, Patricia (Ed.). (1971). *The novels of Mary Delarivière Manley 1704–1714.* Gainsville, FL: Scholars Facsimiles and Reprints.

Legates, Marlene. (1977). The cult of womanhood in eighteenth century thought. *Eighteenth Century Studies, 10*(77), 21–39.

MacCarthy, Bridget. (1944). *Women writers: Their contribution to the English novel 1621–1744.* Cork: Cork University Press.

Pope, Alexander. (1728). *Dunciad in three books.* In Sutherland, James (Ed.) (1963). *The dunciad.* London: Twickenham Edition.

Reeve, Clara. (1785). *The progress of romance.* The Facsimile Text Society Series 1: Literature and Language, vol. IV. 1930.

Richetti, John J. (1969). *Popular fiction before Richardson. Narrative patterns 1700–39.* Oxford: Clarendon Press.

Savage, Richard. (1729). *An author to be lett.* London: Alexander Vint.

Schofield, Mary Anne. (1982). *Quiet rebellion. The fictional heroines of Eliza Fowler Haywood.* Washington: University Press of America.

Schofield, Mary Anne. (1985). "Descending angels." Salubrious sluts and pretty prostitutes in Haywood's fiction. In Mary Anne Schofield and Cecilia Macheski (Ed.), *Fetter'd or free? British women novelists 1670–1815.* Ohio: Ohio University Press.

Snitow, Ann. (1984). Mass-market romance. Pornography for women is different. In Ann Snitow, Christine Stansell, and Sharon Thompson (Eds.) *Desire: The politics of sexuality.* London: Virago.

Spacks, Patricia Meyer. (1974–75). Ev'ry woman is at heart a rake. *Eighteenth Century Studies, 3,* 27–46.

Todd, Janet. (1984). Eliza Haywood. In Janet Todd (Ed.), *A dictionary of English and American women writers 1660–1800.* London: Methuen.

Valverde, Mariana. (1985). The eroticization of domination in formula romance. In Mariana Valverde (Ed.), *Sex, power and pleasure.* Ontario: The Women's Press.

Whicher, George Frisbie. (1915). *The life and romances of Mrs. Eliza Haywood.* New York: Columbia University Press.

Woolf, Virginia. (1916). A Scribbling Dame. In *Virginia Woolf: Women and writing* (1979). London: The Women's Press.

# Sarah Fielding's Self-Destructing Utopia:

## The Adventures of David Simple*

=== Carolyn Woodward ===

If "a utopia always situates itself in the midst of a historical contradiction, combining antagonistic tendencies without synthesizing or resolving them, then every utopia bears within itself its own negation" (Philip Stewart, "Utopias That Self-Destruct": p. 15).

## SARAH FIELDING'S LIFE

Sarah Fielding was born in 1710 in East Stour, Dorset, to Edmund and Sarah Gould Fielding, and spent her girlhood as a middle child in a family of six children, the eldest of whom was her brother, Henry. Their mother died when Sarah was seven and a half, and her father's remarriage caused a breach in the family. From then on, the children were raised by their maternal grandmother, Lady Gould. Sarah and her three sisters attended a boarding school in Salisbury, and Sarah must have augmented the school curriculum by forays in the large library of the Gould home. (Sarah's reading was extensive, as is indicated by frequent allusions in her novels to authors such as William Shakespeare, John Milton, Horace, Virgil, Alexander Pope, and Michel de Montaigne.) During this girlhood, Sarah met Jane Collier, the daughter of a family acquaintance, who became her life-long friend.

Sarah Fielding never married. She achieved a measure of financial self-sufficiency through her writing. But, except for one brief period during the 1740s when she may have shared a house with her sisters, she was all her life dependent on family and friends for shelter. During her adult life, she lived first in Hammersmith (near London) and later in the vicinity of Bath.

In 1742, Sarah likely wrote the letter from Leonora to Horatio in her brother Henry's *Joseph Andrews*. One year later, she seems to have written Anna Boleyn's story for Henry's *Journey from this World to the Next*. In May 1744,

---

*In slightly different form, this essay was first presented at the 1986 meeting of the American Society for Eighteenth-Century Studies, held March 16 in Williamsburg, Virginia.

when she was thirty-four years old, Sarah Fielding published her first novel, *The Adventures of David Simple. . . . By a Lady.* Immediately popular, the novel came out in a second edition that autumn, in a form "revised and corrected" by Henry.

Sarah Fielding's innovative genius, political consciousness, and interest in psychology are reflected in her seven novels. Her fictional experiments include writing the first children's novel and the first British fictional autobiography, as well as creating a new genre she called "dramatic fable." In the 1744 *David Simple,* she experiments with urban picaresque as a vehicle for apologue (an allegorical story intended to convey a useful lesson), and in the completion of the novel, *Volume the Last* (1753), she draws the apologue to its dark conclusion through the use of domestic tragedy. Her other works of fiction include *Familiar Letters between the Principal Characters in "David Simple"* (1747), *The Governess, or The Little Female Academy* (1749), *The Cry: A New Dramatic Fable* (with Jane Collier, 1754), *The Lives of Cleopatra and Octavia* (1757), *The History of the Countess of Dellwyn* (1759), and *The History of Ophelia* (1760).

Although Sarah Fielding worked to earn her own way, she was all her life a needy gentlewoman. In January of 1768, at the age of fifty-eight, she was invited by her friends, Elizabeth Montagu and Sarah Scott, to join a community of women which they were planning to establish. But by then she was too ill to leave her cottage, and in April of that same year, she died. Fielding is buried in the village church of Charlcombe, outside Bath, and tablets are inscribed to her memory in both the Charlcombe church and the Bath Abbey.

## UTOPIAN VISIONS AND FEMINIST THEORY

In *The Adventures of David Simple* (1744 and 1753),[1] Sarah Fielding considers the human need for friendship and criticizes patriarchy for the greed and mistrust fostered by its hierarchies. She finds patriarchal capitalism responsible for the maintenance in society of what she believes are negative feminine virtues: innocence, passivity, and privacy. Further, she presents an alternative system, and is bold in her vision of a utopia that insists on the centrality of what she sees as true feminine values, nurturance, and nonhierarchical sharing. And, finally, she destroys those persons who must fully exhibit the negative feminine virtues, thereby depicting the insidiously oppressive force of such "virtues." In this way, Sarah Fielding examines the historical contradiction present in eighteenth-century ideas about feminine virtue, destroying her utopia through the debilitating underside of the femininity on which it was founded. In so doing, she depicts the need for profound psychological and social change.

In *David Simple,* Sarah Fielding creates a sustained utopian vision, its destruction acting as a critique of the contradictions inherent in a system that taught females powerlessness as a virtue while depending on feminine nurturance for its existence. In several of her other works, Fielding treats this theme briefly, sometimes, as in *The Cry,* offering the hope of utopia but stopping short of its realization; other times, as in *The Governess,* creating a limited utopia that acts as satire on the surrounding patriarchy.

Ann K. Mellor, in an essay on twentieth-century feminist utopias, argues that feminist utopian thinking is inherently revolutionary and "defines the sources and directions of contemporary feminist desire" (1982, p. 243). My exploration of the utopian theme in Sarah Fielding's work was inspired by Barbara Brandon Schnorrenberg's essay (1982) on utopias as imaged in the writings of Mary Astell, Sarah Scott, and Clara Reeve. In general, the thinking of Mary Astell, Sarah Fielding, Sarah Scott, and Clara Reeve helps define the sources and directions of eighteenth-century feminist desire. All four of these writers insist on the importance of education and womanly community to the development of the female identity; this is a central focus of eighteenth-century feminist theory.

## PATRILINEAL INHERITANCE AND WOMAN'S STORY

A brief outline of the plot of *David Simple* is in order. Innocent and passive, David Simple is easily banished from his home through the machinations of his brother. After his uncle restores his inheritance, David settles an annuity for life on the brother, and leaves with the intention of searching for a true friend. In his travels, David is everyone's favorite gull, repeatedly demonstrating the aptness of his name through his utter naivete. Eventually, he meets Cynthia, who has been banished from her home for refusing to be a pawn in a money-marriage. The brother and sister, Valentine and Camilla, next come to his attention, when they are about to be evicted from squalid lodgings. Their stepmother, scheming to gain their inheritance, had turned their father against them and sent them away from their home. Valentine and Cynthia marry, as do David and Camilla, and the friends establish a community based in nurturance and nonhierarchical sharing. Babies arrive, and for some years the community lives in peace. But worldly men use their skill at law and finance to take advantage of David and his friends, finally rendering them destitute. Illness comes to them, too, usually as a result of an inability to confront evil: indirectly when poverty makes medical help inaccessible, or directly when a child is abused by neighbors. One by one the members of the community die, until only Cynthia and her niece remain.

This novel uses the character of David Simple to tell woman's story, a story of some of the complex and subtle ways in which women were silenced by eighteenth-century gender ideology. David is womanly in his embodiment of the accepted feminine virtues of innocence, passivity, and privacy; in his demonstrations of nurturance and nonhierarchical sharing; and in his opposition to and retreat from patriarchal values. Fielding's critique of the oppressive world of *David Simple* centers in the system of patrilineal inheritance and extends to patriarchal capitalism. Eighteenth-century feminine virtues both arose out of and maintained these systems, in which inheritance passed through the male line and where nearly all trades were closed to women. Laboring-class women were sexual prey in trades open to them. Looking toward the marriage market, middle-class parents instilled in their daughters such virtues as ladylike innocence, passivity, privacy, and nurturance. The alternative community in *David Simple* flourishes through feminine nurturance, but Sarah Fielding demonstrates that feminine innocence, passivity, and privacy also allow the system of patriarchal capitalism to destroy the community.

The system of patrilineal inheritance encourages corruption, as David, Camilla, and Valentine are banished from their homes in schemes to rob them of their patrimony. And the system oppresses insidiously, as Cynthia's parents, concerned for her commodity value, caution her against reading: "She had better mind her Needle-work, and such Things as were useful for Women" (Malcolm Kelsall, 1969, p. 101). Ironically, it is because they have been trained only in skills that are "useful" for women that Cynthia and Camilla can't survive on their own. When Cynthia is alone in the world, she can find work only as a lady's companion, a servile "Toad-eater" (p. 113); even through begging, Camilla is unable to support her ill brother. David consistently shows his nonalignment with these patriarchal values. He shares his money with his brother, with friends, with anyone in need. He helps Cynthia leave her demeaning position and find temporary housing, refusing to be stopped by threats of scandal—by the propriety demanded in a system that sees the single woman as sexually available.[2] Believing Cynthia to be the author of her own destiny, he offers respectful nurturance.

Finally, David most clearly rejects patriarchal values when he and his friends establish their alternative community. In this utopia, both fortune and work are shared in common. Late in the story, when Cynthia and Valentine must travel to Jamaica, David divides his money with them: "and this was the first time the Word DIVIDED could . . . have been used, in relating the Transactions of our Society; for SHARING in common, without any Thought of separate Property, had ever been their friendly Practice, from their first Connection" (p. 338). Girls and boys are educated in literacy, the arts, and work. No one person in the community holds authority. The one person the others look to most, however, is Cynthia, whose advanced wisdom is happily acknowledged:

> If *Cynthia* knew her understanding, without being proud of it, *Camilla* could acknowledge it without Envy, and *David* was sensible of it without abating one Tittle of his Love for his Wife; or in the Person of his Wife, desiring to pull down *Cynthia*. And every Advantage or Pleasure arising from any Faculty of the Mind, was as much shared in their Society, as any other Property whatever. (pp. 30–331)

Cynthia, who formerly had to disguise herself with a veil of ladylike passivity and privacy,[3] is able to direct her creativity toward entertaining her friends, often through the telling of stories. In this community, women are recognized as speaking and acting subjects.

Sarah Fielding's utopian vision includes consideration of economic class. Cynthia and Camilla are both representatives of Fielding's own station in life, that of the gentlewoman without means of support. In an early recognition of how capitalism divides and harms people, Camilla laments, "If we were to attempt getting our living by any Trade, People in that Station would think we were endeavouring to take Bread out of their mouths" (p. 169). The utopian community extends to include the struggling Farmer Dunster and his family. Friendship is established, and Cynthia teaches the child, Betty Dunster, to read and write; in return, Betty teaches Cynthia's daughter to knit and spin flax. Not surprisingly, the good capitalists, Mr. and Mrs. Orgueil, seek to ruin this friendship and to keep the Dunsters in their social and economic place.

## FEMININE VIRTUE AS WEAKNESS

Sarah Fielding demonstrates the pervasiveness of eighteenth-century gender ideology by insisting that shelter from a patriarchal world is not, finally, possible. *One must act upon that world* and to do so takes knowledge and considerable self-assertion. This is supremely difficult, for the world demands of women innocence and self-effacement; in taking on these qualities, women oppress themselves. In David's confrontations with those who wield power, we clearly see the crippling effects of the feminine virtues. In patriarchy, one must always look to the powerful men more advanced on the hierarchy, thereby seeking approval and even self-definition specifically from those to whom one is inferior.

This happens to David in his relationship with the manipulative Mr. Ratcliff. In his innocence, David early mistakes Ratcliff's sociability for friendship. Ratcliff controls the destinies of David and the community, exerting power simply for its own sake. Innocent and passive, David is easily dominated. Ratcliff insists on naming David and Camilla's son "Peter," after himself, and on claiming the child as his godson. Ratcliff demands that the boy be sent away to school, while advising that David's daughter learn needlework. When he sends fine clothing to his godson, he throws in discarded damask sacks to be cut up for nightgowns and coats for the daughters. Proud of his connections to men yet more powerful than himself, Ratcliff promises David that he will find him preferment through a certain Great Man. Late in the novel, when the resources of the community have been entirely lost, David learns that Ratcliff has taken the preferment for himself. Just at this juncture, Ratcliff sends "a handsome Present for his God-son" (p. 384), at the same time writing to demand that Peter be sent to him for his further education. David, stunned by Ratcliff's betrayal of friendship, for once asserts himself, insisting to Camilla that the boy not be "educated under the Tuition of such a Man" (p. 384). As Peter has taken ill, Camilla writes that his sickness will not allow the move. Ratcliff replies in a stinging letter accusing David and Camilla of ingratitude, and disinheriting the boy. This letter arrives one day after Peter has died of smallpox.

How are we to read David's insistence that his son not live with Ratcliff? It is one of the very few instances in the whole work in which David shakes off passivity for a moment of self-assertion, and it comes after a long line of passive acquiescences in Ratcliff's design. Sarah Fielding makes David's first acquiescence so passive as to leave it off the page. In the episode concerning Peter's naming, the sole evidence of personal conviction comes from Camilla:

> . . . *Camilla* was brought to bed of a boy, and he was christened by the name of *Peter,* after his God-father; for *Camilla,* although it would have been her Choice, that her first Son should have borne the Name of her much-loved Husband, would not oppose Mr. *Ratcliff's* Request, or even mention her own Choice, whilst there was the least Probability, that her Son's Interest might be forwarded by complying with whatever Mr. *Ratcliff* should in reason desire. (Kelsall, 1969, pp. 317–318)

Camilla's privacy and passivity are such that she is made inarticulate by her recognition of power that is inaccessible to her save through Ratcliff's agency. But David's desires are entirely unspoken, even in his own mind. Sarah Fielding, in an interesting narrative choice, causes the naming of David's first-born son to go by without any note of his thoughts on the matter. She might, for instance, have chosen to make this matter indicative of David's purposeful nonalignment with patriarchal values, which might have been imaged by David's stated preference that his son not be named after him or after any patriarchal figure (such as Ratcliff). This would have been an instance of pacifism, an active refusal to participate in hierarchical systems, the very fabric of which insists on winners and losers and thus promotes violence. Sarah Fielding does provide us with a few demonstrations of David's pacifism; for example, his refusal to play the role of seducer and rapist when he helps Cynthia find lodgings, and his interest in establishing a community based in nonhierarchical sharing. In this novel, Sarah Fielding distinguishes between those behaviors that actively promote peace and health, such as pacifism and nurturance, and those that render good intents ineffective, such as passivity.[4]

The contrast she thus sets up is essential to her critique of eighteenth-century gender ideology in that it demonstrates that the terms of expected female behavior are contradictory, that, for instance, "nurturance" and "passivity" cannot coexist, that real nurturance can only be effected through active self-assertion.

After this initial acquiescence, David endures years of Ratcliff's dominance. Finally, David says "no." But even here, Sarah Fielding points to his passivity. First, David speaks his assertion only to Camilla: *"David* did not design even to take Notice of Mr. Ratcliff's Letter: it was a Correspondence his Soul abhorred, and which had not subsisted so long, had not the State of Timidity . . . taken from him the Power of acting what, in his own Judgment, he thought best" (Kelsall, 1969, p. 385). Camilla writes the rejection letter. Second, Sarah Fielding creates a serious illness for Peter, so that neither Camilla nor David has to speak the real reason for their refusal. And finally, the sudden death of Peter means that David's assertion is never tested; in fact, David sees his son's death specifically in terms of release from Ratcliff's domination: *"David,* in the Joy that his Son had escaped all Possibility of having his young Mind corrupted by being formed under such a Hand, smothered his Grief for his Loss" (p. 390). Death is a certain escape, as it is an ultimate passivity. Peter is sheltered in death as his father was unable to shelter him in life. David's joy in his son's final escape covers the harsh truth, that his own timidity would always render him powerless.

## LAWYERS, FINANCIERS, AND EIGHTEENTH-CENTURY GENDER IDEOLOGY

In David's relations with Ratcliff, Fielding demonstrates the progressively crippling effects of innocence and passivity. In his confrontations with lawyers and financiers, we see David's nonalignment with the values of patriarchal capitalism. But here, again, he is generally without power to assert his own values. In this novel, people need lawyers specifically for protection of patrilineal inheritance rights. After spending five hundred pounds in litigation, Camilla and Valentine lose their inheritance because of a bad mortgage. And when David's right to his uncle's estate is contested in an unjust and intricate lawsuit, David intuits that he should relinquish his claim. Here, again, it is significant to Sarah Fielding's critique that she shows David following not the path of active refusal but that of passive acquiescence: Ratcliff and other "Men of Prudence and Experience" (Kelsall, 1969, p. 324) coerce him to continue, and he assents. After nine years of litigation, the suit is lost, and payments to lawyers leave the community destitute.

In the gender ideology of eighteenth-century patriarchal capitalism, women are sexual goods, their social, legal, and economic status of commodities rather than free agents. Sarah Fielding shows this through events in the lives of Camilla and Cynthia. Early in the novel, we read of Camilla's desperation when her attempts to raise money for her ill brother are met by demands for sexual favors (pp. 165–167) and of the sexual harassment Cynthia must deal with when traveling alone (pp. 175–184). (See Dale Spender, 1986, p. 187.) Late in the novel, Fielding again reminds us of women's commodity status by creating a scene in which the newly widowed Cynthia is propositioned by a lawyer who uses his access to power to try to buy her sexual services. After Cynthia had trusted the lawyer to manage her finances, he presented her with a bill that (falsely) indicated that she had no money coming to her but instead owed him: "he had the Assurance to tell me . . . that he had formed that Account with an Intent of getting me into his Power; and that he would never insist on my paying him the Balance, if I would comply with his Conditions" (Kelsall, 1969: p. 392). When she refused his conditions, he spread rumors about her. Interestingly, Fielding here indicates the complex nature of gender ideology by implicating a woman—"Mrs. *Darkling* (the richest Widow in this Place)" (p. 393)—in the silencing of Cynthia's just complaint. When Cynthia turned to Mrs. Darkling for support, she was advised "not to let my Vanity tempt me to expose myself, by telling such an incredible Story to any other" (p. 393). As theorists such as Rachel Blau DuPlessis (1980, pp. 147–149) and Margaret Homans (1983) have pointed out, middle- and upper-class women often experience a divided consciousness, joined to the dominant culture by their class but excluded by their sex. Fielding represents this divided consciousness in the separate persons of Cynthia, who in her own victimization recognizes woman's powerlessness, and Mrs. Darkling, who must reject a woman's plea in order to protect her (male-identified) position within the dominant group.

Whereas lawyers use their access to knowledge about money to exert power over the less privileged, financiers achieve the same purpose through their access to money itself. Early in the novel, David is shocked to see financiers use "Treachery" to "barter for Interest," and is enraged to learn that "Riches were esteemed Goodness, and Deceit, Low-Cunning, and giving up all things to the love of Gain, were thought Wisdom (Kelsall, 1969, pp. 28–30). Under patriarchal capitalism, values are transposed to commodities, and life becomes a system of debits and gains. David, who simply shares, cannot comprehend this. Very late in the novel, David must turn to a money lender to help his family. The money lender speaks of "Security," "Executions," "Obligations," "Contingencies," and "Substance"; David speaks of "Family," "Enjoyment," and the "Pleasure" of being able to "serve" his "brother" Valentine. Neither understands the other, and at one point, significantly, David says, "You don't talk our Language, Sir" (pp. 368–369). But the money lender has power, and David does not. Money is lent on David's bond for treble the sum. Later, the lender sends a bailiff to claim the family cottage.

## CYNTHIA SURVIVES

In a pattern that is emblematic of their inability to shelter themselves from a patriarchal world, the community is three times forced to give up its home. From an estate, the family moves to a smaller home. From this home, they move to a cottage. Come to posses the cottage, the bailiff in a drunken stupor mistakenly sets fire to it. Losing "their small House, and every Thing in it" (Kelsall, 1969, p. 400), the family is taken in by Farmer Dunster. At the close of the novel, after a long train of corruptions and miseries for which innocent passivity has been no match, everyone in the community has died, save Cynthia and her niece. In a significant act of self-assertion, Cynthia journeys alone to a neighboring town, where she is successful in securing a safe home and sufficient income for both the child and herself. (Surely, however, Sarah Fielding is commenting on woman's powerlessness even here, for Cynthia's success is the success of begging: she visits a family who had once before befriended her and is given promise of help.)

All the friends demonstrate nurturance and harmony, which Sarah Fielding depicts as true feminine grace. All but Cynthia, however, are finally destroyed by an overabundance of other supposedly feminine traits: innocence, self-effacement, and that most "feminine" of all conditions, illness. In their innocence and self-effacement, Camilla and David are repeatedly prevented from turning their good intentions into effective actions. Valentine, a shadow figure who is rarely onstage, is plagued with recurrent illness and passive melancholy. On illness as concomitant to femininity, Sandra Gilbert and Susan Gubar write, "It is debilitating to be any woman in a society where women are warned that if they do not behave like angels they must be monsters. . . . To be trained in renunciation is almost necessarily to be trained to ill health . . . " (1979, pp. 53–54). Janet Todd notes illness as one of the central motifs that mark women in the eighteenth-century novel: "Women fall ill in the eighteenth-century novel alarmingly often. . . . Sickness is a mark of female debility. . . . It is also an excuse for inaction" (1980, p. 407). As an excuse for inaction, illness is linked with the feminine "virtue" of passivity. The negative termination of both illness and passivity is death. It is fitting that Cynthia survive. In her energy and wit, she is able to act upon the world.

## DISGUISE AND THE
## FEMINIST CRITIQUE

In *Sensibility: An Introduction*, Janet Todd discusses a group of novels that depict "the man of feeling who has, in an unfeeling world, avoided manly power and assumed the womanly qualities of tenderness and susceptibility" (1986, pp. 88–89). *David Simple* is the first of these novels, most of which

were written in the 1760s and 70s. Other significant novels of male sensibility include *The Fool of Quality* (1764–1767) by Henry Brooke, *The Vicar of
Wakefield* (1766) by Oliver Goldsmith, *A Sentimental Journey* (1768) by Laur-
ence Sterne, and *The Man of Feeling* (1771) by Henry Mackenzie. In creating the character David Simple, then, Fielding created a model for the man
of feeling as feminine, one whose condition in life is very like that of a woman.
The narrative of David's life tells woman's story, a story that is varied themati-
cally by the stories of Camilla and Cynthia. In disguising woman's story, Sarah
Fielding actually strengthens her critique of eighteenth-century gender ideology. Centering feminine virtues in a male character serves to defamiliarize
them, and we can see that innocence and passivity are, in fact, weaknesses.

David's feminist impulse to retreat from patriarchal values comes from the
combined force of three womanly characteristics. First, his embodiment of
the feminine "virtues" renders him psychologically incapable of confronting
the world; second, each time his innocence is lifted and he sees something
new of patriarchy, he is horrified; and third, he adheres to what we would
term feminist principles—his belief in useful education for both girls and boys,
and his commitment to replacing hierarchy with shared wealth, work, and
ideas. In addition, Fielding's representation of nurturance in the character of
David Simple is pertinent. Today, while nurturance is easily dismissed as a
limiting feminine trait, feminist theorists such as Carol Gilligan (1982) and
Barbara Deming (1984) argue that because females are trained to nurturance,
women have needed healing energy to offer a violent world. It is precisely
this double focus that Fielding gives to her illustration of nurturance. David
is truly nurturing, for example, in the help he originally offers to Camilla and
Valentine, and to Cynthia. The energy he gives comes back to him in loving
friendship and hope for community. But his passivity debilitates him such
that his nurturance eventually becomes little more than good intent—effeminate
in the most stereotypic sense of the word.

Sarah Fielding, then, has here created a man who rejects patriarchy, whose
central beliefs are feminist, and who, finally, is unable to effect his dreams
because he is femininely "virtuous" to an extreme. One disturbing thing Fielding seems to be saying here is that "yes," we women wish men could be more
like women, except that in being like a woman, a man is necessarily weak,
and finally destroyed. (She does, in her later novels, create masculine men
who learn to accept women's values about sex and marriage. Two such are
Lord Dorchester in *Ophelia* and Mr. Bilson in *The Countess of Dellwyn,* both
of whom are taught lessons by the women in their lives. Lord Dorchester in
particular remains basically aggressive, and he does not question patriarchal
values beyond the sexual double standard.) Sarah Fielding's point with David,
the character, and with *David Simple,* the novel, it seems to me, is to hold
the "desirable" feminine virtues up to scrutiny and to demonstrate that these
virtues—innocence, passivity, privacy—are crippling weaknesses that prevent

the social change that would occur with the flourishing of what are, to her, true feminine virtues: nurturance and nonhierarchical sharing. Given her position in mid-century English society, I should think this radical questioning of basic values—had it gone undisguised—would have been dangerous to Fielding's public image and perhaps frightening to her private idea of herself.[5] Her original self-effacing attitude, as evidenced in her advertisement to the first edition of *David Simple,* indicates a timidity of spirit, and even in her later, bolder assertions of self, she is careful to maintain a gentle and light tone.[7] Although Henry Fielding's preface to the second edition of *David Simple* praises the work, it also patronizes it. Henry four times refers to "this little Book" and once to "this little Work"; in physical size, Sarah's novel is equivalent to Henry's *Joseph Andrews.* Further, Henry twice refers to Sarah as a "young Woman," and says that her "Sex and Age entitle her to the gentlest Criticism" (Kelsall, 1969: pp. 5–8). Sarah does not appear to have objected to this patronizing attitude; in her works, she repeatedly expresses her fondness and respect for him.[7] Further, it does not appear to me that she could turn to other mid-century women writers and find ideas as thoroughly revolutionary as were hers.[8] I imagine Fielding must have felt quite alone in her vision, and there is nothing in what we know of her life to indicate that declaring herself "different" could have been anything but painful for her.

The protagonist in *David Simple* looks at his society—specifically at a society centered in patriarchal capitalism—and is saddened; he leaves this society and establishes a new society based on feminist principles; and he and nearly all his society's people are killed off, specifically by manipulations of patriarchal capitalism. To have created that story in the first place has to have hurt. To have created the story with a female protagonist would have been to make obvious, not only to her readers but to herself, as she was writing, that this was woman's story.[9] For all these reasons, it makes sense to me that the use of a male protagonist in a woman's story would be a helpful disguise, as well as a means of examining ideas which might be too painful if imaged in a female body.

Finally, however one interprets the gender of David Simple, it is clear that Sarah Fielding has written a feminocentric novel—feminine at its core, in the characters of David and his friends, and feminist in its critique.[10] It is exciting to try to think back to the reception of *David Simple* among the women and men of eighteenth-century London. Thirteen years after *David Simple*'s publication (and four years after its concluding volume was published), *The Monthly Review* (July 1757), in discussing Sarah Fielding's *Lives of Cleopatra and Octavia,* commented that "It were superfluous to compliment the Author of David Simple upon her merits as a Writer" (Kelsall, 1969, p. xi). Perhaps Fielding's critique of femininity became part of a gradual general questioning of eighteenth-century gender ideology, dramatically demonstrated by Mary Wollstonecraft in her *Vindication of the Rights of Woman* (1792) and imaged throughout the century in novels such as *The Memoirs of Miss Sidney Bidulph* (1761), in which Frances Sheridan (1772) portrays the devastating effects of a daughter's passive acquiescence to her mother's will; *Emmeline* (1788), where Charlotte Smith illustrates woman's dependence (and consequent victimization) in marriage; and *A Simple Story* (1791), in which Elizabeth Inchbald questions how free a woman is to choose her own life.

However, although the woman's story in *David Simple* is today all the more powerful for its hidden qualities, this is in part because it communicates to us the fear that may have been in Fielding's heart, her own dependency on powerful men, and the weight of an eighteenth-century gender ideology that made it impossible for this intelligent and original thinker to act as her own free agent. We cannot know just how her ideas were received by her contemporaries. On the basis of what very few snippets of eighteenth-century comments we have available to us, it does appear that "no one seems to have noticed" Fielding's dangerous critique (comment by Jane Spencer, personal correspondence, September 1986). However, it is always difficult to gauge the effect of a work of fiction on social change. What is clear about *David Simple* is that it was both popular fiction and respected literature and that it offered a (disguised) sustained feminist critique, one that looked back to Mary Astell, was contemporary with the *Sophia* pamphlets, and looked forward to Mary Wollstonecraft.

## BEYOND THE ENDING

The utopian community in *David Simple* tries to exist apart from external oppressions. But the novel shows that retreat has its limits, for no place is free from corruptions in the system of patriarchal capitalism. Further, the novel shows that to the extent that David and his friends embody the feminine virtues of innocence, passivity, and privacy, they are weakened. Because people in the community are not free from this sort of internal oppression, the community is destroyed. Hope resides in the one surviving child, a girl named Camilla, for whom Cynthia may build community anew. But Sarah Fielding's criticism stops just short of fulfilling this hope. We cannot know what will happen in that neighboring town, what sort of patriarchal expectations Cynthia and the child may find in their new home.

Sarah Fielding encourages this uncertainty through both the action of the plot and the texture of her language. In the last pages of the novel, Cynthia makes her successful journey for help, and David faces death with the language of despair. The texture of Fielding's language is richly hopeful as she delineates Cynthia's perceptions after her visit: "Cynthia's Imaginations, on her Journey back, were pleasing beyond Expression. The grateful Veneration which filled her Heart for the Person she had left, was one of those Sensations most capable of giving her Pleasure. The Look of Welcome and the

Words of Kindness she had met with, dwelt on her Fancy, and fixed there the most agreeable Pictures" (p. 428).

Fielding's language is very different, however, in recounting David's death-bed remembrances: "I fancied I had some Constancy of Mind, because I could bear my own Sufferings, but found, through the Sufferings of others, I could be weakened like a Child. — All the Books of philosophy I ever read, afforded me no Relief" (p. 432). It is only in facing his own death, with hope for the Christian hereafter, that David finds relief. Such relief, with its notion of justice beyond the grave, provides a mechanism for the maintenance of a hierarchical system in which many people remain powerless and unhappy during the whole of their (earthly) lives. For David, this relief functions, as had his joy in his son's "escape," as balm against the pain of confronting the damage done by weaknesses inherent in his own innocence and passivity.

In her discussion of sickness as a mark of female debility and an excuse for inaction, Janet Todd writes: "The ultimate symbol of female debility is death, and in the eighteenth-century novel women die in droves. Usually it is the good who die. . . . The saintly death of heroines like Clarissa or Julie is a clean death which neither disfigures nor isolates. It is a slow refining, a gentle easing from life" (Todd, 1980, p. 409). The women, men, and children in David's womanly community have indeed died in droves. In his death, David is very like the heroines Janet Todd describes. The essence of goodness, he experiences death as a saintly and gentle easing towards the hereafter: "These Things did *David* speak at various Times, and with such Cheerfulness, that *Cynthia* said, the last Hour she spent with him, in seeing his Hopes and Resignation, was a Scene of real Pleasure" (Kelsall, 1969, p. 432). David dies in peace, and, with the closing of his life, Sarah Fielding closes her novel. Having decided to "draw the Veil" over David, she writes: "But I chuse to think he is escaped from the Possibility of falling into any future Afflictions, and that neither the Malice of his pretended Friends, nor the Sufferings of his real ones, can ever again rend and torment his honest Heart" (p. 432). In this, the last sentence of the book, life on this earth is presented entirely in a language of despair. What, then, is the reader finally left with? The grateful veneration and agreeable pictures filling Cynthia's heart and fancy? Or the afflictions, malice, and sufferings that rend and torment the hearts of the innocents?

Sarah Fielding's ending is ambiguous, its meaning dependent on where the reader places focus—the finality of David's death or the hope for new life in the persons of Cynthia and little Camilla. Throughout the novel, Fielding's pattern has been to depict despair, then hope, then despair again, and so forth, in a rhythmic narrative. One effect that her ambiguous ending has is to continue this sense of ebb and flow beyond the last pages of her book. Sarah Fielding does not provide closure, but rather an opening out, a story without end. In this way, she refuses to place the woman and child: they are neither one thing nor another, neither hope nor despair, but are open to possibility.

In *Writing Beyond the Ending,* Rachel Blau DuPlessis notes that it is in closure that "Ideology meets narrative and produces a meaning-laden figure of
some sort" (1985, p. 19). Sarah Fielding refuses to give us that one meaning-
laden figure; in this refusal she may anticipate those twentieth-century feminist writers who attempt to leave us with "several different figures at that place
where text meets values" (p. 19). It is interesting that *David Simple* ends as
it had begun, with someone setting off on a quest, illustrative of the "looping-
back motion" (p. 193) that Rachel Blau DuPlessis finds typical of the female
quest. The several different figures in the last pages of *David Simple* may remind us, also, that the narrative line of this story has been multiple and that
the quest had been a search for community in which the self finds meaning
through relationships. Leslie Rabine, (1985) in *Reading the Romantic Heroine,* speaking of a feminine interest in "relations as dynamic movement between self and other," ponders how women can "transform the social world
so that women's self-definition in relationships rather than in transcendent
isolation can become a source of power and fulfillment instead of appearing
as a feminine lack, deficiency, or inferiority" (p. 110). Although the friends
in *David Simple* do experience fulfillment as they build their community, the
chilling message in this novel is that, within the system of eighteenth-century
patriarchal capitalism, women *cannot* transform the social world, because personality traits are gendered to such an extent that women are made powerless simply by their femininity.

    Given Sarah Fielding's emphasis on oppression that controls from within,
the primary effect of her ending is to keep attention focused on the difficult
questions she raises regarding the likelihood of real social change. Through
failure of her utopian community, Fielding speaks to the need for a restruc-
turing of society. She has shown that the feminine "virtues" both have their
base in and are necessary to maintain patriarchal capitalism. In her utopian
vision, she demonstrates the need for what she sees as true feminine virtues,
nurturance, and nonhierarchical sharing. And she repeatedly tells us that ladylike passivity and privacy are deadening weights that block creative responses
to real troubles and thereby prevent feminine nurturance from the healing
it could otherwise bring to a sick society.

    But Sarah Fielding's own need to remain a lady must have made her anal-
ysis painful. In a way her ending suggests this difficulty, in what may be its
recuperation of the very ideology she critiques. David dies quite peacefully,
and neither he nor Cynthia seem aware of the weaknesses by which he dies.
Cynthia believes she faces a hopeful future for herself and her niece, in the
patriarchal home to which they have been welcomed. Perhaps this indicates
a putting aside of dangerous ideas. Sarah Fielding does not again create a
revolutionary community in retreat (see Jane Spencer's rousing analysis [1986:
p. 94] of the contrast in political attitudes between *David Simple* and Fielding's later works). Would that she had once again dared to envision such a

community, and to envision its triumph: how exhilarated, how celebratory we might feel! However, that she could not envision such triumph speaks eloquently to the weight of internal oppression that features so dramatically in *David Simple*.

## NOTES

[1] In this essay, I am considering as one novel Fielding's two separate works *The Adventures of David Simple . . . In the Search of a Real Friend* (1744) and the *The Adventures of David Simple. Volume the Last, in Which His History is concluded* (1753). As the title indicates, *Volume the Last* completes the story begun in the 1744 edition.

[2] Carolyn Burke makes relevant linguistic connections when she speaks of living "beyond the Name-of-the-Father [and] apart from the categories of the 'proper,' 'property,' and 'propriety' " (1981, p. 299).

[3] As a child, Cynthia is constantly harassed by her family for her love of learning, and is consequently forced to disguise her interests. As an adult, she extricates herself from sexual danger by artful use of ladylike disguise (see pp. 101–108 and 179–181).

[4] Regarding the active force of pacifism, Pam McAllister writes in *Reweaving the Web of Life: Feminism and Nonviolence*, "The peculiar strength of nonviolence comes from the dual nature of its approach—the offering of respect and concern on the one hand and of defiance and stubborn noncooperation with injustice on the other. Put into the feminist perspective, nonviolence is the margin of our uncompromising rage at the patriarchy's brutal destructiveness with a refusal to adopt its ways. . . . Together, these seemingly contradictory impulses (to rage against yet refuse to destroy) combine to create a "strength" worthy of nothing less than revolution—true revolution, not just a shuffle of death-wielding power" (1982, iii).

[5] Editor's note: Heidi Hutner makes a similar point in relation to Aphra Behn: women were not free to criticize but women writers found more subtle means to make their meanings known.

[6] *This Excerpt from the Advertisement to David Simple indicates her self-effacing attitude:*

The following Moral Romance . . . is the Work of a Woman, and her first Essay; which . . . will, it is hoped, be sufficient Apology for the many Inaccuracies [the reader] will find in the Style, and other Faults of the Composition.
Perhaps the best Excuse that can be made for a Woman's venturing to write at all, is that which really produced this Book; Distress in her Circumstances: which she could not so well remove by any other Means in her Power. (1744 edition, iii)

See Carolyn Woodward, 1987, chapter one, for discussion of the gentle and light tone in Fielding's later prefatorial remarks.

[7] For instance, Jill E. Grey, in her introduction to *The Governess*, notices the affection Jenny Peace feels for her older brother Harry (1968, 5, pp. 124–28). Martin C. Battestin, "Henry Fielding" (1979, note 22, p. 14), finds complimentary references to Henry in Sarah's remarks before Letters XL-XLIV of her *Familiar Letters*. Further, he notes the following for allusions to Henry's works: *Familiar Letters*, I. 285–87; *The Cry*, I. 16, 169, II. 1, 99, 297, III. 118, 122–24; *The Lives of Cleopatra and Octavia*, ii–iii; and *The History of the Countess of Dellwyn*, I. 6, 53–54, 97, 249n, 258, 282, II. 162.

[8] For example, the author of the wonderfully forthright "Sophia" pamphlets (1739) insists on the excellence of woman's intellect and argues for reform in education but does not so comprehensively question gender ideology as does Fielding—and yet "Sophia" felt it necessary to publish under a pseudonym. One has to go back to the late seventeenth-century women to find

another such disturbing analysis: Aphra Behn's *Oroonoko* (1688), for instance, or Mary Astell's *Some Reflections Upon Marriage* (1700).

[9] Mary Poovey comments, at the conclusion to her discussion of the art of Mary Wollstonecraft, Mary Shelley, and Jane Austen: "The consequences of habitual indirection were undoubtedly serious in personal terms, in political terms, and in terms of the 'unfolding of genius.' . . . Indirection itself [however] is a symbolic action, and, as such, it creates imaginative freedom where there would otherwise be only inhibition, restraint, and frustration" (1984, pp. 243–244).

[10] Nancy Miller discusses the plethora of male-authored eighteenth-century novels such as *Moll Flanders, Pamela, Fanny Hill,* and *Clarissa,* that "predicate the primacy of female experience and thus *pose* as feminocentric writing" (1980, x) while carrying plots that are "neither female in impulse or origin, nor feminist in spirit" (149). After noting that her study forced her to accept "the givens of literary history and its process of elimination" (155), Miller calls for a "new literary history" in which we will recognize "that in the eighteenth century women writers were not the marginal figures they have become in the annals of literary history" (155).

# REFERENCES

Astell, Mary. (1700). *Some reflections upon marriage.* . . . London: John Nutt.

Battestin, Martin C. (1979). "Henry Fielding, Sarah Fielding, and 'the dreadful sin of incest.' " *Novel, 13,* 6–18.

Behn, Aphra. (1688). *Oroonoko, or the history of the royal slave.* London.

Burke, Carolyn. (1981). "Irigaray through the looking glass." *Feminist Studies 7,* 2, 288–306.

Deming, Barbara. (1984). *We are all part of one another: A Barbara Deming reader.* Edited by Jane Meyerding. Philadelphia: New Society Publishers.

DuPlessis, Rachel Blau and Members of Workshop 9. (1980). "For the Etruscans": Sexual difference and artistic production—The debate over a female aesthetic." In H. Eisenstein and A. Jardine (Eds.), *The future of difference* (pp. 128–156). Boston: G. K. Hall.

DuPlessis, Rachel Blau. (1985). *Writing beyond the ending: Narrative strategies of twentieth-century women writers.* Bloomington, IN: Indiana University Press.

Fielding, Sarah. (1744a). *The adventures of David Simple: Containing and account of his travels through the cities of London and Westminster, in the search of a real friend. By a lady.* London: Millar.

Fielding, Sarah. (1744b). *The adventures of David Simple.* . . . *The second edition, revised and corrected. With a preface by Henry Fielding, Esq.* 2 vols. London: Miller.

Fielding, Sarah, (1749). *The governess; or, little female academy.* . . . *By the author of David Simple.* Introduced and edited by Jill E. Grey. 1968. London; facs. rpt. London: Oxford University Press.

Fielding, Sarah. (1753). *The adventures of David Simple. Volume the last, in which his history is concluded.* London: Millar.

Fielding, Sarah. (1757). *The lives of Cleopatra and Octavia. By the author of David Simple.* London: Andrew Millar and R. and J. Dodsley; Bath: J. Leake; facs. rpt. New York: Garland, 1974.

Fielding, Sarah. (1759). *The history of the countess of Dellwyn. By the author of David Simple.* London; facs. rpt. New York: Garland, 1974.

Fielding, Sarah. (1760). *The history of Ophelia. Published by the author of David Simple.* London; facs. rpt. New York: Garland, 1974.

Gilbert, Sandra M. and Susan Gubar. (1970). *The madwoman in the attic: The woman writer and the nineteenth-century literary imagination.* New Haven: Yale University Press.

Gilligan, Carol. (1982). *In a different voice: Psychological theory and women's development.* Cambridge, MA: Harvard University Press.

Homans, Margaret. (1983 Winter). "'Her very own howl': The ambiguities of representation in recent women's fiction" *Signs 9*, (2), 186–205.

Inchbald, Elizabeth. (1791). *A simple story*. London.

Kelsall, Malcolm (Ed.). (1969). *The adventures of David Simple. By Sarah Fielding*. London: Oxford University Press.

McAllister, Pam (Ed.). (1982). *Reweaving the web of life: Feminism and nonviolence*. Philadelphia: New Society Publishers.

Mellor, Anne K. (1982). On feminist utopias. *Women's Studies 9*, 241–262.

Miller, Nancy K. (1980). *The heroine's text: Readings in the French and English novel 1722–1782*. New York: Columbia University Press.

Poovey, Mary. (1984). *The proper lady and the woman writer: ideology as style in the works of Mary Wollstonecraft, Mary Shelley, and Jane Austen*. Chicago: University of Chicago Press.

Rabine, Leslie. (1985). *Reading the romantic heroine: Text, history, ideology*. Ann Arbor: University of Michigan Press.

Schnorrenberg, Barbara Brandon. (1982). A paradise like Eve's: Three eighteenth-century English female utopians. *Women's Studies 9*, 263–272.

Sheridan, Frances. (1772). *Memoirs of Miss Sidney Bidulph. Extracted from her own journal, and now first published* (in 3 vols.). The fourth edition. London: Printed for J. Dodsley, in Pall-Mall.

Smith, Charlotte. (1788). *Emmeline*. London.

Spencer, Jane. (1986). *The rise of the woman novelists from Aphra Behn to Jane Austen*. Oxford: Basil Blackwell.

Spender, Dale. (1986). *Mothers of the novel: 100 good women writers before Jane Austen*. London: Pandora.

Sophia. (1743). *Woman not inferior to man*. London.

Stewart, Philip. (1979). Utopias that self-destruct. *Studies in Eighteenth-Century Culture, 9*, 15–24.

Todd, Janet. (1980). *Women's friendship in literature*. New York: Columbia University Press.

Todd, Janet. (1986). *Sensibility: An introduction*. London: Methuen.

Wollstonecraft, Mary. (1792). *Vindication of the rights of woman*. London.

Woodward, Carolyn. (1987). Sarah Fielding and narrative power for women. Unpublished dissertation University of Washington.

# Elizabeth Inchbald:

## Not Such a Simple Story

Katharine M. Rogers

In the latter part of the eighteenth century, English women developed a novel form that effectively expressed their interests, their values, and their perception of the world. Centered on an intelligent young woman, it asserted her right to determine the course of her own life in terms of choosing her marriage partner. However, almost all these novels are weakened by insipidity in the central character, because eighteenth-century convention demanded that fictional heroines set an example to their sex and that this example be shaped according to the current negative ideal of female virtue: a character whose salient quality is blamelessness cannot convincingly carry the interest of a novel.

In defying this convention, Elizabeth Inchbald's *A Simple Story* (1791) achieves a force, freshness, and authenticity unique in the fiction of its period. Its heroine, Miss Milner, is attractive and lovable but faulty—faulty in modern terms and even more so in those of the eighteenth century. In a time when a woman was not supposed to feel sexual attraction to a man until he had proposed and been accepted by her family, Miss Milner can say of a man she does not expect to marry, "I love him with all the passion of a mistress, and with all the tenderness of a wife" (p. 72). Because she is passionate and self-willed, Miss Milner can engage in conflict with the hero and is responsible for what happens to her; she is not a passive victim and does not set off the maudlin, over-inflated rhetoric that infested sentimental fiction in the period.

Miss Milner is intelligent but frivolous, good-hearted but self-indulgent, and incapable of self-control. A beautiful eighteen-year-old Protestant heiress, she is left under the guardianship of Dorriforth, an idealistic Jesuit priest. (One of the distinctive merits of this novel is that Elizabeth Inchbald, a Roman Catholic herself, represents priests as human beings rather than Gothic stereotypes.) She falls in love with him, despite her recognition that they can never marry. Then he inherits an earldom, becomes Lord Elmwood, and is laicized so he can produce an heir; they realize their mutual love and become engaged. However, she cannot resist trying his love. Even though it is the most impor-

82

tant thing in her life, she risks throwing it away for the pleasure of attending a masquerade in defiance of his orders. The underlying source of conflict in this episode, as it has been from the beginning, is a power struggle: Dorriforth dictates to her in accordance with values that seem to him obviously right, and she resents what seem to her arbitrary restrictions on her harmless enjoyments. In a world where compliance was assumed to be both proper and natural to women, Inchbald's sympathetic presentation of a self-willed heroine, a woman who simply does not want to do what men tell her to do, is extraordinary. Inchbald recognizes that, for women as well as men, self-respect requires ego-gratification and freedom to make one's own decisions.

Nevertheless, she makes clear that Dorriforth's commands are reasonable and that Miss Milner asserts herself over trivial issues: a masquerade is an empty diversion, and, even in her own terms, attending it is unimportant compared to preserving her relationship with Dorriforth. This inconsequence, like her other failings, results in a large part from her fashionable lady's education. Inchbald shared a widespread contemporary concern with women's education—education being broadly defined to include all the social influences that form mind and character. Writers from Mary Wollstonecraft to Hannah More agreed that superficial mental training and overemphasis on their sexual role trivialized women. Given no serious interests or goals, Miss Milner yields to every impulse and squanders her time on diversions she does not really enjoy and her money on things she does not really want. Deprived of intellectual training, she cannot appreciate the logical consequences of her actions. Misled by male gallantry, she thinks that frivolity and caprice are attractive in women.

Taught to value herself primarily as a sexual being, Miss Milner can conceive of no way to gratify her ego except by exerting power over men. Before she fell in love with Dorriforth, she "thought those moments passed in wasteful idleness during which she was not gaining some new conquest" (p. 15). Once engaged to him, she blindly insists on demonstrating her power over him, regardless of consideration for his feelings, rational estimation of the effects of her behavior on a man of his character, or thoughts of jeopardy to the relationship upon which all her hopes of happiness depend. In the limited terms provided by her education, she defines achievement as inspiring uncontrollable erotic passion; that is, passion that will force the most strong-willed, rational man to accept the most provoking behavior in defiance of his own judgment: "I will do something that any prudent man ought *not* to forgive, and yet, with that vast share of prudence he possesses, I will force him still to yield to his love. . . . If he will not submit to be my lover, I will not submit to be his wife—nor has he the affection I require in a husband" (pp. 128, 132). She unthinkingly accepts conventional eighteenth-century prescriptions of morality according to role: appropriate behavior was different for a husband and for a wife, for a husband and for a lover. The gallantry expected in a courtship situation was overestimated because it was supposed to compensate for the subjection of women in every other situation. Dorriforth's character and attitudes have also been molded by his education. As a priest, he has learned to control his feelings to the point that he distrusts his own impulses and has no tolerance for impulsive errors in others. Trained as an authority in moral law, he is very sure of what is right and does not hesitate to impose his views on others.

Yet the conflict between Miss Milner and Dorriforth results from character as well as education. She is generous, impulsive, and undisciplined, while he lives strictly in accordance with his high principles; she errs but forgives freely, while he neither errs nor forgives. He has cast off a once-loved sister for marrying a Protestant and refuses to see his orphaned nephew; his adherence to principle can lead to resolute hardness of heart. Miss Milner goes to see the child and yields (as usual) to temptation, — in this case to the amiable one of bringing him home in hopes of effecting a reconciliation. She cannot anticipate Dorriforth's implacability; he despises her impulsiveness. Although both are good people, the fact that he acts according to upright principle and she from spontaneous goodness of heart leads inevitably to opposition. Often, to use Samuel Johnson's words, it is a case of "the obstinate contests of disagreeing virtues, where both are supported by consciousness of good intention" (*Rasselas,* Johnson, 1981, p. 213). The lovers are kept apart not by the factitious devices common in fiction of the time, such as doubts of the heroine's legitimacy, but by conflicts of character such as strain relationships in actual life.

Because this love conflict is more authentically grounded than any in the English eighteenth-century novel except that of Clarissa and Lovelace, it is profoundly moving. Elizabeth Inchbald can rely on the events of her story to evoke sympathy, without resorting to artificial rhetorical heightening. She has set up situation and characters so adeptly that bare statements or simple gestures can convey the intensity of their feelings. As J.M.S. Tompkins has pointed out, Inchbald, once a professional actress, knew how to communicate feeling through gesture, tone, and facial expression. When Miss Milner has finally provoked Dorriforth into renouncing her, only to realize that she has demolished her happiness, she comes to see him for what she believes to be the last time. Sandford is present, an elderly priest who had been Dorriforth's mentor, who has always disliked Miss Milner and has disapproved of their marriage. He hands her a plate of biscuits; she takes one in return for "the first civility he had ever in his life offered her," and then lays it down without eating it (p. 156). This tiny episode convinces us of Miss Milner's grief and her generosity in spite of it, and of an underlying, almost reluctant kindness in Sandford, at least to a vanquished opponent.

Inchbald excelled in representing intense emotions kept under tight control. While Dorriforth is still a priest and totally unaware of his sexual feelings for Miss Milner, he slaps a rake for forcibly holding and kissing her hand. This violence, so contrary to his character, convinces the reader of his passion, even though he is not yet aware of it himself. It takes the resulting duel to make Miss Milner fully realize her love for Dorriforth.

Often Inchbald intensifies her effects by setting up contrasting reactions among her characters. News of the impending duel is brought to Miss Milner and three other ladies: Mrs. Horton, a stupidly pious Catholic; Miss Woodley, her truly charitable niece; and Miss Fenton, a model young woman in the conventional mold (whom Inchbald uses to satirize the identification of female virtue with lack of passion and will).

> Mrs. Horton exclaimed, "If Mr. Dorriforth dies, he dies a martyr."
> Miss Woodley cried with fervor, "Heaven forbid!"
> Miss Fenton cried, "Dear me!"
> While Miss Milner, without uttering one word, sunk speechless on the floor.
> (p. 67)

After Dorriforth has finally lost patience with Miss Milner and broken off their engagement, and when he is saying his final farewell to her, he takes her hand and cannot let it go. Sandford observes them standing together and suddenly realizes the strength of the bond between them. He orders, "Separate this moment, . . . Or resolve never to be separated but by death" (p. 190). Despite his doubts that Miss Milner is suitable for Dorriforth, Sandford cannot help seeing the force of their love and is too conscientious to ignore it. Again, Inchbald conveys passion with economy and understatement.

In a congratulatory letter to Inchbald, her fellow novelist Maria Edgeworth brilliantly analyzed the emotional power of A *Simple Story* and the methods by which it was achieved.

> "I never once recollected the author whilst I was reading it; never said or thought, *that's a fine sentiment*—or, *that is well-expressed*—or *that is well invented.* I believed all to be real, and was affected as I should be by the real scenes if they had passed before my eyes. . . . By the force that is necessary to repress feeling, we judge of the intensity of the feeling; and you always contrive to give us by intelligible but simple signs the measure of this force. Writers of inferior genius waste their words in *describing* feeling; in making those who pretend to be agitated by passion describe the effects of that passion, and talk of the *rending of their hearts, etc.* . . . You excel . . . peculiarly in avoiding what is commonly called *fine writing* . . . which calls the attention away from the *thing* to the *manner*—from the feeling to the language." (James Boaden 1833, pp. 152–153)

Sandford, the older priest, reveals more markedly than Dorriforth the effects of a clerical education. He can see nothing in Miss Milner but frivolity and insubordination, and years of professional authority have made him expect to dominate his company wherever he is. Miss Milner, coming into the situation as an outsider, sees and is piqued by his need to be master; and soon they are engaged in a power struggle. She and Sandford compete for power and resent their opponent's triumph in exactly the same way; ignoring conventional ideas of decorum, Inchbald makes no distinction between petty self-assertion and hostility in a young woman and in an elderly clergyman. The only difference is that Miss Milner bears no lasting resentment, while he does. Convinced of her unworthiness, Sandford mercilessly works to detach Dorriforth from her. Yet, though this aim causes him to exult in her every mistake, he is too conscientious knowingly to take unfair advantage of an opponent. Had he suspected any want of charity in himself, he would immediately have gone to Dorriforth and tried to rectify any unduly harsh judgments of Miss Milner that he had provoked—but having no such suspicion, "he walked on, highly contented" (pp. 143–44). Both priests assume that moral principle provides an objective guide, but actually, like impulse, it depends on individual feeling.

Elizabeth Inchbald shows another side to Sandford in the second part of *A Simple Story* (Inchbald, 1967, Vol. 3 4): if he is a sore loser, he is a generous winner. After a few years of perfectly happy marriage, Lord and Lady Elmwood are separated, she relapses in dissipation, and finally lets herself be seduced by a previous suitor. When Elmwood returns, he casts her off remorselessly: he has no toleration for an error he would never have committed, and he protects himself from further hurt by guarding against any emotional involvement in the future. He accordingly rejects their daughter, as well as his wife, refusing to let either be mentioned in his presence. Sandford, however, remains their friend, as kind to the repentant, needy woman as he had been harsh to her in her days of vanity and triumph.

This second part unfortunately lacks the unconventional brilliance of the first part of *A Simple Story*. Although Inchbald deplores Dorriforth's transformation into "a hard-hearted tyrant" (p. 195), she softens her treatment of him so as to provide him with a blissful reconciliation with his daughter at the end. In contrast to her questioning of legalistic morality in the first part, she appears to maintain in the second that the appropriate punishment for adultery is ten years of desolate remorse and death at thirty-five. Most unfortunately, the heroine of Part 1 is replaced by her daughter, Matilda, a blameless young person, effusively devoted to the father who treats her atrociously; she is as insipid as the usual late-eighteenth-century heroine and, because she had no character to initiate action, can only be made interesting factitiously, by being made a victim of unnatural parental behavior and abduction. In contrast to her faulty and ruined mother, Matilda is supposed to illustrate the results of "A Proper Education" (p. 294). What this actually means is that her cheerless childhood has inhibited her from developing her mother's will and passion; Matilda's rational self-control is indistinguishable from the dutiful self-suppression that eighteenth-century convention prescribed for women.

In the 1790s, Inchbald became a friend of William Godwin and Thomas Holcroft; and the influence of their radical ideas is apparent in her second novel, *Nature and Art* (1796; see Inchbald, 1849). Here too she contrasted good with bad education, although she drew the contrast more schematically and attacked society's conventional attitudes and institutions more explicitly. Even more than in *A Simple Story*, she preferred spontaneous good feeling to socially determined law, which in the first book is associated with rigid adherence to principle; in the second, with worldly prudence.

*Nature and Art* is actually more a philosophical fiction than a novel, for it presses its message—the influence of education and circumstances on character, the pernicious effects of conformity and class distinctions, the superiority of nature over art, the connection between virtue and happiness—at the expense of character development.

Henry and William set out to make their fortunes at the death of their father, a country shopkeeper. They have no success until Henry's fiddle playing wins him the favor of the best society. He tirelessly works to obtain preferment for his brother, whose talent is scholarship, and finally does so. But no sooner has William begun to rise in the Church than he becomes ashamed of Henry. The final breach comes when Henry marries a professional singer, and William, who has married a vain, empty woman for her family influence, refuses to introduce her to Henry's wife. As a result of various adventures, Henry's son arrives at William's house at the age of thirteen. The contrast between him and his thirteen-year-old cousin, young William, is even more marked than that between their fathers. Young Henry is unselfish, warm-hearted, and able to think for himself. Young William, who has received the best upper-class education, is a total egotist who parrots conventional ideas with polished glibness. Inchbald's plot hammers home Rousseau's point that people are corrupted by society. The older William and Henry start out loving, honest, and tender-hearted; William's appetite for social advancement tempts him to toady to superiors, and his success teaches him arrogance, snobbery, and hardness of heart. All the upper-class characters are corrupted—by conventional education, by adulation because of their position, by the compromises necessary to achieve success.

When the two young men fall in love at twenty, young William seduces Agnes, a beautiful peasant girl, while young Henry aspires to marry Rebecca, the poor and plain, but sensible and good, daughter of the local curate. Young William goes on to become a judge, through a combination of ability, the influence of his wife's family, and long hours devoted to work in order to get away from his wife. He has made a loveless marriage with a dependent of his father's noble patrons, which will end with his wife's adultery and elopement. Agnes is disgraced, flees to London, is discharged from her job as a domestic slave when her employer finds her visiting her illegitimate child, sinks into prostitution, and finally is arrested for passing false bank bills and tried for her life. It is William who presides at her trial, without recognizing her, and passes the death sentence on her. On the emotionally-dead man and the broken-down prostitute he has ruined, Inchbald trenchantly comments: judge and culprit "had passed together the most blissful moments that either had ever tasted!" (p. 411).

This scene in itself is highly effective, but it also indicates the excessively schematic structure of *Nature and Art*. Inchbald never misses an opportunity to press home a didactic point: for example, Rebecca's prettier sisters are spiteful to her and end up as withered old maids, while Rebecca remains everbeautiful to young Henry because her beauty is inward. Nevertheless, Inchbald presents her radical-sentimental message with insight and wit. She demonstrated the stultifying effects of the conformity necessary for worldly success by contrasting the perpetual self-consciousness of the worldly characters with the carefree spontaneity of the unworldly ones. While William and his family are continuously obsessed with what others think of them, young Henry is free to decide what *he* thinks of others. Young William never questions that private happiness is trivial compared to public opinion, or that getting ahead by currying favor with the influential is more dignified than getting ahead by his own independent efforts. As alert to clerical arrogance as she had been in *A Simple Story*, Inchbald deflates the Senior William: he "had a steady countenance, a stern brow, and a majestic walk; all of which . . . this holy calling to religious vows, rather increased than diminished" (p. 305). She neatly derides the hypocritical Establishment's attitude toward the poor: "rigid attention to the religion and morals of people in poverty, and total neglect of their bodily wants, was the dean's practice. He forced them to attend church every Sabbath; but whether they had a dinner on their return was too gross and temporal an enquiry for his spiritual fervour." It is fortunate that he was a magistrate as well as a pastor, "for to be very poor and very honest, very oppressed yet very thankful, is a degree of sainted excellence not often to be attained, without the aid of zealous men to frighten into virtue" (pp. 350–51).

In general, the characters in *Nature and Art* exist to prove points. The only one who moves is young William's victim, Agnes Primrose. She is deeply touching as she painfully struggles to read William's coldly dismissive letter and to answer it in a style free of illiteracies that would arouse his contempt, or as she fights her losing battle to preserve a little self-esteem, while inevitably sinking lower and lower in her own eyes as well as the world's. She is torn between disgust for her trade and a feeling that she ought to conform to the ways of the only women who will accept her. Through Agnes, Inchbald makes a plea for the fallen woman: "Degraded in her own judgment, she doubted her own understanding, when it sometimes told her she had deserved better treatment— for she felt herself a fool in comparison with her learned seducer and the rest who despised her" (p. 403). Self-contempt is a major source of suffering for Agnes, a painful aggravation to the scorn of the respectable world. It almost inevitably follows from that scorn, but that does not mean that it should follow.

Finally, Inchbald gives Agnes an unexpected touch of nature. Desperate and guilt-ridden, she gave birth to William's child in the woods and, though she could not bring herself to strangle it, abandoned it to die. (Significantly, it was this act, not her yielding to William, that first filled her with remorse.) But when young Henry rescued the child, Agnes accepted and mothered it. William's father reluctantly agreed to support her, provided she sent the child away to save the young man embarrassment, and was both outraged and baffled when she refused. He could not understand why a woman who had originally abandoned her child to die would refuse to part with him just because she had started to nurse him. It does not, of course, make logical sense. But psychologically it rings true. Inchbald was never herself a mother, but she understood maternal feeling.

A Simple Story stands out among late-eighteenth-century novels for its emotional power, for it is one of the few in which vividly alive central characters generate a moving plot. Partly at least, the characters' effectiveness results from their having been inspired by actual life: the two principals are not the moral exemplum and the fantasy lover of most women's fiction of the time, but individualized characters derived from the author herself and a man she loved (as Agnes, the only moving character in Nature and Art, was probably drawn from Inchbald's sister Deborah, who also died a miserable prostitute). Inchbald, like her heroine, was beautiful, willful, and much courted by men. She told one of her many suitors that she was too fond of her own way to make him happy as a husband, and, once widowed, she cherished her independence. She had, however, the rational control that Miss Milner conspicuously lacks. Daughter of a farmer, she determined to make her living on the stage, even though she stammered. She managed to become a competent actress and for years worked hard in traveling repertory companies, all the while educating herself. Realizing that she could not go far as an actress in London, she turned to playwrighting and, with difficulty, persuaded a manager to produce her farce The Mogul Tale. This was the beginning of her busy and successful career as an author: she wrote twenty farces and comedies, as well as her novels, and edited The British Theatre, a collection of 125 plays with prefaces, as well as two other anthologies. She also led a brilliant social life, among fashionable aristocrats as well as radical writers. She had to constantly fend off propositions and proposals from men she did not wish to marry and did it so gracefully that they remained her friends afterwards. Her success was in part the result of "proper education," for she was no spoiled heiress like Miss Milner. She had to work hard for everything she had and firmly to control her impulses in order to preserve her character, her independence, and her favored position in society.

If any man in her life tempted her to indiscretion, it would have been the great actor John Philip Kemble. She was strongly attracted to him and hoped to marry him after her husband's death; but he required a more docile wife, although he might have wanted to make her his mistress. He looked like the fictional Dorriforth, was known for his carefully calculated acting and dominating personality, and had actually studied for the priesthood. Inchbald could draw on her own experience for the conflict between two strong wills, the power struggle between a man who needs to exert power and a woman who resists being dictated to; and this adds vitality and authenticity to the struggle portrayed in her novel. Miss Milner is a tragic extension of her author—what Elizabeth Inchbald might have been, had she been born an heiress and had she been unable to control her passions. For this reason, Inchbald can present her with sympathy as well as critical judgment; and she stands as the most intensely human heroine of late-eighteenth-century fiction.

## REFERENCES

Boaden, James. (1833). *Memoirs of Mrs. Inchbald: Including her familiar correspondence* (2 vols.). London: Richard Bentley.

Inchbald, Elizabeth. (1849). *Nature and art*. London: Richard Bentley.

Inchbald, Elizabeth. (1967). *A simple story*. Edited with an introduction by J.M.S. Tompkins. London: Oxford University Press.

Johnson, Samuel. (1981). *The selected writings*. Edited with an introduction by Katharine Rogers. New York: New American Library.

# Charlotte Smith's Feminism:

## A Study of *Emmeline* and *Desmond**

======= Pat Elliott =======

Immediately successful, Charlotte Smith's first novel *Emmeline, or the Orphan of the Castle* (1788) firmly established her reputation as a popular writer. The *Critical Review* comparing *Emmeline* with Fanny Burney's *Cecilia* found it only slightly inferior to Burney's work while praising her style as being in the tradition of Fanny Burney: "a new species, which reflects so much credit on its author." (Vol. 65, 1788, p. 530). By the early 1790s, she was "probably the most popular contemporary novelist in the English-speaking world, but [her] letters testify to the fact that she lived and worked in comparative literary isolation" (Alan Dugald McKillop, 1951–1952, p. 237). Isolated as she was because of personal cares, legal entanglements, and family problems, Smith was well aware of contemporary revolutionary philosophical and political issues. Her first novel addressed the problem of women's position within the family and society at large, while her fourth novel, *Desmond,* which focused on the French Revolution, examined the connection between women's domestic position and political abuse on all levels. In fact, her early novels have less in common ideologically with Burney than with the Jacobins—Thomas Holcraft, Elizabeth Inchbald, Robert Bage, Amelia Opie, William Godwin, and especially Mary Wollstonecraft, whose ideas she respected.

Both Mary Wollstonecraft and Charlotte Smith recognized a crucial link between the political and domestic spheres that rendered women powerless because of institutionalized patriarchy. Both regarded the education of women as the most important step in effecting a personal and social reformation for women. Because of her position on women's issues and the solutions she proposed, Smith should be considered along with Wollstonecraft an important precursor of socialist feminist criticism, which, as Cora Kaplan has pointed

---

*A shorter version of this paper was presented at the South Central Society for Eighteenth-Century Studies Annual Conference in March, 1988, under the title "Testing the Limits: Mature Women in the Novels of Charlotte Smith."

out, "tends to foreground the social and economic elements of the narrative and socialize what it can of its psychic portions. Women's anger and anguish, it is assumed, should be amenable to repair through social change" (1985, p. 152). In 1792 both Mary Wollstonecraft and Charlotte Smith wrote about the status of women, addressing issues of inequality and suggesting solutions for improvement. Both sought to redress the problem of inequality through institutional reform, and they agreed that individual women could improve their lot by cultivating the reason. While many of their ideas are comparable, they differed on the mode of discourse and the question of how women were to be educated to be more rational and autonomous: in so doing, each writer's aesthetic position commented on appropriate language and the uses of fiction.

In her introduction to *Vindication of the Rights of Woman,* published in 1792, the same year as Charlotte Smith's *Desmond,* Mary Wollstonecraft shunned the essentially "feminine" form of the novel in favor of polemical discourse. Problematically, she chose the language of "truth," language stripped of any association with sentiment or feelings, the sort of language she associated with the sentimental novel. In her attempt to "render my sex more respectable members of society," she avoided "these pretty superlatives [the language of novels] [which] dropping glibly from the tongue, vitiate the taste, and create a kind of sickly delicacy that turns away from simple unadorned truth; and a deluge of false sentiments and overstretched feelings, stifling the natural emotions of the heart, render the domestic pleasures insipid, that ought to sweeten the exercise of those severe duties, which educate a rational and immortal being for a nobler field of action" (1982, p. 82).

Cora Kaplan notes "Mary Wollstonecraft . . . first offered women this fateful choice between the opposed and moralized bastions of reason and feeling, which continues to determine much feminist thinking" (p. 155). In "Mary Wollstonecraft and the Search for the Radical Woman," Anna Wilson (1989) theorizes that the failure of Wollstonecraft's polemical work to initiate a movement to redress the wrongs of women can be partially attributed to her rejection of feminine discourse in an attempt to occupy a male ground in language—to apply rational principles to womankind, much as Thomas Paine had done for "mankind." Unlike Paine, who had a clearly identifiable audience, Mary Wollstonecraft's notion of her readership shifted throughout *The Rights.* Without the concept, and the reality, of a politically committed female audience to receive her ideas, Wollstonecraft failed to create common cause with her readers.

Charlotte Smith, on the other hand, had published three novels and had an established female readership by 1792. If her audience was not committed politically, Smith believed it could be educated through fictional example to value rationality and to reject sentimental passivity. With *Desmond* she further politicized the novel as a vehicle for social action, consciousness raising, and change. She used the language available to women while at the same time offering an alternative to the popular, sentimental mindless novel that both she and Wollstonecraft deplored. She knew exactly who her audience was, what they read, and what they were allowed to read. For Smith, then, her novel readers furnished a fertile ground for instruction. Working within the fictional genre, she valorized the combination of reason with emotion as a strong model rather than making the two oppositional; thus her audience was less likely to have been alienated by her language and the familiar form of the popular novel than by rational disquisition.

Her choice of the novel as an appropriate forum for political discussion most surely was prescribed by the economic necessity of providing for her children, but, by including discussions of current political ideas, she used it as a vehicle for social change—and a means whereby women could be given strong, positive role models. Smith and the heroines of her novels were great readers of fiction; in fact, reading was the only means of education available to her heroines, and by way of illustration, she privileged novel reading as an avenue of enlightenment. She chafed at the notion that canonical male writers such as Richardson enjoyed freedoms of subject prohibited to her and her contemporary writers (Smith, 1971, Vol. 11, pp. 172–173) and she condemned, along with Mary Wollstonecraft, many current novels as insipid and improbable, bearing no relation to the real lives of women, and particularly alien to her own experience. But, rather than seeing these novels as corrupting influences as Wollstonecraft did, she believed them an utter waste of time:

> I own, I cannot imagine, that novel reading can, as has been alleged, corrupt the imagination, or enervate the heart; at least, such a description of novels, as those which represent human life nearly as it is; for, as to other, those wild and absurd writings, that describe in inflated language, beings, that never were, nor ever will be, they can (if any young woman has so little patience and taste to read them) no more contribute to form the character of her mind, than the grotesque figures of shepherdesses, or French fans and Bergamot boxes can form her taste in dress. (Smith, 1971, Vol. 11, 166–167)

Such a distinction created at once both a problem and an opportunity for Smith. As her novels show, she focused on problems of contemporary women; writing their lives—"human life nearly as it is"—based on her observation and life experience. The problem lay in the form itself: how was it possible to create a serious discourse concerning women's real experience within the confines of traditional form which demanded a satisfying, if not blissfully happy, conclusion, however improbable? The same problem existed for women writers in the nineteenth century, as well, and it is interesting to observe how later writers managed to solve the problem. Doubtless, the compromise did not sit easily with Charlotte Smith; her characters' comments throughout the novels and her emphasis on social issues suggest that she envisioned a wider range of possibilities for the genre, and for women in society, and conformed with reluctance to conventions of the sentimental courtship novel, which, reflecting the social order, offered no options to the marriage of the heroine to an idealized male, there being no acceptable alternatives for women at the time.

Within the confines of the form, Smith enlarged fictional discourse by clarifying important issues and outlining pressing problems for contemporary women, and by strengthening the image of women in her mature, female characters; although frequently her innovations were couched in well-worn motifs. The problem of women's education, the place for intelligent women in the world, intellectual outlets for woman, marital obligations, unjust laws, abusive husbands, sexual harassment, and the plight of seduced and abandoned women—in short, the tyrannies of patriarchy—were treated as important subjects of her fiction.

Imagining larger possibilities for women to exist effectively in the world, Smith often blurred gender distinctions, presenting intelligent, mature women made strong and resilient through adversity, good men sensitized to women's suffering, weak men effeminate and hysterical, bad women corrupted by power and position. Her admirable female characters are responsible adults whose stamina and rationality often make them stronger than the males in the novels. Invariably the admirable characters, whether male or female, possess refined sensibilities combined with the ability to think clearly and act rationally. Class distinctions, as well, are often played with and revealed to be false in Smith's novels—the requisite Cinderella plot provided ample room for obscuring class difference. She used the form, in other words, as a means of imagining a world in which gender, class, family origin, and wealth were less important than personal integrity and reasonable behavior.

To maintain her readership, Smith had to pay attention to moral restrictions placed on women novelists to appear to stay clearly within prescribed boundaries of decorum. In relation to inhibitions placed on eighteenth-century women writers, Katharine Rogers writes that they ". . . were allowed to publish and retain their respectability, but the price they paid was strict attention to propriety, constant vigilance over the moral implications of their works. . . . The requirement to keep beyond moral reproach combined with the pressure to focus on a female protagonist disastrously to flatten women's novels. For the chastity, propriety, sense of duty, delicacy enjoined on women in real life were doubly enjoined on the fictitious woman who was not worthy to be a heroine if she could not serve as a model" (1977, p. 65). Because the heroine must be a model of virtue, the novel's interest must derive from events surrounding her not of her own creation but beyond her control. Her virtue is then shown in how she meets hardships and handles problems, the plots consisting of difficulties she must overcome to exhibit virtuous behavior and to allow for a satisfactory conclusion—the marriage of the heroine to an appropriate male. The heroic women of Charlotte Smith's novels conform to this recipe with only slight variation.

Emmeline, Mrs. Stafford, (*Emmeline*), and Geraldine Verney of *Desmond* are all very much alike in virtue, standards of behavior, and delicacy of feeling. What distinguishes them from earlier heroines is their maturity, intelligence, and often their spirit. Critics vary in their opinion about the interest of these heroines. Julia Kavanagh was the first to point out that "Mrs. Smith's [heroines] may claim to be the earliest and most successful in personations of the lady . . . of delicate feelings, accomplished mind, and good manners . . . " (1863, p. 203). On the other hand, Charlotte Smith's biographer, Florence Hilbish, writes that "Like the ideal lady of the Elizabethan sonnets, Mrs. Smith's good women are fair, beautiful, and virtuous; her wicked women are ugly, coarse, and bold. Her heroines are all very similar and near relatives of Pamela, Clarissa, and Harriet Byron, Evelina and Cecilia, Sidney Bidulph, and a host of others born in the same century" (1941, p. 356). Still, in her very thorough examination of Charlotte Smith's works, she reads the characters as distinctive from stock heroines, even though they share certain requisite similarities.

Smith's women are traditionally soft-hearted and sympathetic with the good-intentioned and the troubled, but they are capable of overlooking propriety to help another woman in distress. The female characters rarely show the anger of their creator although they frequently weep over their situations, a requisite sign of their sensibility. Responding to an assortment of hardships, they conventionally maintain dignity throughout. But because they are mature for their age or married, events that occur to them and their reactions to those events provide Smith's vehicle for social criticism. Smith's rage at the plight of women in her time is expressed in the bitterness with which she portrays weakness and villainy in many of her male characters—especially attorneys and a host of characters based on her husband Benjamin Smith—and in the situations in which her heroines find themselves because of the disregard or machinations of such men.

When she wrote her first novel, Charlotte Smith was in the process of separating from her husband, a fact which is reflected in *Emmeline*. Concerning the circumstances of the separation, she wrote to the Reverend Joseph Walker: "Tho infidelity and with the most despicable objects had rendered my continuing to live with him extremely wretched long before his debts compelled him to leave England, I could have been contented to have resided in the same house with him, had not his temper been so capricious and often so cruel that my life was not safe" (Alan Dugald McKillop, pp. 238–9). In *Emmeline*, Smith vents her anger about the powerlessness of good women in bad marriages. The novel presents examples of good and bad marriages, but it concentrates mostly on bad ones contracted either for the wrong reasons or before the partners were mature enough to make prudent choices.

Unlike Mary Wollstonecraft, Charlotte Smith does not reject the institution of marriage; instead, she takes a reformist position by setting up exacting criteria for successful unions. In both novels, she opposes early marriage; essentially her thesis is that marriage is a sacred state which must be willingly entered by people mature enough to know their own minds and feelings and with discrimination enough to judge the partner's character. She disapproves of arranged marriages but insists on parental consent. In both *Emmeline* and *Desmond,* women suffer greatly for having married because of parental pressure and disregard for their children's feelings. The lesson Emmeline must learn is to act on her own feelings rather than comply with the desires of Delamere to whom she becomes engaged because *he* wants to, or with the wishes of her guardian, Lord Montreville, who would marry her to anyone to get her off his hands and away from his son, Delamere. As well, the examples of Mrs. Stafford and Lady Adelina teach Emmeline the perils of early marriage.

When the novel opens, Emmeline Mowbray is an orphan reared in rural social isolation at Mowbray Castle; her only companion is Mrs. Grant, the housekeeper, whose death at the beginning of the novel is the first crisis Emmeline faces. She is self-taught, her education derived from books she found in the castle's library—Spenser, Milton, Shakespeare, and Pope have been her teachers. "From them she acquired . . . knowledge . . . which . . . enabled her to support . . . those undeserved evils with which many of her years were embittered" (p. 4). Charlotte Smith emphasized Emmeline's good mind and excellent understanding before giving the reader a physical description of her—she is "interesting" looking rather than conventionally beautiful, "her features not very regular" (p. 5), a deviation from the conventional heroine. Emmeline's character is established with her reaction to Mrs. Grant's death; first she *reasons* what to do about the arrangements, then she allows herself to grieve. This ability to reason her way through difficult situations establishes her pattern of handling problems throughout the narrative and stresses well-developed maturity for a sixteen-year-old: ". . . her understanding was of the first rank. She possessed this native firmness in a degree very unusual to her age and sex" (p. 6). While she had been described as conventional, flat, and not interesting to the modern reader (Katharine Rogers, p. 72), what sets her apart from Evelina or Pamela, for example, and brings an added dimension to the formula heroine, is this emphasis on reasoning, her practical mind balancing conventional sensibility.

More interesting, perhaps, is how Smith employed the device of the orphan to obscure class distinctions and to underscore the fragile position of unprotected women. First, of course, belonging to no one really, since she is thought to be the illegitimate daughter of Montreville's brother, Mowbray, Emmeline is vulnerable to the whims of her uncle, who provides for her more out of obligation than good will or affection. When Mrs. Grant dies, Emmeline is left without companionship, affection, or protection. She is prey to the sexual harassment of the steward Maloney, whose advances force her to retreat to her room for safety where she reads while waiting for her uncle to decide what to do with her.

The point is that females who exist outside protective patriarchal structures are entirely dependent on the benevolence of others while they are targets for the unscrupulous. The orphan's classless status simply emphasizes the position of women in society. Emmeline is also young, unused to the ways of the world, penniless, and alone. There is another side to this coin, however; since she grew up on her own, she had developed self-reliance, the ability to think and act independently, and she is without vanity or affectation. Charlotte Smith uses the convention of the orphan to portray a strong, reasonable young woman whose vulnerability, finally, is not greater than Mrs. Stafford's or Lady Adelina's. In a sense, the orphan becomes metaphor for the position of any woman in society who does not have the protection of good parents, a good husband, or financial security. And even these cannot totally guarantee her well-being.

Protection is finally offered, not by Montreville, but through the friendship of Mrs. Stafford who becomes her companion, mentor, protector, and teacher. With Mrs. Stafford, Charlotte Smith writes her own life—and anger—into the novel: Mrs. Stafford, the mother of several children, is older, mature, and married to an insensitive spendthrift. Living apart from her husband while he oversees unnecessary additions to their home in Dorset, Mrs. Stafford befriends Emmeline. Mrs. Stafford's story is essentially the story of Charlotte Smith; events in the novel concerning Mrs. Stafford parallel Smith's life experience, serve as an example for young women to avoid, add realism to the novel, define her position on marriage, and identify the source of her rage. In addition to protecting Emmeline, Mrs. Stafford offers her advice and provides a living example of the evils of early marriage. Through their friendship and Mrs. Stafford's example, Emmeline receives a practical education in the ways of the world, learning that the place of woman in society depends upon the reliability of the men with whom she is connected. Her relationship with Mrs. Stafford illustrates the importance of friendship between women for protection from predatory or irresponsible men and as a significant vehicle for passing on women's knowledge, a solution to women's problems not imagined by Mary Wollstonecraft. Charlotte Smith stresses the mentor relationship especially: "Mrs. Stafford, delighted with the lively attachments of her young friend, was charmed to find herself capable of adorning her ingenuous and tender mind with all that knowledge which books or the world had qualified her to impart" (p. 45). If Mrs. Stafford is a very thinly disguised Charlotte Smith, then parallels can be drawn between author and reader and between Smith and Stafford mentors. The notion that books, particularly novels, can teach their readers about life is a recurring idea in Charlotte Smith's work. If Mrs. Stafford can save Emmeline from the dangers of patriarchy, what can the reader learn from Smith? Through Mrs. Stafford, Smith very clearly reveals didactic motives in her choice of subject. It was one she felt strongly about, as our later analysis of *Desmond* will show.

Gradually disclosing her situation to Emmeline, Mrs. Stafford tells her that she was married at sixteen at the urging of her father and aunt but soon discovered her husband to be weak and given to excess in gambling, drinking, and womanizing. During the course of the narrative, Mrs. Stafford's patience and endurance are tested by his irresponsible behavior: she is uprooted when their estate is sold to pay his debts, she moves with him to France to escape creditors, she suffers emotionally from his affairs with various women, she becomes responsible for the welfare of her family, and when special pleading with authorities fails to relieve financial distress, she is blamed by her husband for the family's problems. "The derangements of Stafford's affairs, and his wife's unavailing efforts to ward off the ruin every day more visible: while his capricious and unreasonable temper, and a strange opinion of his own sagacity, which would never allow him to own himself in the wrong, made him seek to load his wife with the blame of those misfortunes which he had voluntarily sought, and now as obdurately refused to avoid while it was yet in his power" (p. 293). This story not only provides Emmeline with an example of the importance of making a prudent choice and waiting until she and Delamere are old enough to judge wisely, more importantly it shows how much women's lives are affected physically, financially, and emotionally by their husband's behavior. Mrs. Stafford, finally, is as dependent on her husband as Emmeline is on her guardian; the only difference is that Emmeline is theoretically free not to marry, while Mrs. Stafford is completely trapped. Mrs. Stafford responds to her situation by turning to her children for comfort and attempting to keep the family together, never forgetting her duty to her husband. While her dutiful behavior makes Mrs. Stafford the sort of ideal model Katharine Rogers has described, her forebearance in a completely frustrating situation with a husband who cares nothing about her or their children is grounded in reality by mirroring Smith's experience.

Other actual or potential marriages in the novel underscore the necessity of marrying wisely and for the right reasons. Emmeline receives two inappropriate proposals which she staunchly refuses, declaring that she would prefer to live without any support from Montreville to marrying against her will. The first one comes from the steward Maloney at Mowbray Castle and the other from Mr. Rochely, a wealthy, fifty-year-old businessman whose proposal reads like a legal contract, prefiguring Jane Austen's Mr. Collins. Presented as an absurdly comic figure, Rochely is gently satirized for his personal vanity and misreading of Emmeline's politeness. When her uncle sends Sir Richard Crofts to read the article of her marriage to Mr. Rochely, her response shows the spirit Smith's finest heroines possess:

> "I will not marry Mr. Rochely, though instead of the fortune you describe, he could offer me the world. Lord Montreville may abandon me, but he shall not make me wretched. Tell him . . . that the daughter of his brother . . . yet boasts that nobleness of mind which her father possessed, and disclaims the merce-

nary views of becoming, from pecuniary motives, the wife of a man whom she cannot either love or esteem." (p. 357)

Other examples show unhappy results of marrying for money or position: vanity, pride, greed, and ignorance cause misery to a host of peripheral characters. Most of these marriages show that in the marriage market women are regarded only as commodities to be bartered or sold for profit or convenience.

Another victim of such a marriage is Lady Adelina Trelawny who is found by Emmeline and Mrs. Stafford living in a small cabin close to Mrs. Stafford's house. When the two find her alone and pregnant, Mrs. Stafford immediately thinks that Mr. Stafford must have seduced her. They befriend her and listen to her story; Emmeline even accompanies her to Bath to look after her during her confinement. In Lady Adelina, Charlotte Smith gives her readers an unconventionally sympathetic portrait of a seduced woman. Eva Figes has noted that

> "... it is significant that Emmeline and her independent friend Mrs. Stafford ... befriend the unhappy Adelina and look after her during and after her pregnancy. No Burney heroine would have been allowed to mix in such company, and the normal attitude expressed in the conservative courtship novel is that no young lady should risk her reputation by associating with women of doubtful reputation, and even such women never have illegitimate children. But Charlotte Smith's heroine constantly expresses active sympathy for women in distress." (1982, p. 66)

To elicit sympathy for Adelina, Mrs. Smith portrays her as a victim of early marriage. She tells Emmeline: "Tho' I had not absolute partiality to him, I was totally indifferent to every other man. I married him, therefore; and gave away my person before I knew I had an heart" (p. 213). Trelawny, like Stafford, proves weak and excessive in short order. After her marriage, Adelina discovers her heart, but later when she has the choice to marry her seducer Fitz-Edward, Trelawny having died of excess, she chooses not to. Presumably, Charlotte Smith felt that giving Adelina a happy marriage would have vexed her readers too much; allowing her to reject her lover is an attempt to elevate the character.

In fact, Adelina's portrayal did not escape the critical notice of Mary Wollstonecraft who, in reviewing the novel, objected to Adelina's submitting to passion, then neglecting her duty:

> We will venture to ask any young girl if Lady Adelina's theatrical contrition did not catch her attention, while Mrs. Stafford's rational resignation escaped her notice? Lady Adelina is indeed a character as absurd as dangerous. Despair is not repentance, nor is contrition of any use when it does not serve to strengthen resolutions of amendment. The being who indulges useless sorrow, instead of fulfilling the duties of life, may claim our pity, but should never excite admiration ... this kind of sorrow is rather the offspring of romantic notions and false refinement, than of sensibility and a nice sense of duty. Mrs. Stafford, when

disappointed in her husband, turned to her children. We mentioned this character
because it deserves praise. (*Analytical Review*, 1788, p. 333)

Wollstonecraft's criticism voiced her objection to sensational fiction with its
possibly damaging effects on young readers, a position she maintained but
more thoroughly articulated in *The Rights* four years later. It is interesting to
note that she did not comment on Emmeline and Mrs. Stafford's reactions to
Adelina, who rush to her aid before they know who she is, nor did she comment on the concept of communal support from other women either here
or in her later work.

Adelina's portrayal is important for the reactions she elicits and the ways
the two stronger women can imagine helping her to survive. Without making judgments, they act in concert to rescue her. Adelina is not presented
as a model; if anything, her story is included to illustrate another outcome
of early marriage, and to show that Mrs. Stafford's is not an isolated case. The
point Charlotte Smith makes about Adelina is that she is a victim of the marriage market in which parents choose partners for their children regardless
of their feelings, essentially marrying them off for social position. It is true
that her story is told with sympathy, but she is too consistently passive for
the reader's admiration. One can only surmise that Charlotte Smith took Wollstonecraft's objection seriously, however, since the woman characters in later
novels do not occupy such an ambiguous position.

Emmeline reacts sympathetically to Adelina and her child. At this point
in the narrative, Emmeline believes herself to be illegitimate, occupying a
position as socially marginal as Adelina's or the infant's. In fact, her thoughts
about the similarity of her birth with his lead her to consider the difference
that being born female has made in her life: she wept over "the little infant,
whose birth, so similar to her own, seemed to render it to her a more interesting and affecting object. She lamented the evils to which it might be exposed;
tho' of a sex which would prevent it's [sic] encountering the same species
of sorrow as that which had embittered her own life" (p. 273). Through Adelina, Emmeline meets Godolphin, her ideal partner; as we will see, his reaction to Adelina's situation defines him as a reasonable, sensitive man. A
character of exquisite sensibility, Adelina is hardly a scarlet woman, yet she
would have been regarded as such by her society, as the review indicates.

But what of the men in the novel? Besides the portrait of her husband in
the weak, profligate characters of Stafford and Trelawny, Charlotte Smith's
portrayal of various other male characters shows patriarchy as she experienced
it in her own life, with its deadening effect of subordinating women to defense-
less positions within the family and the state. Her villains guard the preserves
of patriarchy by upholding its institutions—the law, the church, and the class
system. Although they are more vividly drawn than the admirable males, because of their representative functions they are not particularly lifelike, but

their essential natures and condescending attitudes toward women are emphasized. Smith is interested in showing what women are up against when they confront the guardians of the social order. Because the behavior and attitudes of the men illustrate the barriers women faced, a brief survey of the male characters would seem to be in order.

In *Emmeline,* her male characters are not as fully developed as the females, because they occupy subordinate positions within the narrative. The heroic ones are paler versions of their female counterparts; Godolphin is an ideal, his feminized nature is sensitive, his heart as soft as his lady's. In the later *Desmond,* Charlotte Smith attempted to create a more realistic protagonist by flawing his character; still, both are unlike other men in that they respect meritorious behavior and are able to see beyond appearances of class, gender, or birth to judge true worth, They represent ideals of male behavior toward women and children, how men ought to be. While the males may not always seem completely convincing, they serve Smith's didactic purposes: the heroic ones respect women and are delighted with, not threatened by, women's knowledge and abilities. The attitudes and actions those associated with law and aristocracy illustrate the ways in which women are devalued by patriarchy and kept in secondary roles.

Delamere is not an essentially bad character, but impulsive, thoughtless, and often harmful. His imprudence and impetuosity put Emmeline in danger of being misunderstood and condemned by her uncle. When he abducts her to take her to Scotland for a hasty marriage, he shows no regard for her physical well-being or her reputation; he is concerned only with immediately gratifying his desire to have her. Smith's description of him indicates that she wants this character to be appealing and noble, but his dashing about, making bombastic declarations, hitting his head against the wall, and weeping copiously make him a caricature or parody of the man of feeling; he acts like a madman, not a proper partner for Emmeline.

Delamere's charm, good looks, and sensibility appeal to Emmeline and engage her pity initially, although his impassioned outbursts and weeping soon grow tiresome to her. One example will serve to illustrate Delamere's typical behavior: "He stamped about the room, dashed his head against the wainscot, and seizing Mrs. Watkins by the arm, swore, with the most frightful vehemence, that he would see Miss Mowbry though death were in the way" (p. 64). At times, his violent passions are as threatening to Emmeline as Maloney's sexual advances had been. His irrational unwillingness to listen to reason from Emmeline or from his father indicates a character who might later in life (he is not yet twenty-one) create the same sort of problems for Emmeline that have plagued Mrs. Stafford and Adelina. Appropriate to his character, he dies in a duel with his cousin, Bellzone (another unsuitable suitor of Emmeline as well), defending the questionable honor of his elder sister. Bellzone's character is like Delamere's except that since he is unable to have

Emmeline, he indulges his lust by openly having an affair with Delamere's sister, Lady Frances. By contrast with Bellzone, Delamere's "love" for Emmeline seems pure.

The true villain of the novel and the most outspoken defender of patriarchy is the corrupt wily attorney, Sir Richard Crofts, legal advisor to Lord Montreville. Charlotte Smith's lifelong struggle with the courts to secure her children's inheritance of their grandfather's estate is well-documented and need not be related again here; her bitterness and frustration with the legal system resulted in damning potraits of attorneys in several of her novels. The first in a long line of cunning attorneys, Sir Richard has a particular disregard for and condescension to women which are noted on several occasions in the novel. Sir Richard is a social climber, a hypocrite, and a crook who is threatened by anyone with superior understanding or position. Smith's acid portrait of him conveys her hatred of those connected to the law and her personal bitterness about the power of the unscrupulous over others. Charlotte Smith's embarrassment, frustration, humiliation, and anger are related in vivid detail in Mrs. Stafford's and Emmeline's dealings with Crofts. Responsible for concealing Emmeline's legitimate connection to the Montreville family, thus depriving her of her birthright, he especially dislikes her for overstepping feminine boundaries by being too independent and knowing too much. His son, James, tells her: " 'It is,' " said he, " 'a maxim of my father's—and my father is no bad judge—that for a woman to affect literature is the most horrid of all absurdities; and for a woman to know any thing of business, is detestable!' " (p. 236).

As the embodiment of a legal system which had frustrated Charlotte Smith for years, Sir Richard represents patriarchy at its worst; he is described as having:

> less understanding than cunning; less honesty than industry; and tho' he knew how to talk warmly and plausibly of honour, justice, and integrity, he was generally contented only to talk of them. . . . He had that sort of sagacity which enabled him to enter into the characters of those with whom he conversed: he knew how to humour their prejudices, and lay in wait for their foibles to turn them to his own advantage.
>
> To his superiors, the cringing parasite; to those whom he thought his inferiors, proud, supercilious, and insulting and his heart [hardened] as his prosperity increased. . . ." (p. 87)

When she was criticized for too frequently alluding to her own circumstances in basing such characters upon those of her acquaintance, Smith replied: "a novelist . . . makes his drawing to resemble the characters he has occasion to meet with. Thus, some have drawn alehouse-keepers and their wives—others, artists and professors—and of late we have seen whole books full of dukes and duchesses, lords and ladies—I have 'fallen among thieves,' and I have occasionally made sketches of them" (Smith, 1794, p. ix). Smith allows the women to triumph over this character in the end, when Emmeline's estate is restored and Sir Richard is exposed as a scoundrel. Charlotte Smith separates the idea of justice from the reality of the legal system and suggests that true justice is the fruit of wisdom, produced by the experience and maturity of Mrs. Stafford and Emmeline.

By far the most interesting male character, because the most complex, is Lord Montreville, who with Crofts' help has appropriated Emmeline's inheritance by obscuring her legitimacy. The darker side of his nature predominates because of his association with Crofts and his marriage to the family-proud Lady Montreville. Yet he cannot help liking and even admiring Emmeline, even though she threatens his plans to marry Delamere to a young heiress. Her sense of honor in dealing with him and Delamere appeals to his basic goodness. For example, she shows him Delamere's letters to her, because she has promised to be honest with him. She reminds him of his love for his brother, and disappointed to learn about Crofts' underhanded concealment of letters confirming Emmeline's birthright and disgusted about the coldness with which she is treated by his proud wife and haughty daughter, Montreville is finally won over by her. Despite himself, he softens toward her as she reasons with him, convincing him of her honesty and regard for his approval. He wavers between wishing simply to get her out of the way and feeling real affection for his brother's only child. Finally, his good sentiments prevail when he gives Emmeline her inheritance, regrets his condescension toward her, and approves her marriage to Godolphin.

A model of perfection, Godolphin possesses the steadiness of character missing in Delamere. Compared with him, in fact, Godolphin is obviously the ideal match for Emmeline. He truly loves her, long before her fortune and name are restored, *and* he respects her opinions. In turn, his kindness and sympathy for others endear him to Emmeline. To save his sister's reputation, he pretends that Fitz-Edward's son is his, rather than Adelina's, and he proves to be very good with children; he helps a lady in distress in a scene closely paralleling Emmeline's reaching out to Adelina. He is gentle and possesses a poetic nature. Depressed because he believes Emmeline happily engaged to Delamere, he is depicted on more than one occasion sighing deeply and reciting sonnets. He is, of course, handsome and heroic, having proved his courage during his long career in the army. He respectfully withholds his feelings for Emmeline until he is sure she is free and receptive, and when she accepts him: "Godolphin, assured of possessing her affection, left her with an heart which was even oppressed with the excess of it's [sic] own happiness" (p. 457).

When he discovers Fitz-Edward secretly watching Adelina and his son, he offers to fight a duel with him for his sister's honor. Even though he can be passionate in defense of Adelina's reputation, unlike Delamere, he will listen to reason. When Emmeline reasons with him, convincing

him to be careful and handle the situation more responsibly, he responds
with feeling:

> "Ah! lovely Emmeline! more lovely from this generous tenderness than from
> your other exquisite perfection; can I be insensible of the value of a life for
> which *you* interest yourself? and shall I suffer any other consideration to come
> in competition with your peace?"
>     "You promise me then?"
>     "To be calm with Fitz-Edward, I do." (p. 488)

After the two men are reconciled, Godolphin gives Adelina the power of
choice by allowing her to receive a proposal from Fitz-Edward. This is the
only instance in the novel of a male relinquishing his power over a female,
but, of course, Godolphin is exceptional. When Emmeline learns about her
inheritance, Godolphin is unselfishly glad for her because it gives her the
power to *choose* her fate. As a model of the perfect man, Godolphin is
feminized in the sense that his nature is gentle and sensitive, despite his long
career in the military, he speaks the language of sensibility, and his concerns
parallel those of Emmeline and Mrs. Stafford. Charlotte Smith portrays in
Godolphin the sort of behavior a feminist would desire in men; both Godolphin and Desmond may remind the modern reader of the "new man" of the
1980s in their cultivation of sensitivity. Smith implies that with men like these,
women would not be reduced to subservient positions but would be encouraged to use their minds to make positive contributions to family and
society.

The novel ends conventionally, but its conclusion results from choices
Emmeline freely makes. With the blessing of Mrs. Stafford and Lord Montreville, Emmeline marries Godolphin, they retire to Mowbray Castle with Adelina and her son, and, until Emmeline can have her estate restored to her,
Mrs. Stafford joins them. Without seeming too contrived, the novel is structured so that at its conclusion Emmeline does not have to make a choice between love and friendship. Throughout the narrative the three
women—Emmeline, Mrs. Stafford, and Lady Adelina—have relied on one another for support. As the good man who has come to their aid when necessary, Godolphin is skillfully woven into their narratives so that it seems natural
for all these characters to retire together communally to the countryside to
Emmeline's restored property, Mowbray Castle.

In *Emmeline,* Charlotte Smith focused on a small group of characters and
their domestic concerns, particularly those of the women whose lives were
literally controlled by the wishes of parental authorities and the whims of husbands. The world of the novel is the family. With *Desmond,* however, the
same domestic issues and problems with the position of women are situated
in the context of the larger world of social issues and political concerns. Specifically, Smith addresses herself to contemporary controversy concerning the
French Revolution, stimulated in part by Edmund Burke's *Reflections on the*

*Revolution in France* (1790), taking a Jacobite position supporting the overthrow of the French monarchy and aristocracy. Burke's classic critique of the
Revolution, arguing for the maintenance of order through monarchical institutions, more than any other single work had roused England and much of
the Continent against the new France. Since the Revolution signaled the birth
of liberty for the lower classes, by implication, although not in reality, the rights
of women were a part of the ideology which had given rise to the overthrow
of monarchy. Since monarchy and patriarchy are essentially connected, the
justice of Smith's feminist position depends upon showing the wrongheaded-
ness of royalist politics. As the most vocal supporter of the French monarchy,
Burke provides a clear argument for rebuttal. *Desmond* very clearly illustrates
the connection between political advantage and patriarchal rule. Basic to
Smith's liberal political stance, then, is the feminist position that women are
an underclass deprived of basic human rights of choice governing their lives,
and in some cases, the lives of their children as well, that it is necessary to
restructure the system to create the opportunity for women to have legal rights
and thus the opportunity to live responsible lives.

Aware of the restrictions upon women's fiction and of the risks she was
taking by writing about politics, she anticipated detractors by writing in her
preface:

> But women it is said have no business with politics—Why not?—Have they no
> interest in the scenes that are acting around them, in which they have fathers,
> brothers, husbands, sons, or friends engaged?—Even in the commonest course
> of female education, they are expected to acquire some knowledge of history;
> and yet, if they are to have no opinion of what *is* passing, it avails little that
> they should be informed of what *has passed,* in a world where they are subject
> to such mental degradation; where they are censured as affecting masculine
> knowledge if they happen to have any understanding; or despised as insignifi-
> cant triflers if they have none. (pp. iii–iv)

Since women are "damned if they do and damned if they don't" in Smith's
society, it is to their advantage to know as much as possible. The preface also
addressed the issue of female education and its connection to the function
of the novel. It is clear that she saw the novel as a means of informing readers
about political ideas not currently sanctioned by the government, that it was
a useful tool for expressing minority opinion and educating her audience.

*Desmond,* set in 1790 and 1791, is Smith's only epistolary novel. In the
preface she expressed apprehension about publishing it, because it is "so unlike those of my former writing, which have been honored by its [sic] appro-
bation" (p. i). She remarked that she doubted whether she had succeeded as
well in letters as in narrative and that she feared she might displease her readers
with her political remarks. Speculating about Smith's choice of this form, Diana Bowstead (1986) argues persuasively that she may have had two reasons
for using this method. First, the substance of the novel is presented as mono-

logue or quoted dialogue; long speeches which would be very difficult to handle in a dramatic scene seem believable in epistolary fiction, Smith's novel "presents itself rather as a disquisition than a tract" (p. 238). The writer of epistolary novels, then, has the advantage of distance from the subject which an omniscient narrative voice prohibits.

Still, the choice of subject and Charlotte Smith's reservations about addressing political issues (i.e. expressing minority opinion) make her position abundantly clear; she made no attempt to present opposing views, and it might easily be argued that while the epistolary technique removes an authorial voice from the narrative, at the same time it brings the observations and experiences of the narrators closer to the reader. Her apprehension about form might simply have arisen from the difficulty of handling a wealth of material in an unfamiliar way. She was not merely attempting psychological realism and building of suspense, as Richardson had done; she attempted to dramatize the causes of the French Revolution while, by implication, she exposed similar conditions in England thereby indirectly arguing for reform.

In *Desmond* there are two principal sets of correspondents, although letters from peripheral characters appear when necessary, as well as occasional references to letters which do not appear in the text. The exchange between Lionel Desmond and his friend and guardian, Mr. Bethel, occupies almost exclusively the first third of the novel. With few exceptions, the early letters from Desmond contain extended accounts of the political situation in Paris in the summer of 1790 where he has gone, accompanied by Geraldine Verney's brother, Waverly, to see for himself the effects of the Revolution and to lessen his attachment to Geraldine. Meanwhile, in England Bethel responds to Desmond's political commentary while keeping him posted on events in his own country, specifically events concerning the Verney family.

Desmond's reporting of current events along with detailed historical and background information provides the context in which all of the conflicts in the novel are to be understood. The subject of this novel is the abuse of power on all levels and in every type of relationship from king and subject to parent and child. Wherever there is the possibility of one having more power than another in a relationship, Charlotte Smith shows how that power can be abused. Clearly, she is not taking a purely antiaristocratic position, because she includes a portrait of an ideal nobleman in Montfleuri, a friend of Desmond, who has used his wealth and position to create a prosperous and equitable community on his estate; his character is presented to show alternatives to a general abuse of power among aristocrats. Although it is not the purpose here to study the politics of *Desmond* in detail, a brief summary of injustices Desmond describes shows the subjection of women in the broader context of political repression. (For a thorough examination of this subject, see Diana Bowstead, 1986: pp. 237–63.)

Surprised initially to find that French society is not in chaos, as the English press has reported, Desmond instead discovers stability and order. He surmises that the English government wants its citizens to believe the Revolution has failed, so that its own system will not be threatened and its own faults less apparent; thus it has misrepresented the principles of the Revolution to strengthen its own position. Writing to Bethel about conditions leading to revolution, Desmond briefly summarizes French history, specifically detailing the despotic reign of Louis XIV and the debauched court of his grandson, Louis XV. Among other injustices, he writes about the cruelty of aristocrats toward the peasantry, the oppression of the poor by the rich, the corruption of the clergy controlling parishioners through superstition and fear, the inequity of the legal system, deplorable conditions of prisons, and severe punishments for relatively minor crimes. In general, he views the causes of the Revolution as the unequal distribution of wealth and a profligate abuse of power.

Often in Desmond's letters dealing with political injustice, he expresses concern for Geraldine Verney, whom he has known since the early years of her marriage to Richard Verney, a character reminiscent of Stafford and Trelawney in *Emmeline*. Before Geraldine appears directly in the narrative, the correspondence between Desmond and Bethel hints at her marital difficulties. Once her letters to her sister, Fanny Waverly, are included, her story unfolds in a way that clearly connects it with earlier examples of abuses of power.

The position of Geraldine Verney, a married woman, as the heroine is a major departure from convention. There is no precedent in traditional women's fiction for using a mature married woman as a heroine; no one like her appears in the novel of education, the novel of sensibility, the domestic novel, or the courtship novel. In fact, the only previous married heroine was Fielding's Amelia whose tedious, long-suffering faithfulness to Booth was ultimately rewarded after his conversion. Regardless of precedent in contemporary fiction, it is clear that the purpose of *Desmond* dictates the use of a mature, intelligent married woman to illustrate the vulnerability of a woman of good family and sufficient economic means, within an arranged marriage to an unsuitable husband. While her situation is similar to Adelina's and Mrs. Stafford's, Geraldine's central position in the novel allows Charlotte Smith to examine her situation in greater detail and to connect her treatment by her parents and husband with many other examples of abuses of power cited in the novel.

Geraldine is candid in her remarks to her sister, Fanny Waverly, about their family history. She writes about their father's demeaning attitude toward his daughters:

> [He], indeed, would not condescend to suppose that our sentiments were worth forming or consulting; and with all my respect for his memory, I cannot help recollecting that he was a very Turk in principle, and hardly allowed women any pretensions to souls, or thought them worth more care than he bestowed on his horses, which were to look sleek, and do their paces well. (Vol. 111, p. 133)

These remarks comment not only on his attitude toward the value of women but imply that since they were made for decorative uses they are not worth educating.

Similarly, Richard Verney's treatment of his wife reveals much the same attitude. More interested in hunting and gambling with his aristocratic friends than being with his family, Verney first appears in the narrative dishevelled and still intoxicated from the previous night's debauch. He greets Bethel familiarly but is verbally abusive to Geraldine and the children " 'Away with ye all,' " cried the worthless brute . . . " 'there, get ye along to the nursery, that's the proper place for women and children' " (Vol. 11, p. 36). Always in debt, he gambles away everything he has; he spends most of his time in Yorkshire, carousing with aristocratic "friends" such as Lord Newminster and a group of courtesans, while Geraldine's home is confiscated to pay his debts. When he finally leaves for France to take up the aristocratic cause in support of the monarchy, he falls into such debt that he sells the favors of Geraldine to the Duc de la Romagnecourt in payment.

Geraldine's is the story of a lifetime of submitting to the will of others, first her parents, then her husband. Like Mrs. Smith, Mrs. Stafford, and Lady Adelina, Geraldine married because her mother arranged the match. In the same letter to Fanny, she writes about her mother's values: "Riches and high birth . . . were ever the most certain recommendations to the favor of my mother. . . . That *I* have been most unhappily the victim of this mercenary spirit, I do not, however, mean to make matter of reproach . . ." (Vol. 111, pp. 134–5). Her mother's position in the pleasure-seeking leisured class is clarified by Geraldine's further description of Mrs. Waverly's activities:

> Happiness, in her estimation, consists in being visited by the opulent; in giving and receiving good dinners; in having at Bath, or in London, the reputation of having fashionable parties, and very full rooms; of curtsying, at church, to all the best dressed part of the congregation; and being looked upon as a very sensible woman, and one who knows the world. (Vol. 111, p. 135)

With values such as these, it is no wonder her mother she would think Verney a good match, his character not having matured enough at the time of marriage to reveal his tendency to excess. Unable to admit that she has condemned her daughter to "the most dreadful of destinies" (Vol. 11, p. 181), Mrs. Waverly "takes refuge in cards and company against her own heart" (Vol. 11, p. 182). During the course of the novel, she spends the majority of her time planning the wedding of her adored son, Waverly, and admonishing Geraldine not to disgrace the family by refusing to comply with Verney's wishes.

As it is a requirement of the epistolary novel to keep writers separate, Fanny remains in Bath with their mother but writes to Geraldine offering support and sympathy. This exchange reveals both sisters as rational sensitive women. Fanny's letters often sparkle with spirit and satirical wit; Geraldine's describe a gradual evolution in her character from victim to woman of strength. Although she is dutiful to her husband to the end of his life, she does express anger, contempt, and resentment toward him. Most of their letters concern immediate difficulties, but occasionally they digress to other topics, such as women's education and reading of novels. Smith's concern with the value of novels as transmitters of knowledge is most clearly expressed in this correspondence which can also be read as a response to Wollstonecraft's rationalist position. When Fanny complains that her mother's friends have disapproved of her reading novels, Geraldine responds that there are events related in newspapers, on stage, and observable in daily life which are more inimical to innocence than scenes in novels. In their defense she adds, ". . . there *is* a chance, that those who will read nothing, if they do not read novels, may collect from them some few ideas, that are not either fallacious, or absurd, to add to the very scanty stock which their usual insipidity of life has afforded them . . ." (Vol. 11, p. 173). She assures Fanny that novels did no harm in corrupting her imagination or expectations of the world. She remarks with some irony that if novels had such a corrupting influence on their readers, she might have waited until a charming hero appeared in her life, rather than adhering to her mother's directions to marry Verney. "But, far from doing so, I was, you see, 'obedient—very obedient . . .' " (Vol. 11, p. 174).

Later in the novel, obeying Verney's directives to meet him in France, Geraldine travels under the protection of Desmond who knows that Verney is entrapping her to meet the Duc de la Romagnecourt. During the course of the journey, while she is unaware of the plot against her, Geraldine writes to Fanny about the beauty of Normandy and digresses into a discussion of French politics. At this point in the narrative, the central ideas are brought together with Geraldine drawing a parallel between changes in a private family and changes within a country: as tranquility within the family is disturbed when there is an economic change, so changes are felt within a country when property and private interests must be given up for the public good. In the same letter she makes the only negative comment against Verney in the novel, by way of relating an anecdote which brings the issues of domestic and social abuse together. She writes to Fanny about a fashionable French woman, who, being separated from her husband, changed her religion so that she would never have to see him in this world or the next. "Thus it might, perhaps, be said, that I determine never to think on any article . . . like Mr. Verney; and therefore, as he is, he knows not why a very furious aristocrat, that I, with no better reasons, become democrat" (Vol. 111, pp. 131–2). Geraldine needs no better reason to become a democrat since Verney illustrates the worst possible traits of aristocratic pretention and patriarchal abuse. As Smith has shown, the democrat's position squarely opposes undeserved privilege of birth and gender and supports the individual's right to equal opportunity.

This position is most clearly articulated by Desmond, whose letters present a positive view of the revolutionary cause. Desmond is a character who not only holds correct political views (reflecting those of the author) but whose treatment of Geraldine is exemplary. But Smith must have anticipated some negative response from her readers concerning his passion for a married woman. In the preface to the novel, she wrote:

> . . . in representing a young man, nourishing an ardent but concealed passion for a married woman; I certainly do not mean to encourage or justify such attachment; but no delineation of character appears to me more interesting, than that of a man capable of such a passion so generous and disinterested as to seek only the good of its object; nor any story more moral, than one that represents the existence of an affection so regulated. (p. ii)

It is true that Desmond's motives toward Geraldine seem pure, because he never entertains the slightest hope that he can have her for himself. But Desmond's behavior poses difficulties which are left unresolved in the narrative. His passionate attachment to Geraldine is entirely convincing; he is generous both with his money, paying off Verney's debts anonymously to save Geraldine's home, and with his time and energy. He protects her from the duke and his men, accompanies her to France to meet Verney, and saves her from a gang of marauders hired by the disenfranchised aristocrats. Inexplicably, however, he has an affair with Madame de Boisbelle, Montfleuri's sister, who bears him a child. Like Geraldine, she is unhappily married and living apart from her husband whose reported character is similar to Verney's. Had Desmond explained this attachment himself, his motivation would have been clearer; instead, the affair is reported to Bethel by Montfleuri who blames himself and his sister, not Desmond. Perhaps Desmond's willingness to enter a liaison with Josephine Boisbelle illustrates his belief that he will never have more than a friendship with Geraldine, yet this explanation is unconvincing because his devotion to her is consuming. If this departure from dedication to Geraldine is an attempt to humanize the ideal man, the method baffles the reader.

Because the family is shown to be a microcosm of society, the conclusion of *Desmond* focuses on personal relationships. Predictably, Verney dies after being abandoned by his aristocratic "friends," leaving Geraldine free to marry Desmond, for whom she had nourished a concealed passion. The novel ends with Montfleuri married to Fanny and Desmond engaged to Geraldine, who treats his child as her own. Although Smith's readers would have expected a happy ending, the concluding marriages are not merely gratuitous gestures toward convention but significantly illustrate the democratic principle of freedom of choice: mature, intelligent adults have a better chance at happiness when they have the power to choose their own destinies. By implication, as well, healthy family units build a better society.

*Emmeline* and *Desmond* convey strong feminist messages, clarifying and defining women's domestic and social positions, to show how the patriarchal political structure affected women's lives. Charlotte Smith demystified this structure by analyzing it on all levels; on each level, power abusers are represented as hypocritical, greedy, and weak. She gave her readers few examples of powerful but benevolent individuals, although some do exist in these novels. What her works suggest is a call for reform rather than the overthrow of the existing system; there is no vision of a better system to replace the one that was currently in place. What she asked for instead was an examination and rethinking of the present system. Through such characters as Crofts, Montreville, Stafford, Verney, and the Waverlys, she exposed institutionalized social prejudice, based on the false notion that worth is found only in rank, birth, and wealth. Whether the characters are male or female, if they adhere to such false values, they help to perpetuate a powerless underclass of women.

In Charlotte Smith's system of values, power lies in strength and integrity, in characters whose soft hearts and strong minds penetrate appearance to perceive individual merit. Her mature heroines are depicted as intelligent, reasonable, and strong enough to endure hardships while maintaining sympathy for others; her good men are models of exemplary behavior and right thinking. Ideal relationships between such characters serve as models for more equitable treatment of women. If the women are relatively powerless in their immediate situations with privileged men, she emphasized the power they had: Emmeline displays the power of refusal and Geraldine the power of personal integrity.

Hope for the improvement of women's lives lies in more liberal attitudes towards their worth, allowing them the right to acquire good educations and giving them greater power of choice in their personal lives. Not all of Charlotte Smith's novels state the case for women as specifically as *Emmeline* and *Desmond,* but they all argue for a system of values, unbiased by class and gender.

Contemporary reviews praised her for including instructive ideas in her novels and for affirming the importance of women's opinions. *Desmond,* particularly, was commended by the *Monthly Review* for reminding women that in addition to their domestic duties, they should not forget that they—along with their brothers and fathers—were also citizens. The reviewer observed: "Novels . . . are gradually taking a higher and more masculine tone, and are becoming the vehicles of useful instruction. . ." (1792, 9: 14). Charlotte Smith accomplished her goals for the novel: Her work succeeded in elevating its language and scope from the conventional simple tale of love to the novel of ideas.

## REFERENCES

Bowstead, Diana. (1986). Charlotte Smith's *Desmond:* The epistolary novel as ideological argument. In Mary Anne Schofield & Cecilia Macheski (Eds.), *Fetter'd or free? British Women Novelists, 1670–1815.* Athens, OH: Ohio University Press.

Figes, Eva. (1982). *Sex and subterfuge: Women writers to 1850.* London: Macmillan.

Foster, James R. (1928). Charlotte Smith, Pre-romantic novelist. *PMLA, 43,* 463–475.

Hilbish, Florence. (1941). *Charlotte Smith: Poet and novelist.* Philadelphia: University of Pennsylvania Press.

Kaplan, Cora. (1985). Pandora's box: Subjectivity, class and sexuality in socialist feminist criticism. In (eds.). Gayle Green & Coppelia Kahn. *Making A difference* New York: Methuen.

Kavanagh, Julia. (1863). *English women of letters: Biographical sketches. volume1.* London: Hurst and Blackett.

McKillop, Alan Dugald. (1951–1952). Charlotte Smith's letters. *The Huntington Library Quarterly, XV,* 237–255.

Rogers, Katharine M. (1977, Fall). Inhibitions on eighteenth-century women novelists: Elizabeth Inchbald and Charlotte Smith. *Eighteenth-Century Studies, 11*(1), 63–78.

Smith Charlotte. (1794). *The banished man. A novel.* London: Printed for T. Cadell, Jun. and W. Davies, (successors to Mr. Cadell) in the Strand.

Smith, Charlotte. (1971). *Emmeline: The orphan of the castle.* Edited by Anne Henry Ehrenpreis. London: Oxford University Press.

Smith, Charlotte. (1971). *Desmond: A novel.* Edited by Gina Luria. New York: Garland Publishing.

Spencer, Jane. (1986). *The rise of the woman novelist: From Aphra Behn to Jane Austen.* Oxford: Basil Blackwell.

Spender, Dale. (1988). *Mothers of the novel: 100 good women writers before Jane Austen.* London: Pandora.

Wilson, Anna. (1989). Mary Wollstonecraft and the search for the radical woman, *Gender, 6,* 88–101.

Wollstonecraft, Mary. (1982). *Vindication of the rights of woman.* London: Penguin English Library.

# Charlotte Lennox's
## *The Female Quixote:*
### A Novel Interrogation

Helen Thomson

With the appearance of *The Female Quixote* in 1752, Charlotte Lennox became not only one of the early mothers of the novel, but also one of the novel's earliest critics. As in Miguel de Cervantes' great novel *Don Quixote*, to which Charlotte Lennox's title pays tribute, in her second work of fiction she was simultaneously inventing and deconstructing the novel in a manner we might now be tempted to call postmodern, yet at the same time she was apparently bidding farewell to the romance as a superseded form of fiction. (See Margaret M. Doody, 1989, for an authoritative, insightful study of Charlotte Lennox's life and writings.) Romance had served women well, its incorporation of chivalric and courtly codes gave women a position of power and influence they were very unlikely to find in real life. The extreme contrast between the privileged position of women in the romances and the realities of lived experience for most female romance readers of the time, is sufficient explanation for the enduring appeal of the genre. Charlotte Lennox had discovered that in her case the economic protection of marriage was a sham, and by the time *The Female Quixote* appeared she had become the professional author she was to remain for the rest of her life. She had been acknowledged as such since the appearance of her first work, *Harriot Stuart,* in 1750, a tale of female adventure which owed much to Lennox's first-hand knowledge of North America, where she evidently spent part of her youth. (See Margaret M. Doody, 1989: p. xviii, for a discussion of Lennox's first novel and its treatment of romance.)

Samuel Johnson, Samuel Richardson, and later, Henry Fielding welcomed Charlotte Lennox to their writing ranks, but it is not only in relation to her male peers that she interests us now, except as a melancholy demonstration of how their high valuation of her work has not saved it from subsequent neglect. To the complications of her sex and role—as a woman writer her authority was undermined by a patriarchal society which, at least in theory, made "woman writer" a contradiction in terms, then as now—Charlotte Lennox adds the complications of an intensively self-reflexive fiction. Far from

113

being the simple satire on the dangers of romance reading that it has often been taken to be, *The Female Quixote* critically examines the nature of fiction itself, its relation to the imagination and feelings, as well as to the real world. If at the historically critical time of 1752 one form of fiction, the romance, was to be replaced by another, the novel, then Charlotte Lennox dramatizes the event and its significance, but not by simply acquiescing in the supposition that one is inferior to the other.

Charlotte Lennox was as aware as any modern publisher's editor that romance can play a psychological role for women. Her heroine, Arabella, may appear to be deluded by the romances she has read, but they provide her with a way of interpreting her own life and experience. She recognizes a truth in them, a truth to feeling at least, which has nothing to do with probability. *The Female Quixote* is a feminized version of an otherwise masculinist battle between the Ancients and the Moderns. Women may have been barred access to Greek and Latin, but the romances provided alternative versions of an ancient world, one, moreover, where women held sway by virtue of their hold on men's feelings. Thus Lennox pointed the way towards the great mid-eighteenth-century shift in sensibility when the Age of Reason, presided over by Samuel Johnson, crumpled before the onslaught of the sentimental novel. This led in turn not only to the Romantic movement, but to women's fiction in particular developing modes which liberated the feelings and the imagination. Ann Radcliffe dominated Gothic fiction, and other women such as Mary Hays, Mary Wollstonecraft, and Mary Shelley asserted a feminism which elevated the female feeling heart into a badge of moral courage.

On the surface, *The Female Quixote* repudiates the romances with their improbabilities of plot and exaggerations of feeling, in favor of the masculine world of reality and, furthermore, uses the voices of male authority, Samuel Johnson and Samuel Richardson, for example, to bring about its validation and its heroine's change of mind. Yet, as we shall see, another woman has prepared the way for Arabella's recognition of error which also comes about only when her own heart has given her definitive proof that the romances have served their purpose, and it is time to replace a fictional prince with a real husband.

The price of this is marriage, a legal loss of identity for the woman and a subjugation to the will of the man. No wonder the courtship novel became the dominant form of women's fiction in the remainder of the eighteenth century, the didacticism serving to consolidate patriarchal authority, but also asserting for women not only a right to choose, but a right to love, and the necessity for careful evaluation. The first way in which the romances serve Arabella is in protracting her period of courtship, that critical time when she will enjoy power over her lover, which may vanish after marriage and in which she can ensure that the most crucial choice of her life is the correct one. Further, by turning herself into a heroine of romance, Arabella makes of her lover

Glanville a hero whose sole function is to serve his mistress. This is a fantasy any woman might cherish, because it represents a reversal of the normal power relationship between the sexes.

It is little wonder the masculine characters, Arabella's father, uncle, and Glanville, resist. Her persistence has its risks—her uncle thinks her mad more than once—but it succeeds in testing Glanville's heart and in teaching him to be her loyal knight, whose function is solely to please his mistress and shield her from criticism. This process is conducted through the romance texts; Arabella succeeds in getting Glanville to speak to her through the language of romance, a metaphoric language of love. Arabella's husband is chosen for her by her father, a family and property alliance which is to be brought about by a few weeks of courtship, during which Arabella will be brought to acquiescence. She is extremely shocked at what amounts to the theft of the romantic courtship she had imagined for herself:

> . . . for, though she always intended to marry some time or other, as all the heroines had done, yet she thought such an event ought to be brought about with an infinite deal of trouble; and that it was necessary she should pass to this state through a great number of cares, disappointments, and distresses of various kinds, like them; that her lover should purchase her with his sword from a crowd of rivals; and arrive to the possession of her heart by many years of service and fidelity. (p. 29)

She shows considerable ingenuity in bringing about a more interesting courtship for herself, despite the fact that her cousin is attractive to her, her father is not tyrannical, and that no real heroine ever submitted to parental choice: "What lady in romance ever married the man that was chosen for her?" (p. 29). Her choosing to construct herself and her life as a romance is an act of rebellion, more covert than outright defiance, but ultimately more effective. The constraints under which she lives may have been considered unremarkable for the time, but they are considerable. She has, in fact, been shut up in a castle quite as totally as any fairy tale princess (indeed the Cinderella motif is in the background; she is motherless, with Miss Glanville playing the role of the Ugly Sister and the Countess of—the Fairy godmother), and her father has total power over her. He can force her to write to Glanville, recalling him after his first repulse, and forbid her freedom of movement—he allows her only an occasional ride or visit to church. These are the same constraints endured by her mother during her mercifully brief marriage, and the romances which helped her endure her solitary life are the only maternal inheritance Arabella has (Margaret M. Doody, p. xxi). It's not surprising that she'd cling to this, particularly when, as the single female child, she is only the means by which the paternal inheritance will pass, on her marriage, to her husband.

The romances have enriched Arabella's life with their imaginative possibilities, and it is the possession of a strong imagination which is Arabella's best weapon. Dr. Johnson may have feared the imagination's power and its alliance to madness, but female writers such as Charlotte Lennox correctly recognized its liberating potential, at least for her own sex. The 18th century's private madhouses and their female inhabitants constituted the dark side of this possibility, as Mary Wollstonecraft was to uncover in her *Maria: and the Wrongs of Woman*.

Some of the novel's episodes discover Arabella's libido at work constructing wish-fulfillment sexual fantasies. Before Glanville appears, she sees two young men who interest her and sets about creating adventure and excitement for herself. Mr. Hervey, first seen at church, is encountered on one of her rarely permitted rides, whereupon ". . . her imagination immediately suggested to her, that this insolent lover had a design to seize her person" (p. 21). Her response to the young man's puzzled question, "What do you take me for?" is comic in its apparently inappropriate romance exaggeration:

> For a ravisher, interrupted Arabella, an impious ravisher! who, contrary to all laws, both human and divine, endeavour to possess your self by force of a person whom you are not worthy to serve; and whose charity and compassion you have returned with the utmost ingratitude. (p. 22)

This may be the stuff of romance, but Charlotte Lennox's readers know, even if they have not read *Clarissa*, that rape and abduction were real and not fanciful dangers for unprotected women. Arabella then achieves two things which reinforce her delusion. Struggling in the hands of her servants, Hervey is driven to threats of real violence, ". . . if I can but free one of my hands, I'll stab the scoundrel before your face" (p. 22). Arabella's response is calm, and she insists upon the appropriate romance power relationship: "A little more submission and respect would become you better; you are now wholly in my power: I may, if I please, carry you to my father, and have you severely punished for your attempt" (p. 22). Here, as in every instance of Arabella's so-called romance delusion in the novel, reality impinges on the fantasy. Well aware that she could, in fact, make good her threats, Hervey submits to her orders ". . . knowing that an attempt of that nature upon an heiress might have dangerous consequences" (p. 22).

This kind of demonstration of a common underlying truth shared by both fantasy and fact is a very good reason for Arabella's slowness to be convinced she is in error. The later encounter with the highwaymen on the road to Bath is an all too common eighteenth-century adventure for travelers. Arabella's comic misapprehension—she thinks they are knights mistakenly trying to rescue the two women from the hands of abductors—underlines the tendency of romance to convert everything into a sexual currency (albeit in the form of literary metaphor), which forces men into one of two roles, villain or protector. The highwaymen want to rob them of their money, but in the moneyless world of the romance, chastity may be a woman's only fortune. Lennox makes sure we understand in many other episodes that this is still precisely the case for women of her own time.

Arabella's encounter with Miss Groves (whose name ironically evokes the world of the pastoral, another kind of romance), is a case in point. Charlotte Lennox's inclusion of a subtextual "Ruined Woman" story is in tune with the didactic function assumed by the novel, but her treatment of it subverts, to a degree, the support it usually gives the patriarchal disposition of power and the sexual double standard. Arabella's own purity, chastity, modesty, and innocence ensure her misunderstanding of the common story of a young girl betrayed by her passions, and she has little difficulty in finding a romance precedent with which to innocently interpret the tale. But Charlotte Lennox includes two mitigating circumstances in the story. Miss Groves has been badly brought up, allowed her own will and boisterous pursuits by a mother whose task should have been to tutor her daughter in restraint and decorum. Instead she ". . . was sent up to London, and allowed to be her own mistress at sixteen; to which unpardonable neglect of her mother she owes the misfortunes that have since befallen her" (p. 80). In spite of her two illegitimate births (the absolute power of her faithless lover demonstrated by his taking the second, live infant and refusing her access or even knowledge of the child) ". . . he will not be persuaded to inform her how, or in what manner, he has disposed of the child" (p. 84), Miss Groves is married in the end and not allowed to suffer the usual tragic fate of the fallen woman. But having been married for her looks and her money does not make her fate any more than ordinary for the time.

More importantly, however, this episode is used to introduce the novel's far more effectively subversive demonstration that language is not always the straightforward tool of philosophical empiricism it was claimed to be, that the reality it names is complex and ambiguous. When Miss Groves's maid, Mrs. Morris, tells her mistress's secrets to Arabella, we are treated to the comedy of the dual perspective of the one story being told and understood by us, while quite another is being heard and misunderstood by Arabella. Her high-flown language, borrowed from the romances, has been employed to comic effect from the start, but when Mrs. Morris tells her story in the ordinary language of the 18th century, we suddenly understand that much of the romance vocabulary has been appropriated and devalued by conversion into a series of euphemisms for sexual misbehavior. Thus a woman who has a "history" full of "adventures" and who accepted "favors" is a woman of ill-repute, not the heroine of an exciting romance whom Arabella takes her to be. It is language that has changed, not human nature or behavior. Thus the reliability of language to convey the truth is weakened and its fixity made uncertain. In this episode, Charlotte Lennox effectively deconstructs the language of romance, but in doing so also destabilizes current usage. There is not much to choose after all between the romance usage, recording improbable happenings, and the contemporary usage, clothing reality in the disguise of euphemistic metaphor. Once again, it is hardly surprising that Arabella persists in her delusions, when the alternative seems no closer to the "real" world.

Charlotte Lennox appears to have been familiar with the philosophy of John Locke, and indeed he is invoked in Arabella's final conversion, but Lennox's fine intelligence understood that his empiricism had not pinned down reality any more firmly than hitherto. In the episode of Edward, the gardener, she demonstrates that what the eye sees is not necessarily the same as what another eye sees, or rather, how another observer interprets sensory data. Princes are always handsome, and Arabella understands at once, when she sees the good-looking young gardener in her employ, that he is a disguised prince who naturally aspires for her hand. All princes are handsome; Edward is handsome; therefore, Edward is a disguised prince. Given the narrowness of Arabella's experience, this is no more ridiculous than some of the social games the bewildered heroine sees played in Bath and London.

Arabella's unwavering adherence to the high ideals of romance saves her from succumbing to the villain of the novel, Glanville's friend, Sir George Bellmour, who loves Arabella's fortune and pretty face, yet does not have Glanville's superior regard for her character. He sees his own familiarity with Arabella's romances as a means to win her favor, and in the telling of his "history" in the approved romance style, hopes to win her heart. He is fittingly defeated, not by any discrepancy between the real and the fantasy version of it, but because in ironically translating his own sexual transgressions and emotional infidelities into the vehicle of romance—which he presumes will amusingly disguise them—he is detected by Arabella, because his faithlessness breaks the rules of romantic fidelity. Once again, it is hardly surprising that Arabella's belief in the romance world is not shaken: it has a clear moral superiority to the alternative "real" world.

In this episode, Charlotte Lennox reverses her heroine's narrative metaphor; she sets up a complex, metafictional situation in which real adventures are presented as fiction, where the true is told as "false" to part of the audience, and the false romance tale told as true to the credulous Arabella. It is a clear demonstration of the dangers as well as complexity of fiction. It is amusing for those listeners who already know Sir George's history to hear his attempted seduction of Dolly, the milkmaid, converted into an Arcadian idyll with Dorothea, the shepherdess. Yet it is entirely fitting that Sir George should fail to disguise the moral ugliness of his womanizing in the idealized form of romance, for its empowerment of women seems less dangerous than the use men make of their power over women in ordinary life. In fact, the crucial turning point in Arabella's final conversion comes about only when it is pointed out that the exaggerated power of women in the romances could result in the needless suffering and destruction of men. These books "teach women to exact vengeance" and expect "human sacrifices," the Doctor tells her.

It is hardly surprising that a female author, bidding farewell not simply to a time-honored form of fiction, but also to all the "women's knowledge" contained within the romance, should ask us to consider the form which is replacing it, and how it might serve women. If the novel is to possess verisimilitude, probability and a didactic function, as well as entertaining its readers, then the heroic role becomes a virtual impossibility for women, given their position in eighteenth-century society. Arabella is a transitional figure, the last to claim romantic status for herself (until Jane Austen makes Catherine Morland victim to romance delusion in *Northanger Abbey*), and she must be divested of this in the end. Within this novel, Lennox holds out little hope of heroism being found amongst modern young women. Charlotte Glanville has had all the advantages of wealth and class and, presumably, an education considered appropriate to her rank, yet she is infinitely inferior to Arabella, most crucially in terms of her moral nature. That the romances have produced the highest moral character in Arabella is constantly stressed—but can the novel, this novel subtextually asks, achieve the same things for women?

The linguistic misunderstandings in the Miss Groves story are used to comic effect. The apparently similar episode of the "chocolate quarrel" between Miss Glanville and Arabella points to the qualitative difference of character between two women of equal rank. Arabella, having rejected Sir George's advances and received a parodic, hyperbolic letter from him threatening to take his own life, following first her notions of honor and secondly the dictates of compassion, decides to visit him and command him to recover, as many of her romance heroines had done in similar circumstances. Miss Glanville is shocked at this impropriety, while Arabella decries modern courtship practices. Arabella sums up their quarrel:

> Miss Glanville maintains, that it is less criminal in a lady to hear persons talk to her of love, allow them to kiss her hand, and permit them to write to her, than to make a charitable visit to a man who is confined to his bed through the violence of his passion and despair; the intent of this visit being only to prevent the death of an unfortunate lover, and, if necessary, to lay her commands upon him to live. (p. 206)

Underlying the clash of codes here and complicating judgment is the genuine good feeling on the one hand, and the cynical husband-hunting flirtatiousness, on the other. Further complicating all this and allowing a comic resolution are the facts that Sir George is lying, and Charlotte and Glanville are jealous. Yet again, however, Arabella is surely right in preferring to adhere to the code of the romances, understanding as she does its underlying moral idealism. It is to Glanville's credit, despite his refusal to read the romances and readiness to condemn them unread, that he does gradually learn not only to comply with the desirable rules of behavior for a lover, but to see that in Arabella, at least, they have produced a morally superior character. He has already perceived her intelligence and beauty. What better education, does the eighteenth century offer for a woman? This is a challenge which the women novelists were themselves to take up as the century proceeded.

The romances, and Arabella, are really put to the test when she ventures into the world of society, in Bath, for the first time. Once again she is victorious, not only in thwarting Charlotte's malice by eliciting admiration not derision in her dress, modeled on that of a romance heroine (her costume the outward sign of her construction of herself in a fictional role), but in routing, with superior wit, logic, knowledge, and devastatingly effective conviction, the phony male "intellectuals" of Bath. The universally admired historian, Mr. Selvin, in reality very poorly read in the Ancients he cites as authority, is unmasked as a sham in conversation with the better (romance) read Arabella. Here the Ancients are quite clearly associated with the masculine, the Moderns with the non-canonical romances of the feminine discourse—which is victorious. At this point in the novel, above all, Charlotte Lennox seems in possession of a postmodern sense of history: "History is no longer a movement along the files of time. It is a set of myths inhabiting the present" (Helen Carr, 1989, p. 11).

In the artificial world of Bath, Arabella shines not only because she adheres to a higher code of behavior, but because her candor and honesty are in such welcome contrast to the practices of hypocritical display there. The question of the appropriateness and the usefulness of female romance reading, as an alternative to the normative social employment of women, is explicitly raised when in Bath Arabella surprises Charlotte by regretting the loss of her books and solitude. In reply to Charlotte's catalogue of the pump-room, the parade, the parties of pleasure, Arabella replies:

> What room, I pray you, does a lady give for high and noble adventures, who consumes her days in dressing, dancing, listening to songs, and ranging the walks with people as thoughtless as herself? How mean and contemptible a figure must a life spent in such idle amusements make in history? Or rather, are not such persons always buried in oblivion; and can any pen be found who would condescend to record such inconsiderable actions? (p. 314)

As is so often the case in this novel, the question goes beyond that of female education, of women's role in their society, to raise the question of the fictional depiction of women. If the novel is to be deprived of Arabellas and is left merely with Miss Glanvilles, how can it fulfill the highest aim of fiction, its didactic purpose? And where are women writers and readers to look for role models? The women novelists who followed were to take up the challenge, but Charlotte Lennox seems to have understood the difficulties which, in fact, led to some decades of female writing that complied with masculine notions of decorum, rather than challenged them. It was not until the revolutionary years of the 1790s that this changed.

From Eliza Haywood's *The History of Miss Betsy Thoughtless* (1751) to Fanny Burney's *Evelina* (1778), there were many examples of female writing which warned young women of the dangers of rebelling against the constraints of the socially accepted female role. One of the first voices raised against the tyranny of female "duty" which made young women powerless was Frances Sheridan's *The Memoirs of Miss Sidney Bidulph* (1767) where compliance to the ideal of filial duty had disastrous results for the heroine. In the main, however, it was the much later writing of Mary Wollstonecraft, along with novels such as Mary Hays's *The Memoirs of Emma Courtney* (1796), which made a powerful plea for women's entitlement to a fuller and more honest emotional life. Female fiction in the 18th century can be read as a series of alternations between conservative strategies of survival on the best terms offered in a male-controlled world, and brave voices of radical protest. Charlotte Lennox's play with woman as already textualized (the romance heroine), assuming the power of fiction extended to real life (the novel heroine), represented a remarkably sophisticated subversive technique in this ongoing debate about women's problematical social role.

In suggesting that a loss of authority in the heroines of fiction would inevitably result in a loss of authority for the woman writers, Lennox indicates her impressive understanding of the problems of gender and writing. Sir George's history, which is merely and unsuccessfully parodic, provides us with one example of a confident but inept male fiction-maker. His interpolated story is false fiction, a kind of ingenious plagiarism: his attempt is to seduce Arabella by using her own literary codes. Charlotte Lennox's triumph, in contrast, is to have created a wonderfully original story and heroine out of the very problems of fiction-making itself. She indicates quite early in the novel that such a task has its difficulties, in the comic parody of the female romancer tutoring a disciple in the craft and its rules. When Lucy is instructed how to relate her mistress's history, the girl's naivety is used to question authorship itself. Lucy, like Cervantes' Sancho Panza, has an imperfect knowledge of the romance originals and lacks the essential imaginative act of faith that has blurred the distinction between real and fictional in her mistress.

"How can I make a history about your ladyship?" she asks, only to have Arabella deny the necessity for fiction at all. "There is no occasion, replied Arabella, for you to make a history: there are accidents enough in my life to afford matter for a long one: all you have to do is relate them as exactly as possible" (p. 134). The motif of the servant telling her mistress's story has already been used with Miss Groves, where the actual happenings of her life had reduced a "history" to scandalous gossip. Arabella's high-minded understanding of the word is ludicrous, only in the absence of immortality and scandal in her own life, not in its intention to valorize female experience. Yet Lennox reveals that the novel has jettisoned the higher version of "history" for the version that only records sexual misdemeanors. As for the authoritative masculine version of history, grounded in the classics, to which Mr.

Selvin appeals in Bath, Arabella triumphs thereby revealing its sources to be "made" and as much the discourse of power and fiction as the romances.

The naive Lucy is used to subvert authorship even more thoroughly when she replies to Arabella: "Indeed madam, . . . I can't pretend to tell his thoughts; for how should I know what they were? None but himself can tell that" (p. 136). Here is the novel writer questioning the authority of authorship itself. Lucy's literal-mindedness satirizes the necessity to invent what cannot empirically be known by one human of another. The question invites us to deconstruct authorship in a postmodern fashion, and the key value it appeals to is the imagination—the exercise of it in the author and the shared belief in the reader. Arabella's imaginative act of faith in her reading of the romances is not really different in kind from the same act of faith required of novel readers, who are at one level believers in the "reality" of the fiction. After all, the central irony of *The Female Quixote* is that Arabella all along sees her life as furnishing material for a romance, with herself as heroine, when, in fact, her "history" is made into a novel, a form of fiction which sets itself in opposition to the so-called improbabilities of romance.

Some readers of *The Female Quixote* are disappointed that Arabella's conversion is not brought about by her female mentor, the Countess of—(whose excellence of character as well as "sense, learning and judgment" [p. 360] suggest her real-life counterpart was Margaret Cavendish, Duchess of Newcastle). However, this is not a fairy tale with a convenient all-powerful fairy godmother, but a novel, reflecting the patriarchal realities of power relations between the sexes and the formal relinquishing of the feminine values of the romance to the masculine requirements of "reality." The Countess reveals the awful truth to Arabella, that a woman of "honor" in the eighteenth century can have no history at all, for her worth in the eyes of the world hinges totally on her chastity.

"But custom, madam, said Arabella, cannot possibly change the nature of virtue or vice: and since virtue is the chief characteristic of a hero, a hero in the last age will be a hero in this" (p. 366). The reply points, as many other incidents in the novel have done, to the unreliability of naming, of language as a medium of truth. "Though the natures of virtue or vice cannot be changed, replied the Countess, yet they may be mistaken; and different principles, customs and education, may probably change their names if not their natures" (p. 366). She later adds, "It is certain, therefore, madam, that what was virtue in those days, is vice in ours" (p. 367). It is hardly surprising that this fails to convince Arabella, whose life experience has only reinforced her impression of the comparative superiority of fictional experience offered in the romances. Modern life has consistently disappointed Arabella, and ironically the Countess fails, because she appeals to the masculine attributes of "wit and good sense" (p. 363) in Arabella. It is, in fact, from masculine teachers that she will learn the truth conveyed through the feminine mode of feeling.

It is her heart that converts Arabella, not her head, and in that Lennox perhaps scores her final triumph for the romances over the ultimate victory represented by the novel as the emergent and dominant fictional form.

It is Sir George's second attempt to ensnare Arabella through a false romance, that begins the crucial change of heart. His prostitute who successfully convinces Arabella not only that she is the Princess of Gaul, but that her lost lover is none other than Glanville, arouses a strength of emotion in Arabella which surprises her. Discovering, as the wily Sir George well knows, that the laws of romance demand that she should relinquish Glanville to the Princess (shortly after Arabella has contested the supremacy of the laws of the land with Glanville, maintaining the absolute sovereignty of the "empire of love," p. 357), she is quite overcome. "Our charming heroine, ignorant till now of the true state of her heart, was surprised to find it assaulted at once by all the passions which attend disappointed love. Grief, rage, jealousy, and despair, made so cruel a war in her gentle bosom, that, unable either to express or conceal the strong emotions with which she was agitated, she gave way to a violent burst of tears" (p. 391).

Quite suddenly, the emotional temperature of the novel itself is raised. A rapid series of life-and-death adventures take place, so that for a time the characters could as well be in a romance as in a novel. Charlotte disguised as Arabella precipitates a duel between her brother and Sir George, who is seriously injured. Meanwhile, Arabella, in fear of four horsemen riding towards her, imitates the heroic Clelia who swam across the Tyber to save her honor (her source Adrien Thomas Perdu de Subligny, *The Mock-Clelia: Being a Comical History of French Gallantries, and Novels, in Imitation of Don Quixote*, 1678) and plunges into the Thames.

It has been argued that the reality of sexual danger for unprotected women of the time and the absolute necessity of intact chastity in an unmarried woman could justify what the learned Doctor describes as a product of "wild imagination(s)" (p. 412; Doody, 1989, p. xxi). It seems also that Lennox provides her novel with two endings, one a romance adventure (which is "real" because it occurs within a novel), and the other the renunciation of romance in favor of probability and contemporaneity. The Doctor has a difficult time dealing with an adversary whose intelligence and learning are a match for his own. He is hardest pressed when Arabella herself uses the theories of contemporary philosophers to argue against him. Locke, for example, is evoked when she points out to him that: "Universal negatives are seldom safe, and are least to be allowed when the disputes are about objects of sense; where one position cannot be inferred from another. That there is a castle, any man who has seen it may safely affirm. But you cannot, with equal reason, maintain that there is no castle, because you have not seen it" (p. 414).

When urged to prove that the romances are fictions and vicious, the Doctor must first counter a Shaftesburian claim for innate benevolence, which requires an equal motive be given for falsehood: "There is a love of truth in the human mind, if not naturally implanted, so easily obtained from reason and experience, that I should expect it universally to prevail where there is no strong temptation to deceit . . ." (p. 417), Arabella points out. The Doctor counters by invoking the patriarchal authority of Charlotte Lennox's real-life male mentors, Samuel Johnson and Samuel Richardson, who in the novel (specifically, *Clarissa*), have discovered a mode of fiction which does not injure truth and can convey "the most solid instructions" (p. 417). If both forms of writing are fictions, Arabella insists, why is one censured as absurd? And here, at last, the new rules for the novel, the supplanter of the romance, are described by the Doctor: "The only excellence of falsehood . . . is its resemblance to truth: as therefore any narrative is more liable to be confuted by its inconsistancy with known facts, it is at a greater distance from the perfection of fiction; for there can be no difficulty in framing a tale, if we are left at liberty to invent all history and nature for our own convenience" (p. 418).

What the Doctor fails to deal with here is the different use made of the creative imagination in two kinds of fiction. The romance story was often well known and its excellence thus measured according to the novelty of the manner in which it was told. The novel, on the other hand, as its name implies, was an invention which was validated by the unique conjunction of novelty and verisimilitude. Arabella has recognized the romances' emotional verisimilitude, a method of telling the truth of the heart and, therefore, in Shaftesburian terms, indicating moral truth as well. She trusts this rather than the claim to verisimilitude made on the basis of "known facts" partly because of the unreliability of language itself, its sometimes dubious ability to name the world truthfully, as so many of the novel's incidents have proved to her.

Thus it is, finally, that Arabella is only convinced by an appeal to her feelings, to the values of the heart which are the basis of the romances. When their *emotional* verisimilitude is demonstrated to be, if not false, then certainly dangerous, her resistance collapses at once. When the Doctor deconstructs the romance into its prevailing passions of revenge and love, points out that the price of women's love is very often the death of men, Arabella's consciousness of how nearly she may have lost Glanville in the duel overcomes her and she cries, "My heart yields to the force of truth" (p. 421). Better a live husband, after all, than a dead hero.

If this is a surrender to the needs of reality, there is triumph here, too. Arabella has got what her heart really desires, if not on the terms of the romance reversal of power relations between the sexes, then at least on terms very much better than the bald property transfer originally proposed for her. Her assertion of autonomy via the romances has ultimately excited the admiration of all the men she has encountered. Her uncle's words of praise ". . . if she had been a man, she would have made a great figure in parliament, and . . . her speeches might have come, perhaps, to be printed, in time . . ."

(p. 348) constitutes one of Charlotte Lennox's metafictional jokes, but she has as author so exercised her authority that the masculinist "joke" has a different resonance for her readers. Arabella out-heroes all the men in the novel and her male-despised romances are, in postmodern fashion, given equal status in the competing forms of fiction contained within this self-consciously "made" novel. She may, as Jane Spencer (1986) has pointed out, be one of the eighteenth century's "reformed heroines," but her author's exceptional awareness of the complexities of her narrative art saves her heroine from unconditional surrender to contemporary decorum (p. 140).

It seems extraordinary that such a remarkable novel as *The Female Quixote* should have been allowed almost to disappear from accounts of English literary history. It is a wonderfully entertaining record of a perfectly self-aware and deliberate transition from one kind of fictional writing to another, with the added complexity of aesthetic and moral value being firmly gendered. Modern feminist theorists could teach Charlotte Lennox little she didn't know about binary oppositions and their relative values. In seeing, at its very inception, that the novel was part of the masculine hegemony, she accurately, if unwittingly, foretold the subsequent historical construction of a masculine canon. The reclamation of a female writing tradition is the challenging task that still lies ahead, and Charlotte Lennox's sharp insights into the fiction-making process provide us with important tools of analysis as well as crucially gendered measurements of value.

## REFERENCES

Carr, Helen (1989). Introduction to *From my guy to sci-fi: Genre and women's writing in the postmodern world*. London: Pandora.
Doody, Margaret M. (1989). Introduction to *The female quixote*. Oxford: Oxford University Press.
Lennox, Charlotte (1986). *The female quixote*. London: Pandora. (Originally published in 1752.)
Spencer, Jane (1986). *The rise of the woman novelist. From Aphra Behn to Jane Austen*. Oxford: Basil Blackwell.

# Fanny Burney:
## The Tactics of Subversion

### Judy Simons

"I would a thousand times rather forfeit my character as a writer than risk ridicule or censure as a female," confided Fanny Burney in a letter to her mentor, Samuel Crisp. Throughout her long literary career the sense of conflict between her authorship and her gender was to prove a source of tension that was never fully resolved. Struggling to reconcile her urge towards self-expression with the demands of an age that required young women to be silent and self-effacing, Fanny Burney discovered within herself a latent feminism which made her deeply uneasy. It is, however, this tension between radical and conservative impulses that establishes her as one of the most provocative of eighteenth-century women writers. When Burney started out on her literary career in 1778, women, if they published fiction at all, tended to do so anonymously to guard themselves against charges of immodesty. By the time she produced her last novel in 1814, an identifiable female fictional tradition had emerged. The intervening twenty-five years were years of social and political change in Europe, incorporating fierce debates about women, their nature, and their social roles. Fanny Burney's work contributed centrally to that debate, and in her development of certain literary strategies, which subtly undermined approved models, she initiated a distinctive fictional approach which many subsequent women novelists were to take up and develop.

Although she produced four novels only—and it is on the first two of these that she made her name—Fanny Burney was also an outstanding diarist who kept journals faithfully for over sixty years. In addition, she wrote for the stage brilliant, witty comedies of which only one, *Love and Fashion* (1799), was produced, and in her eighties she tried her hand at a new form of writing with a memoir of her father. In comparison with many popular writers of the time, her published output was small. Yet her reputation eclipsed all others. *Evelina,* her first novel, was thought to be better than Henry Fielding's; it was so stylish and clever that people assumed it must have been written by a man! "In an age distinguished by producing extraordinary women," wrote Edmund

Burke with mock modesty to Fanny Burney in 1782, "I hardly dare tell you where my opinion would place you among them" (July 29, 1782). It is the novels and diaires which have jointly contributed to Burney's subsequent critical reputation, works which by their very nature reflect that division between the private and public aspects of self that permeates all her work and which is a vital ingredient of her approach to women's issues. When in 1778, at the age of twenty-five, she published her first novel, *Evelina,* she was already sensitive to the problems of being a woman writer in the eighteenth century, a time when the terms "woman" and "writer" appeared to many to be mutually exclusive.

Fanny Burney was born in 1752, in Kings Lynn, Norfolk, the daughter of Dr. Charles Burney, a highly respected musician. After her mother's death (when Fanny was ten years old) and her father's remarriage, Fanny was brought up in London where the Burney family had moved in 1760, and it was amongst the cultivated, informed intelligentsia of metropolitan life that she received her education. The lively, erudite conversation that filled the household was a more than adequate substitute for formal schooling, and Fanny, with the run of her father's library, acquired a scholar's knowledge of the classics and a love of literature that never left her. By the age of fifteen, she had already begun, secretly, to write a romantic novel, *The History of Caroline Evelyn,* but when her stepmother discovered the manuscript, she was forced to destroy it on the grounds that the novel was an utterly degrading form of literature. Yet she later described how "even in childhood, even from the moment I could hold a pen" (Preface to Fanny Burney, *The Wanderer,* 1988), she had been impelled by a burning desire to write.

How then could she manage to reconcile these opposing forces: to find approval in the eyes of the world, while also satisfying her impetus for artistic creativity? This was the problem which dogged her all her life. One solution was to be found through the medium of her journal. Although she was advised by a friend that to keep a journal was "the most dangerous employment young persons can have—that it makes them record things which ought *not* to be recorded but instantly forgot" (Annie Raine Ellis, 1907, p. 20), Burney began her extant adolescent diary on March 27, 1767 so she claimed, "To have some account of my thoughts, manners, acquaintance and actions, when the hour arrives in which time is more nimble than memory" (p. 5). During the next six decades, she was to produce an eloquent record of contemporary events from the perspective of her own exceptional circumstances—moving from the glittering life of the London literary circles to "slavery" at the British Court of George III, where she was Second Keeper of the Robes to Queen Charlotte; to life in Paris after the Revolutionary War; to the battlefields of Waterloo to find her wounded husband; and, ultimately, returning to England. But in addition to the unique nature of the historical material the diaries comprise, they also indicate the ways in which eighteenth-century women were creating new forms of expression that reflected their ambivalent cultural position, for Burney's diaries in their focus on personal female experience powerfully dramatize the issues which also form the subject of her fiction. Not tied by formal literary requirements, they show us a woman who, in negotiating techniques for survival in her own life, developed a literary mode which encoded those techniques in its recourse to privacy.

The development of women's articulacy throughout the eighteenth-century is to some extent bound up with the history of their private writings during this period. The diary, the letter, and the autobiographical memoir all proved popular forms of expression for women who were denied a public voice. Contemporary educational tracts, offering models for perfect female behavior, emphasized the values of silence and modesty if women were to conform to expected standards. With their freedom of movement severely limited, financial independence virtually impossible, and when they were forbidden by the weight of social codes to voice their opinions in public, many women turned to personal writing as their only outlet for self-validation. As Felicity Nussbaum (1988) has observed, "In writing to themselves, eighteenth-century women could create a private place in which to speak the unthought, unsaid and undervalued" (p. 154). The appearance of outrageous "autobiographies" by women such as Laetitia Pilkington (1748) and Charlotte Charke (1755) were sufficient guarantee that respectable women would continue to shun the limelight. In the mid eighteenth century, the act of publication in itself was often equated with immorality. As the influential "Queen of the Bluestockings," Mrs. Montagu, sourly remarked, "The generality of women who have excelled in wit have failed in chastity" (Katharine Rogers, 1982, p. 243). No wonder that most women who wanted to state their own views, sought a form of writing that relied on secrecy and disclaimed an audience.

When Fanny Burney, at the age of fifteen, addressed her diary to "a certain Miss Nobody," she was unconsciously following the pattern adopted by others in her position, using the journal as a means of creating an imaginary confidant to whom she could unburden herself of her secret fears and anxieties. A journal was the place where "I must confess my *every* thought, must open my whole heart!" she avowed in her opening entry. For only to her journal dared she "reveal my private opinions of my dearest friends; my own hopes, fears, reflections and dislikes" (Ellis, 1907, p. 5). In this she showed herself eager to establish her identity as an independent-minded being, with thoughts that often diverged from the compliant exterior of demure femininity she presented to the world. It was in her diary that Fanny Burney first drew the wickedly satirical portraits of her contemporaries that were subsequently to figure in her novels. It was here too that she could express her cynicism over social institutions. "O how short a time does it take to put an eternal end to a woman's liberty! (Annie Raine Ellis, 1907, p. 17) she commented caustically after a friend's wedding. Her decided views on marriage led her to resist all attempts to provide her with appropriate suitors, but it was only to her diary that she disclosed the full extent of her fears at taking such a wayward stance. "I was terrified to death," she admitted when urged by her father to look favorably on a Mr. Barlow as a prospective husband. "I felt the utter impossibility of resisting not merely my father's *persuasion*, but even his *advice*" (Ellis, 1907, p. 69). This use of the diary as a clandestine mode of expression was later confirmed by Burney's half-sister, Sarah Harriet Burney, who noted how she "looked and generally spoke with the most refined modesty," but "what was kept back and scarcely suspected in society, wanting a safety valve found its way to her private journal" (Sarah Kilpatrick, 1980, p. 184).

*Evelina,* Burney's first novel, which took London society by storm, had its basis in this potentially subversive form of expression. Characteristically, it was published anonymously, not even her father knowing of his daughter's authorship, and Burney only acknowledged responsibility for the work when she was assured of its success. In her diary, she argued with typical defensiveness that in *Evelina,* "I have not pretended to shew the world what it actually *is,* but what it *appears* to a girl of seventeen:—and so far as that, surely any girl who is *past* seventeen may safely do?" (January 1778). Like Burney's journal, *Evelina* presents a view of life through the eyes of an apparent innocent, a girl whose only defense in a society which is in many respects hostile to her interests is her exploitation of the traditional attributes of femininity. Yet, again like the journal, the novel creates in its narrator a young woman whose acuity and intelligence offer a searching critique of establishment values and behavior, but who suppresses overt expression of her views. In this way, the subjective narrative method that Burney employed, a continuation of the tradition of private writing she was familiar with, becomes integrated into the matter of the text. Evelina, bewildered but mostly quiescent in social situations, reveals her true feelings only in the letters she writes home to her guardian. In the caricatures she creates of the men who intimidate her at balls, at the theater, or out walking, she discovers a weapon that invests her with a degree of power over them. Her contempt and anger, hidden from view in public, surface in her private comments, which allows her a freedom of expression never detected by those whom she secretly judges. As Harriet Martineau was to write over fifty years later, "I want to be doing something with my pen since no other means of action in politics are in a woman's power" (Ellen Moers, 1977, p. 4). This was a truth Burney knew instinctively. Despite the apparently conservative tenor of her novels, they do address radical issues in their analyses of female power, and the mutinous subtext that can be detected is often at odds with their surface conventionality.

Burney's novels might, at first glance, seem merely to amalgamate features from other contemporary fictions in a way that appealed to public taste; certainly they show evidence of Burney's literary heritage. The letter form of *Evelina* and its interest in a young girl's experience can be traced back to the novels of Samuel Richardson. The savage satire and the commentary on manners find their roots in the work of Henry Fielding as well as in periodical essays, such as were to be found in *The Spectator*. The burlesque elements and the witty dialogue owe much to theatrical farce, of which Burney was something of an addict, and the romantic scenes accord with the popular taste for sentimental literature. However, Burney's fictions are much more than technical *tours de force*. In placing the center of her first novel within the consciousness of her heroine, Burney introduced a genuinely female perspective on contemporary experience and showed the transforming effect on the world when seen through a woman's eyes. She did not imitate the male overview of female experience, but, in drawing on a mode of writing that had been developed in her own personal struggles for concealment, she exposed the problems that faced women in their attempts to accomodate the demands of society with their own, often rebellious, desires.

*Evelina* is indeed a startling first novel. Its subtitle, "A Young Lady's Entrance into the World," spotlights the dilemma in which all Burney's heroines find themselves. Like Evelina, the women in her later novels, *Cecilia* (1782), *Camilla* (1796) and *The Wanderer* (1814), operate in situations which emphasize female defenselessness in its first encounter with the powerful social structure which determines and limits their behavior. This subject of the conflict between the youthful heroine and the society around her can be read as a paradigm of women's problematic situation in late-eighteenth-century England. Evelina, an orphan, comes to London from the country, where she has been brought up in seclusion, only to find herself having to manipulate situations for which she is totally unprepared. In presenting her heroine with problems which range from the apparently trivial—how to book seats at the theater for instance—to the directly threatening—how to ward off unwelcome male advances—Burney embraced a spectrum of issues which bore a surface resemblance to the contents of the conduct books of the time but which incorporated a far more deep-seated skepticism about the male-dominated society. To some twentieth-century readers, Burney's emphasis on etiquette might seem trifling, but not if we recognize its emblematic function in her fictions. For in her metonymic concentration on details of social decorum, Burney was in fact probing the real uncertainties that related to women's perceptions of their role and their identity in a world which offered them such contradictory images of self.

Burney was deeply interested in the mechanics of survival for single and unprotected women. Without father or husband, Evelina is encouraged to mold herself on a male stereotype of womanly perfection, to cultivate the qualities of modesty, delicacy, and purity as advantages in the society which values such commodities in women. Yet these are double-edged benefits, for while they are Evelina's only equipment in the fight for social recognition, they also mark her as a ready victim for unscrupulous seducers. The ambiguity of sexual politics is thus delineated and the novel is fraught with equivocal signals as Evelina simultaneously tries to attract and repel male attention. The corresponding confusion the novel depicts regarding Evelina's identity reveals the uncertainties about female self-hood that is at its heart. The demands made on her by the vulgar Branghton family and Mme. Duval underline this confusion in showing the heroine as a product of different social classes, each with its separate behavioral code.

As Evelina progresses through the maze of complications Burney establishes for her, she provides a demonstration of the strategies that Burney herself adopted as a means of survival and which are to be found in the pages of her journal. The terms that are ascribed to Evelina at the beginning of the book emphasize her innocence and her artlessness. To some extent, Burney was providing here a female variant of the favorite eighteenth-century life versus art theme. However, the book contains a paradox, for Evelina's artlessness, the quality so admired in women, initially leads her into unacceptable actions. At first, ignorant of the rules which govern London's stratified society, she commits social faux pas, refusing a partner who asks her to dance, because she dislikes him and laughs openly at what she finds to be ridiculous behavior. In order to win the approval of the patrician hero, Lord Orville, who represents the acceptable face of what frequently emerges as a bizarre world, she must repress her spontaneous reactions and cultivate a passive image. By the time Evelina has reached the end of the novel, much of her original vitality has faded, and she has become a much more reticent version of the girl who, fresh from the country, "almost wished to have jumped on the stage and joined" the actors on her first visit to the London theater (Burney, 1907, p. 22). This toning down process, in which their freedom of choice is gradually weakened, is the price that all Burney's heroines have to pay for social protection. It forms an essential ingredient in Burney's realist vision, as she presents a series of potentially energetic and independent young women who must sacrifice their individualism for financial security and respectability.

All Burney's novels focus on the subject of female isolation, and all depict English society as built around a patriarchal structure that is inimical to women's interests. Evelina's lack of parentage and her ignorance of her true name reflect her vulnerability in a world in which women's status is dependent on male protection. It is significant that in finding her father at the end of the novel, Evelina also finds a husband, the magic combination of the two endowing her with a firm identity and a social security which had previously seemed elusive. For in the male world that Fanny Burney describes in all her fictions, lone women are marginalized figures. Cecilia, lost in London at the end of the novel, is taunted, robbed, degraded, and confined as a mad woman; Camilla, having become separated from her family, falls victim to malicious rumors, becomes destitute and nearly dies from a brain-induced fever; in *The*

*Wanderer,* Juliet's disguise and her unknown origins effectively bar her from her rightful claim to her family inheritance, and, like the others, she has to endure humiliations and extreme poverty in her attempts to survive. All these characters contribute to Burney's investigation into the complexities of gender relations in a society whose rules are weighted against women.

*Cecilia,* Burney's second novel, is a more outspoken and often more trenchant work than *Evelina,* dealing with many of the same issues. Left an heiress, Cecilia is bound by the terms of her father's will—a nice example of the power of dead men over living women—to renounce her inheritance if, when she marries, she adopts her husband's name. As in *Evelina* and *The Wanderer,* the question of a name helps to lay bare the instability of female identity. The story focuses on the plight of a woman whose wealth and family position should guarantee her security, but who in effect finds herself dependent on men who undermine that position and consequently her hold on self. For Cecilia's guardians have control over her fortune until she reaches the age of twenty-one, and in succession each shows his incompetence at handling her affairs. The book is highly innovative in its analysis of the way economic forces shape women's destiny, and in this it proved an influential force on subsequent women novelists, most notably Jane Austen whose *Pride and Prejudice* is often seen as a direct descendent of *Cecilia.*

Cecilia herself is also a forerunner of the spirited heroines of many nineteenth-century fictions. Unlike Evelina, she makes no secret of her intelligence and her independent spirit. She is resourceful, capable, energetic, and charming, but these qualities do not ultimately help her. By making Cecilia fall in love with a man whose family pride prevents him from exchanging his name for hers, Burney sets up an opposition between the massed forces of masculine tradition and the heroine's attempt to retain her individuality. Allowing herself to be inveigled into a secret marriage, Cecilia places herself in her lover's power, and her social impotence is exposed when her subsequent reputation is endangered and all forms of support are withdrawn. The frightening scenes towards the end of the novel, when Cecilia is lost and bemused in the city, parallel the episodes in Burney's first book when Evelina is both metaphorically lost in the strange urban environment and actually lost in the dark alleys at Vauxhall pleasure gardens. Similarly, in her journal, Burney frequently portrays herself as panic-stricken in an alien world, trapped with no means of escape, a nightmarish projection of women's real powerlessness.

After the publication of *Cecilia,* Fanny Burney was hailed as a celebrity wherever she went, an experience she did not relish. She had already noted after the appearance of *Evelina* how "the more the book is drawn into notice, the more exposed it becomes to criticism and remark" (Lewis Gibbs, 1971, p. 6). Public acclaim, however, wasn't for the range and depth of Burney's social critique but for her virtuosity, both as a comic writer of genius and as a sentimentalist who could tug at her readers' heart strings in affecting scenes, such as the suicide of Mr. Harrel in *Cecilia*. It is worth noting that Burney was by no means the last, but certainly one of the first of women writers, to recognize the value of comedy as an incisive tool. In part, her achievement rests on this combination of traditional elements with new and exciting subject matter.

Despite their plot resolutions, both *Evelina* and *Cecilia* reveal a suspicion of orthodox conventions in their view of gender and culture. The heroines, who ultimately conform to the romantic narrative direction of the text, are flanked by minor characters who suggest alternative female models. Strong unconventional women, such as Mrs. Selwyn, in *Evelina,* and Mrs. Delvile in *Cecilia* are invested with a degree of power that is denied the central figures. Mrs. Selwyn, for instance, though mocked for her cleverness, is the architect of Evelina's eventual happiness, managing to engineer the reunion with her aristocratic father that her guardian has for years been unable to effect. Similarly, Mrs. Delvile is established as an intellectual woman who is contemptuous of fashion and "feminine" pursuits. She has successfully created her own conditions for living, which rely little on the traditional boundaries of women's roles. In both these figures, Burney begins to explore the strength of women's friendship and the debate about women's education, topics which were to form the central subject of her next work, *Camilla*.

By 1796, when *Camilla* appeared, Burney's situation had changed dramatically. She had spent five years at Court, had virtually given up her literary career, was married to a French emigré, Alexandre D'Arblay, and had a child. She returned to novel writing, as did so many women of her generation, purely because she needed money to support her family. In this, most interestingly, her private actions contradicted the message of female passivity her books seemed to encode. *Camilla* differs from Burney's other novels in presenting its heroine within a family structure. Subtitled "A Picture of Youth," it reveals the impact of Romantic thinking with its extended enquiry into the upbringing of children, a favorite topic in literature of this period. As Burney's own social and political awareness intensified, through her precarious financial circumstances and through her pragmatic mistrust of revolutionary ideals, so her attitudes towards women's roles became increasingly ambivalent, and *Camilla* seems, at first glance, a much less adventurous work than her first two novels. In it, Burney takes up subjects considered particularly appropriate for women writers: education for girls and the tension between nature and environment as developmental forces. The first section of the novel deals with the main characters as children, the second shows them as the young people they have become.

Once again, however, it is the ambiguous portraits of women that mark Burney's challenge to contemporary mores. Despite the lengthy sentimental episodes and the passages of moralizing, the book imparts a cynicism that fits oddly with much of the dominant tone. This is particularly evident in the portrayal of the minor characters, the forceful Mrs. Arlbery who is clear-sighted about the vicissitudes of marriage, witty and sympathetic; the romantic Mrs. Berlinton, forced by her parents into an incompatible match with an elderly husband who "supposed he had engaged for life a fair nurse to his infirmities" (Burney, 1983, p. 686); the young Miss Dennel, who enters unthinkingly into marriage in order to gain independence from her authoritarian parents, only to find herself trapped in a bondage she never imagined, having become "the property of another, to whom she made over a legal right to treat her just as he pleased" (p. 910). Against this background of skepticism about marriage are placed single women, the sour old maids of tradition, whose desperation for marriage as the only possible route to respectability for women, complicates the pattern as a whole.

It is in this context that we find Camilla, a prototype of later impulsive, but misguided, fictional heroines. Her story discloses the pitfalls women must navigate as it follows the development of her romance with the priggish hero, Edgar. He is accompanied by his misogynist tutor who acts for Burney as devil's advocate, putting forward contemporary stereotypic views of women (as weak, thoughtless, frivolous, petulant, and mentally unsound) against which Camilla's actions are measured. It is this sort of assumption about gender difference, Burney implies, that women have to combat. Together these two men monitor the unwitting Camilla's every move and judge her accordingly, so that Edgar's love is held out as a reward for Camilla's good behavior, a reward that she almost forfeits in her spontaneous gestures for independence.

*Camilla* remains a work which defies easy classification in its combination of orthodox morality and nonconformist ideas, which cannot be simply dismissed. The same sort of critical difficulty occurs with *The Wanderer*, Burney's last novel, composed over a period of several years. Artistically, as most readers would agree, it is patchy. Intellectually, however, it is one of the most controversial of Burney's books in its overtly political approach to the subject of *Female Difficulties*. The opening of the novel is given a precise historical setting, Revolutionary France, a context which directs the ideas and sympathies of the text. Its heroine, Juliet Granville, arrives in England, penniless and unprotected, and with her adventures Burney returns to her favorite theme of woman alone. The novel's range is ambitious, and in it Burney draws a bitter picture of British society as insular, stratified, and antipathetic to women. As Juliet struggles literally to survive in a series of paid occupations, each more menial than the last, Burney exposes the limited opportunities available to women trying to earn their own living, their lack of training for gainful employment, and the inevitable dangers they run from predatory men who are everywhere lying in wait.

The current feminist debate, to some extent a product of the whole unsettling process of the French Revolution, had surfaced in a series of English publications of the turn of the century, such as Mary Wollstonecraft's *A Vindication of the Rights of Woman* (1792) and Mary Anne Radcliffe's *The Female Advocate* (1798). In *The Wanderer*, Fanny Burney explicitly addresses this debate through the character of Elinor Joddrel, an aggressive spokeswoman for the feminist cause. Elinor provides a foil for Juliet, the heroine of the text, and in the contrast between them, Burney presents her mistrust of militancy and the opposing case for moderation. For Elinor, possibly modeled on Wollstonecraft herself, is an unruly termagant, who alienates society's sympathy by her forceful methods of self-promotion. She is, however, undeniably, a character with more vitality and energy than Juliet, and one whose arguments are reasoned and generally incontrovertible. She vigorously attacks the injustices of the situation that Juliet suffers uncomplainingly, but her directness and unconventionality are proved to be counter-productive. In the end, it is Juliet who wins love and fortune. It is also highly significant that Elinor's social position is assured; she can afford the luxury of voicing her challenge. Burney's own attraction to the rationalist cause is evident in the clarity of the arguments she places in Elinor's mouth and in the narrative importance of the character—she cannot be ignored as a minor figure. But the final tactics of the text are registered in the words of the hero, who advises Elinor that "Unbridled liberty . . . cannot rush upon a state without letting it loose to barbarism. Nothing, without danger, is suddenly unshackled" (Burney, 1988, p. 10).

Such an attitude reflects the policy that Burney herself had successfully adopted throughout her own difficult career. The mask that Juliet wears at the beginning of *The Wanderer* symbolizes the concealment that women must employ if they wish to insinuate themselves into society's good graces. Burney's writing continually suggests the opposing tensions which formed her views and which mirrored the transitions of the age in which she lived. The contrary signals transmitted by her novels correspond to the enigmatic self-projections of her journals. In these, Burney emphasizes her own helplessness, her indecision, and her bewilderment in the face of circumstance. We find her in middle age traveling to France, surrounded by threatening crowds on arrival in Calais; in Paris, a city in turmoil, during the chaos of Napoleon's Hundred Days; isolated among strangers as she tries to reach her husband who is away at the battlefield; terrified in an innocuous English seaside resort when the incoming tide suddenly traps her almost beyond recovery. Yet this claim to frailty is offset by the power of her descriptions and by the very fact of her repeated survival. For her personal courage was extraordinary. She endured, for instance, an operation for breast cancer without anesthetic in 1811, an event she recounts graphically and unsentimentally in a lengthy journal letter written six months afterwards.

Her journals themselves constitute a process of resistance to a milieu that threatened to encroach on Burney's sense of self. While presenting the front of deference to the world, she retained her private writing as a means of control, placing menacing experiences at bay as she recorded her triumphs over them. Similarly her novels are double edged in their representation of women's interests. Her work fully recognizes the "female difficulties" of contemporary life, and the techniques of subterfuge she developed for dealing with this complex subject encode both her own policy and an oblique mode of expression that she was to leave as a legacy for the women writers who followed her.

# REFERENCES

Burney, Fanny. (1907). *Evelina*. London: Dent.
Burney, Fanny. (1987). *Cecilia*. London: Virago.
Burney, Fanny. (1983). *Camilla*. Oxford: Oxford University Press.
Burney, Fanny. (1988). *The wanderer*. London: Pandora.
Ellis, Annie Raine (Ed.). (1907). *The early diary of Frances Burney, 1768–1778*. London: Bell.
Gibbs, Lewis (Ed.). (1971). *The diary of Fanny Burney*. London: Dent.
Hemlow, Joyce, et al. (Eds.). (1972–1984). *The journals and letters of Fanny Burney (Madame D'Arblay), 1791–1840*. Oxford: Oxford University Press.
Kilpatrick, Sarah. (1980). *Fanny Burney*. London: David & Charles.
Moers, Ellen. (1977). *Literary women*. London: The Women's Press.
Nussbaum, Felicity. (1988). Eighteenth-century women's autobiographical commonplaces. In Shari Benstock (Ed.), *The private self*. London: Routledge.
Rogers, Katharine M. (1982). *Feminisms in eighteenth century England*. Urbana, IL: University of Illinois Press.

# Daddy's Girl as Motherless Child:

## Maria Edgeworth and Maternal Romance; An Essay in Reassessment

===== Mitzi Myers =====

"A new path is thus open for female exertion. . . . Man no longer aspires to an exclusive dominion in authorship. . . . Who . . . does not contemplate with enthusiasm . . . the fine character painting, the practical instructions of Miss Edgeworth, the great KNOWN, standing . . . by the side of the great UNKNOWN [a reference to Sir Walter Scott, who tried to conceal his authorship to the Waverley novels]?" (Joseph Story, 1826, p. 17)

"The one serious novelist coming from the upper class in Ireland, and the most finished and famous produced by any class there, is undoutedly Miss Edgeworth." (William Butler Yeats, 1891, p. 27)[1]

Criticism of women's writing is inevitably preoccupied with patriarchy (however diversely that historically slippery concept may be defined), for man-made language, culture, and literary formats shape the environment within which—or against which—female authorship defines itself. The rather slender body of scholarship on Maria Edgeworth's writing is an exemplary case, because it is literally obsessed with paternal lineage: the remarkably energetic, inventive, opinionated, and optimistic Richard Lovell, very influential over his enormous family and very much beloved by his eldest daughter, though Byron was neither the first nor the last outsider to pronounce him a bore or a tyrant. Ever since Maria emerged as an author, virtually every discussion has centered on the extent and direction of her father's indisputable impact. Without any evidence, some early critics thought he had ruined her work by inserting passages on "unfeminine" subjects like politics, while others took the equally unfounded view that she was merely a ventriloquist's puppet, mouthing daddy's words. For instance, a reviewer of her last novel (*Helen* [1834], a woman-centered tale, now recognized as among her finest) insisted that its production after her father's death in 1817 demonstrated that she couldn't have written the strong, "masculine" works previously attributed to her: "Ay! it is just as we expected! Miss Edgeworth never wrote *the* Edgeworth novels;—we mean that portion of them which gave life, and will

137

confer longevity on the whole mass. All that, as we long have had a suspicion, was the work of her father" ("A dozen of novels," 1834, p. 483).[2]

The old dichotomy is replicated in subsequent debate. Did the father constrain the daughter's lively genius within moralistic paradigms, or did he generously encourage her career and provide her with the knowledge of the larger world that makes her (as recent male critics seek to compliment her) the "least feminine of female novelists" or the "most masculine English woman novelist" (Watson, 1980, p. x; Welsh, 1972, p. 281)?[3] Marilyn Butler's 1972 literary biography has established the authorative position on Maria as daddy's girl by espousing the latter position. Although Butler's study makes rich use of family papers not available to prior critics, her model of the father-daughter relationship was in fact anticipated by a number of earlier researchers, who also found Richard Lovell's influence empowering.[4] After all, it was Maria herself who repeatedly and enthusiastically gave her father credit for raising her from the dust (the implied image is of God breathing life into inanimate clay), for creating her as a writing woman.[5] Given this union of opinion between official family biographer and biographee, attempts to read Edgeworth's work as simplistically subversive of her father's rationalist intellectual stance, or patriarchy in general, run the risk of seeming thin or downright perverse. Examples of critics hampered by preconceptions and careless with facts about the life and works they seek to reassess include Mark D. Hawthorne's pre-Butler study and even Sandra M. Gilbert and Susan Gubar's brief analyses of Edgeworth's achievement in their pioneering and often admirable *The Madwoman in the Attic: The Woman Writer and the Nineteenth-Century Literary Imagination* (1979) and *The Norton Anthology of Literature by Women* (1985).

Mark Hawthorne's *Doubt and Dogma in Maria Edgeworth* (1967) caricatures Richard Lovell as reason and Maria as feeling and tries to demonstrate that her work covertly romanticizes his position. (If it were less reductive about human nature and literary structures and more theoretically informed, it might qualify as an early deconstructive reading.)[6] Comparably thesis-bound in their search for Maria's particular "madwoman," Sandra Gilbert and Susan Gubar sometimes fail to recognize the historically situated linguistic ironies of the texts they cite, thus transforming Maria Edgeworth's arguments for female rationality into misogyny. Paradigms universalized from Victorian fiction cannot fully account for women's writing generated from and contingent on a different historical situation. Establishing a false dichotomy between Edgeworth's so-called "feminine" fiction and "her father's commitment to pedagogically sound moral instruction," Sandra Gilbert and Susan Gubar also make much of the fact that *Castle Rackrent* (1800)—usually cited as Maria's masterpiece—was written without her parent's being in on the composition process, but so were other works, including some created specifically as surprises for the father (1979, pp. 146, 150).[7] All the same, even though their anthology misdates Maria's birth and tangles up Richard Lovell's four wives (a third stepmother a year younger than Maria hardly qualifies to have problematized a thirty-year-old daughter's *upbringing*—and the relationship between the two was deeply fond), even though they say she wrote nothing aside from her father's biography between Richard Lovell's death in 1817 and her last adult novel in 1834 (she produced many volumes of juvenile fiction), Sandra Gilbert and Susan Gubar legitimately wonder whether Butler's zeal to rescue Richard Lovell from widespread critical distaste hasn't turned Maria's biographer herself into daddy's girl who finds the father more compelling than the daughter and frankly says so.[8] Similarly, despite his gaffes and gaps, Mark Hawthorne is right to interrogate models of female authorship that reduce the writing daughter to the brainy father's eager pen, however much Maria herself enjoyed and cannily used that posture to win the attention and esteem of the father whose early neglect no amount of later familial affection ever quite erased.

If those recent theoretical approaches aligned under the rubric of the "New Historicism" remind us that *all* writing is culturally determined, a product of specific time and place, revisionist critics must recall that women's writings require tactful and nuanced contextualization even more than the texts of their male counterparts.[9] Social proprieties press more firmly on their work; familial circumstances more clearly imprint their careers and their themes, though not in one monolithic pattern. Crude binary oppositions of reason and feeling, male and female, father and daughter, adult and child, teacher and pupil, or text and subtext fail to engage the ambiguities in Edgeworth's writing that Mark Hawthorne and Sandra Gilbert and Susan Gubar rightly sense, for, more than any other woman writer of her day, Maria Edgeworth managed to have things two ways, to keep her cake and enjoy it too. Unlike Mary Wollstonecraft, she was a feminist thinker who didn't offend; unlike Jane Austen, she was at home in diverse class, regional, and masculine milieus; unlike most of her sister authors, she evaded the staple sentimentalities of female fiction while valorizing generous feeling. And she did so in a style remarkably supple and often epigrammatic, as quotable as her lively letters. She was a thorough mistress of her day's multiple discursive practices and hence of multiple possibilities for self-constitution through writing, as my reassessment will argue.

Although literary history has been oddly grudging in recognizing such gifts (everyone who *does* write about Edgeworth describes what amounts to a conversion experience), it seems stranger still that a writer so oriented to the relational maternal thinking familiar to us all from the work of Nancy Chodorow (1974, 1978), Carol Gilligan (1982), Sara Ruddick (1980, 1989), and other recent feminist theorists, so dedicated throughout her career to the role of mother-teacher, and so obsessed with development and nurturing in both life and art should forever be pigeonholed as daddy's girl. Whether we interpret what theorist Jane Gallop (1982) would label the "daughter's seduction" scenario positively or negatively, there is more to Maria than that alone.[10] Few other writers have been so vitally concerned with formative years and family fictions; whether in her tales for children or adults, the *Bildungsroman* or growing-up format is the staple plot with which she is always most comfortable. Wise maternal pedagogy—or the lack of it—and orphans, actual or psychic, loom large in her writing with good reason, from her children's stories to adult novels like *Belinda* (1801) and *Helen: A Tale* (1834), in each of which the relationship between an orphaned adolescent and her female mentor displaces a conventional heterosexual romance plot.[11]

Edgeworth remembered her own ineffectual and permissive mother, the least loved of her father's wives, as "always crying," a detail discreetly canceled from the official family *Memoir* (1867).[12] Left a motherless child at five, Maria had three stepmothers and a much adored aunt as maternal surrogates. Intense female friendships and a variety of mother-daughter relationships textured her life. Her first stepmother, Honora Sneyd, beautiful, brilliant, and coolly just, left plain little Maria with a rational maternal ideal she tried to live up to in her fiction and a starving child's need for motherly nurturance, a need richly satisfied during her many decades with her last stepmother, Frances Beaufort, who shared with Maria the mothership of her symbolically named firstborn, Frances Maria (Fanny). Passionately beloved, Fanny was Maria's sister, daughter, and friend, while Frances provided for her year-older "daughter" both loving friendship and the petting Maria had missed as a child. Although we may disagree with Richard Lovell's characterization of his daughter's leading traits as "the defect of [her] disposition," he and all her family were keenly aware of her warm "sensibility" behind the rational public persona and her "inordinate desire to be beloved."[13]

Marilyn Butler justly gives Edgeworth credit for her pioneering sociological fiction, her empirically grounded representations of reality, the fruits of her father's public experience, and her own role as his right hand in conducting the business of the family estate. But encoded within many of Edgeworth's realistic tales is another mode of writing, an idealist pattern of wish-formulation and wish-fulfillment that might be termed maternal romance. Issues of power and pedagogy lie at the heart of Edgeworth's life and work, but they are not exclusively patrilineal; they have a psychically resonant maternal dimension as well. Much concerned with maternal themes in her own life and art, Edgeworth was, moreover, the almost unacknowledged mother of several interlinked Anglo-American literary traditions. Despite Jane Austen's well-known encomium in *Northanger Abbey* (1818, chapter 5), Edgeworth is typically eclipsed among British female nurturers of the novel by the more conservative Frances Burney and Austen, who ground their literary structures in heterosexual romance paradigms as Edgeworth does not. In American feminist literary criticism, she receives the barest mention as an inspirational foremother, though she provided models for several overlapping genres of American women's writing, a debt warmly acknowledged by her sister writers themselves, pioneers in the female *Bildungsroman,* local color fiction, and what one recent critic has termed the "narrative of community."[14]

Revisionist work from varied perspectives is necessary before Maria Edgeworth rightfully assumes the significant place in English literary history that Yeats accords her—and that place should be enlarged to accommodate her work's diversity. For him, she was a cross-cultural pioneer in Irish fiction (and we remember Sir Walter Scott's generous tribute to her as the inspiration for his own regional ventures), but she was a notable and neglected pioneer in other genres than adult and regional fiction as well. Long before Louisa May Alcott, Edgeworth established the definitive form of the realistic juvenile tale, the family story which still remains a staple of Anglo-American literary culture. In tandem with her storytelling for the young, Maria was also a notable educational thinker; on her own and in collaboration with her father, she canvassed pedagogy from the primary years to female accomplishments to professional training for young men. Indeed, English educational historians perpetually rediscover her and wonder why such a forward-looking native educator has been displaced in favor of Johan Heinrich Pestalozzi and Friedrich Froebel.[15] Her fictional and expository educative projects, each of which comments on the other and each of which became the woman writer's métier, are not peripheral but central to her accomplishment. No one would disagree that the "manly" public scope and sociological realism distinguishing much of her fiction were innovative in her day (though not the whole of her achievement), and not just for a woman writer, but for any author, as Marilyn Butler warmly argues. However, except for Edgeworth's last novel, *Helen,* Butler (like Richard Lovell before her) shows less enthusiasm for those tales specifically targeted for a feminine audience and (unlike Richard Lovell) does not expend much energy on Maria's stories for the young.[16] Nonetheless, I want to argue, it is precisely in exploring these "minor" works that a more nuanced and contextualized feminist reading of Maria's literary achievement might usefully be initiated. (Not coincidentally, the same "feminine" genres demonstrate that Edgeworth deserves credit as a woman writer per se as well as the "most masculine" novelist of her sex.)

Rather than an "images of women approach" assuming that literary language transparently mirrors reality, that there is a unitary "female experience" somehow separate from the discursive practices of its period, that fully integrated female selves universally define their being in opposition to a monolithic "patriarchy," or that heroines unequivocally reflect authorial aspirations and rage, I want to historicize and to problematize one of Edgeworth's *Moral Tales for Young People* (1801)—"Angelina; or, L'Amie Inconnue." This seemingly transparent cautionary tale about an idealistic young woman's unconventional behavior turns surprisingly complex when considered in the context of its familial, historical, and literary specificity.[17] Examining the psychic patterns and linguistic structures that Edgeworth's *Bildungsroman* for teenagers exploits and subverts does more than forward our reassessment of its author's niche in the canon. It helps us think about the social construction of gendered subjectivity through language. This socialization story's multiple idioms and parodic romance paradigms exemplify the linguistic construction of the female self, showing a period's conventional discursive strategies in the very process of governing and being resisted. Angelina is more than a guileless girl who misreads the world as a sentimental fiction, a female quixote to amuse and warn the reader. As she quests her way through a veritable map of misreadings encoded in the jarring dialects and mistaken assumptions of character after character, she elucidates the interplay of language and identity: how selves are constructed and how they may be reconstructed. Angelina's ordering of the world according to a set of conventions, her entanglement in allusion and illusion, emblematizes—and critiques—her fictional world's mode of social interaction as much as her own adolescent confusion.

The story as the subtitle suggests is about ways of knowing, especially women's ways of knowing, to adapt the title of a recent feminist study, which like Edgeworth's tale, explores a cultural preference for connected knowing and the known community, as opposed to the objective and the abstract (Mary Field Belenky et al., 1986).[18] Knowing is thus interwoven with friendship, the other charged word in the subtitle, particularly female friendship. Because, in common with much children's fiction, the tale's world is matriarchal, almost literally textualizing maternal space—or women's utopian wish for it—it also helps us think about how current popular theories of mother-daughter relationships such as those of Nancy Chodorow might relate to women's literary as well as psychic structures.[19] Chodorow's observation that "a woman identifies with her own mother and, through identification with her child, she (re)experiences herself as a cared-for child" has obvious implications for women's writing (1974, p. 47). Edgeworth is both mother and daughter in composing her tale, and as with much writing for the young, the audience is at once child and adult, the structuring myths both personal and cultural. The birth of Fanny, Maria's daughter-sister, on a visit to Clifton in 1799 intertwines with Angela's birth as a fictional heroine of the same place and time, much as Edgeworth's private myth of reconciliation and renewal resonates in the story's public implications.

As a product of the French Revolutionary years, "Angelina" is suffused with political meanings. The letters recording Edgeworth's composition of her juvenile tales also dramatically recount the family flight during Ireland's 1798 French invasion and insurrection. Seen against the backdrop of bloody revolution and reactionary literary propaganda (much of it delivered in alarmist fiction), Angelina's independence and self-determination, even though initially articulated in the "wrong" language, convey a strikingly positive message for girl readers. The story's witty satire on the fashionable world's values and its celebration of maternal tolerance and community offer lessons for national as well as gender reformation. Appearing at the height of English counter-revolutionary paranoia, the work gets away with its lighthearted liberalism, because it's a philosophical tale in the guise of moral improvement for adolescents. Maria's often-deplored didacticism enables her intellectuality, her engagement with public issues. Like so much of Edgeworth's oeuvre, then, "Angelina" richly demonstrates how the woman writer's appropriation of "marginal" literary forms like stories for young people opens up important issues for a feminist theory of reading.[20]

Historically, educational access has always come first on feminist agendas, but we are only beginning to interrogate educational thematics and structures in women's fiction. Pedagogical relations narrowly conceived as a father-teacher and daughter-learner dyad outside the text have hitherto dominated Edgeworth criticism. Extending our attention to educational dynamics between characters within texts and between the author and her text suggests pedagogy's more encompassing role in Edgeworth's art and life, and by extension in those of many other women writers of her period too.[21] Written *by* adults *for* children, and for those child readers' parents as well, and by adults peculiarly drawn to identification with the juvenile protagonists their stories purport to socialize, children's literature inevitably problematizes pedagogy. Simultaneously present on different narrative planes, its author must be at once child and adult, learner and teacher, untutored feeling and enlightened wisdom. No matter how overtly the story declares its moral meaning, its writer is necessarily the "changing and contradictory subject" familiar to us from postmodern theory, a self in process whose experience is never definitively fixed, but always subject to redefinition (Chris Weedon, 1987). Not for nothing have recent critics of children's literature pronounced such works "of all texts . . . the most 'self-deconstructing,' " or discovered in this fiction "the remarkable characteristic of being about something which it hardly ever talks of": "the impossible relation between child and adult" (Peter Hunt, 1985, p. 121; Jacqueline Rose, 1984, p. 1). Although Edgeworth deserves her reputation as the first producer of realistic child characters for a real child audience, there is also a sense in which Sir Walter Scott was right: her "moral narrations . . . are really fitter for grown people than for children," because only adults can fully appreciate the relational complexities (Scott, 1934, p. 7, 312).

The inherent structural tensions of Edgeworth's fictions for youth thus specially illuminate the contradictions central to Georgian female life and to recent feminist criticism: the relation between nurturance and autonomy, connectedness and individuation, dependence and dominance, feeling and reason, and, finally, between experience and the discursive practices that configure it. For Maria Edgeworth, language literally equals power, love, identity. As a lonely little girl in boarding school far from her family, she tried to win that family's affection first through letters and later through fictions. Her earliest stories were written for younger siblings, about families, and circulated among her relatives. She was the mother of stories which she presented as children to her family audience, and her tales knit the emotional bonds she needed, making her a focus of attention, affection, and respect. This genesis of her writing not only makes her juvenile fiction particularly crucial in evaluating her career, but also implies larger dualities of mothering and daughtering in women's texts, both inside the stories, with fictional mothers and daughters who are often the thematic subject, and outside the stories, toward which the author assumes a maternal stance, mothering herself through mothering her heroine, and often correcting her heroine so as to rewrite her own life. These psychic complexities and structural tensions manifest themselves in the language of "Angelina"—literally in talk, the idioms and dialects available to the orphaned heroine as she flees from English high society to the wilds of Wales and back again; in the varied mother-teacher and daughter-learner relations centering the story; and in literary structure, the dialectic between conventional quixotic romance and the more realistic maternal fantasy of a renovated domestic community that overwrites it. If Edgeworth speaks in the wise voice of Lady Frances Somerset, she is equally present in the posturings of sixteen-year-old Anne Warwick, who christens herself "Angelina" in true sentimental style.[22] Amused yet sympathetic toward the girl in search of the mother-friend-romantic novelist styled "Araminta," Edgeworth as clearly enjoys the rambunctious brandy drinker and incessant talker that this spurious maternal surrogate turns out to be. The author who mothers herself through her text is not narrowly coterminous with the enlightened mother valorized in the text.

Although heroines ask to be read as their author's daughters, as at once self and other, protagonist and author are not as seamlessly conjoined as Sandra Gilbert and Susan Gubar's practice suggests. Nor is Edgeworth's most quoted statement about herself as artist the embodiment of passivity and repression that they imply in prefacing their discussion with an epigraph borrowed from Marilyn Butler's longer citation: "I am like the 'needy knifegrinder'—I have no story to tell" (1979, p. 146; 1972, p. 9; *Edgeworth Family Memoir* 1867, 3 p. 259). Edgeworth's letter replies to publishers who wanted new prefatory material for a reprinted edition of her work. Stating that she is a woman whose domestic circumstances are not the stuff of public display, she distances herself from the Romantic cult of the author, familiar to us from Byron's posturings or Wordsworth's egotistical sublime. She claims that her work speaks for itself and describes her relation to it in characteristically allusive fashion. To those who know the context, the language she borrows is multilayered and resonant, for "The Friend of Humanity and the Knife-Grinder" is George Canning's famous 1797 parody of Robert Southey's "The Widow," written in revolutionary youth before the poet's lapse into conservatism. Southey's poem is about a mature "orphan" ("Once I had parents. . . . I had a home once") unheard and neglected by authority figures; Canning's parody metamorphoses the widow into a drunken knifegrinder, a knowing rogue too worldly wise for the easy answer of "republican enthusiasm and universal philanthropy" (Lionel Madden, 1972, pp. 56–58). As with the dualities of "Angelina" and her other tales of unconventional youth, which critique society, imagine an alternative, and yet sidestep militance, Edgeworth's authorial disclaimer epigrammatically situates her in a double position re her own texts.

Similar patterns appear in a nursery rhyme Edgeworth used more than once to characterize her status as woman writer. Refusing her long-time American correspondent Rachel Mordecai Lazarus an engraved likeness, Edgeworth told her, "I would rather you took your idea of me from my writings." Yet if her work is a version of herself, her child, it is also curiously parentless: "*Maria Edgeworth* always looks to me, when I meet it accidentally in print, as a foreign German name and I feel like the little woman in the nursery story, whose petticoats were cut short when she was asleep, and who, on wakening and finding herself in that condition, sang, 'Oh, says the little woman, this is none of I' " (in Edgar F. MacDonald, 1977, pp. 175, 300). As Edgeworth, who knew her children's literature, was aware, in most versions the little woman is befuddled and her nakedness revealed because she has been lying drunk on the market road.[23] Not an innocent child, she knows the ways of the world, and the peddler who tricks her tempts us toward a feminist conclusion Edgeworth discreetly does not draw.

Warning us of hasty conclusions in reading women's writing, such oblique authorial self-representations reveal Edgeworth's characteristic doubling of an innocent response and a sophisticated situating of that innocence within a larger linguistic context. This technique is a staple of her work, from the charmingly garrulous, relentlessly revelatory old Thady M'Quirk in *Castle Rackrent* (1800)—who deconstructs the feudal dynasty he claims to glorify; to the adolescent heroes and heroines like Angelina and her male counterpart in "Forester," another of the *Moral Tales*—who challenge the social order and are both chastened and celebrated for their daring; on through the serial portrayals of her autobiographical child character, Rosamond, forever chattering and precipitous; and Rosamond's unfailingly rational mother (a version of Maria's first stepmother, Honora, she insists that the girl correct her naiveté through learning to think for herself.) But Rosamond's improvement in rationality never contains her generous embracing of experience, any more than Edgeworth's notorious "didacticism" drowns the clamorous voices who compete in her texts for the reader's attention. Alternative modes of interpreting the world and alternative textualizations of the female self vie in the richly rendered conversations that are the basic structural unit of her fiction. It is noteworthy that Edgeworth's longest and most considered appraisal images her novelistic art as dialogue, talk, the literary form of a woman's relational mode of interconnecting herself with the world. She was well aware of what her critics often told her, that her genius lay in letting her people talk what they were, in the revelation of ethical values through clashing verbal styles. Plot for her is typically conventional (and sometimes creaky), and what she does best, as in "Angelina," is to let someone grow up, to achieve some balance of subjectivity and commonality through the languages the period made available.[24]

The competing languages in the *Moral Tales* are framed by the paternal preface usual in Maria's books. Written to appeal to parents, the introduction objectively justifies the role of entertaining fiction and the unexceptionable morality of the tales. Richard Lovell links "Angelina" and the rest to the educational experimentation of *Practical Education* (1798), the family's collaborative manual for enlightened parents: "These tales have been written, to illustrate the opinions delivered" in the treatise (*Moral Tales* 1801, 1974, 1, p. xi). Like the stories for younger children Maria had previously published, her fiction for adolescents is self-consciously presented as part of a larger educational project, and even more than her children's literature, these young-adult works are rightly presented as innovative, an early attempt to shape and exploit what is now a huge market. The *Moral Tales* were among the first fictional ventures specifically designed to appeal to a teenage audience's reading interests and psychic needs.[25] Like the Edgeworths' modern successors, Richard Lovell is aware of the difficulties: such stories must be "suited to the early years of youth, and, at the same time, conformable to the complicate [sic] relations of modern society" (1801, 1974, 1, p. v). [26] They must initiate their readers into the social order, somehow reconciling the individual's claims to freedom and authenticity and society's pressure on the individual to comply with institutional codes. By this implicitly political nature of its subject matter, young-adult fiction takes part in the period's raging ideological debate about the relation between private person and public order that Butler (1975) had dubbed the "war of ideas." (The late 1790s and the early 1870s had much in common—controversy over social structure, warring factions at left and right, a lively feminism, and an upsurge of works priming the young to deal with a society increasingly seen as problematic.)

The two most politically charged tales, the matched male and female *Bildungsroman* "Forester" and "Angelina," are explicitly linked by Richard Lovell. The first pictures an "eccentric" young man, "who scorns the common forms and dependencies of civilized society" and might well have turned out "a fanatic and a criminal." " 'Angelina' is a female Forester. The nonsense of *sentimentality* is here aimed at with the shafts of ridicule, instead of being combated by serious argument," and with the heroine's "romantic eccentricities . . . are contrasted faults of a more common and despicable sort." The father-educator's voice that mediates between Maria and her audience concludes with the hope that the stories "will be thought—what they profess to be—*Moral* Tales" (1801, 1974, 1, pp. viii–ix, xi). Informative, enlightened—and reductive, Richard Lovell's equation of treatise and tale had often been taken as gospel by critics, who expend their energies on measuring the fit between precept and story. Certainly, the pedagogic principles provide backbone—the characteristic Edgeworth stress on education as learning to think, judge, and act for oneself (girl and boy alike)—but the stories are far richer than their dehydration to moral example suggests. Usefully boosting the volumes to an educationally concerned audience (and wisely skirting the charged political issues with which the stories are alive), Richard Lovell's paternal exposition certifies Maria's material as innocuous and screens its complexities. The father's prefaces, always sought by his daughter, like the appropriation of children's literature itself, allow Maria a protected space within which she can explore serious issues. Mrs. Sarah Trimmer, canny conservative and literary watchdog, wasn't fooled. An educational innovator like the Edgeworths but as staunchly religious as they were secular-minded, she scrutinized all the family productions in detail in her pioneering venture at reviewing children's books, The Guardian of Education (1802–6). Trimmer thought Maria and her heroine got away with too much, because no patriarchal religious message overwrites the lesson Angelina painfully learns for herself; for want of "serious argument," "Angelina" "does not appear to us what the general title of the work announces, a Moral Tale" (1803, 2, p. 428).

God's language may be missing, the male characters reduced to marginality, and the technique allusive and amusing, but the tale's theme is nevertheless serious. It involves not just a critique of Angelina's misplaced idealism, but also of patriarchal aristocratic court culture, whose hegemony a progressive, bourgeois, family-centered ideology was contesting in this period. Edgeworth's code word for the cultural and linguistic systems she deplores is "fashion," and her very popular six-volume Tales of Fashionable Life (1809; 1812) exemplify the satire she directed toward decadent institutional and behavioral practices throughout her career.[27] As in the adult novels Belinda (1801) and The Absentee (in the 1812 Fashionable Life series), "The Good French Governess," another of the adolescent Moral Tales (1801), features the reclamation of a mother from fashionable dissipation to enlightened domesticity; as surrogate mother, the governess regenerates the young people and their mother too. Angelina has no such help; her orphaned state literalizes the individual choices she must make. Unlike many of the period's young heroines, she doesn't just do what mother says. She escapes from her bad surrogate mother, who epitomizes fashion, and runs away in search of a fantasized mother and an idealized maternal space. She ultimately gets rewarded with her dream of a good mother-friend come true, but only after she had learned for herself that her inaugural choice— "Araminta," the mother-friend as sentimental author—is a preposterous fraud. Angelina may be fooled by literary romance initially, but she is vindicated in deploring the values that rule the world. Though she begins by searching in the wrong place, the idealized maternal romance she seeks really does exist, it turns out, or at least the author textualizes that maternal space for her daughter-heroine—and herself. As Clair Kahane (1988) has suggested of recent feminist attempts to reclaim and empower the mother, such representations assert the potency of a dream, speaking to the "need for a rescue fantasy in which the writer-daughter becomes the mother of her mother, a female version of the family romance in which the daughter gives birth to the mother she always wanted" (p. 82).

Angelina is the ward of Lady Diana Chillingworth, whose name signifies her hard heart and effect on her surrogate daughter, and whose fashionable cant reveals the linguistic pressures that draw women toward conformity with what the "world" will say, in this case about the girl's running away, still a troubling act for a sixteen-year-old and truly shocking in its period, when reputation was all. Egotistic, irresponsible, slavishly dependent on convention for her behavioral standards and set phrases, Lady Di becomes a trope for her class's decadence as well as neglectful mothering: " 'Oh, what will the world say! . . . The world will lay all the blame upon *me*'. . . . Lady Diana Chillingworth went to calm her sensibility at the card-table" (2, pp. 148, 151). Lady Di's sister, Lady Frances Somerset, one of Edgeworth's numerous ideal mother figures, loving home and its pleasures, yet rationally enlightened, thinks for herself and gives us a colloquial language informed with idealism and natural feeling with which to interpret Angelina's bizarre actions: "a simpleton of sixteen is more an object of mercy than a simpleton of sixty" (2, p. 243). (The name "Frances" pays tribute to Maria's last stepmother. Initially jealous, Maria became her loving friend and accompanied her and Richard Lovell on their belated honeymoon trip to the Bristol-Clifton area where Fanny was born in 1799 and the action of "Angelina" takes place.) The story begins with the talk of the two sisters, with contrasting value systems revealed through a conversational dialectic, the linguistic ground where ideological content—Edgeworth's interrogation of patriarchal social and literary structures—and of gendered subjectivity—her examination of this society's ways of writing woman—come together. Always Edgeworth's strong suit as a novelist, dialogue in this story functions as much more than a convenient mode of exposition or character portrayal. Throughout the tale, as with the exchange between the good and bad mothers which opens it, oppositional voices embody oppositional ethical, class, and gender systems; the cultural cacophony that every adolescent must learn to translate into sounds of sense and selfhood literally echoes in the reader's ears.

Like Edgeworth's play with conventional romance paradigms, her use of multiple competing sociolects converts formal element into ideological statement. The comic cross-purposes of Welsh, Scottish, Irish, French, Quaker, and Somerset speech, as well as fashionable cant, middle-class, country, and children's phraseology, along with an extraordinary range of literary and cultural allusion, are all functional as well as funny. The linguistic and structural way that the story gets told is, quite literally, what the tale is all about—reading as wish-formulation, fictionalizing the world, writing yourself into the world on your own terms. Anne Warwick yearns to be the author and agent of her own life, not the dependent of a woman who has no "higher ideas of excellence" and wants her to "behave like other people" (2, p. 152). Like many previous heroines (the deluded girl reader was a conventional eighteenth-century satiric target), she has overdosed on sentimental fiction and tries to live out her dream.[28] She talks, thinks, and defines herself in the rhetorical language of sensibility, right down to being reborn under the more fitting name of Angelina, and she expects the real world to conform to the organizing principles she has imbibed.

But so does just about everyone else. They all play parts, read the world in terms of their own scenarios, and (mis)interpret Angelina in fictions of *their* making—as pathetic victim, runaway slut, barmaid on the make for a rich nobleman lover, madwoman, sentimental friend—not *hers*. Unlike most female quixote variants, the heroine of Edgeworth's tale isn't the sole deluded role player. Only Lady Frances sees lucidly from the first, insisting that Lady Di's "self-willed, unaccountable, romantic girl" really possesses "great abilities," "generosity of temper," and "warm affections," that her true stength of mind is temporarily obscured because her mistaken education has scanted her "knowledge of realities" (2, pp. 148, 157). And even Lady Frances is intially very much mistaken about the cause for Angelina's flight, dumbfounded to find that "there is no love at all in the case." "Incredible!" she exclaims when she learns that Angelina's dream does *not* involve "some admirer, some lover" (2, p. 150). It's female friendship that Angelina elopes to find; she wants a mother, not a man. By writing for adolescents, Edgeworth evades the entrance-into-the-world-to-get-married plot which has always been the staple of heterosexual romance. Her variant on the deluded reader as quixote sidesteps male-female relationships to foreground issues of connection and individuation central in girls' growing up.

Since Angelina's experience is focal, we might expect that, as in most modern young-adult fiction and in many eighteenth-century novels too, we would get a first-person confessional narration. But such confinement to the heroine's vision would prevent the reader's awareness of alternative interpretations of her conduct and, important for Edgeworth's larger cultural theme, of the world which presses on her.[29] Her view of reality does not constitute the whole of the novella's reality, just as the prenuptial girl is only one element in the negotiation among gendered roles that the book offers. Unlike many late-eighteenth-century women writers, Edgeworth does not chain herself to the virgin of sensibility, but gives us females of many ranks, ages, nationalities, and moral characters. We have to laugh as the heroine literally bangs her head against reality—Welsh cottage doors are low and a mystic bard turns out to be "a mere modern harper!—He is not even blind" (2, pp. 172–73, 163)— but we also warmly sympathize. The reader's and narrator's stances re the heroine thus structurally reproduce the mix of separation and relation that female maturation entails. Rather than the independence which patriarchal

Western culture has typically defined as individualism, the story dramatizes a more woman-centered view. As Jessica Benjamin (1986) expresses it, "[I]ndividuality is properly, ideally, a balance of separation and connectedness, of the capacities for agency and relatedness. . . . Infancy research . . . suggests that the self does not proceed from oneness to separateness, but evolves by simultaneously differentiating and recognizing the other, by alternating between 'being with' and being distinct. . . . The vital issue is whether the mother herself is able to recognize the child's subjectivity, and later whether the child can recognize the mother" (p. 82).

Just as the woman writer's voice is not an idiolect solely of her own making, but partakes of the linguistic structures available, so female identity is a dialectic between freedom and nurturance, between learning self-reliance and retaining affiliation. Thus Angelina has to mouth the jargon of phony "feminine" sensibility before she recovers her "natural feeling" and abandons her "accustomed cant"; she must leave home in order to find home. It's important that she needs to identify her own errors before she can recognize in Lady Frances the previously unknown friend-*cum*-mother whom she has always wanted (2, pp. 304–5). She ran away, wishing "for a friend, to whom I could open my whole heart, and whom I could love and esteem, and who should have the same tastes, and notions with myself," she tells Lady Frances at the tale's conclusion; and Lady Frances smilingly reminds her and us that women's friendship is not symbiotic identification, that mother and daughter figures must "recognize" both difference and connection (2, p. 241).

Angelina's quest puts her up against a multiplicity of languages and systems of ordering the world (much of the plot has to do with linguistic misunderstandings), and Edgeworth multiplies mother-daughter dyads to set her choices in perspective as well. Maternal helpers and hindering witches proliferate along her route, and so do daughters, from Betty Williams, the hilariously ignorant Welsh girl playing Sancho for Angelina's Quixote, to Scottish Clara Hope, another little girl lost, whom Lady Frances has taken under her wing. If Betty's materiality—imaged in her clumsiness and hunger for "heggs and pacon and toasted cheese"—usefully teaches Angelina about life's realities, the schoolgirl Clara offers an opportunity for Angelina to mature through nurturing an emigrant French lad (2, p. 193). " '[T]is a sad thing to be in a strange country, far away from one's ane kin and happy hame—poor wee thing!" observes Clara (2, p. 203), and Agelina's generous recognition of their mutual displacement converts these two into *real* "unknown friends," who are ultimately pivotal in uniting her with Lady Frances. But the most striking of the daughters against whom Angelina is measured is a very different unknown, another runaway who shows us how we must value Angelina's idealism despite her delusions. Miss Burrage, Lady Di's sycophant companion who had been as determined to shed her bourgeois identity and kind aunt to ape the fashionable world as Angelina was eager to abandon it, is ultimately unmasked as only "daughter to a drysalter, niece to a cheese-monger" (2, p. 253). Should

Lady Di prove stiff about Angelina's indiscretion, strong-minded Lady Frances has her *sister's* unknown friend, the now banished Hetty Burrage, in reserve: "[I]t always provokes me, to see a person afraid to do, what they think right. . . . What signifies the uneasiness we may suffer from the idle blame or tittle-tattle of the day," she warns Lady Di (2, p. 215).

In his introduction to Maria Edgeworth for the English Novelists Series almost forty years ago, P. H. Newby remarked that "whereas Jane Austen was so much the better novelist Maria Edgeworth may be the more important." Newby notes that Austen brought to perfection realist ground that had already been tilled, whereas Edgeworth subdued new territory: child psychology, the peasant mind as well as that of the resolute woman of affairs, and regional fiction (1950, pp. 93–94). He does not mention her colonizing the now-flourishing field of adolescent literature, though as "Angelina" richly demonstrates, she was a poineer here too. Without denigrating Austen, feminist critics are in a position to challenge that "so much" and to revaluate Edgeworth's artistry as a founding mother of the novel—as does Austen herself in *North-anger Abbey* (1818). Similarly, even as we continue to explore the significance and complexities of Edgeworth's literary partnership with Richard Lovell (a partnership she insisted on more than he), we should also expand the daddy's girl paradigm to accommodate the motherless child who triumphantly created in both art and life the nurturance she needed. If the historical linkage of authorship and paternity that Sandra Gilbert and Susan Gubar outline has been a constraining metaphor of creativity against which women writers have had to struggle, their literature for youth implies an alternative association of gender and generativity, of textual production and reproduction. Few female authors assume the male voice so convincingly as Maria Edgeworth in her daddy's girl mode, but many of the genres she developed and the role that those genres played in her life delineate a maternal model of authorship, an intertwining of art and life in which creativity and nurturance (of self and reader), story and child, are homologous. In writing, "Angelina" at the crucial beginning of a marriage that mattered so much to her domestic happiness, Edgeworth gives birth to a story that both dreams and predicts an idealized mother-daughter relationship. And just as Lady Frances and Angelina come home to Bristol together, so Maria found in Frances a loving mother-friend and in Fanny a daughter-sister who became "100,000,000,000,000,000,000,—in short incaluclably dearer to me . . . than any infant could be to the most unreasonably fond mother" (Edgar F. MacDonald 1977, p. 98).

## NOTES

[1]Story's tribute in his Phi Beta Kappa discourse nicely demonstrates two points: the woman writer's rise in standing during the key years of Edgeworth's career, a progress toward which her fame contributed much, and Edgeworth's own stature and transatlantic reputation. The American Story is ranking her with what the period acclaimed its greatest novelist. Yeat's commentary

is riddled with factual error, yet his artistic assessment still rings true. Almost a century later, Edgeworth is once again being rediscovered as a major Irish writer; see for example the anthology of essays by Cóilín Owens (1987) and the studies by W. J. McCormack (1985) and Anthony Cronin (1982). Surprisingly, she had seldom been the topic of sustained feminist attention; exceptions include Iain Topliss (1981); Dale Spender (1986); Mitzi Myers (1988); and Beth Kowaleski-Wallace (1988).

[2]John Ward, who had reviewed Edgeworth's fiction perceptively and favorably, was taken by Austen's more traditionally feminine focus when her novels began to appear: "She has not so much fine humor . . . Miss Edgeworth, but she is more skillful in contriving a story, she has a great deal more feeling, and she never plagues you with any chemistry, mechanics, or political economy, which are all excellent things in their way, but vile, cold-hearted trash in a novel, and, I piously hope, all of old Edgeworth's putting in. . . . I heard some time ago that the wretch was ill. Heaven grant that he may soon pop off" (1814 letter, p. 251).

[3]This mode of flattery harks back to the eighteenth century's use of "manly" to praise the intellectual woman; Mary Wollstonecraft uses it, as do many male critics. The vicissitudes of Maria Edgeworth's reputation—her extraordinary fame in her own day, her surprising neglect in ours, as well as the varied explanatory models of her achievement predicated on one relation or another with her father—solicit investigation from an enlightened historical and feminist perspective. For a typical overview focused primarily on attitudes toward Richard Lovell, see chapter 1 of James Newcomer's 1967 study. Additional examples of the critics' father fixation include Rowland Grey's 1909b and Patrick Murray's 1971 essays and the sections on the Edgeworths in Frank Swinnerton's 1966 and Maggie Lane's 1989 studies of literary fathers and daughters. It seems symbolically appropriate that Lane has reproduced a spurious portrait of Maria without knowing that it's purely an artist's invention (bound between p. 160 and 161)! A note about nomenclature: in contrast to most studies, I use "Edgeworth" to refer to the daughter; when confusion might result, I refer to "Maria" and "Richard Lovell."

[4]P. H. Newby's is a good example of the statement obligatory in all discussion of Maria: "But there is only one way of approaching Maria Edgeworth. Because of the extraordinary influence he wielded over his daughter's mind we have, first of all, to make the acquaintance of her father" (1950, p. 10). Anticipating the lines of Butler's argument, Newby finds that Richard Lovell's undue influence resulted not from coercion, but from his having been "one of the most successful husbands and fathers on record" (twenty-two children by four wives, two of them sisters, and all the commingled families living cheerfully together), "he so conducted himself as to cause his daughter to love him uncritically and therefore adopt his precepts on literature and life unquestioningly" (pp. 18–19). Whether Maria's work is in fact this unquestioning must be a central question in feminist reassessment.

[5]"Where should I be without my father? I should sink into that nothing from which he has raised me" (Butler, 1972, p. 207). Maria's letters abound in such extravagant statements of affection for her father. The coolly rational persona she presented to the public was very different from her volatile private self; her Aunt Ruxton, her last stepmother Frances, and her sister-daughter Fanny, among others, were also recipients of Maria's unbounded family affections. Despite its elisions about her neglected early childhood, Maria's own account of her writing partnership with her father in the *Memoirs* that she completed for him rings true. She thought of him not as a dictator, but as the encourager who signed himself, "your critic, partner, father, friend" (*Memoirs,* 1821 ed., 2, p. 198).

[6]For example, Hawthorne writes, "According to Mr. Edgeworth, a personality that is neither wholly reasonable nor wholly passionate does not and cannot exist" (p. 32), though the personality emerging from Richard Lovell's engaging *Memoirs* (admired by Virginia Woolf) conflates precisely these supposedly incompatible orientations. Hawthorne's thesis requires that Richard

Lovell be a rigidly Utilitarian, ultra-rational scapegoat. In fact, father and daughter shared a resilience, impulsiveness, and volubility that Hawthorne's outmoded faculty psychology can't accommodate.

[7]Gilbert and Gubar's readings predicate one archetypal female text, as their title indicates, and one archetypal conflicted stance of the woman writer toward her profession: "Maria Edgeworth must have struggled with the conflict between her desire to fulfill her father's wishes by living out his plots and her need to assert her own talents" (1979, p. 152). As a matter of fact, Maria was more given to moral instruction than her father, whose startlingly frank *Memoirs* still gives one pause. Of *Leonora* (1806), perhaps her most "feminine" fiction, she observed in 1818, "He never liked Leonora—he thought it too prosing in morality—he though it would not succeed" ("Letter of Maria Edgeworth," 1923, p. 488). Every feminist critic must recognize Gilbert and Gubar's achievement, but that need not prevent us from also recognizing its lapses, especially where pre-Victorian work is concerned. As Jane Spencer (1986) points out in her survey of the woman novelist's rise, "In the eighteenth century we can detect the presence of a view of writing that links it to the feminine literary production" (1986, p. xi). Myra Jehlen and Rachel Blau DePlessis's review of Gilbert and Gubar provides an excellent assessment of *Madwoman's* strengths and weaknesses. Acknowledging the author's "tongue of power," the reviewers investigate how the study's one "universal psyche" makes earlier works richly accessible to modern readers at the expense of translating their writers out of their own history, "so that finally both work and writer seem taken out of context, the context, that is, of their particular situation as it is *not* part of our world or congruent with our meanings" (Jehlen and DePlessis, 1981, p. 543). Other recent critiques of Gilbert and Gubar's governing assumptions include Toril Moi's (1985); and Janet Todd's (1988); see also June Howard's 1988 review essay for a relevant survey of recent feminist critical thinking.

[8]Gilbert and Gubar observe that "its meticulous research and its fine insight into Edgeworth's literary and pedagogic writings notwithstanding, Marilyn Butler's literary biography seems dedicated to justifying Richard Lovell Edgeworth against the charges of female Victorian biographers who cast him in the role of a villain" (1979, p. 655, note 4).

[9]For a useful overview of the difficulties involved in assessing women's writing, see Ruth Perry's 1988 study.

[10]Given the extraordinary impact of Richard Lovell's mother on his character and educational ideas (fully documented in his *Memoirs*), not to mention that of his second wife, the deeply beloved Honora (the maternal originator of the family educational enterprise), or that of his fourth, Frances, whom he praised from his deathbed, one wonders whether Richard Lovell shouldn't be termed "mamma's boy"; and, given Maria's address in using her writing to forge a paternal partnership, whether the "father's seduction" isn't just as apt a term. Jane Gallop's *The Daughter's Seduction* (1982) is a relevant critique of our tendency to mythologize the father's power.

[11]Edgeworth's fictions abound in idealized country gentlemen, good landlords, and informed educators like Richard Lovell, but they are never focal in the way that Lady Delacour in *Belinda* and Lady Davenant in *Helen* are. Notably, too, these maternal figures, though worldly wise, powerful, and witty mistresses of language, are flawed characters who learn from their "daughters." In each novel, both a real daughter and a surrogate daughter highlight the mentoria's lapses. Indeed, for an author obsessed with domestic affection, Edgeworth displays extraordinary insight into parental error and family dissension. *Belinda* and *Helen* have recently been reprinted in Pandora Press's "Mothers of the Novel" series.

[12]The manuscript draft page is among the Edgeworth papers, Bodleian Library, Oxford, along with an enormous amount of other material (including many family letters) recently deposited through the generous gift of Mrs. Christina Colvin, who shared her intimate knowledge of family history.

[13]All Edgeworth's biographers, from the Victorian women whom Butler denigrates to Butler herself, have much to say about Edgeworth's domestic circumstances. See Myers, 1988, for feminist theoretical perspective on these circumstances (especially notes 12–13 and 22). An 1811 letter refers to "my father who says the defect of my character is an inordinate desire to be beloved," and Richard Lovell's 1817 deathbed injunctions reiterate the same motif: Maria writes that "his last exhortation was against the indulgence of weak and vain sensibility . . . the defect of my disposition" (letters in Butler 1972, p. 477; and Grey 1909a, p. 260, respectively).

[14]*Northanger Abbey*'s defense of the woman novelist praises Edgeworth's *Belinda* (1801) for its language, wit and humor, knowledge of human nature, and the "greatest powers of the mind" (1818, p. 38). In characterizing the unspectacularly feminist American "woman's fiction" that "represented a protest against long-entrenched trivializing and contemptuous views of women," Nina Baym gives passing credit to English women moralists, "especially Maria Edgeworth, with her combination of educational intention, moral fabulating, and description of manners and customs." Women brought up on Edgeworth attempted to adapt to the American scene the "clarity of Edgeworth's exemplary fiction blended with the accuracy of her regional novels" (1978, p. 29). Similar brief credits can be found in Josephine Donovan (1983, pp. 21–23) and Sandra A. Zagarell (1988, pp. 500–01), but Beverly R. Voloshin (1984) fails even to mention a prime source for the female *Bildungsroman* tradition she opposes to restrictive domesticity. Yet Catharine Maria Sedgwick, one of Voloshin's key examples, pays tribute to Edgeworth's inspiration by dedicating *A New-England Tale* (1822) to "Maria Edgeworth, as a Slight Expression of the Writer's Sense of her Eminent Services in the Great Cause of Human Improvement."

[15]The Edgeworths' collaborative manual of 1798, *Practical Education*, a very readable how-to-teach-children-to-think-for-themselves guide for enlightened parents, especially mothers, has won extraordinary praise from educational historians for its innovative approach. Brian Simon (1960) terms it "the most significant contemporary work on pedagogy"; Alice Paterson pronounces it the "most important work on general pedagogy" to appear in England between Locke and the mid-Victorian periods (1960, p. 25; 1914, pp. v–vi, respectively). Steven Shapin and Barry Barnes (1976); Geraldine E. Hodgson (1912); and Bertha Coolidge (1936) similarly stress how far in advance of its period the book was, Coolidge judging it "almost as modern as if it had been conceived today" (p. 609). Recognizing femininity as a social construction, the Edgeworths differentiate as little as culturally possible between male and female education; girls too must relfect and judge for themselves. The educational treatise is not only significant in itself, but also because Edgeworth's fiction for young women has frequently been read as illustrating its tenets.

[16]In 1805, for example, Maria wrote to her cousin Sophy, "My father has excited my ambition to write a *useful* essay upon professional education: he has pointed out to me that to be a mere writer of pretty stories & novelettes would be unworthy of his partner, pupil & daughter" (Butler 1972, p. 209).

[17]I have explored the story more fully in Myers, 1989b.

[18]The relation between the "rational," abstract epistemologies most highly valued in Western culture and the more personal and empirical strategies our gender symbolism associates with women is explored more theoretically by Mary Hawkesworth (1989), a useful analysis of a large body of recent work; and Alison M. Jagger and Susan R. Bordo (1989). Undoing simplistic binary oppositions of reason and feeling is essential to understanding Georgian women like Edgeworth, whose model of ideal womanhood unites rationality and empathy.

[19]Chodorow argues for the "central importance of the mother-daughter relationship for women" (1974, pp. 43–44). Because of a girl's indentification with her mother, the female personality is more oriented toward the "communal" than the "agentic." It is characterized by more flexible ego boundaries and a more relational cognitive style, empathetic qualities continually reproduced

by cultural patterning, as Chodorow elaborates in her 1978 study. Despite the tendency toward psychoanalytical totalizing and ahistoricism, Chodorow's observations are richly applicable to writing for children.

[20]An enormous amount has been written about the French Revolution's impact on English literature, most of it relating to male Romantic poets or to Jane Austen. Except for radicals like Mary Wollstonecraft and Mary Hays, women writers' fictions have usually been read as defending the status quo. Marilyn Butler's classic formulation of the conservative reading in *Jane Austen and the War of Ideas* (1975) has recently been challenged by Claudia L. Johnson's *Jane Austen: Women, Politics, and the Novel* (1988). Despite their differences, both usefully establish how seemingly domestic female fictions may encode political commentary.

[21]Late-eighteenth-century and nineteenth-century women writers' "didacticism" was often the object of their male contemporaries' amused commentary. Byron skewered his day's outstanding female authors (among them Edgeworth) in *Don Juan* (1819; canto 1, line 15) for their obsession with education and improvement, and the minor poet Samuel Rogers similarly jested: "How strange it is that while we men are modestly content to amuse by our writings, women must be didactic. . . . Miss Edgeworth is a schoolmistress in her tales" (Robinson, 1938, p. 436, 6 Jan. 1834). However, teaching genres sustain both personal fantasies of being cared for and public projects of caring for others which allow the woman writer to speak with cultural authority; see Myers, 1988, p. 78, and 1986.

[22]Names often have rich symbolic associations for Edgeworth; she returns to the same names for her heroines over and over. Several seem variants on the name of "Honora," her chillingly perfect first stepmother. "Rosamond," the autobiographical child character whose growing up she traced in stories written over many years, is indebted to her own passion for flowers and gardening. "Frances" here compliments Frances Beaufort, who became Richard Lovell's fourth and last wife in 1798; she contributed illustrations for the five-volume first edition. Frances is also the name of "The Good Aunt," the mother-teacher in another of the *Moral Tales* (1801, 1974, 2, pp. 1–144).

[23]The "little woman" appears again in *Memoir,* 1867, 1, 233. For the history and multiple variants of the rhyme, see Iona Opie and Peter Opie, 1951, 1975, pp. 427–29.

[24]For fuller discussion of the Rosamond series, see Myers, 1986; 1989a. Edgeworth's discussion of her fiction is in *Memoir,* 1867: 3, pp. 144–60. Maria's involvement in relational interaction also extends to letter writing; she composed over 2,000 to her family alone and many are very long. Although Cronin tries to make Edgeworth's fascination with talk and paucity of plot distinctively Irish—"Maria stands at the beginning of that devouring interest in speech, which was to run right through to the twentieth century"—gender seems to me more important here than nationality (1982, p. 25). The typical form of the Georgian juvenile tale is a dyadic interaction between mother and child, and many other women writers have confessed to difficulties with linear plots. For a typical example, see Elizabeth Ammons on Sarah Orne Jewett (1983).

[25]The stories went through many editions and were also often reprinted separately, even into the 1930s. In his study of American popular fiction, Frank Luther Mott (1947) lists them among the "better sellers" in America as well (p. 317).

[26]"Conformable" means not "conformist," but presenting a complex world realistically. Like his modern counterparts, Richard Lovell assumes that young adult stories need to address social realities even more than realistic children's stories do, because adolescent readers are becoming social participants. Modern young-adult fiction extends this realistic bent to brutally frank "problem" fiction about everything from sex to drugs to parental abuse.

[27]Conservative reformers like the Anglican Trimmers and the Evangelical Hannah More shared much with the radical Mary Wollstonecraft and the liberal Edgeworths, despite religious and political differences, because all promoted emergent middle-class professional and domestic values, including an emphasis on mothering and childhood. (See, e.g., Myers, 1982; Kelly, 1986; Armstrong, 1987; and Davidoff and Hall, 1987.)

[28]Useful overviews of mock romances deriving from Don Quixote as deluded reader include Shepperson, 1936 and Staves, 1972.

[29]For a useful survey of narrative voice in literature for youth, see Kuznets, 1989, Otten and Schmidt, 1989.

# REFERENCES

A dozen of novels. (1834). *Fraser's magazine for town and country 9:* (52) (April), 456–87.

Ammons, Elizabeth. (1983). Going in circles: The Female geography of Jewett's *Country of the pointed firs. Studies in the Literary Imagination 16:* (2) (Fall), 83–92.

Armstrong, Nancy. (1987). The rise of the domestic woman. In Nancy Armstrong and Leonard Tennenhouse (Eds.), *The ideology of conduct: Essays on literature and the history of sexuality* (pp. 96–141). London: Methuen.

Austen, Jane. (1818). *Northanger abbey and persuasion.* In R. W. Chapman (Ed.), 3rd ed. 1933, rpt. 1959. *The novels of Jane Austen* (Vol. 5). London: Oxford University Press.

Baym, Nina. (1978). *Women's fiction: A Guide to novels by and about women in America, 1820–1870.* Ithaca: Cornell University Press.

Belenky, Mary Field; Clinchy, Blythe McVicker; Goldberger, Nancy Rule; and Mattuck Tarule, Jill. (1986). *Women's ways of knowing: The development of self, voice, and mind.* New York: Basic Books.

Benjamin, Jessica. (1986). A desire of one's own: Psychoanalytical feminism and intersubjective space. In Teresa de Lauretis (Ed.), *Feminist studies/critical studies* (pp. 78–101). Bloomington, IN: Indiana University Press.

Butler, Marilyn. (1972). *Maria Edgeworth: A literary biography.* Oxford: Clarendon Press.

Butler, Marilyn. (1975). *Jane Austen and the war of ideas.* Oxford: Clarendon Press.

Byron, Lord (George Gordon). (1819–1824, 1958). *Don Juan.* Edited by Leslie A. Marchand. Riverside Editions. Boston: Houghton Mifflin.

Chodorow, Nancy. (1974). Family structure and feminine personality. In Michelle Zimbalist Rosaldo and Louise Lamphere (Eds.), *Women, culture, and society* (pp. 43–65). Stanford: Stanford University Press.

Chodorow, Nancy. (1978). *The reproduction of mothering: Psychoanalysis and the sociology of gender.* Berkeley: University of California Press.

Coolidge, Bertha. (1936). Practical education. *The Colophon new series 1* (4), 604–609.

Cronin, Anthony. (1982). Maria Edgeworth: The unlikely precursor. *Heritage now: Irish literature in the English language* (pp. 17–29). Dingle, Ireland: Brandon Book Publishers.

Davidoff, Leonore, and Hall, Catherine. (1987). *Family fortunes: Men and women of the English middle class, 1780–1850.* London: Hutchinson.

Donovan, Josephine. (1983). *New England local color literature: A woman's tradition.* New York: Continuum; Frederick Ungar.

[Edgeworth family]. (1867). *A memoir of Maria Edgeworth, with a selection from her letters by the late Mrs. [Frances] Edgeworth* (3 Vols.). Edited by Her Children. London: Privately printed by Joseph Master and Son.

Edgeworth, Maria, and Edgeworth, Richard Lovell. (1798). *Practical education* (2 Vols. in 1). London: Joseph Johnson.

Edgeworth, Maria. (1801, 1974). Angelina; or, L'amie inconnue. In *Moral tales for young people* (2nd ed. of 1802 rpt. in 3 Vols.). London: J. Johnson. The Feminist Controversy in England 1788–1810 Series. New York and London: Garland, 2, 147–255.

Edgeworth, Maria. (1801,1974). Forester. In *Moral tales for young people* (2nd ed. of 1802 rpt. in 3 Vols.). London: J. Johnson. The Feminist Controversy in England 1788–1810 Series. New York and London: Garland, 1, 1-194.

Edgeworth, Maria. (1801, 1974). The good aunt. In *Moral tales for young people* (2nd ed. of 1802 rpt. in 3 Vols.). London: J. Johnson. The Feminist Controversy in England 1788–1810 Series. New York and London: Garland, 2, 1–144.

Edgeworth, Maria. (1801, 1974). The good French governess. In *Moral tales for young people* (2nd ed. of 1802 rpt. in 3 Vols.). London: J. Johnson. The Feminist Controversy in England 1788–1810 Series. New York and London: Garland, 3, 1–144.

Edgeworth, Maria. (1801, 1986). *Belinda*. Mothers of the Novel Series. London: Pandora.

Edgeworth, Maria. (1809). *Tales of fashionable life* (3rd ed. 3 Vols.). London: J. Johnson.

Edgeworth, Maria. (1812). *Tales of fashionable life* (3 Vols.). London: J. Johnson.

Edgeworth, Maria. (1834, 1987). *Helen*. Mothers of the Novel Series. London; Pandora.

Edgeworth, Maria. (1923). Letter of Maria Edgeworth to Mr. Hunter, 1818. *Notes and Queries* 12th ser. 12 (June 23), 488.

Edgeworth, Richard Lovell, and Edgeworth, Maria. (1820, 1821). *Memoirs of Richard Lovell Edgeworth, Esq: Begun by himself and concluded by his daughter, Maria Edgeworth* (2 Vols. in 1). Boston: Wells and Lilly.

Gallop, Jane. (1982). *The daughter's seduction: Feminism and psychoanalysis*. Ithaca: Cornell University Press.

Gilbert, Sandra M., and Gubar, Susan. (1979). *The madwoman in the attic: The woman writer and the nineteenth-century literary imagination* (pp. 146–53). New Haven: Yale University Press.

Gilbert, Sandra M., and Gubar, Susan. (Eds.) (1985). *The Norton anthology of literature by Women: The tradition in English* (pp. 187–94). New York and London: W. W. Norton.

Gilligan, Carol. (1982). *In a different voice: Psychological theory and women's development*. Cambridge: Harvard University Press.

Grey, Rowland. (1909a). Maria Edgeworth and Etienne Dumont. *Dublin Review 145*, 239–65.

Grey, Rowland. (1909b). Heavy fathers. *Fortnightly Review 86*, 80–89.

Hawkesworth, Mary. (1989). Knowers, knowing, known: Feminist theory and claims of truth. *Signs: Journal of Women in Culture and Society 14* (3) (Spring), 533–557.

Hawthorne, Mark D. (1967). *Doubt and dogma in Maria Edgeworth*. Gainsville: University of Florida Press.

Hodgson, Geraldine E. (1912). *Rationalist English educators*. London: Society for Promoting Christian Knowledge.

Howard, June. (1988). Feminist differings: Recent surveys of feminist literary theory and criticism [a review essay]. *Feminist Studies 14* (1) (Spring), 167–190.

Hunt, Peter. (1985). Necessary misreadings: Directions in narrative theory for children's literature. *Studies in the Literary Imagination 17* (2) (Fall), 107–21.

Jagger, Alison M., and Bordo, Susan R. (Eds.). 1989. *Gender/body/knowledge: Feminist reconstruction of being and knowing*. New Brunswick: Rutgers University Press.

Jehlen, Myra, and DuPlessis, Rachel Blau. (1981). "The tongue of power." *Feminist Studies 7* (3) (Summer), 539–46.

Johnson, Claudia L. (1988). *Jane Austen: Women, politics, and the novel*. Chicago: University of Chicago Press.

Kahane, Claire. (1988). Questioning the maternal voice. *Genders 3* (Fall), 82–91.

Kelly, Gary. (1986). Jane Austen and the English novel of the 1790s. In Mary Anne Schofield and Cecilia Macheski (Eds.), *Fetter'd or free? British women novelists, 1670–1815* (pp. 285–306). Athens: Ohio University Press.

Kowaleski-Wallace, Beth. (1988). Home economics: Domestic ideology in Maria Edgeworth's *Belinda*. *The Eighteenth Century: Theory and Interpretation 29* (3) (Fall), 242–262.

Kuznets, Lois R. (1989). Henry James and the storyteller: The development of a central consciousness in realistic fiction for children. In Charlotte F. Otten and Gary D. Schmidt (Eds.), *The voice of the narrator in children's literature: Insights from writers and critics* (pp. 187–98). New York: Greenwood Press.

Lane, Maggie. (1989). *Literary daughters* (pp. 51–74). New York: St. Martin's Press.

MacDonald, Edgar E. (Ed.) (1977). *The education of the heart: The correspondence of Rachel Mordecai Lazarus and Maria Edgeworth*. Chapel Hill: University of North Carolina Press.

Madden, Lionel. (Ed.) (1972). *Robert Southey: The critical heritage*. London: Routledge and Kegan Paul.

McCormack, W. J. (1985). *Ascendancy and tradition in Anglo-Irish literary history from 1789 to 1939* (pp. 97–122). Oxford: Clarendon Press.

Moi, Toril. (1985). *Sexual/textual politics: Feminist literary theory*. London: Methuen.

Mott, Frank Luther. (1947). *Golden multitudes: The story of best sellers in the United States*. New York: Macmillan.

Murray, Patrick. (1971). Maria Edgeworth and her father: The literary partnership. *Eire-Ireland 6* (3), 39–50.

Myers, Mitzi. (1982). Reform or ruin: "A revolution in female manners." In Harry C. Payne (Ed.), *Studies in Eighteenth-Century Culture* (pp. 119–216). Madison: University of Wisconsin Press.

Myers, Mitzi. (1986). Impeccable governesses, rational dames, and moral mothers: Mary Wollstonecraft and the female tradition in Georgian children's books. In Margaret Higonnet and Barbara Rosen (Eds.), *Children's literature* (pp. 31–59). New Haven: Yale University Press, 14,

Myers, Mitzi. (1988). The dilemmas of gender as double-voiced narrative; or, Maria Edgeworth mothers the *Bildungsroman*. In Robert W. Uphaus (Ed.), *The idea of the novel in the eighteenth century* (pp. 67–96). East Lansing, MI: Colleagues Press.

Myers, Mitzi. (1989a). Quixotes, orphans, and subjectivity: Maria Edgeworth's Georgian heroinism and the (en)gendering of young adult fiction. *The Lion and the Unicorn: A Critical Journal of children's literature, 13* (1), 21–40.

Myers, Mitzi. (1989b). Socializing Rosamond: Educational ideology and fictional form. *Children's Literature Association Quarterly, 14* (2) (Summer), 52–58.

Newby, P. H. (1950). *Maria Edgeworth*. English Novelists Series. London: Arthur Barker.

Newcomer, James. (1967). *Maria Edgeworth the novelist, 1767–1849: A bicentennial study*. Fort Worth: Texas Christian University Press.

Newman, Gerald. (1987). *The rise of English nationalism: A cultural history, 1740–1830*. New York: St. Martin's Press.

Opie, Iona, and Opie, Peter. (Eds.) (1951, 1975). *The Oxford dictionary of nursery rhymes*. London: Oxford University Press.

Otten, Charlotte F., and Schmidt, Gary D. (Eds.) (1989). *The voice of the narrator in children's literature: Insights from writers and critics*. New York: Greenwood Press.

Owens, Cóilín (Ed.) (1987). *Family chronicles: Maria Edgeworth's* Castle Rackrent. The Appraisal Series. Dublin: Wolfhound Press.

Paterson, A[lice]. (1914). *The Edgeworths: A study of later eighteenth century education*. London: W. B. Clive; University Tutorial Press.

Perry, Ruth. (1988). Some methodological implications of the study of women's writing. *Harvard Library Bulletin 35* (2) (Winter), 230–248.

Robinson, Henry Crabb. (1983). *Henry Crabb Robinson on books and their writers*. Edited by Edith J. Morley. 3 Vols. London: J. M. Dent.

Rose, Jacqueline. (1984). *The case of Peter Pan, or The impossibility of children's fiction*. London: Macmillan.

Ruddick, Sara. (1980). Maternal thinking. *Feminist Studies 6* (2) (Summer), 342–367.

Ruddick, Sara. (1989). *Maternal thinking: Toward a politics of peace.* Boston: Beacon Press.

Scott, Sir Walter. (1934). *The letters of Sir Walter Scott, 1821–1823* (vol. 7 of 12 Vols.). Edited by H. J. C. Grierson. London: Constable.

[Sedgwick, Catharine Maria]. (1822). *A New-England tale* (2nd ed.). New York: E. Bliss and E. White.

Shapin, Steven, and Barnes, Barry. (1976). Head and hand: Rhetorical resources in British pedagogical writing, 1770–1850. *Oxford Review of Education 2* (3), 231–54.

Shepperson, Archibald Bolling. (1936). *The novel in Motley: A history of the burlesque novel in English.* Cambridge: Harvard University Press.

Simon, Brian. (1960). *Studies in the history of education 1780–1870.* London: Lawrence and . Wishart.

Spencer, Jane. (1986). *The Rise of the woman novelist from Aphra Behn to Jane Austen.* Oxford: Basil Blackwell

Spender, Dale. (1986). *Mothers of the novel: 100 good women writers before Jane Austen* (pp. 270–300). London: Pandora Press.

Staves, Susan. (1972). Don Quixote in eighteenth-century England. *Comparative Literature 24* (3), 193–215.

Swinnerton, Frank. (1966). *A galaxy of fathers* (pp. 154–218). London: Hutchinson.

Todd, Janet. (1988). *Feminist literary history: A defense.* London: Polity Press.

Topliss, Iain. (1981). Mary Wollstonecraft and Maria Edgeworth's modern ladies. *Études Irlandaises,* 6, 13–31.

Trimmer, Mrs. [Sarah]. (1802–6). *The guardian of education; Consisting of a practical essay on Christian education and a copius examination of modern systems of education, children's books, and books for young persons* (5 Vols.). London: J. Hatchard.

Voloshin, Beverly R. (1984). The limits of domesticity: The female *Bildungsroman* in America. *Women's Studies 10* (3), 283–302.

Ward, John [Earl of Dudley]. (1905). In S. H. Rommilly (Ed.), *Letters to "Ivy"* [Mrs. Dugald Stewart] *from the First Earl of Dudley.* London: Longmans, Green.

Watson, George. (1980). Introduction. *Castle Rackrent.* By Maria Edgeworth. 1800. Edited by Watson. The World's Classics (pp. vii–xxv). Oxford: Oxford University Press,

Weedon, Chris. (1987). *Feminist practice and poststructuralist theory.* London: Basil Blackwell.

Welsh, Alexander. (1972). Maria Edgeworth and more Dickens [review essay]. *Yale Review 62* (2) (Dec.), 281–87.

Yeats, W. B. (1891, 1979). Introduction. In Mary Helen Thuente (Ed.), *Representative Irish Tales.* Atlantic Highlands, NJ: Humanities Press.

Zagarell, Sandra A. (1988). Narrative of community: The identification of a genre. *Signs: Journal of Women in Culture and Society 13* (3) (Spring), 498–527.

# Joanna Baillie and Mary Brunton:

## Women of the Manse

Mary McKerrow

## JOANNA BAILLIE 1762–1851

Her life was sheltered from all harsh contact with the world, she herself was never shaken by any of the passions that stir the soul of man to the depths. And yet she devoted the best years of her life to delineating those emotions which were personally unknown to her, and produced characters whose chief fault is that they show too plainly the power of emotion. (Margaret Sprague Carhart, 1923, p. 190)

While today it would be difficult to substantiate the assertion that Joanna Baillie's *own* emotional experiences were not of the same order as those which shook the soul of man to his depths, the above quotation from Margaret Carhart's 1923 biography of the Scottish poet and dramatist highlights one of Joanna Baillie's remarkable achievements: that in the context of a relatively sheltered life—as an eighteenth-and nineteenth-century lady and "daughter of the manse'—she went beyond the limits of her direct experience and produced manuscripts which encompassed the range of human passions.

She was born in Bothwell, Lanarkshire (September 11, 1762) the daughter of the Presbyterian minister of Shotts, Bothwell, and Hamilton, the Reverend James Baillie, and his wife Dorothea Hunter. The fact that Joanna had little parental affection in her childhood and was firmly repressed, as were her elder sister Agnes and her brother Matthew (all being subjected to the strictly religious regime which was a feature of the ministerial parenthood of the day), made it virtually essential for her to rebel in her own fashion, by finding self-expression in her writing.

At the age of ten, Joanna was sent to boarding school in Glasgow where she displayed many talents—musical, mathematical, and dramatic. (She was very good at creating characters, using dialogue, and acting, and she was soon writing plays which were performed by her schoolmates.) Then at the age of fourteen, her father was appointed Professor of Divinity at the University of Glasgow, and the family moved, conveniently, into university accommodation. But before Joanna could really benefit from the academic environment,

160

James Baillie died (only two years after his promotion), Dorothea and the children were thrown upon the generosity of her brother, Dr. William Hunter (one of the two famous Scots physician-surgeon brothers who practiced in London. He was obstetrician to Queen Charlotte).

The Baillie family moved to Long Calderwood in Lanarkshire, and then to London in 1784 where they settled in Windmill Street in the house which Matthew had inherited under the will of his Uncle William, as well as the Windmill Street School of Anatomy. After Matthew's marriage in 1791, Dorothea and her daughters moved to Hampstead where, after her death in 1806, Agnes and Joanna continued to live together.

London provided Joanna Baillie with the opportunity to launch a literary career. Moving away from the emerging genre of the novel she favored the more traditional forms of poetry and play-writing; her first volume of poems (*Fugitive Verses*) was published in 1790, and she also wrote a play during this period (*Arnold*), which did not survive.

Religious honesty—as a result of her Presbyterian indoctrination in childhood—was as important to Joanna Baillie as was intellectual honesty; she was a product of her time and, as a consequence, a deeply religious note was to appear in all her dramas. Between 1798 and 1812, her *Plays on the Passions* were published, a series in which an attempt was made to delineate the stronger passions of the mind, each passion being the subject of a tragedy and a comedy, so that each passion was allocated two separate plays. This was an ambitious exercise, an intellectual undertaking.

Like so many other women writers of her time, Baillie experienced the contradictions inherent in being a woman *and* a writer (and as an intellectual writer, one who dealt with human passions in the poetic and dramatic form, she was a writer who trespassed on the traditional territory of men). Not surprisingly, she elected to publish the first edition of *Plays on the Passions* anonymously, in the wake of the strong feeling that persisted at the time against a decent woman gaining a "reputation" as a writer.

But *Plays on the Passions* produced the kind of reaction which could only be described as a furor. Because of its supposedly "masculine" nature and the Scottish influence, it was at first thought to be the work of Sir Walter Scott; and, says Barbara Brandon Schnorrenberg (1984), "the discovery that the author was a woman caused considerable amazement for there seemed to be nothing "feminine" about its subject matter or style" (p. 36). By 1802, Joanna Baillie felt sufficiently brave to let her name appear on the title page of the second volume of the plays.

As a result of her unexpected acclaim as a newcomer to the literary scene, and with her name as a writer so flatteringly linked with that of the man whose name was on the lips of all lovers of Scottish writing—Walter Scott—it was inevitable that a correspondence should spring up between the two and that they should become close friends. Having respected each other's literary achievement, they met in Edinburgh in 1908. In his third canto of *Marmion*, Scott refers to Joanna Baillie as "the bold enchantress" and compares her to Shakespeare.

Concerned more with an analysis of the passions (she stated in the "Introductory Discourse" that she wanted to develop the noble view of emotion and self-knowledge, without the distraction of "bustles of plot, brilliancy of dialogue, and even the bold and striking in character"), Joanna Baillie's plays probably had more appeal to readers than to theater audiences. Yet her dramas still achieved considerable success.

The five-act play *De Montfort* (from the first volume) was produced by John Kemble at the Drury Lane Theatre in 1809, and he cast opposite himself Sarah Siddons (a close friend of Joanna Baillie's), as the leading lady, Jane. And from the second volume of plays, the comedy on hatred was produced at the English Opera House.

Other *Plays on the Passions* also had well-received showings; *Constantine and Valeriae* was staged successfully in London, Liverpool, Edinburgh and Dublin; *The Separation* appeared at Covent Garden; *Henriquiez* at Drury Lane; and, in 1810, *The Family Legend*—with a prologue by Walter Scott—was produced in Edinburgh.

With these performances, Joanna Baillie's fame spread. When Lord Byron was dining with Samuel Rogers, the banker, in St. James' Place, London, he discussed her in the same breath as Walter Scott. Byron admired her greatly and enjoyed her confidence.

Joanna Baillie earned her living by her pen. By the time her mother died in 1806, she was making enough money to support herself and her sister—and to give half her income to charity. She had a stimulating circle of friends and acquaintances from the world of science and letters (with Laetitia Barbauld, another close friend), and she was readily acknowledged as the leading British woman dramatist during the first part of the nineteenth century.

All in all, it was a pleasant and satisfying existence; Joanna Baillie must be counted among the women writers who were both successful and secure.

In 1826, at the age of sixty-three, she produced a drama, *The Martyr* (which was translated into Singhalese); this was followed by another tragedy, *The Bride* (1828), a story about Ceylon, and one which was dedicated to its people. These followed her collection of poems, chosen from the manuscripts of living authors and published in 1823. Her complete collection of poetical works appeared in an American edition in 1832, the year that she was penning, with great personal sadness, her *Lines on the Death of Walter Scott*. (Scott, the ballads of Robert Burns, and Scotland, were all influential in her poetry writing.)

Three volumes of her dramas were published in 1836 (*Miscellaneous Plays*); *Ahalya Baee: A Poem* was published in 1849 and *Dramatic and Poetical Works* in 1851.

In 1831, appeared *A View of the general tenour of the New Testament regarding the nature and dignity of Jesus Christ, including a collection of the various passages in the Gospels, Acts of the Apostles and the Epistles which relate to the subject,* but it was too late to be appreciated by Joanna's "younger admirer," Mary Brunton, who died in 1818, and who had been, like Sir Walter Scott and Lord Byron, a humble admirer at Joanna Baillie's feet. That Joanna had met William Wordsworth, Humphry Davy—and Maria Edgeworth—and that she had associated with some of the greatest poets of her day (such as Samuel Coleridge and Robert Southey), even that she had traveled on the continent with her sister, gave her a distinctive aura. But basically she was a Scot, with a strong moral and religious commitment—a daughter of the manse—and a woman of literary accomplishment. It was these qualities which influenced Mary Brunton to dedicate her first novel, *Self Control,* to Joanna Baillie when it was published in 1810. There were many motives behind her decision to also be an anonymous author. So Joanna Baillie did not know to whom she owed the compliment of the dedication, but she acknowledged it in a letter that she sent to the publishers which included her own criticisms of the novel for the benefit of the author, whoever he or she might be. Mary Brunton replied in her own name, giving a clear statement of her motives for producing the book and explaining how it came to be written. She agreed with most of the older woman's criticisms but explained at considerable length why she found it impracticable to make use of them.

It seems unlikely that these two women ever met. Joanna Baillie was in Edinburgh in 1808, but at that time *Self Control* was just being put together as an amusing exercise, with little thought of publication. After their initial contact by letter in 1810, there was a lively correspondence between the two; on Mary Brunton's death in 1818, Joanna Baillie penned a forty-seven line obituary poem for her literary friend. (It is included in Alexander Brunton's tribute to his wife, in his *Memoir* which appeared with her unfinished novel, *Emmeline,* in 1819.)

Inevitably Joanna Baillie had to face criticism of her work. The editor of the *Edinburgh Review,* Francis Jeffrey, wrote a long article on *Plays and Passions* in 1803, condemning her for trying to describe a person's character solely through passion, and criticizing her intention of giving her audience a moral uplift. (This reviewer could have been ahead of his time in seeing plays designed for amusement and not simply for serious purpose.) Later, perhaps with a sense of guilt at his damning words, he made certain expiation by referring to Joanna Baillie's talents as "superior to those of any of her contemporaries among the English writers of tragedy." But, understandably affronted by his earlier remarks, Joanna Baillie was disinclined to meet such a caustic critic. It was not until 1820 that she could agree to make contact with Francis Jeffrey, and she was surprised to find the man sufficiently fascinating to invite him to her home.

Undeterred by his daunting comments, she continued with her writing, producing *Metrical Legends of Exalted Characters* in 1821; in which she took as her subjects Wallace, Columbus, and Lady Grizel Baillie (1665–1746), the daughter of Sir Patrick Hume who had displayed such courage by feeding him for a month while he was hiding in the family vault after the discovery of the Rye House Plot against Charles II.

Like so many other female authors, Joanna Baillie tried to sidestep the stigma of the pointed finger at female intrusion into the masculine world, by plunging into a pattern of domesticity, making a point of presenting herself in the image of a knitter, a maker of puddings, and all the necessary trappings of the spinster lady of the nineteenth century. In 1814, when she was fifty-two, she—like Mary Astell before her—sent out notices requesting that she should be known as Mrs. Baillie as a mark of respect for her age and achievement. This was far from an eccentric indulgence; it was a device which many maiden ladies adopted in order to establish themselves as reputable citizens, possibly in exasperation at ever having been considered otherwise.

When she was 89, Joanna declared that she was tired of life, went to bed and died; so managing her own death as completely as she had her family's livelihood—no mean achievement in an age which disapproved of women earning their living.

Joanna Baillie was a woman writer whose works rank among the classical British dramas: "Her status is currently that of a virtual unknown, but renewed interest in literature written by women should reveal her to be an innovator whose efforts inspired both Scott and other Romantics to redefine the type of drama to appear on the English Stage" (Priscilla Dorr, 1988, p. 16).

When it is considered that Joanna Baillie's earnings from her writings equaled those of Sir Walter Scott in the early years of the nineteenth century, that she was hailed as a second Shakespeare and Scotland's greatest playwright, it does not seem too early for a reassessment of her work. Where, otherwise, is a nineteenth-century female dramatist of her caliber to be found?

## MARY BRUNTON—1778–1818

Whey should an epic or tragedy be supposed to hold such an exalted place in composition, while a novel is almost a nickname for a book? Does not a novel admit of as noble sentiments—as lively description—as natural character—as perfect unity of action—and a moral as irresistible as either of them? I protest, I think a fiction containing a just representation of human beings and of their actions—a connected, interesting, and profitable story, conducting to a useful and impressive moral lesson might be one of the greatest efforts of human genius. (Mary Brunton, Letter to Mrs. Izett, August 15, 1814)

Mary Brunton's forebears on her mother's side were Ligoniers, from Castres, near Toulouse; on her father's side, they were Balfours from Orkney. In the spring of 1776, a new officer was commissioned as Ensign in the 9th Regiment of Foot—Thomas Balfour (Army Lists, 1777). He came from an honorable and respected Orkney family, mainly resident there since 1560, with distinguished records in military service. The young Ensign was soon courting the Colonel's sister, Frances Ligonier, quickly winning her affection, for they were married within a year. That she was thirty-four, and he twenty-four, seemed of little importance. Thomas Balfour took his bride to Orkney to make her a new home on the tiny island of Burray. By January 1778 Frances Ligonier Balfour found that she was pregnant. Her brother Edward (himself childless) asked to be godfather so as to "accept the care and morals of my nephew" (Earl Ligonier to Thomas Belfour, Jan. 9, 1777). After Mary arrived on November 1, 1778—All Saints Day—he wrote to his sister:

> It is better than having a boy . . . for few mothers see much of their sons after five years of age. . . . (Earl & Lady Ligonier to Frances Balfour, December 6, 1778)

Edward's wife, Mary, was the godmother and wasted no time in telling Frances to take care of the baby's beauty. Her warm devotion to Mary was to put her in an awkward situation twenty years on.

Frances Balfour had a son, John Edward, fourteen months later, and another son William, in 1781 (Ligonier to T. Balfour, 1782). When Edward Ligonier died in 1782, Thomas Balfour decided to leave the army and concentrate on farming in Orkney. He moved his family to Elswick on Shapinsay Island and built a family house there called "Cliffdale." He was an extremely successful and popular laird (Patrick Bailey, 1974). Mary grew up happily there and later went to school in Edinburgh, staying with one of her father's sisters, enjoying reading poetry and fiction but writing nothing except what she called "vile rhymes" and letters.

Her first known letter is to her Aunt Mary, wife of Captain George Craigie of Saviskail, Orkney, dated February 4, 1795; it is beautifully written and composed. Another followed it on March 6 (Balfour Archives The Orkney Library). Just past sixteen, she was not too young to find a boyfriend, and so her association with Alexander Brunton, a student of classics and theology at the University of Edinburgh, began. He was six years older than she.

Leaving school at sixteen, Mary returned to Elswick to help with the housekeeping. Three years later there was a crisis. Her godmother, who after Edward's death had remarried and become Viscontess Wentworth, invited Mary to go and live with her in London. Frances might have been behind this offer, seeing life in Orkney as too restricted for her daughter and anxious for Mary to experience the social highlights of London which she enjoyed herself in her youth. Mary was devastated by indecision, for Alexander Brunton had asked her to marry him. She knew very well that marriage to a young Church of Scotland minister on a low stipend did not fit into the category of a "good" marriage which every mother wishes for her daughter, so she quickly and quietly arranged her marriage for December 4, 1798 (Francis James Grant,

1922), weeks after her twentieth birthday. That her mother was upset would be an understatement—"blackest ingratitude and perfidy" (Frances Balfour to Elizabeth Manson, 1798), were the words used. Thomas, in London at the time of the wedding, kept his feelings to himself.

This was the significant turning point in Mary's life which was to influence her future. She had behind her the ancestry of two distinguished families— French and Scottish—the right of entry into the highest London society. But, whether led already into a dedicated Christianity by the influences of her husband or led by her own philosophy of life that it was necessary to be useful, she moved with thankfulness into her role as the minister's wife in Bolton, East Lothian, in such pretty, country surroundings. She told another of her Orkney aunts, Elisabeth Manson, just six weeks after her marriage:

> . . . the world for me may bustle in vain. I shall join in its bustle no more. There is an excellent neighbourhood in which Mr. Brunton is much beloved. But where is he known and not beloved? (Mary Brunton to Elizabeth Manson, 1799)

Tackling the domestic economy with cheerful determination, she was never too busy to join her husband in his study every morning, listening to him reading aloud from works of criticism, history, and philosophy. A new dawning, a new realization of her need to read more and learn more had arrived. Studying German and mathematics failed, so she concentrated on drawing.

When two East Indian protégés of her husband's stayed at the manse, Mary found herself responsible for their religious instruction as well as their material needs (Alexander Brunton, 1819). To instruct them, she had to examine her own beliefs. This convinced her that Christianity must be an active principle in everyday life, something of brightness and peace—never dull and dutiful piety.

But the idyllic life in Bolton came to a close when Mr. B. (as Mary liked to call her husband) passed his thirtieth birthday and, seeking promotion, successfully applied to become one of the ministers at the New Greyfriars Church in Edinburgh. Mary felt that her world was falling apart. Her much-loved father had died at the early age of forty-six (Orkney Library, D2/12/5 1799). Her elder brother, John, had been killed in the Netherlands as Captain of part of the English Expeditionary Force which was defeated by the French. He was nineteen.

Frances, distraught and inconsolable in Larkney, sent long, depressing letters which Mary found difficult to answer. (Orkney Library, Ref. D2/53/20). Mary sent her own distress signal to her mother at the beginning of October 1802:

> I heartily regret the loss of my little quiet residence. . . . But when I think that Mr. B., without any object in view, might sink into indolence,—live neglected,— and die forgotten,—I am in part reconciled to a removal. . . . I think I could endure anything rather than see him, to please me, consign himself with regret to solitude and inaction. (Mary Brunton, 1802)

Dreading the Edinburgh move, Mary could not foresee that there she was to find a fulfillment which the quiet life of Bolton could never have produced. In Scotland's capital city, their circle of friends widened. They settled at 3 St. John's Street, Canongate. Neighbors at Number 6 were Mr. and Mrs. Chalmers Izett. He had a successful hatter's business, and she was an English-woman. Mary's friendship with Mrs. Izett was to influence her writing life. They had much in common: they read together, worked together, shared opinions, and helped each other, as neighbors do, whether they were in agreement or not. For fun, they discussed how to go about writing a novel. Mrs. Izett was often socially involved, so Mary started to write, purely for experiment and amusement. She knew that whatever she wrote had to be useful. But how did one put this into a novel that would attract the non-churchgoer? Perhaps it was on Mrs. Izett's advice that she decided that she must cloak any moral message in a blanket of romanticism, drama, human weakness, suffering, self-denial and pain. Agatha Christie, in *Mystery of the Blue Train*, has made her immortal hero, Hercule Poirot, remark that moral worth is not romantic, "it is appreciated, however, by widows." But Mary Brunton set about, in her leisure time, contriving a romantic novel with a moral message. Hercule Poirot would have been agreeably surprised.

Mary kept what she was writing from Mr. B. for some time, but, unable to keep it a secret, she was delighted that his surprise at her work was mingled with pleasure, and that he praised "the beauty and correctness of her style, her acuteness of observation and loftiness of sentiment" (Alexander Brunton, 1819). He, a little grudgingly, attributed his wife's successful manipulation of the English language to the teachings of her mother, which he had often thought more suited to a life at court than in a Scottish manse.

Publication was never in Mary's mind until a publisher friend came to dinner. She wanted Mr. B. to get into print and suggested that their friend might publish her husband's sermons and lectures. But Mr. B. was not ready for that. His best work, the *Persian Grammar,* was not to be published until 1822. Their friend told Mary that he would willingly publish a book of hers. This possibility had never occurred to her before, and she asked more than once if he was in earnest (Alexander Brunton, 1832). She returned with renewed purpose to her writing, faced with new problems as a result, but coping with them as they arose. If her book was to be published, she couldn't put her name to it, convinced as she was that it would be a failure, and fearing for repercussions on Mr. B. And because it mustn't have a misleading title, she called it *Self Control,* which she considered honest and *not* misleading. She carefully planned Chapter One so that any readers who idly flicked over the pages would find the virgin heroine, Laura Montreville, assailed, but not quite seduced by the wealthy rake, Colonel Hargrave, whom she loves. She is "throbbing with Hargrave's rapture for her" until he clasps her to him in a vehemence of passion and she sees him as her seducer. "Are you so base?" she cries, and sinks without motion to the ground—deathly pale. She banishes

Hargrave for two years, knowing that to marry him would solve her father's financial problems. Hargrave's predictable jealousy when he discovers that she had another suitor leads him to have her kidnapped and shipped off to Canada, where she is set afloat in an open boat down a fast-flowing river, alone.

As a preface to the book, Mary chose a piece from Book VI of William Cowper's mammoth poem, *The Task* (The Winter Walk at Noon):

> His warfare is within; There unfatigu'd
> His fervent spirit labours. There he fights,
> And there obtains fresh triumphs o'er himself,
> And never with'ring wreaths, compar'd with which
> The laurels that a Caesar reaps are weeds.

Mary, like many of her contemporaries, had felt a close affinity with Cowper, with his gentle spirit, his humanity, and his doubts about the welfare of his soul. She dedicated *Self Control* to another of her idols, Joanna Baillie, the Scottish poet and dramatist.

Mary's holiday with Mr. B. and the Izetts in Harrogate and the Lake District late in 1809 refreshed her. Her letters to her relations in Orkney give a lively picture of this tour (Mary Brunton, Letter to Frances Balfour, November 21, 1809).

The Edinburgh publishers, Manners & Miller, accepted *Self-Control* even though Mary had not quite finished her thirty-four chapter novel, but they wanted the book to appear during the commercially profitable part of the season. So meticulous was her composition that it was printed from the first copy. But she was upset and distracted because the Izetts had moved from Edinburgh to Kinnaird, near to Dundee. She tried to settle her prepublication nerves by a letter to her friend:

> Ask for me . . . that I may neither be elated by its success, nor fretted by its failure! Its failure! The very thought makes my flesh creep! I cannot express to you what a fellow-feeling I now have with the poor wretches whose works fall dead from the press. Well—well—by the end of February, or beginning of March, my rank in the scale of a literary being will be determined by a sentence from which there is no appeal. (Mary Brunton, 1810)

But she had no cause for worry. Within five days of publication, 240 copies of *Self-Control* were sold. A second printing was called for in just over a month and a third followed. She was a bestseller. By the beginning of February 1811, the news was out that she was the author. Jane Austen, by the end of April, had tried in vain to get a copy (Chapman, 1932). Mary told Mrs. Izett that the best parts of the book were attributed to Mr. B. and the defects to her. But she managed to deal with praise and criticism without finding herself "destitute of decent humility" (Mary Brunton, 1812).

On eventually obtaining a copy of *Self-Control,* Jane Austen was worried. She was revising *Sense and Sensibility* and felt afraid that her story might have been all forestalled, expressing her fears in a letter to her sister Cassandra on April 30, 1811. (Chapman, 1932, p. 278). By the autumn of 1813, *Self-Control* was still on her mind and she was telling Cassandra:

> I am looking over *Self-Control* again, and my opinion is confirmed of it being an excellently-meant, elegantly-written Work, without anything of Nature or Probability in it. I declare I do not know whether Laura's passage down the American River, is not the most natural, possible, everyday thing she does. (Chapman, 1932, p. 344)

Another year passed before Jane was telling Anna Lefroy of her intentions:

> writing a close imitation of *Self-Control* as soon as I can; — I will improve upon it, my Heroine shall not merely be wafted down an American river in a boat by herself, she shall cross the Atlantic in the same way, and never stop till she reaches Gravesend. (Chapman, 1932, p. 423)

As far as we know, Mary and Jane Austen never met. Clerical and ministerial environments strongly influenced the writings of nineteenth-century women novelists. Joanna Baillie's father was a minister and then Professor of Divinity at Glasgow University; Mary Brunton's husband was a minister at the Tron Church in Edinburgh and Professor of Hebrew and Oriental Studies at Edinburgh University; and in England, Jane Austen was a daughter of the rector of Stevenson. The Brontës produced their immortal novels in the religious atmosphere of their father's house at Haworth, as did Mrs. Gaskell under the roof of her Unitarian husband. The quiet atmosphere of the rectory or the manse could be very conducive to writing.

The Bruntons celebrated the success of Mary's first novel by going to London in 1812, Mary's first visit there. The entrancing descriptions of her experiences have to be read to be enjoyed (Mary Brunton, 1812). She visited Yorkshire, Doncaster, Sherwood Forest, Stamford, and Burleigh, went to an oratorio in Covent Garden, heard 7,000 children singing in St. Paul's, walked on Hampstead Heath and Richmond-hill, before seeing Windsor, Henley, Oxford, Magdalene College, the Radcliffe Library, and the Pomfret Marbles, coming home via Stratford and Warwick, where she saw and described the magnificent Warwick vase. Mr. B. reported that she suffered from "an anguish ailment" (Alexander Brunton, 1819) during this holiday which affected her health and spirits for a time, but she recovered from it.

The year 1813 was to bring the sadness of Frances' death. Mary and Mr. B. moved house to 35 Albany Row, later to become Albany Street, Edinburgh. Restless to start writing again, Mary could not decide on a subject. Eventually she took Mr. B.'s advice to continue the theme begun in *Self-Control:*

To show the means through which, when self-control has been neglected, the mind must be trained by suffering ere it can hope for usefulness or for true enjoyment. (Alexander Brunton, 1819)

Writing and composition were more laborious this time. Ellen, the heroine, made slow progress even though Mary tried to write every day. She was convinced that her "stock of wits" was not her own but was "under the management and controul of a higher power" (Mary Brunton, 1812). *Self-Control* had begun as a pastime. This book had been work from the beginning.

This time, the title—*Discipline*—was no more seductive than before, but now her readers could guess what to expect. Ellen Percy suffers a frustrated elopement, bereavement, penury, and a period in a madhouse before finding happiness in Scotland. Mary enjoyed writing the part of the book which was based in the Highlands. By the end of 1814, she thought that six weeks of hard work would finish the book. She told Aunt Craigie:

When I have ended, I will dance on top of it, as the man in the song was to do with his dead wife. I am sure she was not half such a plague to him as my book has been to me. (Mary Brunton, 1814)

But when she had nearly finished Ellen's adventures in the Highlands, what seemed a kind of disaster struck. Sir Walter Scott's *Waverly* was published. It thrilled Mary when she read it, before she was struck with the realization that her Highland episodes were far inferior to those of Scott, and worse still, she might be accused of borrowing from his material. It took all Mr. B.'s persuasion to overrule such thoughts, and, low in spirits, and without much hope for its future, Mary finished writing *Discipline*. She woke Mr. B. at three o'clock one morning to tell him of Ellen's wedding (1814). On December 13, 1814, the book was published, again printed from the first copy. Its success greatly exceeded Mary's expectations. It had 30 chapters and 476 pages, each chapter headed with a carefully selected verse from twenty different poets including Scott, Byron, Cowper, Crabbe, Gray, Goldsmith, and Shakespeare. This time, she was known to be the author and was doubtful of the sincerity of all the praise she received. She was never to know that eighteen years later, the book would be enjoying publication in London, Edinburgh, Dublin, and Paris. It reappeared in paperback in 1986.

The repairing of the Tron Church in the summer of 1815 gave the Bruntons another opportunity for a holiday in England. Mary kept her journals again, pages and pages of varied, interesting, and entrancing descriptions of what she saw—Somerset House, Salisbury, Southhampton and the Isle of Wright, Portsmouth and the *Nelson* where they went aboard. She described it in meticulous detail: measuring 240 feet from its stem to stern, rating at 2,800 tons and 120 guns with 1,200 tons of ballast on board. Monmouthshire was her favorite place as they returned home:

> From the top of a steep hill, which forms its bank on the side opposite to the town, we had a view of a most splendid valley—varied by rising grounds—skirted by hills which are gay with every sort of cultivation—and terminated by the Welsh mountains at a distance of from fifteen to twenty miles. No scene of greater richness, variety, and beauty have I seen in England. The whole is like Mosaic work, without one blank. There are no frightful squares and straight lines in Monmouthshire fences. The colours too are much richer than those of Scottish landscape. The wheat is a more golden yellow; the grass is unspeakably green; the very fallows are of a rich purpleish brown. The woods are natural, and therefore they are more feathery, and less formal than our plantations. Nothing could be added to the beauty of this country. . . . (Mary Brunton, 1815)

Mary had a feeling that she would not visit the south again. At home in the winter, aware that she should start writing again, she couldn't decide on a subject. Mr. B. suggested that she might undertake a series of essays on Cowper, but that was discarded. Her own idea of writing a collection of short stories beginning with "The Runaway," the account of a truant boy whose hardships were to teach him the value of home, had to be rejected also. She had thought of situating that story in Orkney but, after so long away, she couldn't recall as much of the place as she wished. So she turned again to the type of story which had already won her many readers, and began to write *Emmeline,* which tells how little chance of happiness there is for a divorced wife who marries a seducer.

Endless visitors made it difficult for her to "take her talent out of its napkin," as she told Mrs. Izett when she wrote to her in September 1817, but after four months of lethargy she made a synopsis, beginning Chapter One with lines from John Newton (1725–1807), the clergyman friend of her favorite William Cowper:

> Do you find the paths in which you are led, or rather hurried and driven on, to be 'paths of pleasantness and peace?'. . . . You know that you are not happy, and we know it likewise.

Emmeline is preparing for her "nuptial hour" with Sir Sidney de Clifford, a "soldier of high fame . . . a lover who adored her . . . yet the sigh which swelled her bosom was not the sigh of rapture . . . for Emmeline had, before, been a bride." (Emmeline, pp. 3–4).

Mary tried to develop the story with the romantic drama of her former novels, each chapter preceded by a verse, but this time the effort was more of a strain. Mr. B. and Mrs. Izett were worried about her. When she found in the spring of 1818 that she was pregnant, there was great rejoicing. Even though she was approaching her fortieth birthday, everyone saw this as the solution to her lethargy. Mr. B. offered prayers of thankfulness. But Mary was convinced that she would die. She chose the clothes which she would be buried in, the tokens of remembrance for her friends, and went serenely about her daily tasks. On December 7, 1818, she gave birth to a stillborn son. After recovering well for a few days, she took a fever and died on the morning of December 19th.

The five chapters of the unfinished *Emmeline* were published in 1819, prefixed by a Memoir of her life by her husband, and dedicated to her brother, Captain William Balfour, R.N., who succeeded to the Trenaby estates, became Provost of Kirkwall and Vice-Lieutenant of Orkney, and for the last three years of his life was adjudged head of the Balfour family by the Lord Lyon Court. Some of Mary's letters to William are within the Memoir (pp. lxvii, lxxvii, lxxxi).

Alexander Brunton lived on until 1854, when he died at the age of eighty-one at Meigle, near to Cupár Angus, Fife. His will contains no reference to any of Mary's manuscripts, his whole estate passing to his niece, Anne Stevenson.

Maurice Lindsay in his *History of Scottish Literature* considers that *Discipline* was Mary's best novel; the unfinished *Emmeline* suffering the misfortune of being eclipsed by Susan Ferrier's *Marriage* (Maurice Lindsay, 1977). *Marriage* was being written the year that Mary died.

Also in the Memoir, there can be found Mary's self-analysis which instantly disperses any conception of her as the strait-laced, moralizing wife of a Presbyterian minister:

I believe nobody was ever better formed for enjoying life than I, saving and excepting in the construction of an abominable stomach, for I delight in travelling, yet I can be happy at home; I enjoy company, yet I prefer retirement. I can look with rapture on the glorious features of nature—the dark lake and the rugged mountains—the roaring cataract—yet can gaze with no small pleasure on the contents of a haberdasher's window. (Mary Brunton, 1812)

Her obituary in the *Edinburgh Evening Courant* confirms her candor, good sense, and charm, and is worth reading, especially for its statement that since her books were published, immorality in novels ceased for some years.

The books also possess a variety of excellence, independent of the moral aim which fostered them. They show a vigorous judgment, an intimate knowledge of the human heart, and an accurate perception of character and manners which can be ranked in composition with the most celebrated novels in the same class.

It would be difficult to find in any of those depths of English literature, which have employed the pens of female authors, better specimens of a pure and vigorous style.

# REFERENCES
## Joanna Baillie

Carhart, Margaret Sprague. (1923). *The life and work of Joanna Baillie*. New Haven & London: Yale University Press and Humphry Milford, Oxford University Press.

Chapman, Robert William. (1932). *The life and letters of Jane Austen, 1796–1817*. (Pages 278, 344, 423). Oxford: Clarendon Press.

Dorr, Priscilla (1988). *Joanna Baillie*. In Paul Schlueter & June Schlueter (Eds.), *An encyclopaedia of British women writers*. New York: Garland Publishing.

Lindsay, Maurice. (1977). *A history of Scottish Literature*. London: Robert Hale.

Russell, Rosalind. (1987, February 2). *The 'immortal' who fell from literary grace. The Scotsman*.

Schnorrenberg, Barbara Brandon. (1984). *Joanna Baillie*. In Janet Todd (Ed.), *A dictionary of British and American women writers 1660–1800*. London: Methuen.


# REFERENCES
## Mary Brunton

Brunton, Mary. Letter to Mrs. Izett, August 15, 1814. In Alexander Brunton's Memoir of her life and extracts from her correspondence, published with her unfinished novel, *Emmeline* by Manners & Miller, Edinburgh, 1819.

Ligonier, Edward Earl to Thomas Balfour from Cobham, Surrey, January 9, 1777. Balfour Archives, The Orkney Library, Kirkwall. Ref. D2/4/12.

Ligonier, Earl & Lady, to Frances Balfour, December 6, 1778. Balfour Archives, The Orkney Library, Kirkwall. Ref. D2/4/12.

Ligonier, Edward, Earl, to Thomas Balfour, February 6, 1782. Balfour Archives, The Orkney Library, Ref. D2/4/12.

Bailey, Patrick (1971, 1974). *Orkney* (pp. 112–113). Devon: David & Charles, Newton Abbot.

Brunton, Mary. Letter to Aunt Mary Craigie, February 4, 1795. Balfour Archives, The Orkney Library, Ref. D2/8/16.

Balfour, Frances, to Elizabeth Manson, December 12, 1798. Balfour Archives, The Orkney Library.

Brunton, Mary, to Elizabeth Manson, January 18, 1799. Balfour Archives, The Orkney Library, Ref. D2/8/16.

Brunton, Alexander, in *Emmeline* Memoir, March 3, 1819, p. xii.

Doctor's account of last illness of Thomas Balfour. Balfour Archives, The Orkney Library, Ref. D2/12/5.

Balfour, Frances, to Mary Brunton, 1801. Balfour Archives, The Orkney Library, Ref. D2/53/20.

Brunton, Mary, to Frances Balfour, October 6, 1802. In Alexander Brunton's Memoir in *Emmeline*, p. xiv.

Brunton, Alexander, Memoir, March 2, 1819, p. xviii.

Brunton, Mary. *Self-Control*, Pandora Press, London & New York, 1986, p. 8.

Brunton, Mary, to Frances Balfour, November 21, 1809. Alexander Brunton's Memoir, p. xx.

Brunton, Mary, to Mrs. Izett, October 4, 1810, Memoir, p. xxxviii.

Brunton, Alexander, Memoir, p. liv.

Brunton, Mary, to Mrs Izett, November 3, 1812. Memoir, p. lxvi.

Brunton, Mary, to Mrs Mary Craigie, May 31, 1814. Memoir, p. lxxii.

Brunton, Mary, to Mrs Izett, August 15, 1814, Memoir, p. lxxiii.

Memoir, p. 145, 14 August 1815.

The John Newton quote (p. 324) is used opposite to the title page of *Emmeline*.

Emmeline, pp. 3–4
Brunton, Mary, to her sister-in-law, March 21, 1812. Memoir, p. li.
Grant, Francis James, W.S. (1922). Register of Marriages in the City of Edinburgh 1751–1800.
*Edinburgh Evening Courant,* Monday, December 28, 1818.


*Footnote:* A second edition of *Emmeline* was published in 1820 with some other pieces by Mary
Brunton, author of *Self-Control* and *Discipline,* to which is prefixed a memoir of her life, including some extracts from her correspondence. Printed for Manners & Miller, and Archibald
Constable & Co., Edinburgh, and John Murray, Albemarle Street, London, by James Ballan-
tyne & Co.

# Part Two

# The Issues

# "The Witchery of Fiction":

## Charlotte Smith, Novelist

Mary Anne Schofield

Charlotte Turner Smith (1749–1806), the eldest daughter of Nicholas Turner, a landed gentleman in Sussex, was the author of several collections of poetry, two translations, ten novels, and several children's stories— twenty-six volumes in total. (See Schofield, 1989 for previous studies of Charlotte Smith.) The runaway success of her first novel, *Emmeline; or the Orphan of the Castle,* 1788 (the first 1500 copies of the first edition were sold so quickly that a second edition of 500 copies was printed in the same year, while a third was out by June, 1789), often obscures the great triumphs of her other early pieces. Throughout her writing career, be it with the best-selling *Emmeline* or the later, darker *Marchmont* and *Montalbert,* Smith maintains her avid concern for presenting an accurate picture of the female condition. She has written the feminine life through the amalgamation of her own experiences superimposed upon the fictional adventures of her characters. Carefully and meticulously, she charts the life and movements of a prototypical eighteenth-century woman.

The eighteenth-century female—and Smith was no exception—was a superb needlewoman. (Pamela was certainly not the only heroine to be dexterous with her needle.) Smith's own "education"—schooling first at Chichester and afterwards at Kensington, ending when she was twelve—was superficial by twentieth-century standards, but she was proficient at painting, reading, and needlework. Interestingly enough, a major topos in Smith's novels involves metaphoric matrices of mending and sewing. Smith pieces together a fictional life from the scraps, facts, and pieces of her real life, thus creating an entire corpus that can be read as romanticized biography.

This pervasive metaphor of mending is an important one on several counts. First, Smith is able to piece together extraordinarily effective and important feminist statements and texts because of the interweaving of her personal life and the fictional lives of her heroines. Specifically, in each of the novels (with one exception), there is always a "writing," literary character—that is, one who is in the throes of literary creation and composition, fitting together in a nar-

177

rative pattern the various pieces and fragments of a life. In the later works, this mending and mentoring presence gives way to the actual appearance of Smith herself in the text, specifically in the voice of the prefaces. From the unhappy events of her own life, she sews a "happy" romance story, thus combining the pervasive needlework topos with her feminist stance.

Second, this topos continues on as she pieces together a feminist tradition in writing, thus acting as a keystone for the new breed of feminist writers. She becomes a "mothering mender and mentor" between the often insecure, fragmented, feminine writer who had preceded her (Barker, Davys, Collyer, Haywood, Fielding) to those who follow Lennox, (West, Inchbald, Burney, Austen). She pieces together the feminine novel tradition before the reader's eyes.

Her sewing, together with the weaving of the novel tradition, becomes an imaginative act. She deconstructs, deciphers, reconstructs, and reinterprets *the* feminine story. Both Charlotte Smith and her women learn how to rebuild and structure a female life. Smith's own reconstructing is evident when one considers the "facts" of her life. She was raised at Bignor Park, Sussex, and quickly developed a love for the English countryside. Such enthusiasm was cut short when her father remarried. A fifteen-year-old daughter was intolerable to the new stepmother, and Charlotte was hurled into a precipitous marriage to Benjamin Smith, the second son and business partner of Richard Smith, a wealthy West Indian merchant and director of the East India Company. Her husband's philandering and harebrained schemes soon left the couple destitute, and Charlotte turned to her writing in an effort to alleviate some of their debts.

Smith's necessity of transforming such dire facts into plausible fictions is evident in her second work, *Ethelinde, or The Recluse of the Lake* (1789), which, ultimately, becomes the love story of Montgomery and Ethelinde. Ethelinde is well-versed in the popular literature of her day, having "read . . . every book that is to be had at a circulating library" (Smith, 1974, vol. II, p. 129). She often is able to see the world through heroine-colored eyes and frequently finds herself in heroine-harrowing situations (that is, Lord Danesforte takes her to the lake, but is so violent in his rowing demonstration that Ethelinde is thrown overboard and must be rescued by Montgomery). Immediately, Ethelinde begins to weave her fantasy, romance text.

> Disgusted by the useless and unmeaning parade with which she was surrounded, and weary of society where friendship and sincerity were forgotten, she suffered her imagination to wander towards scenes more adapted to her taste, and more soothing to her heart . . . To be the wife of Montgomery! she dared not trust herself with an hope *so romantic*—so enchanting—*so impossible!* She tried to drive it from her; but her *busy fancy* was still in spite of herself *employed in dressing scenes of visionary happiness,* from which she returned to feel with *awakened anguish* the melancholy and depressing circumstances of her *real situation.* (Smith, 1974, II, p. 28) (Emphasis added.)

But such unbridled romantic fantasies cannot be stitched in such an unrestricted fashion. Ethelinde is imprisoned and tortured by the Woolastons, who are in league with Lady Newenden (they want to match her with Lord Davenant). After a climactic scene with Davenant, who rips Montgomery's letter to her from Ethelinde's hand, Smith as Ethelinde records:

> Montgomery's letter . . . the fragments of which she had folded up in a sheet of paper, and put into her bosom, she now anxiously took up; but too much agitated *to attempt to re-adjust the pieces and decypher it,* she could only kiss the torn relicts, and bathe them with tears. (II, p. 63) (Emphasis added)

Smith continues:

> she began with painful pleasure *to put together* Montgomery's letter, which had been written on several sheets of long paper; some pieces were still wanting; but these *Ethelinde by her imagination supplied* and read with satisfaction, that as his departure became inevitable his mind had acquired courage to bear his separation from her with more calmness. (II, pp. 71–2) (Emphasis added)

So too, Smith pieces together the fabric of her story. In fact, this picture becomes symbolic of Smith's entire corpus. Her own imagination supplies the missing facts from the pages of real life, the raw material with which she works, as she fills in the pieces with facts of her own life.

Charlotte Smith's novels concentrate on this image of mending, of presenting and piecing together both a fictional and a real life. And, as such, she writes *the* romance story (by definition the discovery of a self from a journey of no one from no place to being someone from someplace), weaving together her strands of fictional and real lines. Thus, unlike the first and more popular Emmeline (protagonist of her first novel), who is controlled by men throughout the novel, Ethelinde, like Smith, is the maker and controller of her own fate.

Charlotte Smith herself had much to control. Her married life with Benjamin Smith was intolerable. (She was only sixteen; he, twenty-one.) Bound by contemporary marriage laws that gave her philandering and economically unstable husband nearly total control over her money, her twelve children, and her body, Smith was unable to adjust and become submissive, dependent, and financially indigent in order to accommodate the male image of the female. She had been raised in a respectable residence in an aristocratic Westminster neighborhood and in a rambling Sussex estate. Taken care of by an aunt after her mother's death when she was three years old, Smith was unused to the autocraticism of her invalid mother-in-law, whom she cared for and with whom the couple lived. (The young Smiths lived above the elder Smith's place of business in the City of London far from the Sussex countryside.) Fortunately (though it was a mixed blessing), Smith did get on with her father-in-law, who made her joint executor and trustee of his will; however, the provisos, codicils, and so forth created more trouble and anxiety than she gained from his death, and the final settlement did not occur until after Charlotte's death, when her children were too old to benefit from the will. Smith's own inability to benefit lucratively from the will, coupled with her husband's failure to secure or hold jobs, made their finances extremely shaky and culminated in her husband's seven-month imprisonment for debt in 1783. During this time, in an effort to reduce the debt, Charlotte first found her way into print (with the help of William Hayley), producing *Elegiac Sonnets and Other Essays* (1784). None of her efforts, however, succeeded in making them solvent again, and so in 1786 Charlotte Smith left her husband of twenty-three years. Until her death in 1806, she supported herself and her nine surviving children through her writing. As she notes in the preface to *Marchmont*:

> Still continuing . . . under the necessity of earning by my pen the subsistence of my remaining family, I began some months afterward the present work. (pp. ix–x)

*Marchmont* is not her only work where she so blatantly and openly comments upon the state and fate of her own life. In fact, it is her prefaces, the first appearing in the 1794 *Banished Man,* which provide Smith with the raw material she weaves into the fabric of her fictions. Thus it is that she writes about the inequities of lawyers, the falseness of the government, the hunger of her children. Smith realistically and scrupulously handles these facts and those frequently labeled inappropriate to the female that is, she discusses French politics in *Desmond* (Smith, 1974; p.162; see also Elliott, this volume and the French Revolution in *The Banished Man*).

Smith's concern with the art of fiction includes not only her weaving together fact and fiction, piecing together the facts of the preface with the fictional escapades of her heroines, but also the creation of fictional writing characters and authors. For example, in *Ethelinde* we meet the simply delicious Miss Clarenthia Ludford, budding novelist and romancière. Through Ludford (and the other characters like her), Smith examines the ever-popular romance genre. Through her manipulation of Ludford et al. Smith is able to tear the fabric of romances and reveal the realities of her unromantic life, tantamount to the long-suffering life of every female. In a word, Smith creates a subtext of the actual realities of the eighteenth-century woman's life. Clarenthia tells us that she turns to novel writing because of her displeasure with the contemporary literary scene, noting that, "the thing I like is to be carried out of myself by a fiction quite out of common life, and to get among scenes and people of another world" (Smith, 1789: p. 166).

She then goes on to catalogue *her* romance story:

> My heroine falls in love with a young man; quite a divine creature of course, who is obliged to go [as an] ambassador to Tripolia. She knows not what to do, but at length determines to hire herself into the family of the Tripoline Ambassador here, to learn the language, and accompany her love as his valet de

chambre. This plan, by help of walnuts to change her complexion, and a pair of black mustacios, she accomplishes; then she meets with an amazing number of adventures in France, where she kills two or three men in defence of her lover; and her sex being discovered, a French nobleman becomes enamoured of her, and carries her away by force into a chateau in a wood. But I will not tell you a word more of it, because I will surprise you with the catastrophe, which is quite original; only one event is borrowed from the Arabian nights, and one description from Sir Charles Grandison. Rupert, indeed, says, that with a little application, my pen will become truly Richardsonian. (pp. 167–8)

The adventures almost read like Ethelinde's own (at least with all the plot complications), or even more to the point, like so much of the mid-century fiction (I am reminded of numerous Haywood plots that could be synopsized thusly).

Smith has it both ways. First, she can make Clarenthia look foolish and her novel techniques even more so when the plot is described so inanely. Yet the inanity disguises some very sophisticated, important issues that will continue to interest Smith in her later novels. Clarenthia's story, the fiction she makes, is the surface one of female exploitations, that is the male story; yet feminine aggression is also there. Her heroine kills men—certainly a desire of the women protagonists since Penelope Aubin. She disguises herself as a man and lives, for a while at least, the freewheeling life of one. Though Clarenthia's story is fiction, she unmasks what is at the heart of women. Further, by claiming to study or imitate the Richardsonian style, she indicates that what is of concern here is a psychological novel that probes the inner female psyche. On closer inspection, one sees that the vaporish, overly imaginative heroine that Ethelinde is sometimes close to becoming is not the Clarenthia Ludford heroine type at all. Clarenthia's own position as "a young lady of science" (p. 123) affords her a seriousness that in some ways Smith approves of.

For Smith does take her craft very seriously. Desmond (1792), her next novel and the only one to be cast in epistolary form, is, perhaps, her most extensive investigation of the creative process. The majority of the correspondence is between Lionel Desmond and Erasmus Bethel, though in the second and third volumes there are large numbers of letters exchanged between Geraldine Verney and her sister, Fanny Waverly.

Desmond is the romantic composer of the piece, and he frequently uses his imagination to help in the creation of a scene for his letter readers, yet it is Geraldine who can claim "recourse to my pen and my pencil, to beguile those hours, when my soul, sickening at the past, and recoiling from the future, would very fain lose its own mournful images in the witchery of fiction" (Smith, 1974, III, p. 162).

This witchery for Smith, then, involved the blending together of romance fiction and personal fact. It is impossible, she finds, to have one without the other. Thus, Fanny Waverly (Desmond) is unable to become a heroine, because she has no text (that is, Geraldine puts restrictions on what she writes; her mother on what she reads). She is allowed no avenue of imaginative escape that would allow her to project her exploits on another. Therefore, she has no text. Contrarily, Geraldine, because she is Smith herself, sometimes has too much text, as she writes:

> I got up into my own room, and devoured with an eager appetite the mawkish pages that told of damsels, most exquisitely beautiful, confined by a cruel father, and escaping to an heroic lover, while a wicked lord laid in wait to tear her from him, and carried her to some remote castle. Those delighted me most that ended miserably; and having tortured me through the last volume with impossible distress, ended in the funeral of the heroine. (Smith, 1974, II pp. 173–74)

Here she creates the subtext of all eighteenth-century feminine fiction.

Geraldine's unmasking of her fictional tastes is tantamount to Smith's own revelations. At this juncture, then, I think it is important to note the advances that have been made in the "woman's story" since the early years of the century. Though still adhering to the proper fictional forms, Smith need not distort these forms as much as say Haywood did in the majority of her romances. Smith is freer to express her opinion. Thus, unlike Haywood, who could only articulate her anger and aggression about the plight of the female through disrupting the romantic text and exposing the accepted, euphoric, love story, Smith can express her feelings about fiction and about women in the fiction itself in a less antagonistic way. She creates characters who critique the very sort of fiction that Eliza Haywood (et al.) was writing, and simultaneously writes a euphoric, happily-ever-after text. Smith enters her fictional world unlike any of her predecessors.

Smith becomes her heroines as her heroines become her. She blurs the line between fiction and real life in order to present the true female fiction as she notes in her first preface (*The Banished Man*): "The work I now offer to the Public has been written under great disadvantages . . . at a time when long anxiety has ruined my health, and long oppression broken my spirits" (Smith, 1794, p. A3). Her financial predicaments continue, she tells us; the lawyers have confiscated most of her grandfather's estate, and she and her children continue to be poverty-stricken. Smith claims that she still tries to correct this injustice, but in the meantime, she must survive and does so by writing fiction, by yoking together the two plotlines of realism and romance. Her preface assures the reader that it is the realistic story that is the most important, as she writes:

> I have in the present work, aimed less at the wonderful and extraordinary, than at connecting by a chain of possible circumstances, events, some of which have happened, and all of which might have happened to an individual, under the exigencies of banishment and proscription. (p. xv)

*The Banished Man* gives us Mrs. Charlotte Denzil, poet, writer, and clearly one of Smith's most magical "mending" figures. Denzil is Smith, Smith Denzil. Smith weaves her own real life facts into the fictionalized life of Charlotte Denzil—she is the magical figure, who, by her own admission, acts like Prospero (p. 216), uniting the diverse strands of the story. Mrs. Denzil is Charlotte Smith.

> Driven from my home twelve years since, with a large family wandering without any fixed plan, was long a matter of necessity and may now, for ought I know, be grown into habit, and be a fault of temper. (p. 220)

The "disguise" is successful—is it Mrs. Denzil or Smith herself? The answer is not important. What is important to note is that this material is transferred to the character and is not confined merely to the revelatory preface material. Smith does not hide. Mrs. Denzil is harassed by creditors, Mr. Thomas Tough and Humphrey Hotgoose. And because of all the financial worry, she sickens. But it is not just Mrs. Denzil who is ill; Smith too, is the victim.

> Thus harassed by pecuniary difficulties, driven about the world without any certain home, she experienced, from day to day, the truth of the adage, 'That the ruin of the poor, is their poverty;' for she was thus made liable to much greater expenses, than would have happened in a settled establishment; perplexed by creditors, and sickening from the sad conviction that her power of supporting her family by her literary exertions must every year decline, while her friends become more and more weary of her long continued sorrows. (pp. 117–18)

There is no mask; they are one and the same person.

Through Mrs. Denzil, Smith catalogues and examines the trials of being an author. The disguise is barely perceptible. For example:

> After a conference with Mr. Tough, she must write a tender dialogue between some damsel, whose perfections are even greater than those 'Which youthful poets fancy when they love,' and her hero, who, to the bravery and talents of Caesar, adds the gentleness of Sir Charles Grandison, and the wit of Lovelace. But Mr. Tough's conversation, his rude threats, and his boisterous remonstrances, have totally sunk her spirits; nor are they elevated by hearing that the small beer is out; that the pigs of a rich farmer, her next neighbor, have broke into the garden, rooted up the whole crop of pease, and not left her a single hyacinth or jonquil. . . . Melancholy and dejected she recollects that once she had a walled garden well provided with flowers, and the comforts and pleasures of affluence recur forcibly to her mind. She is divested from such reflections however, by hearing from her maid that John Gibben's children over the way, and his wife, and John himself have all got the scarlet fever; and that one of the children is dead on't, and another like to die. She is ashamed of the concern she felt a few moments before for a nosegay, when creatures of the same species, and so near her, are suffering under calamities infinitely more severe. . . . Compassion for these unhappy persons is now mingled with apprehensions for her own family. . . . With the earliest dawn she sends her servant . . . to enquire at their door how they do? (pp. 225–26)

This is an important passage not only because it uncovers the very thin disguise that Smith has adopted as Mrs. Denzil, but also because of what it reveals about the novel and fiction. The romantic exploits and escapades of the hero and heroine seem far removed from the everyday reality that faces her readers. Such detailing of her existence, then, supports the entire notion of romance's *raison d'être*: necessary disguise. In order to deal with the awfulness of life, one disguises in a romance—both author and character. The romance provides escape—for both writer and reader. As Smith records following her bout with the infectious neighbors:

> The rest of the day is passed as before; her hero and her heroine are parted in agonies, or meet in delight, and she is employed in making the most of either; with interludes of the Gubbin's family, and precautions against importing the infectious distemper into her own. (p. 229)

Smith unmasks, it must be noted, in order to reweave the fictional fabric of romance and reality. Perhaps she is able to best accomplish this desire in her 1795 and 1796 pieces respectively, *Montalbert* and *Marchmont*. I would suggest that *Marchmont* is the most personal of her novels, while *Montalbert* is the most timely, with its pervasive theme of mothering and the concept of the creation of a female history. It is a romance that teaches how to read the female text. Rosalie Lessington, the protagonist, must not only discover her real biological mother, but she also learns to read, interpret, and write women's history while in the process: she keeps a journal in which she records her imprisonment (she is incarcerated by the family of her supposed suitor), her search for her mother, and for an understanding of the female text. It is a journal that warmly weaves together the strands of Smith's biography, her career, and the creation and fate of her heroines. It is a journal of female survival in a male world. Rosalie Lessington is the exploited orphan, abandoned by her real mother, forced into a marriage with the Reverend Philbert Hugson, and further cast off by her surrogate mother, Mrs. Lessington. The first generation of mothers, like Smith's own, have left their daughters. Smith writes to alleviate her own pain of being orphaned so early to help the next generation of women writers and to instruct the readers. Without strong models, without independent mothers, women are almost certainly doomed to male control and the constant repetition of imprisoning patterns.

She continues this female investigation with *Marchmont: A Novel* (1796) and its critical preface, which not only codifies her novelistic theory but simultaneously reveals the real Charlotte Smith. It is her most personal work, her most thinly disguised. It contains the most "facts" turned into "fiction" and is, I think, Smith's most sustained attempt to understand her fate.

In the preface, she speaks to the reader both as an ordinary woman, beset with domestic problems and tragedies, and as a novelist, an artist trying to create a believable story in the midst of humdrum reality. The preface is a true scene of unmasking, and no one who reads it cannot hear the besieged voice of Smith. She observes that this is her thirty-second volume presented to the public; she writes "from necessity and by no means from choice" (p. vi); she apologizes for the state of both *Montalbert* and *Marchmont* and goes on to explain that "these volumes, therefore, have been written under the disadvantages of wanting a friendly critic on those errors of judgement which occur in every long work entirely dependent on the imagination" (p. x). Further on in the preface, she disclaims the use of the imagination and notes that she teaches morality and reality:

> It is a fault frequently imputed to novels, that they are directed to no purpose of morality, but rather serve to inflame the imaginations, and enfeeble by false notions of refinement the minds of young persons. I know not what share of those faults may be found in the present production, but my purpose has been to enforce the virtue of fortitude: and if my readers could form any idea of the state of my mind while I have been writing, they would allow that I practise the doctrine I preach. (Smith, 1796, pp. xv–xvi)

*Marchmont* becomes a story of fortitude and patience as it tells of Althea's long and arduous struggle to win Marchmont and of the almost insurmountable difficulties of their married years.

Althea, the protagonist, was raised in the country by her aunt, Mrs. Trevyllian. She is not allowed the luxury and peace (and freedom) of such an idyllic, independent existence for long. Her halcyon days end abruptly with Mrs. Trevyllian's death, and Althea is forced to go to live in London with her father, Sir Audley, and stepmother, Lady Dacres. Her father tries to force her to marry the scurrilous lawyer, Mr. Mohum, but her "native integrity, her soul revolted at the idea of selling herself to any man, and Mohum was in his person, manners, and morals equally disagreeable to her" (I, p. 151). Later she muses, that had she married him:

> Privileged by her sex, he might have dissipated my fortune, and his own, and possibly have beat me, or locked me up; or sold me if he could have met with a purchaser, to give cause to his brutal humor or contribute to his selfish indulgence. (IV, pp. 279–289)

Sir Audley, like may of Smith's males, is a tyrant and is not used to having his demands ignored:

> he could not endure to find opposition where he thought he had a right to implicit obedience. . . . The refusal of his daughter . . . seemed the most unpardonable offense that ever was committed against him. . . . Therefore in very angry and peremptory terms he declared to her, that though he had first condescended to speak to her rather as a friend than as her father, she should find that he would be obeyed. (I, pp. 152–153)

Part of Smith's purpose here is to learn how to deal with autocrats, despots, and tyrannical fathers. Althea's fate is the typical one of the eighteenth-century female. She is homeless, moneyless and, with the death of Mrs. Trevyllian, motherless. Though her protagonist is cut from the same cloth as so many of the age's heroines, Smith writes that she struggled to make Althea interesting:

> How difficult then is it for a novelist to give to one of his heroines any very marked feature which shall not disfigure her! Too much reason and self command destroy the interest we take in her distresses. It has been even observed, that Clarissa is so equal to every trial as to diminish our pity. Other virtues than gentleness, pity, filial obedience, or faithful attachment, hardly belong to the sex, and are certainly called forth only by unusual occurrences. Such was undoubtedly the lot of Althea, and they formed her character; for in the hard school of adversity, she acquired that fortitude and strength of mind which gave energy to an understanding, naturally of the first class. (I, pp. 178–179)

She must learn how to avoid the matrimonial pitfalls Sir Audley arranges for her and how to keep herself until such time as she can become as free in person as she is in mind.

The reader watches Althea develop her own self. Of course, on a textual level, it is these trials and tests that make her adventure interesting, the plot so entangling and entrapping. Subtextually, Smith probes the female psyche in order to see exactly how much suffering, how many near violations a woman can endure. *Marchmont,* like *Montalbert* and her last novel, *The Solitary Wanderer,* is less outwardly revolutionary; the focus is on interior state of mind and how the inner being deals with the frustration and violence that is so much a part of life. What *Marchmont* teaches is strength of mind; Althea is able to turn her exile, her punishment, to a positive state:

> Accustomed insensibly to her solitude, Althea passed her time without murmuring. Her mind compelled thus to exert its strength at so early a period, and her education having been such as had not enfeebled while it ornamented her excellent understanding, she not only became reconciled to a situation which to most young women would have been intolerable, but every day learned to rejoice at the election she had made, and compare the melancholy tranquility of her present situation with the splendid wretchedness to which a union with Mohum would have condemned her. (II, p. 234)

This is the strength of mind and character that she learned from Mrs. Trevyllian; this is the mind set that Smith would have her readers adopt as well.

What Smith offers with these heroines of her later novels is alternatives. She is trying to show her readers that they do not have to accept the lies men offer, that they have a right to their own minds, selves, and lives. Smith probes the facade of the "typical" romance, the fiction that women have come to believe is true, and like Eliza Haywood and Sarah Fielding, she exposes the myths which have proliferated in the pages of the century's fiction. She dispels notions of female dependency and Gothic entrapment as she reveals these notions for the fabrications that they are. Here, in *Marchmont,* she will not allow her hero to be romantically, unrealistically, heroic; instead, he is chased by creditors, poverty-stricken, homeless, but he proves himself in spite of such obstacles. Althea is not cast in the heroine mold either; though homeless, poor, and incarcerated in a country estate, living single, she is happy.

Smith's concern throughout has been on instructing her women readers to find the correct mix of fact and fantasy, reality and fiction. The anonymous reviewer of *The Old Manor House* certainly gets it right when he observes:

> To conduct a series of familiar events so as to rouse and preserve attention, without a violation of nature and probability; to draw and support the different characters necessary for an animated and varied drama in just and glowing colours; to hold the mirror of truth in the moment of youthful intemperance, and to interweave amidst the web of fable, pictures to instruct, and morals to reform. (*Critical Review, VIII,* May 1793: p. 45)

This is Smith's *raison d'être*—admirably achieved.

# REFERENCES

Schofield, Mary Anne. (1989). *Masking and unmasking the feminine mind.* Newark, DE: University of Delaware Press.

Smith, Charlotte. (1789). *Ethelinde, or the recluse of the lake.* London: T. Cadell.

Smith, Charlotte. (1794). *The banished man.* London: T. Cadell, Jr., and W. Davies.

Smith, Charlotte. (1796). *Marchmont: A novel.* London: Sampson Low.

Smith, Charlotte. (1795). *Montalbert: A novel.* London: S. Low for E. Booker.

Smith, Charlotte. (1971). *Emmeline; or, the orphan of the castle.* London: Oxford University Press. (Originally published in 1788)

Smith, Charlotte. (1974). *Desmond. A novel.* New York: Garland Publishing. (Originally published in 1792)

# Romancing the Novel:

## Gender and Genre in Early Theories of Narrative

=== Ros Ballaster ===

In a novel written in the late 1680s, *The Unfortunate Bride; or, the Blind Lady a Beauty*, Aphra Behn puts into the mouth of her heroine, Belvira, a critique of the commodification of women by men. In order to illustrate her argument against marriage to her lover, Belvira draws an analogy between the way in which men "consume" women sexually, and the way in which readers consume particular narrative forms:

> . . . women enjoy'd, are like romances read, or raree shows, once seen, meer tricks of the slight of hand, which, when found out, you only wonder at your selves for wondering so before at them. 'Tis expectation endears the blessing. . . . When the plot's out, you have done with the play, and when the last act's done, you see the curtain drawn with great indifference. (Aphra Behn, 1986, p. 233)

Belvira recognizes here that men perceive woman as an enigma, which they believe sexual possession alone will solve. Paradoxically, however, it is only the enigma that makes women interesting, and once possessed, they have to be discarded in favor of another woman or text whose "secret" has yet to be discovered. Like narrative itself and the reader's response to it, it is only in pursuit of resolution and mastery that women are of interest to men. When we get to the end of a narrative, our interest and compulsive attention necessarily stops.

Behn's use of a textual analogy to describe men's sexual relations with women is by no means a singular incident in the early "novel." Conversely, textual pleasure, particularly that which narrative offers, is frequently described in terms of sexual pleasure. Unsurprisingly perhaps, it is the thrills that romance narratives give their female readers that are the main target for attack. On Tuesday, April 29, 1712, *The Spectator* solemnly warned its "fair Readers to be in a particular manner careful how they meddle with Romances, Chocolate, Novels and the like Inflamers; which I look upon as very dangerous to be made use of during this Carnival of Nature" (Joseph Addison & Richard Steele, 1965, III, p.374).

I hope to illustrate that the struggle to define a new genre, the novel, in the late-seventeenth and early-eighteenth centuries was primarily conducted in terms of gendered oppositions and analogies. The key terms in this critical debate were those of the "romance" and the "novel," whether presented as two conflicting fields of narrative prose at war with each other for both popular and literary supremacy, or, as in *The Spectator* above, dismissed as equally degenerate forms of fictional seduction upon young minds. I would suggest that while the terms themselves are subject to endless redefinitions and negotiations in the critical and literary writing of both men and women throughout the eighteenth century, they are underpinned throughout by a relatively stable association of the romance with female readers and writers. While this may be anything but an accurate description of female reading patterns in the period, it acts as a powerful ideological weapon in the war of words. I will go on to argue that it is through this gendering of a debate over literary forms in the eighteenth century and a consistent identification of the romance with female literary production and consumption, that the term "romance" comes to acquire its more contemporary meaning of idealized love relations between men and women and "romance fiction" to be associated with popular narratives of love for women readers.

Significantly the 1910 edition of the *Oxford English Dictionary* contains no such definition of romance. The *New English Dictionary* edited by James Murray "With the Assistance of Many Scholars and Men of Science" defines romance as "to compose in verse," "to exaggerate or invent," "to have romantic ideas," "to say hyperbolically," "to persuade into something" or "to translate into a Romance tongue" (*OED*, 1910, VIII, p. 767). It is not until the *Supplement* of 1982 that we find the more common contemporary definition of romance as "a love affair; idealistic character or quality in a love affair; a love story; that class of literature which consists of love stories" (Burchfield, 1982, III, p. 1334). The 1910 edition sticks firmly with the "original" meaning of romance from the medieval period, a text written in a vernacular tongue derived from the Latin, and some of the term's later developments along the same lines, averting its eyes from the somewhat less reputable connections of the term with mass-market formula fiction for women.

In her book-length gloss to the romance, Gillian Beer insists:

> We need to recognize at the start that there is a distinction between "the romance" and "romance" as an element in literature. The history of the romance . . . could almost be epitomized as a shift from form to quality. We tend to speak of "medieval romances" but of "the Elizabethan romance" and then of "romance" in nineteenth century novels. . . . Perhaps we can best understand the significance of the romance by considering what kinds of experiences it persists in offering the reader through its many guises. (Beer, 1970, p. 5)

This shift from form to quality takes place with the advent of the novel as an alternative form of narrative fiction around the end of the seventeenth century. Its difference from the romance lies ostensibly in its dependence upon fact rather than imaginative idealism as Lennard Davis' *Factual Fictions* (1983) admirably demonstrates, but even this distinction comes to be articulated in terms of the novel's involvement in the masculine "real" of the political and economic public sphere, versus the romance's concern with the feminine "real" of the love-oriented, domestic, and social private sphere.

Probably the most important book of the period for the purposes of argument is Clara Reeve's *The Progress of Romance* published in 1785. Reeve sets about tracing the history of narrative fiction from the classical period to her own times. The text is an ostensible transcription of a debate about the respective merits of the romance and the novel between three late-eighteenth-century readers, two women and one man. Over the course of twelve evenings, Reeve's spokeswoman, Euphrasia, defends romance against the misogynist attacks of the male reader of the supposedly "masculine" prose tradition, Hortensius, with their mutual friend and secret romance reader, Sophronia, acting as arbiter. It rapidly becomes clear that the battle between modern novel and romance is as much a sexual-political as a literary one. On the second evening, when Euphrasia arrives with her dictionaries, a brief exchange demonstrates the fact that this is a battle of the sexes:

> *Hort:* I see *Euphrasia* has brought her artillery and is placing them to advantage.
>
> *Euph:* You know your advantages, and that a woman is your opponent. (Reeve, 1930, I, p. 11)

Hortensius identifies Richardson and Addison as authors for women when he says "*Richardson* is a writer all your own; your sex are more obliged to him and *Addison,* than to all your other man-authors" (I, p. 135). Euphrasia is quick to respond that "no man is degraded by defending us, for the female cause is the cause of virtue" (I, p. 136). It is, however, clear that male writers may not have felt themselves degraded by defending the female cause of virtue, but their literary reputations were at stake if they were perceived to be writing to an audience solely made up of women readers.

Male writers in the mid-eighteenth century seem to have been caught between the demands of populism and their own wish to obtain literary posterity. In order to sell their works they needed to secure a female audience, for throughout the eighteenth century women were the major consumers of fiction,[1] Hortensius highlights this point when he comments to Euphrasia, "your [sex] are most concerned in my remonstrance for they read more of these books than ours, and consequently are most hurt by them" (II, p. 81). However, in order to be read as "serious" fiction rather than popular fodder for love-sick girls, it seems to have been necessary for the male and female author to deny his or her connections with exclusively female forms. Thus, Richardson's postscript to *Clarissa* goes to considerable lengths to establish the narrative's debt to Aristotelian theories of tragedy in order to avoid its being "looked upon . . . as a mere novel or romance" (Richardson, 1985: p. 1498).

The jostling over terms in this debate is precisely one of an association between the "literary" and the masculine, and the "popular" and the feminine. Formal difference is transparently equated with sexual difference. When Hortensius expresses a liking for Tobias Smollett's *Humphry Clinker,* Euphrasia seizes her chance for counterattack:

*Euph:* Then you do condescend to read Novels sometimes, especially when they are written by men?

*Hort:* Spare your raillery – it was *Romances* that I made war against. (II, p. 11)

Hortensius cloaks his sexual prejudice by insisting that he is arguing against a literary genre rather than the female gender.

Euphrasia's history of the romance identifies the connection in the public and critical mind between femininity and romance as a modern phenomenon, originating with the dissemination of the seventeenth-century French romance in Britain. This connection she analyzes as being the result of a change in the gender of the romance's readership from the 1660s onwards. She cites both epic and medieval chivalric poetry as examples of the romance, but it is only when she turns to a discussion of seventeenth-century romance that she begins to identify the romance reader as female. Interestingly, it is only here that Sophronia, the reader rather than the critic of the triad, begins to feel at home.

When, on the third evening of the discussion, Euphrasia lists Homer, Diogenes, Tatius, Xenephon, and Damasius (I, p. 32) as romance writers, Sophronia comments in despair, "I thought myself well read in Romance, but I know nothing of any work you have yet mentioned" (p. 32). The works of Honoré d'Urfé, Gauthier de Costes de la Calprenède and Madeleine de Scudéry find her on surer ground, however, as she remembers her mother and aunts reading them together.[2] Sophronia describes how "they us'd to meet once a week at each others houses, to hear these stories; – one used to read while the rest ply'd their needles" (I, p. 69). This picture of communal reading activity on the part of women is somewhat nostalgic; consumption of the emergent novel appears to have been a solitary and intimate reading experience carried out in the *boudoir.* At the same time as this allowed reading for women to become more salacious and erotically charged as in the work of Mary Delarivière Manley and Eliza Haywood, it returned women to their isolation in the home and to an exclusively "private" sphere of literary consumption and pleasure.

Sophronia also makes a clear link between the French romance and the writings of Aphra Behn, Delarivière Manley and Eliza Haywood, asserting that they provided the sole reading matter of late-seventeenth and early-eighteenth century women readers (I, p. 38). Dorothy Osborne and Lady Mary Wortley Montagu are probably the two best-known readers of and propagandists for the French romance.[3] However, there is little or no similarity between the works of these early British women writers and their female precursor, Madeleine de Scudéry, except perhaps in their shared use of traditional "romance" names (Clelia, Artaxander, Idalia, Philadelphia, Rivella, etc.) and, on occasion, exotic locations. Most strikingly perhaps Delarivière Manley and Eliza Haywood's novels are steeped in a voyeuristic eroticism that Madeleine de Scudéry, with her strictly decorous system of *bienscéance* and courtly love ethic would have shunned in horror. It seems more likely that their identification with the French romance is the product of a powerful late-eighteenth-century critical orthodoxy about the novel and romance, which *The Progress of Romance* admirably demonstrates. The former was represented as given to prolixity, idealization, literary shoddiness and, most importantly, acted as the reading fodder of "ladies," while the latter was seen as virile, robust, developing a moral and formal realism lacking in its predecessor, and, of course, the natural reading matter of the gentlemen.

This orthodoxy was by no means so firmly in place in the early-eighteenth-century when women were first beginning to produce and publish prose fiction. Rather, the romance and the novel seem to have shared the same marginal and illegitimate status in relationship to "art." As Ioan Williams points out in his introduction to *Novel and Romance: A Documentary Record 1700–1800*, "As far as most commentators were concerned novel and romance remained on the outskirts of literature, to be treated perfunctorily, merely with reference to their potential moral danger" (Williams, 1970, p. 7). One of the ways of escaping this kind of condemnation was to claim that the narrative was fact, and this is a consistent ploy used by both men and women in the early novel. In her "Epistle Dedicatory" to *Oroonoko*, Aphra Behn writes "What I have mentioned I have taken care shou'd be truth, let the critical reader judge as he pleases," (Behn, 1986, p. 25) and again in *The Fair Jilt*, "every circumstance, to a tittle, is truth" (p. 105). As Lennard Davis points out, claiming fiction to be fact gave the author considerably more freedom to create improbable events than declaring a work fiction and then being forced to make its action and characterization consistent.

One of the recurrent charges against the French romance was its improbability. In 1740, Lord Chesterfield wrote to his son dismissing the romance on the grounds that it "generally consists of twelve volumes, all filled with insipid love nonsense, and most incredible adventures" (Williams, 1970: p. 100). William Congreve was one of the first prose writers to try and differentiate between novel and romance when he wrote in his preface to *Incognita* in 1691:

> Romances are generally composed of the Constant Loves and invincible Courages of Hero's, heroines, Kings and Queens, Mortals of the first Rank, and so forth; where lofty Language, miraculous Contingencies, and impossible Performances, elevate and surprise the Reader into a giddy Delight . . . Novels are of a more

familiar nature; Come near us, and represent to us Intrigues in practice, delight us with Accidents and odd Events, but not such as are wholly unusual or un-presidented. . . . (Williams, 1970, p. 27)

Behn, Manley, and Haywood were clearly on the side of Congreve's novel, dealing in intrigue, marital strife, and, in the main, bourgeois morals and manners, and yet they are consistently relocated as part of a romance tradition.[4] The explanation for this reaction again lies both in the perceived "female-ness" of their writing in terms of their subject matter, reader address, and narrative voice, and in gender-determined definitions of what qualified as the "real" as opposed to the "fictional" in this period.

What was at stake in the suppression of the French romance in favor of the mid-eighteenth-century "realist" novel was precisely the question of female power and reading identification. The French romance presented love as the sole motivation and engine of change behind every major historical event and centered its attention upon the more obscure female characters in conventional history. It thus fictionalized history at the expense of the masculine "public" sphere and privileged women as the primary force in culture and civilization by their judicious use of their power to inspire love in the nation's heroes. This is by no means an unusual strategy in romance, linking these early fictions with twentieth-century "historical romance" for women, which involves, as the authors of *Rewriting English* put it, "a reversal of the common view of history, allowing the usually marginalized female sphere to dominate" (Batsleer, Davies, O'Rourke, and Weedon, 1985, p. 96).

As early as 1664, Samuel Pepys, whose wife was an avid reader of French romance,[5] reports a discussion with a certain peer who "among other things did much enveigh against the writing of Romances; that five hundred years hence, being wrote of matter generally true, . . . the world will not know which is the true and which the false" (Latham & Matthews, 1970, V, p. 319).

Eighteenth-century prose abounds with depictions of young female romance readers who are unable to separate fact from fiction due to this "corruption" of history and thus assume women to have boundless power and influence in the public sphere through the devotion they command in their lovers.[6] As Clara Reeve frequently reiterates, the "romantic" turn of mind is seen as a peculiarly female phenomenon, which encourages young girls to get ideas above their station in life. Hortensius complains that:

A young woman is taught to expect adventures and intrigues—she expects to be addressed in the style of these books, with the language of flattery and adulation.—If a plain man addresses her in rational terms and pays her the greatest of compliments,—that of desiring to spend his life with her,—that is not sufficient, her vanity is disappointed, she expects to meet a Hero in Romance. (Reeve, 1930, II, p. 78)

Charlotte Lennox in her novel *The Female Quixote*, published in 1752, dramatizes this fiction of the romance's iniquitous effect upon the female reader far more sympathetically than many of her male contemporaries. (See also Helen Thomson, this volume.) Arabella, the heroine of Lennox's novel has been brought up in the country, and her only education has been in the reading of the French romances her dead mother left her. Like her namesake, Miguel Cervantes' Don Quixote, Arabella cannot separate fact from fiction and is convinced the romances are "true." She is thus horrified to hear Cleopatra condemned as a whore (Lennox, 1986, pp. 114–115) and Thalestris, Queen of the Amazons as "a terrible women . . . a very masculine sort of creature" (p. 139). Arabella rejects her solid bourgeois suitor, Glanville, because of his lack of respect for the romance and the absolute authority of the female sex. Her conversion is finally brought about by a suitably paternalistic figure, the doctor, who attends her following a disastrous attempt to imitate Scudéry's heroine, Clelia, who swam the Tiber to avoid a rapist. The doctor, through long consultations, weans Arabella from the romance to the sentimental novels of Richardson, persuading her that the French romances "teach women to exact vengeance, and men to execute it; teach women to expect not only worship, but the dreadful worship of human sacrifices" (p. 420).

Charlotte Lennox's moral conclusion is, however, not an unequivocal or unsympathetic condemnation of her heroine. Arabella's "imaginary" world is presented to the reader as stemming from a fine moral integrity, courage, and sense of self. Glanville, we are told, "admired the strength of her understanding, her lively wit, the sweetness of her temper, and a thousand amiable qualities which distinguished her from the rest of her sex: her follies, when opposed to all those charms of mind and person, seemed inconsiderable and weak" (p. 128). Yet Arabella's charms are paradoxically the *product* of her follies, because the models of romance, the female heroines Arabella takes as her ideal, offer up the prospect of agency and autonomy for the female reader. If "love" is the *raison d'être* of the romance view of history, women are accorded absolute power in determining the course of that history. Arabella's constant citing of precedents for female heroism is clearly a search for fame, a desire to commit an act of greatness to commit her name to posterity. Unfortunately for her, as George Eliot pointed out over one hundred years later in her preface to *Middlemarch*, non-chivalric society provides no opportunities for women for "an epic life wherein there [is] a constant unfolding of far-resonant action" (Eliot, 1977: p. 25). Arabella is obliged to recognize female heroism as a *fiction* with no place in male historiography, and, having been stripped of her imaginary delusions, is reinserted into patriarchal order through the comic novel's conventional resolution of bourgeois marriage.

The reality of female desire and fantasy is contrasted throughout Charlotte Lennox's novel with the reality of patriarchal power and social order. This struggle is then relocated in a battle over the definitions of fact or history and fiction. The realist novel is represented as bringing an end to the blurring of boundaries between history and fiction that is the stock in trade of romance.

And yet those women writers who did present their fictions as fact in reaction to the romance, continued to be classified as producing the romance. The answer to this seeming illogicality on the part of commentators on the novel lies in the reality that female desire and fantasy are in and of themselves considered "unreal" by patriarchal society, rather than in the question as to whether women's writing in the early-eighteenth century was either more or less true to the requirements of "formal realism" of men's writing as Ian Watt defines it.[7] Thus, as Jane Spencer comments, "The feminocentric novel of the century was . . . inescapably bound to the 'unreality' as well as the love-theme of romance" (Spencer, 1986, p. 183).

The writer of the new novel or history required, according to Samuel Johnson in the *Rambler* (4, Saturday, March 31, 1750): "together with that learning which is to be gained from books, that experience which can never be attained by solitary diligence, but must arise from general converse and accurate observation of the living world" (in Williams, 1970, p. 143). In addition to this list of accomplishments, the writer was obliged to convey "the most perfect idea of virtue" (p. 146) to the impressionable young minds he is serving. This is an impossible requirement for a professional woman writer of the eighteenth century: knowledge of the world and virtue in a woman are irreconcilable opposites according to patriarchal logic. The woman writer seems to have been caught in a cleft stick. Her personal reputation was cleared if she dealt in the mythologized, idealized world of the romance, but her literary status was minimal. Yet if she wrote the kind of novelistic fiction that Johnson describes, she would be indicted as a prostitute of the pen for displaying the worldly knowledge which was a prerequisite for the text's moral function.

There were other reasons than the question of the slur of fiction's seeming duplicity and corruption of history for early British women writers rejecting the French romance structure. The lengthy romances of Madeleine de Scudéry asserted female autonomy at a considerable cost to the female character, that of a total repression of female sexuality and desire. Scudéry's heroines are idealized virgins who gain power by denying sexual passion and subjecting their male lovers to long and protracted deferrals of gratification. While the complex weavings of the plot provided a form of erotic suspense for the female reader, the possibility of female desire itself is rigorously purged from the text. Mary Delarivien Manley in her preface to *The Secret History of Queen Zarah* (1705) recognizes the problems of the desireless rationalism which lies at the heart of Scudéry's heroinism for the women readers who might chose it as a model. Manley comments wryly:

> The Authors of *Romances* give Extraordinary Virtues to their Heroins, exempted from all the Weakness of Humane Nature, and much above the Infirmities of their Sex; . . . It wou'd be in no wise probable that a Young Woman fondly beloved by a Man of great Merit, and for whom she had Reciprocal Tenderness,

> finding her self at all Times alone with him in Places which favour'd their Loves,
> cou'd always resist his Addresses; there are too Nice occasions. . . . " (Williams,
> 1970, p. 35)

As well as writing for a generation of female readers of the French romance,
Behn, Manley, and Haywood were seeking to satisfy a growing market of bourgeois female readers whose tastes may have been less well-served by the
protracted niceties of aristocratic courtship.

It is as much this aspect of the French romance, I would argue, which contributed to its demise in popularity, as its supposedly intolerable length (after
all in the 1750s Richardson's *Clarissa* seemed to manage to maintain interest
through its 1,500 pages) and artificial language. The writings of Behn, Manley, and Haywood in the early-eighteenth century in Britain are an attempt
to fulfill the sexual promise of the romance for women readers, to represent
female desire within the romance's framework of female heroism. Their novels
constitute the return of the repressed in the romance, utilizing female desire
as a means of undoing the romance while exploiting its formal device of deferral of a conclusion to its full erotic potential. In doing so, they produce a new
fictional economy, in which the female libido substitutes as the structuring
principle of romantic writing.

Behn, Manley, and Haywood's fiction brings us far closer to the formula
romance of the twentieth century associated with publishing houses such as
Mills and Boon and Harlequin. Eliza Haywood's novels in particular are satu-
rated in narcissistic descriptions of the female body convulsed with desire
against the heroine's better judgment. Desire now becomes an irresistible unconscious force of the type common to seduction scenes in romantic fiction
of the present day. In *Love in Excess*, Amena, who is later abandoned by her
lover, meets him illicitly in the Tuilleries and finds herself unable to resist
her own unconscious wishes:

> . . . she had only a thin Silk Nightgown on, which flying open as he caught her
> in his arms, her found her panting Heart beat measures of Consent, her heaving
> Breast swell to be press'd by his, and every Pulse confess a Wish to yield; her
> Spirits all dissolv'd, sunk in a Lethargy of Love; her Snowy Arms, unknowing,
> grasp'd his Neck, her Lips met his half way and trembled at the Touch. (Hay-
> wood, 1725, p. 26)

This kind of writing was, however, seen as no less "unreal" than the dam-
sels and knights of the French romance. Dieter Schulz, in his essay, " 'Novel',
'Romance,' and Popular Fiction in the First Half of the Eighteenth Century,"
argues that the *real* object of Daniel Defoe's, Henry Fielding's and Samuel
Richardson's attack on the "romance" and the "novel," was this early fiction
by women in Britain rather than its French precursor. He comments that, "The
salient features of the 'novel' before 1740 are sensationalism and erotic sen-
sualism, thinly veiled by the rhetoric of romance. The 'extravagancies' of romance were thus replaced by new outrages against 'common sense,' 'nature,'

and morality" (Schulz, 1973, p. 90). Dieter Schulz fails to recognize that these "outrages" and the continuing label of "romance" may in some way be connected to the fact that these early novels maintained the feminocentric structure of the romance, and were still, though differently, acting as vehicles for the female reader's fantasy.

The major difference between the French romance and the early woman's novel in Britain remains, however, its location of femininity on the side of nature or of culture. Female aspirations to fame and glory through a civilizing influence upon the masculine world of war and military conflict which is acted out in the romance, is substituted by an erotic depiction of natural female sexual desire which threatens the world of male rationalism and self-seeking gratification. In her *New Atlantis* (1709), Delarivière Manley tells the story of Polydore and Urania, a brother and sister who conduct an incestuous relationship. The lovers are discovered by a jealous cousin and condemned by a corrupt society; they themselves live in utter seclusion and, according to Manley, are simply following their natural and unquenchable desires. While Manley endeavors to frame the story with moral disquisitions on the evils of brother-sister incest, her highly eroticized portrayal of the romance undercuts the ostensible critique. Her attention focuses on Urania, the sister, which intensifies her representation of sexual desire as a female force for subversion of the given order. Manley rhetorically challenges her reader: "Thus excluded from Conversation, with that dear softness of Constitution, plainness of Nature, and unaffected Sweetness, what should she do for some Body to Love?" (Manley, 1971, I, p. 552).

The implication that the natural course of female sexuality has been silenced or misdirected by a masculine social order is common in Behn, Manley, and Haywood's novels. While this means that their fiction both recognizes and valorizes the unconscious power of female desire, however, it also fixes the feminine on the side of nature in the commonplace nature versus culture opposition of the period. It thus accords women no instrumentality in either sphere, because they are the victims of both; the abstract greedy "natural" force of love and the repressive, manipulative power of male culture.

This swing from a rationalist to a desiring representation of women in what might better be described as "romantic fiction" by this stage, brought with it its own perils, not least the attendant collapse of an outlet for female heroism. Behn, Manley, and Haywood's heroines are subjected not only to the dangers of masculine desire, but their own, and the demise of the French romance in Britain was accompanied by the loss of a fiction which provided women with an image of their own purchase on culture. Perhaps this may have been the reason for the massive popular success of Richardson's *Clarissa* (1747–8) which, with its debilitated, suffering female heroine as icon, restored the possibility of female heroic action. Renunciation of desire, whether in its sentimental or romance form, seems to be the prerequisite of heroism.

Throughout the late-seventeenth and early-eighteenth centuries then, we can see a long-standing struggle within the romance form, metaphorically associated with femininity at every stage, to produce a workable fantasy of female power, either by denying or foregrounding female sexual desire. Here too the techniques of modern romantic fiction for women evolve in the shape of a protracted deferral of heterosexual union and stasis, a voyeuristic attention to the female body and manifestations of unconscious desire, and a mythologizing and idealized portrayal of history under the sway of a feminine capacity for love. (For twentieth-century feminist theories of romantic fiction, see Modleski, 1984; Batsleer et al., 1985). Perhaps the last word should go to Euphrasia, as it does in *The Progress of Romance*, where she ably illustrates the liberatory possibilities of the veil which the French romance drew over the female body and the peril's of the modern romance novel's reintroduction of the female form and feminine desire at the heart of its narrative:

> Notwithstanding the absurdities of the old Romance, it seems calculated to produce more favorable effects on the morals of mankind than our modern Novels. If the former did not represent men as they really are, it represented them better. . . . its heroines were distinguished for modesty, delicacy, and the utmost dignity of manners. The latter represent mankind too much what they really are . . . they expose the fair sex in the most wanton and shameless manner to the eyes of the whole world, by stripping them of that modest reserve, which is the foundation of grace and dignity, the veil with which nature intended to protect them from too familiar an eye, in order to be at once the greatest incitement to love, and the greatest security to virtue. (Reeve, 1930, II, p. 87)

## NOTES

[1] The view that women were inveterate readers of fiction may have been somewhat of an exaggeration on the part of male critics displaying a moral panic that they were neglecting their domestic duties to indulge escapist fantasies. For example, in 1772 the *Critical Review* complained: "When a farmer's daughter sits down to read a novel, she certainly mispends her time, because she may employ it in such a manner, as to be of real service to her family . . . " (*Critical Review 33*, p. 327). In 1760, the *Monthly Review* declared it was no longer able to review every new book published, complaining that: "So long as our British Ladies continue to encourage our hackney Scribblers, by reading every Romance that appears, we need not wonder that the Press should swarm with such poor insignificant productions" (*Monthly Review 23*, p. 523). For a more sociological twentieth-century analysis of the female reading market see Watt, 1957.

[2] Aphra Behn frequently used and was referred to under the romance pseudonym of Astraea, Honoré d'Urfé's eponymous heroine, which suggests popular familiarity with the book. Other highly successful French romances in Britain were Gauthier de Costes de la Calprénède's *Cassandra* (translated 1642) and *Cleopatra* (translated 1652–8), and Madeleine de Scudéry's The *Grand Cyrus* (translated 1653–55) and *Clelia* (translated 1678). Their association with women readers was firmly established by the early nineteenth century when Walter Scott wrote, " . . . while Addison was amusing the world with his wit, and Pope by his poetry, the ladies were reading *Clelia, Cleopatra* and the *Grand Cyrus*" (Scott, 1870, p. 215). For a further discussion of the French Romance in Britain, see Davis, 1983.

[3]Dorothy Osborne's letters to William Temple are both a record of their own romance between 1652 and 1654 and her own penchant for French romance fiction, which she read in the original French, volume by volume, and frequently sent on to her lover. Madeleine de Scudéry, whom Osborne presumed to be a man since she published under her brother's name, emerges from the letters as her favorite romance writer. (See Smith, 1928.) Lord Wharncliffe in his 1861 edition of Mary Wortley Montagu's letters comments on her romance addiction: "she possessed, and left after her, the whole library of Mrs. Lennox's female Quixote—Cleopatra, Cassandra, Clelia, Cyrus, Pharamond, Ibrahim etc.,—all, like the Lady Arabella's collection, 'Englished,' mostly by persons of honour" (Smith, 1935, pp. 87–88).

[4]After the 1750s, the involvement of men in the production of the new novel, and Richardson's feminocentric epistolary fiction in particular, seems to have raised the prestige of the form. In 1751, Haywood turned to Richardsonian moralism and sentiment with her *The History of Miss Betsy Thoughtless*. However, when her *The Agreeable Caledonian* was reprinted in 1768, forty years after its original publication, the *Monthly Review* dismissed it on the grounds that:

> It is like the rest of Mrs. Haywood's novels written in a tawdry style, now utterly exploded; the romances of these days being reduced much nearer the standard of nature, and to the manners of the living world. (p. 412)

Whatever she wrote, it appears Eliza Haywood could not slough off association with the French romance.

[5]See Spender, 1991, Latham & Matthews, 1970, for further discussions of Elizabeth Pepys's reading habits. Pepys describes his wife, Elizabeth, reading Madeleine de Scudéry's *The Grand Cyrus* while he read a history of abbeys (I, p. 312), listening to him read a piece of the same book when she has a cold (VII, p. 225) and reading a letter from Gauthier de Costes de la Calprénède's *Cassandra* to him when he returns home and she is sick in bed (IX, p. 545). On two occasions he records buying French Romances for her (IX, pp. 247–365). One of the most amusing incidents occurs when his wife insists on narrating plot synopses from *The Grand Cyrus* to him:

> At noon home, where I find my wife troubled still at my checking her last night in the coach in her long stories out of *Grand Cyrus*, which she would tell, though nothing to the purpose nor in any good manner. This she took unkindly, and I think I was to blame indeed. . . . (VII, p. 122)

[6]See in particular, Samuel Johnson whose hero, Hymenaeus, in no. 115 of *The Rambler* (April 23, 1751) comes into contact with the arrogant Imperia in his search for a suitable wife. Imperia, we are told, "having spent the early part of her life in the perusal of romances, brought with her into the gay world all the pride of Cleopatra; expected nothing less than vows, altars and sacrifices; and thought her charms dishonoured, and her power infringed, by the softest opposition to her sentiments, or the smallest transgression of her commands." Bate and Strauss, 1969. Hymenaeus gives up all hope of marrying after this encounter.

[7]A useful synopsis of Ian Watt's definition of the characteristics of formal realism can be found in Lovell, 1987, pp. 20–21. They are: i—traditional plots are replaced by plots which conform to the "truth of individual experience" and are drawn from life rather than literary precedent; ii—plots are acted by people with a distinctive particularity, rather than types; iii—the past experiences of characters were the cause of present actions, narrative cause and effect comes from the relations between characters; iv—the action was located in an identifiable time and place; v—referential and denotational language was used in preference to the language of poetry.

# REFERENCES

Addison, Joseph & Steele, Richard. (1965). Donald Bond (Ed.). *The spectator*. Oxford: Clarendon Press. (Original work published 1711–1712.)

Batsleer, Janet, Davies, Tony, O'Rourke, Rebecca, and Weedon, Chris. (1985). *Rewriting English. Cultural politics of gender and class.* London: Methuen.

Bate, Walter Jackson & Strauss, Albrecht. (Eds.). (1969). *The Rambler IV.* London: Yale University Press.

Beer, Gillian. (1970). *The romance.* London: Methuen.

Behn, Aphra. (1688). Maureen Duffy (Ed.). 1986. *Oroonoko and other stories.* London: Methuen.

Burchfield, RIchard (Ed.) (1982). *A supplement to the Oxford English Dictionary, Volume III.* Oxford: Clarendon Press.

Davis, Lennard J. (1983a). The romance, liminality and influence. In *Factual fictions. The origins of the English novel.* New York: Columbia University Press.

Davis, Lennard J. (1983b). *Factual fictions. The origins of the English novel.* New York: Columbia University Press.

Eliot, George. (1977). *Middlemarch.* Middlesex: Penguin Books. (Originally published in 1871–1872)

Haywood, Eliza. (1719–1720). Love in Excess. In *Secret Histories, Novels, and Poems, Second Edition, Volume 1.* 1725. London: Browne and Chapman.

Haywood, Eliza. (1986). *The history of Miss Betsy Thoughtless.* London: Pandora. (Originally published 1751.)

Johnson, Samuel (1969). *The rambler.* Walter Jackson Bate and Albrecht Strauss (Eds.). London: Yale University Press. (Originally published in 1750–1752)

Latham, Robert & Matthews, William. (Eds.). (1970). *The diary of Samuel Pepys.* London: G. Bell & Sons.

Lennox, Charlotte. (1986). *The female Quixote or the adventures of Arabella.* London: Pandora Press. (Originally published in 1752)

Lovell, Terry (1987). *Consuming fiction.* London: Verso.

Manley, Mary Delarivière. (1971). The new Atalantis. (1709) In Patricia Koster (Ed.), *The novels of Mary Delarivière Manley 1704–1714.* Gainesville, FL: Scholars Facsimiles and Reprints

Modleski, Tania. (1984). *Loving with a vengeance. Mass-produced fantasies for women.* London: Methuen.

Murray, James (Ed.) (1910). *New English dictionary, volume VIII.* Oxford: Clarendon Press.

*Oxford English Dictionary (OED).* (1910). Oxford: Oxford University Press.

Scott, Sir Walter. (1870). Essay on romance. In *Miscellaneous prose works, Vol. VI, Chivalry, romance and the drama.* Edinburgh: Adam and Charles Black.

Small, Miriam Rossiter. (1935). *Charlotte Ramsay Lennox: An eighteenth century woman of letters.* London: Oxford University Press.

Smith, George C. Moore. (1928). *The letters of Dorothy Osborne to William Temple.* Oxford: Clarendon Press.

Spender, Dale (Ed.) (1991). *The diary of Elizabeth Pepys.* London: Grafton Books.

Watt, Ian. (1957). The reading public and the rise of the novel. In *The rise of the novel: Studies in Defoe, Richardson and Fielding.* London: Chatto and Winus.

# "Of Use to Her Daughter":

## Maternal Authority and Early Women Novelists

Jane Spencer

Adrienne Rich has argued that while the relationships between father and son, mother and son, and father and daughter have been explored in the most highly revered works of Western literature and art, the relationship between mother and daughter, "minimized and trivialized in the annals of patriarchy," remains the "great unwritten story" (Rich, 1984, pp. 225–226). Yet not so much unwritten, maybe, as unread: for although they have received little recognition for it, many women writers in the late 1700s and early 1800s were using their new forum, the novel, to express their sense of this relationship. Frances Sheridan's *Memoirs of Miss Sidney Bidulph* (1761) set the trend, by making the heroine's relationship with her mother, rather than her lover, the emotional focus. Sidney rejects Orlando Faulkland and marries Mr. Arnold on the advice of Mrs. Bidulph, who remains, despite Sidney's consequent unhappiness, "the best of mothers" in her daughter's eyes (Sheridan, 1761, II, p. 65). Later novelists like Charlotte Smith, Jane West, Mary Wollstonecraft, Mary Hays, and Amelia Opie followed Sheridan in emphasizing the emotional importance of a mother's advice. Though their novels, in this didactic age, carried widely varying "morals," all these writers were centrally concerned with the interplay between mothers and daughters.

An important issue in their works was the mother's authority—how far, and in whose interests, should she exercise control over her daughter? How far should a daughter be encouraged to follow in her mother's footsteps? The various answers reveal a fundamental ambivalence in eighteenth-century attitudes to the mother: she appears as the guardian of moral values, yet the representative of the frailer sex. The division reflects the dual view of woman, long entrenched in patriarchal society, in the particular form it takes at a certain historical moment, when the tradition of woman's depravity is being ousted by the belief in her special virtue. The change offered opportunities, as well as pitfalls, for women; and my concern here is with the use women writers made of the authority vested in the mothers of daughters. I will argue that this neglected subject was important to early women novelists not only

201

as a reflection of the domestic life of their time, but because it presented them with a paradigm for their own literary authority. In this way, the study of fictional mothers and daughters should help in the exploration of a complex problem in feminist criticism: the means by which women are accepted as writers within patriarchal society, and our feelings about the result.

We have been alerted to the extent to which a writer's authority in our culture is based on masculine, and especially paternal authority: the author is father to his text (Gilbert and Gubar, 1979, pp. 3–7). According to this model, women's writing is in and of itself transgressive of patriarchal rules. Yet many of the early British women writers managed to be accepted and praised within their society. How do we account for their achievements? I suggest that a model for female literary authority was developing over the eighteenth century, which worked—and has continued to work—in a double-edged fashion. On the one hand, it made it possible for women to write without altering the basic structure whereby authority lay in the hands of the father; but at the same time it contained the potential for radically subverting that authority. The basis for this model was the authority of the mother.

Female authority, as well as male, is acknowledged in the metaphors we use about writing: it can be pregnant as well as seminal. The analogy between writing a book and giving birth to a child was often drawn in the eighteenth century: sometimes with a sneer at "our newly-delivered Authoress and her literary bantling" (Monthly Review, 1763, p. 162); but also with an uneasy sense of the power of the mother as writer. In 1759, the reviewer of the anonymous novel Jemima and Louisa, "By a Lady," commented on the recent growth of women's writing as indicating "that this beautiful sex are resolved to be, one way or other, the joyful mothers of children. Happy it is, that the same conveyance which brings an heir to the family, shall at the same time produce a book to mend his manners, or teach him to make love, when ripe for the occasion" (Critical Review, 1759, p. 165). While this critic treated maternal authority with defensive sarcasm, other writers were taking it more seriously. Popular moralists like James Fordyce (Sermons To Young Women, 1766) and Thomas Gisborne (Enquiry into the Duties of the Female Sex, 1797) wrote of the mother's duty to teach her children and the importance of her influence on them; and, as the novelist Elizabeth Bonhote pointed out, if women were to fulfill this educational role they needed a position of authority:

> The department of a woman [she wrote] consists in regulating the economy of her family, and in a still-more important charge,—that of forming the minds of her children, and rearing them up in the paths of innocence and truth. But to enable her to do this, and to preserve the authority of a preceptress and the mistress of a family, she must be treated with respect and attention by her husband. (Bonhote, 1796, III, p. 45)

Through a conceptual link between writer and mother, the "authority of a preceptress and the mistress of a family" became the model for the woman writer's authority and the basis for her claim to "respect and attention" from the reading public.

Elizabeth Bonhote's own work demonstrates the short step from mother's to writer's authority: the remarks quoted above come from her book *The Parental Monitor* (published in 1788), consisting of miscellaneous moral observations addressed to her children. Other eighteenth-century titles offer evidence of similar moves. Women were held especially responsible for their daughters' education, and educational works were written as from mother to daughter, such as the anonymous *The Polite Lady: or a Course of Female Education; in a Series of Letters from a Mother to a Daughter* (1762). The eighteenth-century novel was deeply affected by this kind of educational model. To escape the common charge that their tales of love dangerously awakened their young readers' sexuality, women novelists presented their works as a fictional extension of the didactic tract; and one obvious way to base a fictional work on a mother's teaching was to dramatize maternal wisdom within the novel.

Jane West is one writer who exemplifies the maternal authority established in the eighteenth century. As the mother of three sons, she disarmed criticism by claiming that her domestic duties always came before literary ones, and a letter by one of her friends in the *Gentleman's Magazine* pointed out that while she was reading she would knit stockings for the family at the same time (*Gent. Mag. 72*, pt 11, p. 99). One of her published works, *Letters Addressed to a Young Man* (1801), grew directly out of her maternal role. She had no daughters of her own, but her *Letters to a Young Lady* (1806) were written as motherly advice to a Miss Maunsell, the daughter of a friend of hers who had died. Jane West's novels are explicitly aimed at a readership that stands in the same daughterly relationship to her. In the preface to *The Advantages of Education* (1793), she writes that her design is "to enstruct, rather than to entertain" her audience, which is envisaged as "the inexperienced part of her own sex." The story itself dramatizes a similar mother-daughter exchange: the heroine, Maria, is "an amiable unaffected girl, who, to all the enthusiasm of youthful innocence, unite[s] all its impetuosity and inexperience" (West, 1793, I, p. 7). She must learn to follow her mother's sage advice before reaching prudence and contentment. The advice is all to do with curbing her natural impulses and learning to accept hardships with fortitude. The examples of good conduct held up for Maria's edification are examples of filial duty—in particular, that of a woman who married a man she disliked for the sake of saving her parents from financial troubles. Maria's education bears fruit when she discovers that the man she loves wishes to seduce her. She rejects him, manages to overcome her unhappiness, and marries a more worthy man with the approval of her mother, who now turns to advising her on proper submission to a husband's temper: "Men are but men, nor must a wife always expect the behaviour of a lover, even from an affectionate husband" (II, p. 234).

As the education offered Maria suggests, the maternal authority so crucial to West's oeuvre finally operates under the authority of the patriarchal system. Adrienne Rich points out that "patriarchy depends on the mother to act as a conservative influence, imprinting future adults with patriarchal values" (Rich, 1984, p. 61), and West, writing to educate her daughter-readers and daughter-heroine in their duty to parents and society, is a good example of the mother who exercises this influence. Her express aim is to encourage women to accept their established place in society: "That philosophy which I wish my readers to possess," claims her narrator, "is constantly occupied in assimulating [sic] our desires with our situations" (West, 1793, I, p. 109). It is not surprising, then, that she was highly praised by conservative critics in her own day, and that her writings were considered, in a telling phrase, "monuments of *well-directed* genius" (my italics) (*Critical Review,* 2nd series, vol. 26, p. 452). Her maternal authority submitted to society's directing.

Such a use of the mother's authority in West and other writers suggests that the woman novelist's accepted role was bought at a high price to women in general. However, even within its conservative moral ethic, *The Advantages of Education* does suggest the feminist potential of the mother-daughter theme. Maria's mother is far more important to her than her father, who was a wastrel unable to give guidance to anyone; more important than the lover who proves unworthy; and more important than the man she eventually marries, whose main attraction seems to be that he is the son of a woman who, years before, offered maternal guidance to Maria's mother. The novel thus celebrates the establishment of a kind of maternal line of moral worth. As we will see, the establishment of such ideas of motherly goodness opened the way for writers like Mary Wollstonecraft to use maternal authority to challenge the patriarchal system.[1]

Any subversive use of the writer's motherly role needed to take account of the ambiguous status of maternal authority in the eighteenth century. The mother's disruptive potential was clearly felt as a threat, and this is probably one reason women like West disarmed criticism by stressing the conservative role of the good mother. Misogynist views held an important place in religious life: people were very conscious that the blame for mankind's Fall devolved on "our first mother," Eve, and that every "daugher of Eve" was implicated in her mother's guilt. James Fordyce, even while emphasizing the mother's role as her daughter's teacher, is haunted by the idea of mother Eve. He praises Milton's portrait of Eve and challenges the mothers who are reading his book for advice on bringing up their daughters to remember their descent from her: "Is there nothing in your own minds," he asks, "that whispers the frailty of your sex?" (Fordyce, 1766, I, p. 89). According to this influential view, maternal authority is fundamentally divided against itself: the good mother is the one who guards her daughter against tendencies inherent in her own female nature.

The image of the mother, then, was split, like other images of women in patriarchy, into "good" and "bad" halves. The split is neatly articulated by the repentant heroine of Amelia Opie's novel of mother-daughter relations, *Adeline Mowbray* (1804):

> There are two ways in which a mother can be of use to her daughter: the one by instilling into her mind virtuous principles, and by setting her a virtuous example: the other is, by being to her in her own person an awful warning, a melancholy proof of the dangers which attend a deviation from the path of virtue. (Opie, 1986, p. 244)

This double image of the mother complicates the development of maternal authority. The division Adeline makes here between different uses of the mother is reflected in differences in the mother's significance in the novels of the period. The mothers in Frances Sheridan and Jane West are "good" mothers, instilling virtuous principles in their daughters' minds. Women novelists were equally interested in the opposing type: the mother who has in some way failed and become an "awful warning" to her daughters. So we have novels in which the heroine's moral progress is measured, not by how well she follows her mother's good advice, but how well she succeeds in avoiding her mother's errors.

A brief look at two novels will suggest some implications of this alternative image of the mother. Fanny Burney's first novel, *Evelina* (1778), offers one example. The heroine's mother, Carolyn Evelyn, died innocent but socially disgraced when Lord Belmont refused to acknowledge her as his wife. Mr. Villars, Evelina's guardian, has tried to shelter her from the world so that she will be in no danger of becoming, like her mother, the victim of a lover's deception. When Evelina does enter society, she is plagued by her maternal grandmother, the bad mother who is to blame for Carolyn Evelyn's original mistake (she ran away with Lord Belmont to escape being forced into an unwanted marriage by her mother). Burney depicts Madame Duval as a grotesque figure of fun, and Evelina does all she can to dissociate herself from her mother's mother. Madame Duval is the butt of the cruellest jokes in the book—jokes at which both Evelina and her creator seem uncertain whether or not to laugh. In the end, the grandmother is routed and Evelina finishes her story with a redundancy of fatherly protection, from her guardian, her husband, and her father.

Elizabeth Inchbald's first novel, *A Simple Story* (1791), has a striking instance of a daughter's quest to atone for her mother's errors. The first two volumes of the novel contain the story of Miss Milner, witty, passionate, and defiant, who fascinates Lord Elmwood, the former Catholic priest, into marriage. The final volumes resume the story after sixteen years, to show the working-out of Miss Milner's story a generation later. After her adultery, disgrace, and early death, her daughter Matilda replaces her as heroine. Her father refuses to see Matilda, thus making her bear the punishment for her mother's crimes; but by her intense devotion to her father's will, she atones for her mother's transgression, and the climax of the novel is the reconciliation between father and daughter.

In both *Evelina* and *A Simple Story*, the heroine honors her dead mother, but the emotional focus is on the separation from and reconciliation to the father. The heroines resemble their mothers—in both novels the father, confronted by the daughter he has denied, thinks he sees her mother risen to life—but they are reincarnations with a difference. They are dutiful daughters who will not err, either flagrantly like Lady Elmwood or simply from imprudence like Carolyn Evelyn. Both novels criticize the tyrannical father, but they do not offer any alternative to him in the mother's authority.

It appears, then, that the ideological pattern of many women's novels in the late-eighteenth century is that of a recurrent return to the Law of the Father, whether through the mediation of the mother's authority or by avoidance of the mother's example. This results from pressure on women writers to become acceptable to their society by taking on a maternal authority granted only on condition that it reinforced the authority of the father. Nevertheless, the image of the mother, whose experience the daughter must avoid, was, like that of the mother as preceptress, capable of being appropriated for feminist use; and in the radical decade of the 1790s, several writers offered a more subversive version of maternal authority, by reintegrating the split image of the mother so that she could serve both as teacher and as warning example.

The most thorough attempt to revise the concept of maternal authority was Mary Wollstonecraft's, in her unfinished novel *Maria: and The Wrongs of Woman* (1798). Following the tradition of the female conduct-book and the didactic novel, Wollstonecraft dramatizes the mother's advice to her daughter and makes the mother's educational role serve within the fiction as the source of her identity as a writer. The heroine, whose imprisonment in a madhouse by her husband is a metaphor for the world's oppression of women, finds writing her only consolation. She begins by "some rhapsodies descriptive of the state of her mind," but soon turns to writing her memoirs, because they "might perhaps instruct her daughter, and shield her from the misery, the tyranny, her mother knew not how to avoid" (p. 82). This instruction is diametrically opposed to that offered by the mothers in Frances Sheridan or Jane West—it is not instruction in accommodation to the existing structures of society but in defiance of them. Maria's lesson, repeated over and over again in the stories of all the women she encounters, is that because of men's tyranny women are rendered unable to mother their daughters. Maria's own mother, subject to her father's ill-treatment, valued her son far above her daughter. Maria's husband, George Venables, seduces a servant whose only recourse, after he has thrown her out, is prostitution. She dies within a year and her baby daughter, left in the charge of the parish, suffers in mind and body from neglect: "She could hardly support herself, her complexion was sallow, and her eyes inflamed, with an indescribable look of cunning, mixed with the wrinkles produced by the peevishness of pain" (p. 149). When this child is brought to Maria, she is given a terrible warning of how the father, Venables, will treat their daughter. When she does give birth, she knows enough of the oppression of women to lament that her baby is a girl. Her separation from her baby is the culmination of all these injustices to mothers and daughters. The image of the baby torn from her breast recurs several times in the narrative and becomes a powerful metaphor for the many ways in which society denies women the right to nourish their daughters.

Maria's memoirs, written for the daughter who has been taken from her, are an attempt to provide the mothering that has been denied her. Maria holds herself up to her daughter as a warning, hoping her child will avoid her mistakes; but hers are not errors of transgression, but the error of failing, through lack of resolution, to challenge existing laws. In the passage introducing her memoirs, Maria tells her daughter that she is a mother

> who will dare to break through all restraint to provide for your happiness who will voluntarily brave censure herself, to ward off sorrow from your bosom. From my narrative, my dear girl, you may gather the instruction, the counsel, which is meant rather to exercise than to influence your mind.—Death may snatch me from you, before you can weigh my advice, or enter into my reasoning: I would then, with fond anxiety, lead you very early in life to form your grand principle of action, to save you from the vain regret of having, through irresolution, let the spring-tide of existence pass away, unimproved, unenjoyed.—Gain experience—ah! gain it—while experience is worth having, and acquire sufficient fortitude to pursue your own happiness; it includes your utility, by a direct path. (p. 124)

Maria's "instruction" is radically antiauthoritarian. Her only advice to her daughter is to exercise her mind and to act for herself. She tells her story not, as Adeline Mowbray would have it, as either the vehicle for moral advice or as a warning to avoid her own wicked conduct, but as an example of the oppression society visits on women, which she hopes will help her daughter to avoid becoming a victim in her turn. She is not advising self-restraint, but herself "breaking through restraint" in order to write; and she is not seeking to placate masculine disapproval of her boldness, but "braving censure" in order to pass on her liberating message to her daughter. Maria's memoirs are Wollstonecraft's model, within this novel, of women's writing. She takes the existing model of acceptable, didactic maternal authority and transforms it into a radical, challenging motherly permissiveness.

Maria's memoirs are abruptly broken off, and so was the novel itself at Wollstonecraft's early death. Like the heroine's memoirs, the novel itself is a fragmented legacy offered to daughters, opening up new possibilities for women's fiction. Its influence can be seen in similar radical transformations of the mother-daughter relationship in novels by Mary Hays and Charlotte Smith, which appeared soon afterwards. In Hays's second novel, *The Victim of Prejudice* (1799), the heroine's mother has been driven to prostitution. Eventually she is executed for her part in a fatal tavern fight; yet the legacy she leaves to her illegitimate daughter is not one of shame. She warns her daughter to avoid men's oppression rather than sin, asking her daughter's guardian to "cultivate her reason . . . rouse her to independence . . . teach her to contemn [sic] the tyranny that would impose fetters of sex upon mind" (Hays, 1799, I, p. 169). In Charlotte Smith's *The Young Philosopher* (1798), the heroine's mother expresses the hope that her daughter will not follow the "good advice" of the mother figures who serve patriarchal authority, but will "dare to have an opinion of [her] own, and not . . . follow one formal tract, because [her] grandmother and aunts have followed it before" (Smith, 1798, II, p. 14).

In making these explicit challenges to the version of authority which eighteenth-century society had accepted in women as mothers and writers, these women ran the risk of cutting off the branch they were sitting on. The critical outcry against Mary Wollstonecraft and Mary Hays, in particular, showed how quick critics were to deny women the right to write once they stopped upholding conventional moral wisdom in their novels. At the turn of the century, with the climate of conservative reaction deepening in Britain, many women writers turned away from Wollstonecraft's feminism (Butler, 1975; Kelly, 1976). There was a return to more acceptable pictures of maternal authority. This can be most clearly seen in a novel I have already mentioned for its presentation of the split image of the mother: Amelia Opie's *Adeline Mowbray; or, the Mother and Daughter* (1804). Written by one of her old friends several years after Mary Wollstonecraft's death, the novel is haunted by the ghost of Wollstonecraftian feminism.

Criticism of *Adeline Mowbray* has always focused on the heroine's decision to live with Glenmurray outside marriage—a decision which echoes the concerns of the feminists Mary Hays and Mary Wollstonecraft in the previous decade, and which allows the liaison to be interpreted as a fictional rendering of Wollstonecraft's with Gilbert Imlay. As Amelia Opie's subtitle indicates, though, she is more concerned with Adeline's relationship with her mother than Glenmurray. Mrs. Mowbray's delight in radical theories such as Glenmurray's attack on marriage is seen to be to blame for her daughter's action, and her rejection of Adeline afterwards therefore reveals cruel inconsistency. It is the separation from her mother, rather than society's condemnation or a sense of guilt, which makes Adeline miserable. Mrs. Mowbray betrays her daughter by letting a man come between them. Her second husband, Sir Patrick O'Carroll, is more attracted to Adeline than to the mother; and when his attempted rape of Adeline prompts the daughter to leave home, the mother is forced to realize this. Her extreme anger at Adeline's flight with Glenmurray is not attributed to outraged morality or concern for her daughter's welfare, but to jealousy, which prompts her to the curse which ruins

Adeline's life. She cries: "until you shall have experienced the anguish of having lost the man whom you adore, till you shall have been as wretched in love, and as disgraced in the eye of the world, as I have been, I never will see you more . . . not even were you on your death-bed. Yet, no; I am wrong there— Yes; on your death-bed" (Opie, 1986: p. 109). After this, Adeline's whole life becomes a series of self-punishing moves to fulfill the conditions her mother has laid down for a reconciliation. She is not happy with Glenmurray, because she cannot forget her mother. When, years later, she finds herself deserted by Berrendale, she rejoices to find herself "forsaken, despised and disgraced," and so a candidate for her mother's forgiveness (p. 203). It is hard not to see her final illness, which is given no organic cause, as willed on herself for the purpose of being able to claim the reconciliation with her mother which she achieves shortly before she dies.

With its intense commitment to the mother-daughter relationship, Amelia Opie's novel is like Mary Wollstonecraft's: both suggest what Adrienne Rich has recently claimed, that "the loss of the daughter to the mother, the mother to the daughter, is the essential female tragedy" (Rich, 1984, p. 237). But where Mary Wollstonecraft blames man's tyranny, Amelia Opie blames the mother. It seems likely that there is an autobiographical significance to Amelia Opie's portrait of the troubled mother-daughter relationship: from the account given by Opie's biographer, her mother seems to have displayed Mrs. Mowbray's combination of progressive ideas on most social issues with a sternly traditional view of parental authority; and lines written after her mother's death, which occurred when Opie (then Amelia Alderson) was fifteen, show her still haunted by her mother's criticisms.[2] In her exploration of a mother's proper authority, though, we find Opie confronting not only her natural mother but her literary "mother," Mary Wollstonecraft. Adeline is usually considered a portrait of Wollstonecraft, drawn by an old friend who sympathized with her but could not condone her "immoral" actions. In one sense, though, Wollstonecraft is represented more by Mrs. Mowbray than by the heroine. Mrs. Mowbray's first fault as a mother is to neglect her daughter's practical welfare in favor of writing a huge work of education intended for her future benefit: only the attention of a more traditionally-minded woman, Mrs. Mowbray's mother, saves Adeline from ignorance. Moreover, the ideas she introduces to her child are dangerous, because they encourage her to break social restraints. The reflection on Wollstonecraft's *Vindication of the Rights of Woman* (1792) is clear, and there may also be a reference to *Maria: and The Wrongs of Woman*. These works must have seemed, in the reactionary early 1800s, dangerous theoretical speculations which ignored women's practical needs.

The rejection of Mrs. Mowbray's motherly writings comes close to a rejection of the woman writer's authority altogether. The good Quaker Mrs. Pemberton accuses her of self-love in preferring her writing to her daughter. Mrs. Mowbray claims eagerly:

"I am sure that I paid the greatest attention to my daughter's education. If you were but to see the voluminous manuscript on the subject, which I wrote for her improvement—"

"But where was thy daughter; and how was she employed during the time that thou wert writing a book by which to educate her?"

Mrs Mowbray was silent: she recollected that, while she was gratifying her own vanity in composing her system of education, Adeline was almost banished from her presence. . . . (Opie, 1986, p. 257)

Where does Mrs. Pemberton's judgment leave women novelists like Opie herself, who were using an authority based on the mother's? Doesn't it suggest that they, too, should get back to a purely domestic role and stop extending their maternal influence in publication? Not quite, for there is an alternative model of the mother-writer to set against Mrs. Mowbray: Adeline herself, when she becomes a mother. Adeline's writing does not interfere with her devotion to her daughter but is, rather, an extension of her self-denial, as we learn that "wholly taken up all day in nursing and in working for [her baby], and every evening in writing stories and hymns to publish, which would, she hoped, one day be useful to her own child as well as to the children of others, [Adeline] soon ceased to regret her seclusion from society" (p. 187). Self-sacrifice instead of vanity, and hymns instead of speculative educational theories: Adeline's choice is the choice of an early-nineteenth-century writer disappointed in the revolutionary hopes of the 1790s. In relation to Mary Wollstonecraft, Amelia Opie enacts the very estrangement between mother and daughter that her novel explores. With the publication of *Adeline Mowbray*, the revolutionary potential for maternal authority which Mary Wollstonecraft had outlined was once again submerged.

# NOTES

[1]In the political division of Britain in the years following the French Revolution, Wollstonecraft and West (a firm supporter of Church and State) were at opposite poles. However, their ideas on female education shared some features, especially in the emphasis on women's need for fortitude, and Wollstonecraft praised West's fiction of domestic life. Commenting on West's novel *A Gossip's Story* (1796), she wrote: "The great merit of this work is . . . the display of the small causes which destroy matrimonial felicity & peace" (Letter to Mary Hays, January 1797, in Wardle, 1979, p. 375).

[2]Opie's biographer reports that Mrs. Alderson "was possessed of firm purpose and high principle; a true-hearted woman, and somewhat of a disciplinarian . . . Her daughter . . . frequently referred to her, even in her latter days, and usually with reference to some bad habit from which she had warned her, or some good one which she had inculcated" (Brightwell, 1854, pp. 6–7). Details of Mrs. Alderson's discipline suggest liberal political views: among her reproofs to Amelia was one for screaming at the sight of a black man who lived opposite. The child was encouraged to make friends with him and was told about the slave trade. Opie attributed her later involvement with the campaign against slavery to this incident. Her poem, "In Memory of My Mother," indicates the mixed feelings with which Opie looked back, and includes these lines:

I heard thee speak in accents kind,
And promptly praise, or firmly chide;
Again admir'd that vigorous mind
Of power to charm, reprove, and guide.
Hark! clearer still thy voice I hear!
Again reproof, in accents mild,
Seems whispering in my conscious ear,
And pains, yet soothes, thy kneeling child! (in Cecilia L. Brightwell, 1854, p. 10)

# REFERENCES

Anonymous. (1759). Review of *Jemima and Louisa*. By a lady. *Critical Review 8:* 165.

Anonymous. (1763). Review of Mrs. Woodfin, *History of Miss Harriot Watson*. *Monthly Review 28:* 162.

Anonymous. (1799). Review of Mary Hays, *The Victim of Prejudice. Critical Review 2nd ser. 26:* 452.

Anonymous. (1802). Letter in *Gentleman's Magazine 72* (1): 99.

Bonhote, Elizabeth. (1796). *The Parental Monitor*. London: William Lane.

Brightwell, Cecilia L. (1854). *Memorials of the life of Amelia Opie*. Norwich: Fletcher and Alexander.

Burney, Frances. (1970). *Evelina*. London: Oxford University Press.

Butler, Marilyn. (1975). *Jane Austen and the war of ideas*. Oxford: Clarendon.

Fordyce, James. (1766). *Sermons to young women*. London: A. Millar.

Gilbert, Sandra M. and Gubar, Susan. (1979). *The madwoman in the attic: The woman writer and the nineteenth-century literary imagination*. New Haven and London: Yale University Press.

Gisborne, Thomas. (1797). *An enquiry into the duties of the female sex*. London: T. Cadell.

Hays, Mary. (1799). *The victim of prejudice*. London: J. Johnson.

Inchbald, Elizabeth. (1977). *A simple story*. London: Oxford University Press.

Kelly, Gary. (1976). *The English Jacobin novel, 1780–1805*. Oxford: Clarendon.

Opie, Amelia. (1804, 1986). *Adeline Mowbray: Or, the mother and daughter*. London: Pandora.

Rich, Adrienne. (1984). *Of woman born: Motherhood as experience and institution*. London: Virago.

Sheridan, Frances. (1761). *Memoirs of Miss Sidney Bidulph, extracted from her own journal, and now first published*. Dublin: G. Faulkner.

Smith, Charlotte. (1798). *The young philosopher*. London: T. Cadell, Jun. and W. Davies.

Wardle, Ralph M. (1979). *Collected letters of Mary Wollstonecraft*. Ithaca: Cornell University Press.

West, Jane. (1793). *The advantages of education*. London: William Lane.

West, Jane. (1801). *Letters addressed to a young man*. London: T.N. Longman and O. Rees.

West, Jane. (1806). *Letters to a young lady*. London: Longman.

Wollstonecraft, Mary. (1976). *Mary: And the wrongs of woman*. London: Oxford University Press.

# Violence Against Women in the Novels of Early British Women Writers

Katherine Anne Ackley

Contemporary writers of fiction have explored the subject of violence against women, from Murial Spark's *The Driver's Seat,* through Diane Johnson's *The Shadow Knows,* to Margaret Atwood's *Bodily Harm.* These works are critiques of male aggression and violence against women and the cultural supports for such behavior. In reading the works of early British women writers who have recently been recovered, one discovers that those writers also addressed the issues of overt physical violence and more subtle forms of abuse as they described the social milieu in which such behaviors flourished. While the novels are entertaining and delightful reading, they also record certain realities of women's experiences: their lives were characterized by psychological, legal, and social victimization, as well as the constant danger of physical assault.

Though not explicitly feminist outcries against the injustices of patriarchal tyranny, many early novels by women are populated with characters who have been seduced, abused, or traumatized by men.[1] In the process of writing about the social and personal dynamics of women's lives, women writers have also transmitted information which readers today reinterpret from their own perspectives. Knowing what we do about sexual politics and power-structured relationships between men and women, for example, these texts are useful for illuminating the variety of ways in which the earliest female fiction writers perceived women's oppression. Their aim may not have been to "expose" the violent nature of women's lives, taking for granted that limitations and potential dangers were standard fare of everyday life, but their novels, nonetheless, adumbrate a dark reality.

Mary Brunton's *Self-Control* (1811), is almost entirely about sexual harassment. Other novels in the process of treating different topics also say much about the ways in which women are victimized. The primary subject of both Eliza Haywood's *The History of Miss Betsy Thoughtless* (1751) and Fanny Burney's *Evelina* (1778), for instance, is the education of young women into the ways of the world, but that process teaches the heroines about sexual harassment and the precarious nature of a woman's reputation in a male-dominated world. Maria Edgeworth's *Helen* (1834) is principally about how far one ought ethically to go to protect a friend but makes some pointed observations on the ways in which patriarchy limits and manipulates women. Even a book like Mary Hamilton's *Munster Village* (1778), which argues for educational opportunities for women, includes references to seduced and abandoned women. Indeed, no matter what their ostensible subject, novels by early women writers almost always contain women who have been victims of male aggression and control, in one form or another. Even when these writers seem to be nonjudgmental about or even subscribe to the limitations society places on women, modern readers find subtexts that those writers, perhaps, had not anticipated. Reading these novels reminds us of how constant have been the ways in which men aggress against women and commit real violence, both psychological and physical.

One of the most striking characteristics of eighteenth and early nineteenth-century novels by women is the chilling accuracy with which they portray the same kinds of aggressive behavior against women and the men who are driven to possess them that feminists today are decrying. For example, Mary Brunton's depiction of Villiers Hargrave's maniacal determination to possess Laura Montreville in *Self-Control* is little different from case studies of the many contemporary men who tyrannize in an effort to control the women in their lives. Hargrave is a fully drawn villain who will stop at nothing to have Laura, using more and more violent means in an effort to break her spirit. In fact, breaking Laura's spirit becomes almost more important to him than gaining her love: " 'Though the deed bring me to the scaffold, you shall be mine,' " Hargrave vows at one point. " 'You shall be my wife, too, Laura—but not till you have besought me—sued at my feet for the title you have so often despised. I will be the master of your fate, of that reputation, that virtue which you worship—' " (p. 391). He expresses this sentiment repeatedly and with increasing hostility.

Hargrave's determination to conquer Laura unfolds from a scene in the first chapter when he proposes not marriage, but a sexual relationship, to the seventeen-year-old Laura. As a pious Christian, Laura is so shocked to find that this man she has adored to the point of idolatry is a degraded seducer, that she faints. Hargrave, having decided that seduction would take too long, offers marriage to atone for his transgression, but he has not reckoned on the strength of Laura's character. She will have nothing to do with the immoral man, though at first she agrees to give him two years in which to prove himself worthy of her.

Hargrave is a handsome, weak, self-centered man, heir to a large inheritance and a lordship, and therefore accustomed to having his way in every matter, particularly with women. He finds Laura's refusal to marry him impossible to accept. It wounds his pride, fills him with a resentment bordering on hatred, and compels him to follow her relentlessly. The degree to which he harasses her is truly astonishing. With the complicity of Lady Pelham, the aunt who takes Laura in after her father dies, Hargrave becomes an object of real dread to Laura.[2] He hounds her at every opportunity so that finally she resorts to simply refusing to leave her room in order not to be open to his pursuits, becoming "a sort of prisoner" (p. 298) for weeks. Then he comes up with an elaborate scheme to have her transported to him by two men posing as law officers who have come to arrest her for a debt her uncle was supposed to have left unpaid. Hargrave shows up and offers to pay the debt, but Laura would rather go to prison than owe Hargrave anything. This rejection humiliates and enrages him so much that he orders the men to carry her off bodily, but Laura escapes to her room. What follows is a harrowing period in which the men pound on the door, Hargrave entreats her to come out, and Laura screams for help. The two men finally succeed in knocking the door down, and Laura, who has stood pushing against it on the other side, is taken down with it. The poor victim is gagged and dragged downstairs but is saved by the arrival of Lady Pelham's man of business, whom one of Laura's maids had secretly run to for assistance.

This horrendous event has no legal repercussions for Hargrave, but his uncle, Lord Lincourt, hears of it and arranges to have Hargrave's entire regiment sent to America. Relieved by this knowledge and engaged to marry De Courcey, Laura is still not yet at peace: before he leaves, Hargrave wounds De Courcey with a pistol shot. Finally, thinking Hargrave is out of her life at last— for news reaches her that he has sailed to America—Laura takes leave of the convalescing De Courcey one evening, in preparation for a journey to Scotland, only to be kidnapped, blindfolded, and spirited away to a ship that carries *her* to America. While Laura's last-minute escape in an Indian canoe down a river that takes her over a thundering waterfall borders on the melodramatic, the anguish she suffers during her captivity and the villainy of Hargrave are quite plausible.

The incident that had turned Laura from Hargrave forever is his affair with Lady Bellamer, whose pregnancy forces her to reveal Hargrave as her lover. This proof of Hargrave's "incorrigible depravity" (p. 225) is so stunning that Laura, after going through the process of examining her own motives and laying a large portion of the blame for Hargrave's actions on herself, is seized by a fever and almost dies. This particular episode illustrates not only the way women will assume blame for inviting unwanted sexual harassment, but also exemplifies that typical "blame-the-victim" attitude and double standard which has prevailed strongly until modern times and which still lingers today. Lord Bellamer turns his wife out of his home, challenges Hargrave to a duel, is wounded, recovers, and eventually is awarded 10,000 pounds for his trouble. Lady Bellamer's reputation is ruined, of course, and no mention is made of the fate of the unfortunate offspring. Furthermore, Hargrave always refers to Lady Bellamer as the wanton who had seduced *him*.

Hargrave's history of successful seductions also includes the young Jessy Wilson, daughter of Montague De Courcy's servants. In her case, however, it was not seduction but rape. Jessy's mother relates to Laura that her poor child arrived home following her undoing in a woeful condition, with a cheek turned blue and a mouth bloodied from Hargrave's blows. Now a ruined woman, she vowed to live only long enough to give birth to the child that resulted from the union. As her mother says, Jessy " 'could never wish to live to be "a very scorn of men, an outcast and an alien among her mother's children" ' " (p. 376). While Lady Bellamer may have been a willing participant in the illicit relationship with Hargrave, Jessy Wilson was not. Yet the world would condemn them both equally, while Hargrave continues to be received in polite society.

Indeed, the most outrageous aspect of Laura's final, most terrifying adventure is this matter of assigning blame to the victim of seduction or rape. Like the hapless Jessy Wilson, Laura knows the world will scorn her as a fallen women, once it learns she has gone to America. She prepares for this disgrace upon her return to Scotland by writing De Courcey and releasing him from their engagement and by arranging to live in solitude for the rest of her life. Never mind that she was abducted, bound, and dragged kicking to the ship, almost dead from fright and heartsick at being wrenched away from home and friends, to be taken deep into the wilds of a foreign country. Fortunately for Laura, just before he commits suicide in his grief over what he thinks is Laura's death, Hargrave—in the only unselfish gesture he ever makes—writes a letter absolving Laura of any blame in her excursion to America and the connection with him it seems to imply.

Laura's father explicitly states this double standard in the passage in which, exasperated by his insistence that she marry Hargrave, Laura blurts out:

> How can my father urge his child to join pollution to this temple, (and she laid her hand emphatically on her breast) which my great master has offered to hallow as his own abode? No! the express command of Heaven forbids the sacrilege, for I cannot suppose that when *man* was forbidden to degrade himself by a union with vileness, the precept was meant to exclude the sex whose feebler passions afford less plea for yielding to their power. (p. 175)

Her father responds: " 'My dear love, . . . the cases are widely different. The world's opinion affixes just disgrace to the vices in your sex, which in ours it views with more indulgent eyes' " (p. 176). Laura is placed in a serious double bind: she must disobey a parent whom she had regarded as godlike by refusing to marry a man they both know is a libertine; or she must obey her father and lose her self-respect. Though it pains her keenly to oppose her father on any point and though it gives her acute mental anguish to be guilty of filial disobedience, Laura opts for self-respect.

A similar conflict is experienced by Betsy Thoughtless in Eliza Haywood's *The History of Miss Betsy Thoughtless.* Her dilemma also involves her own sense of self in opposition to the demands of family. Betsy is convinced that her own moral strength is enough to protect her reputation, but her brothers, her guardian Sir Ralph Trusty, and especially Lady Trusty, all press on her the absolute necessity of preserving the appearance of virtue. The anxiety of Betsy's family and friends grows as Betsy finds herself in increasingly difficult situations, with men forcing themselves on her, trying her virtue, involving her in near scandals. At first Betsy enjoys her power to attract men. Perhaps naively, she enjoys teasing them, flirting with them, and generally driving them into a frenzy over her beauty and charm—not in order to seduce them but simply because it is fun. She has not yet learned that men perceive her behavior as invitations to take sexual liberties with her and that they will refuse to let her say "no" once she had behaved in this manner. Betsy is perplexed, annoyed, and eventually outraged at the behavior of men the moment they have her alone. While Betsy may view her sport with men as harmless fun, the world perceives it as evidence of licentiousness.

The conflict for Betsy occurs when her brothers insist that her reputation will ruin them, stressing the importance of *appearing* innocent. For Betsy, it is a matter of self-respect to know herself virtuous despite what the world believes; for her brothers, it is the appearance that counts. Betsy says, "with some warmth": " 'The loss of innocence must render a woman contemptible to herself, though she should happen to hide her transgression from the world.' " When her brother Francis points out that " 'a woman brings less dishonour upon a family by twenty private sins, than by one publick indiscretion,' " Betsy replies: " 'Well, I hope I shall always take care to avoid both the one and the other, for my own sake' " (p. 352). While the novel generally seems to accept and even support the customs of the time, a passage such as this suggests a subversive censure of the kind of hypocrisy her brother endorses.

Haywood is really exploring the emotional impact of restrictive social constraints on a bright, vivacious young woman. Besty must learn the folly of vanity in a society that places high value on beauty, at the same time it condemns women who "give in to" the men they are trained to attract. One of her closest calls serves as an example of the predicaments Betsy frequently finds herself in. This is the scene in which she is almost married to the devious Sir Frederick Fineer but is rescued at the last moment by the fortuitous arrival of Trueworth, brandishing his sword. Like Laura in *Self-Control*, Betsy suffers physical abuse at the hands of accomplices of the man who is determined to marry her. Two men, posing as a surgeon and a parson, push her "with so much violence as almost threw her down" and Sir Frederick himself, in trying to pry her loose from the bedpost, uses such "rough means" that he "was very near breaking both her arms" (p. 391). Betsy learns that not only will men try to get their way with her, but they will resort to violence if they must, in order to get it.

Contemporary researchers are interested in the ways cultural attitudes toward women encourage violent behavior in males. For example, Martha Burt's 1980 study "Cultural Myths and Supports for Rape" determined that when traditional sex-role attitudes are combined with the notion that sexual relationships are fundamentally exploitative or manipulative, and that force and coercion are legitimate ways to gain compliance in intimate and sexual relationships, then such violence as rape, battering, and acceptance of rape myths is inevitable. That is, the psychological availability of violence, in combination with deeply held attitudes about women's submissive nature, normalizes violent aggression against women. This conclusion has been reached by many other researchers as well.[3] If the observations of these researchers is accurate today, then it is likely that they were also accurate in the eighteenth and nineteenth centuries. A large number of encounters between men and women in the novels under examination reflect the reality that violent male aggression is one effect of traditional sex-role expectations and assumptions.

Many passages, such as the scene in *Betsy Thoughtless* with Fineer and Betsy's encounter with a gentleman commoner at Oxford, are filled with the language of sexual assault. In the Oxford incident, Besty is left alone in a room with a man who begins to kiss her against her will. Her struggles only increase his persistence. He seizes her roughly and cries, " 'You are in my power,' " then forces her to sit down, "holding her fast" (p. 47). Likewise, almost all of the passages in which Hargrave tries to manipulate Laura Montreville in *Self-Control* also contain the language of force. Then, as now, violence seemed a natural option available to men as a way of getting what they wanted, particularly sexually.

While physical force is useful for gaining one's immediate goal, psychological violence is more effective in the long run as a means of control. It also leaves deeper scars. Lenore Walker, in her book *The Battered Woman* (1979), says that most of the women in her studies described "incidents involving psychological humiliations and verbal harassment as their worst battering experience, whether or not they had been physically abused" (p. 72). Novels by early British women writers are full of women whose husbands tyrannize them verbally without ever physically touching them; though sometimes they do both. In *Betsy Thoughtless,* for example, Lady Mellasin's lover's wife had been kept under his thumb both physically and emotionally. Though her husband beats her, he maintains control by humiliating and degrading her. Such treatment destroys her self-esteem and leaves her feeling insecure and dependent on the man who abuses her. In Brunton's *Self-Control,* Laura's trauma is much more emotional than physical. As strong as she is and as healthy as her self-esteem is, she says to De Courcey: " 'I cannot tell you to what degree he [Hargrave] has embittered the last years of my life' " (p. 301).

Another example of psychological abuse is a character mentioned in Mary Hamilton's *Munster Village.* Mrs. Lee was married off by her family to a wealthy man who grew impatient and ill-tempered and soon tired of her. Not only did his verbal assaults grow increasingly abusive, but "his very footmen were taught to insult her, and every one in the family knew the most effectual way to ingratiate themselves with him, was to disregard his wife" (p. 46). This woman bore much contempt, neglect, and distress until the tyrant Lee wounded a man he accused of loving his wife and she left him, ruining not her husband's reputation but her own. Repeatedly in these novels, women are accosted by men or harassed by them; they are verbally abused and frightened by men who want to seduce them, control them, and own them completely.

Although Besty Thoughtless is rescued from being "a victim to the most wicked stratagem that ever was invented" in the bedroom scene with the plotting Sir Frederick Fineer (p. 392), the event convinces her brothers that she must marry at once to save her reputation. The most available and acceptable man at the moment is Mr. Munden. Her marriage to Munden comes after many protestations by Betsy against marriage. She has had no intention of marrying until she loves someone; she is too young and enjoys the attentions of a variety of men too well to give herself to any one man. Betsy realizes what marriage means to women: the end of personal liberty, the end of individuality, the loss of even a legal identity, and of course, the end of fun as a single woman. As she thinks to herself:

> I wonder . . . what can make the generality of women so fond of marrying? It looks to me like an infatuation; just as if it were not a greater pleasure to be courted, complimented, admired, and addressed, by a number, than be confined to one, who, from a slave, becomes a master; and, perhaps, uses his authority in a manner disagreeable enough. . . . Mighty ridiculous! they want to deprive us of all the pleasures of life, just when one begins to have a relish for them. (pp. 451–52)

In fact, Betsy at first gives up the man she ultimately loves and eventually marries, Mr. Trueworth, because of her haughty treatment of him, her disdain of his advice about her behavior, and her insistence that she is too young to marry. When she finally is pressured into marriage, she agrees reluctantly, sadly, and only because she does not want to lose the good will of her brothers and her most devoted friends, the Trustys, all of whom insist that marriage is the only way she will avoid ruining her reputation and, consequently, that of her brothers.

Munden, who marries Betsy as a matter of pride, not love, turns out to be verbally abusive, parsimonious, and potentially physically violent. At one point, in a rage, he dashes Betsy's pet squirrel against the fireplace mantle, shattering its little body. He is also unfaithful to her. When Betsy discovers this fact, especially when one of his paramours is staying in Betsy's own home, she can no longer live with him and, in a daring act, moves out. Interestingly, her close female friends advise her to make the best of a bad situation, which Betsy does until she is pushed too far. Leaving their husbands was not a solution available to many women, given the absolute control men had over them. Because wives were their husbands' legal property, husbands had the right to order their wives home—and into their beds—with the full backing of law officers to ensure their compliance, an option Munden considers but finally rejects. Thus, Betsy is guilty of violating both social and legal sanctions when she leaves her husband.

What keeps *Betsy Thoughtless* from being a feminist tract against the customs of the society it depicts is the way Betsy rarely questions the lessons she learns. As she matures, she no longer challenges accepted standards as she does in the passage in which she argues with her brother about what the world thinks versus what she knows of her own behavior. Nor can we assume that Haywood intended to decry the double standard or the incredible limitations of women's lives. Her intent must surely have been to write an engaging narrative about a subject guaranteed to be of interest to the reading public. In Haywood's time, that public was limited to the leisured class who had both the time and money to educate their daughters and sons. Haywood's novel remains a delightful, fast-paced, eminently entertaining work. Those fortunate women who read the novel in 1751, when it was first published, very likely were drawn to the character of Betsy, who is strong-willed, beautiful, and in need of lessons about the world.

Indeed, not only did Betsy's close calls with disgrace stand as lessons to young women, but also the sordid lives of several women of easy virtue served as stern warnings of what would befall women of loose moral character. Betsy's unfortunate friend Miss Forward becomes a prostitute to support herself after having given birth to an illegitimate child who dies. When Betsy is seen in public with Miss Forward, unaware of her friend's profession, Trueworth warns her that her own reputation is in imminent danger of irreparable damage. Betsy drops her friend. This same Trueworth knows that his beloved friend, Sir Bazil Loveit, is a frequent visitor of Miss Forward. Trueworth himself sexually uses Flora Mellasin to get over his disappointment at losing Betsy. Once he begins an attachment with the chaste Harriot Loveit, however, he abandons Flora remorselessly. While Betsy and everyone else seem to accept the rightness of this double standard, the evidence of its devastating consequences for women abound. Flora, her mother Lady Mellasin, Mademoiselle de Roquelair, and the unhappy Miss Forward are all punished for their promiscuity.

The heroine in Fanny Burney's *Evelina* is also warned of the dangers of associating with loose women. After being frightened by a group of men, Evelina unwittingly seeks help from two prostitutes. These rude women force Evelina to walk with them until she sees the friends from whom she had been separated. Lord Orville sees her in their company and makes a special visit to her in the morning to inquire if Evelina were aware of the women's reputation. Evelina had already been reminded by her guardian that "nothing is so delicate as the reputation of a woman: it is, at once, the most beautiful and most brittle of all human things" (p. 152).

There are other parallels with *Betsy Thoughtless* in *Evelina*. Evelina's mother Caroline, a ruined woman, was deserted by her husband Sir John Belmont and died of a broken heart. This same husband also fathered an illegitimate son, Mr. Macartney, whose unhappy mother sought exile in Scotland and lived in isolation there for the rest of her life. Furthermore, there are also men who test the virtue—and the patience—of the heroine. One notable example is Lord Merton, who, engaged to Lady Louisa Orville, nevertheless harasses poor Evelina, first in private and then in public, much to the embarrassment and distress of Evelina. Drunk one evening, he "frequently and forcibly seized [her] hand, though [she] repeatedly, and with undissembled anger, drew it back" (p. 289). The fop Mr. Lovel makes a real pest of himself at her first assembly, and Sir Clement Willoughby will not leave her alone.

The case of the rude, obnoxious, and cruel Captain Mirvan is different. While Lovel and Willoughby are not particularly dangerous, just immensely irritating, Captain Mirvan causes real damage, both psychological and physical. His wife is half afraid of him, and his fondness for practical jokes results in a truly frightening hoax perpetrated against Evelina's grandmother. Disguised as a bandit, Mirvan drags the terrified Madame Duval from her carriage, shakes her viciously and repeatedly, ties her feet with a rope that he fastens to the upper branches of a tree, and, knocking her wig off, leaves her there. Madame Duval, rather than being solaced, is treated is a ridiculous figure. Even the servants, "in imitation of their master, held her in derision" (p. 137). While Burney clearly means both Duval and Mirvan to be comic figures, the incident is fraught with terror. This is a truly vicious dirty trick.

Nothing can match *Betsy Thoughtless* for sheer numbers of men who pester, harass, and fight over the beautiful heroine, however. Betsy does successfully save her virtue and avoid, usually at the last minute, being ruined. More importantly, from Haywood's point of view, she learns not to be so "thoughtless" as she grows into a mature young woman who learns the ways of the world. Betsy's moment of insight comes after the attempt of her husband's patron to seduce her. Betsy finds herself in a real fix when Lord **** arranges to have Munden called away from a private dinner party he has for them. The two of them are left alone when the woman who Betsy thought was a kinswoman of the lord leaves the room. This "kinswoman," it turns out, is really "no more than a cast-off mistress of his lordship's; but, having her dependance [sic] entirely upon him, was obliged to submit in every thing to his will, and become an assistant to those pleasures with others which she could no longer afford him in her own person" (p. 510). Here is an example of a character who, though presented almost as an aside, serves to remind the reader of the tyranny of powerful, self-indulgent men like Lord ****. Notice the language of the passage: once his mistress and since "cast-off," she is now dependent on him and must "submit in every thing to his will." This involves the humiliation of participating in laying a trap for a new sexual partner for this man whom she "no longer affords" pleasures.

Betsy is chased around the room by the lecherous lord but is saved from his advances by quick thinking. Later, in reviewing the evening, she

> now saw herself, and the errors of her past conduct, in their true light. "How strange a creature have I been!" cried she; "how inconsiderate with myself! I knew the character of a coquet both silly and insignificant; yet did every thing in my power to acquire it. I aimed to inspire awe and reverence in the men; yet, by my imprudence, emboldened them to the most unbecoming freedoms with me." (p. 519)

The result of this self-examination is that she blames herself for all the unwanted advances she had experienced and becomes a serious, sensible, well-behaved woman.

While Haywood may very well have meant this as a positive step for Betsy, readers today see it as compromising her spirit. Besides, the novel's occasional dark tones suggest that Haywood did not wholly endorse society's condemnation of Betsy's behavior.[4] For example, she has strange dreams the night she agrees to marry Munden: "Sometimes she imagined herself standing on the brink of muddy, troubled waters; at others, that she was wandering through desarts [sic], overgrown with thorns and briars, or seeking to find a passage through some ruined building, whose tottering roof seemed ready to fall upon her head, and crush her to pieces" (p. 452). Her marriage to Munden turns out to be truly a nightmare from which she is rescued only by his early death. The future that lay before her, had he not died, was grim indeed, for Betsy had agreed to return to him once he became gravely ill. His death and the death of Trueworth's wife allow for a tidy happy ending to the novel, with Betsy marrying Trueworth. Still, the tyranny of men and their possessiveness if glaring throughout.

An excellent example of the way men rule women without being physically violent or even thought of as cruel is Maria Edgeworth's *Helen*. While it is not overtly concerned with male violence against women, the society Edgeworth depicts is patriarchal and, therefore, bound up in power structures characterized by male dominance and female submission. This is most clearly illustrated in the relationship between Clarendon and Cecilia, where a kind of psychological violence is operating. As husband, as general, as head of his household, Clarendon holds absolute power over his wife. His particular insistence on marrying a woman who has loved no other man adds an additional criterion to the usual requirements of chastity, fidelity, and beauty in potential wives. As a result, Cecilia is put in the position of either admitting the truth that she once was enamored of another—thereby losing the highly desirable Clarendon—or she must lie, and get her man. Clarendon's requirement is a strongly self-centered one, which he admits, and Cecilia's lie to secure a husband does not seem extreme, given the opportunity she would miss by telling the truth. Although at one point he implies he would have forgiven Cecilia had she confessed early on, it is abundantly clear that Cecilia is operating out of real fear of his power over her: she believes he would cast her aside, as indeed he says he will until the last page of the novel.

Because of the disparate power relationships between men and women, Cecilia not only lies to get a husband and then again and again to keep him, but she is forced to betray the trust of her friend Helen. Cecilia's insecurity in her marriage, that is, her consciousness of the relative power positions of Clarendon and herself, is responsible in large part for the predicament she gets herself and Helen into. Weakness of character also accounts for it, but the fact that men are the real authorities and whatever idiosyncrasies they have go unquestioned is a strong contributing factor to Cecilia's lying. Both her economic and social positions are tenuous, dependent on a man who insists on total possession of his woman's affections including the time before she knew him. She has not nearly the freedom her husband has and is reduced to desperate lies and evasions, not just to save face but to keep her very real fears from becoming reality.

An interesting thing happens to Cecilia, however. She tells Helen that her love for Clarendon decreased when she realized how completely she had fooled him. She says that she had always looked up to him for his superior judgment, but when she saw that he had been so fully duped by her, he was lowered in her opinion. When he began to catch her in her lies and speak harshly to her, she says, " 'all my love—all my reverence—returned . . . my passion for him returned in all its force' " (p. 419). That passage illustrates another dynamic of power-structured relationships. Cecilia has viewed Clarendon not as her equal but as some larger-than-life, imposing authority figure whom she adored as long as she felt unworthy of him, as long as she had to struggle to meet his standards. When she realized she could manipulate him, that *she* had the power to weaken his judgment, then she lowered her opinion of him. Her regard for and love of her husband rises and falls in relation to how much control he has over her. Cecilia is attracted to her husband as someone she can fear but repulsed by him as someone she can control. The social conditions that produce such an attitude and such a marriage prevent female autonomy and cause deception and betrayal. Communication between men and women becomes impossible.

No matter what its outward form, male aggression against women has its roots in the basic inequality between men and women. Fiction by early women writers reflects the real world where such inequity results in battered and embittered women, powerless women, spiritually imprisoned women. This world is uncomfortably familiar to modern readers, who know that women's experience of male power and victimization must inherently be different from male depictions of such experiences. Reading male writers of the eighteenth and nineteenth centuries does not afford us the perspective on women's lives that novels by these early women writers give us. Along with the pleasure of reading well-written, carefully crafted, lively narratives by early British women writers, our historical understanding of women's realities is immeasurably enriched by their recovery.

## NOTES

[1]For an excellent discussion of the seduction theme in eighteenth-century novels, see Spencer, 1986. Spencer notes that in the first two decades of the eighteenth century, Delarivière Manley and Eliza Haywood, while seeming to capitalize on the sensationalism inherent in explicit descriptions of seduction, were in fact challenging the accepted male view of women. But from 1720 to the 1760s, Spencer says, female novelists did not express much sympathy for their seduced heroines. The novels in this period reinforced the ideology of femininity by praising subordination in women and scorning "fallen" women. With the sentimentalism of the 1760s, 1770s, and 1780s came a renewal of sympathy for the seduced woman, but she was no longer the heroine of the novel. The last two decades saw a radical feminist which strongly attacked the patriarchal social structure that supported the double standard.

[2]Interestingly, Lady Pelham is a study in female tyranny as well, particularly when it is motivated by a desire to gain male approval and to benefit from male privilege. Determined that Laura will marry Hargrave and completely unmoved by the knowledge that he is a libertine and an adulterer, Lady Pelham colludes with Hargrave in several of his nefarious plots. Not only does she conspire to get Laura alone with him, but she also is physically violent to her. Once she slaps Laura's face viciously, and another time she pinches her arm until it bleeds. The terror Laura experiences under her aunt's protection is not merely exasperating; it is dangerous.

[3]One of the most thorough studies of the subject is the research by Cannie Stark-Adamac and Robert E. Adamac, whose review of literature from seventeen different fields was published in their 1982 article. They specifically limited their research to studies of rape and aggression by men against female intimates and concluded that "the data suggest that there has to be a climate in which aggression is both conditioned and reinforced, a climate in which asymmetrical sex roles are adopted and the female devalued, for men to choose aggression as a response and to choose a woman as the target of aggression" (p. 1).

[4]Ros Ballaster, at a 1987 summer conference on early British women writers in London, remarked that in all of Eliza Haywood's works there is a consistent cynicism about heterosexual love affairs that presents a far bleaker picture of women's existence under patriarchy than her reputation as a romance writer might indicate. Such relationships are characterized in part by exploitative men who lose interest once they made their conquest. Rape, seduction, and betrayal abound. See also "Preparatives to Love: Seduction as Fiction in the Works of Eliza Haywood" and "Romancing the Novel: Gender and Genre in Early Theories of Narrative" by Ros Ballaster, this volume, pp. 188–200.

## REFERENCES

Brunton, Mary. (1811, 1986). *Self-control*. London: Pandora.

Burney, Fanny. (1778, 1958). *Evelina*. London: J. M. Dent & Sons.

Burt, M. R. (1980). Cultural myths and supports for rape. *Journal of Personality and Social Psychology 38* (2), 217–230.

Edgeworth, Maria. (1834, 1987). *Helen*. London: Pandora.

Hamilton, Mary. (1778, 1987). *Munster village*. London: Pandora.

Haywood, Eliza. (1751, 1986). *The history of Miss Betsy Thoughtless*. London: Pandora.

Spencer, Jane. (1986). *The rise of the woman novelist: From Aphra Behn to Jane Austen*. Oxford: Basil Blackwell.

Stark-Adamac, Cannie and Adamac, Robert E. (1982). Aggression by men against women: Adaptation or aberration? *International Journal of Women's Studies* 5 (1), 1–21.

Walker, Lenore (1979). *The battered woman*. New York: Harper Colophon.

# Part Three
# The Achievements

# The Triumph of the Form

## Rosalind Miles

Who can deny that the novel is unique among literary forms in owing its birth, survival, and success at every stage as much to women writers as to men? Yet Colin Wilson (1975) could only find three women (Jane Austen, Daphne du Maurier, and Sigrid Undset) worthy of inclusion in *The Craft of the Novel*, while in Martin Seymour Smith's *Fifty European Novels: A Reader's Guide* (1980), which purports to "outline the development of the novel since Rabelais" (p. 5), only one female name is to be found. It is clear that not enough recognition has yet been given to the courage and resources of the pioneer women novelists in their two-fold task—for in addition to the struggle to write undertaken by any writer, they also had to fight a much deeper and usually unacknowledged battle within the predominantly masculine tradition, first to find a permitted place, and second to find a voice that could make itself heard.

In the centuries following the work of the early women novelists, a very great deal of effort was expended in claiming and reclaiming the novel as a vehicle for women writers and for exploring their distinctively female experiences and preoccupations. Given the number of exciting innovations in women's writing in recent years, any critical observations have to be in the nature of an interim report. This stunning explosion of female talent has created a new wave of women writers, most of whom are only beginning to realize their potential and who will go further in directions as yet unimagined. There is also much work for women writers still to do in continuing to explore the intimate aspects of their lives as women: as daughters, as mothers, in sexual relations with men and with each other, or as women alone—besides the ongoing challenge of mapping those areas of experience still under the patriarchal taboo (for example, power structures and vested interests, whether of oppressive religious ideologies or those of big business).

For all these reasons and many more besides, the novel has from its earliest days engrossed the attention of women writers to the virtual exclusion of any other art form. This fact has been of substantial significance to all who

work in this area. The sex of a novelist has always been in question somewhere, sometime, in the course of the critical response—the sex of a woman
novelist, that is. Whatever a woman has produced as a writer, she will still
be judged as a woman (see Spender, 1989, for further discussion.) Roland
Barthes (1972) in *Mythologies* examined a photograph of a group of women
novelists that appeared in the magazine *Elle*. Every single one of the seventy
writers represented was described as "Jacqueline Lenoir, two daughters, one
novel; Marina Grey, one son, one novel; Nicole Dutreuil, two sons, four
novels," and so on. Twenty years later, what has changed?

As Dale Spender demonstrates in *Mothers of the Novel* (1986) and *The
Writing or the Sex?* (1989), the "lady novelist" initially picked up her pen and
staked out the novel as female territory *before* her male colleagues. But a funny
thing happened to her on the way to posterity: "We have a splendid but suppressed tradition of women writers," says Spender, when "Jane Austen is
presented as a solitary figure and starting point of women's literary achievement" (p. 145). This contention is endorsed and echoed by the work of other
women scholars. Janet Todd's *Dictionary of British and American Women
Writers 1660–1800* (1984) lists nearly 500 names, while Lisa Mainiero's *American Women Writers* (1979–1981) runs to four large volumes. But by the nineteenth century, the sustained onslaught of males on women's right to write
had largely done its work; the idea that the novel was man's "proper sphere"
was so entrenched that the very suggestion of a "lady novelist" was enough
to prompt suspicion, scorn, surprise, or roguish gallantry all around. Considerable interest was aroused by the hope of spotting a female hand at work,
as Dickens did with George Eliot's *Scenes from Clerical Life* (1858). Masculine opinion combined to produce an impression of the woman writer as an
aberration; the philistine gibe of W.S. Gilbert in *The Mikado* at the "lady novelist" as a "singular anomaly" who could well be spared from the cultural scene,
both illustrated the entrenched prejudices of the operetta's audiences and confirmed their limitations of taste.

Many would concede that the sense of sex difference was strong in the
past but would like to think that things are different now. The idea of the "lady
novelist," like the phrase itself, has a whiff of stale elegance and misplaced
chivalry about it. The days are gone in which a male critic could no more
bring himself to dispraise a lady's novel than he could disparage her bonnet.
Those familiar with Norman Mailer's critique of Marcy McCarthy in *Cannibals
and Christians* (1967) and his general response to his female critics in *The
Prisoner of Sex* (1971) will be aware that they are long gone indeed; Mailer
proved that he could bring himself to the entire critical gamut that lies between the left hook and the right cross.

And for all this, the part-playful, part-hostile nineteenth-century distinction
of women writers as "lady novelists" has stayed very much alive. The distinction, however, has become hallowed as "writers" and "women writers," the

phrase still operating to confine creative women to a pejorative subsection of the real thing, the great world of literature, when, as Mary Ellmann remarked, "criticism embarks upon an intellectual measuring of busts and hips" (Ellmann, 1968, p. 29). The great artists may illustrate the pettiness and absurdity of such classification, but they seem to be able to do little to undermine it. The novel is masculine territory, over which men must keep control. So to Norman Mailer (1967) the novel is "the Great Bitch"; writing is fucking and mastering her, good writing is "making her squeal": "Man, I made her moan" (pp. 104–105). David Lodge made a similar claim to masculine sexual possession in *The Language of Fiction* (1966): "Fiction is never virgin: words come to the writer already violated by other men" (p. 71). The French structuralist Jacques Derrida was not only speaking for the nation of lovers when he identified the pen with the penis on the virgin page. But the American writer William Gass found solace in a more domestic metaphor when he gave his version of the *Boys' Own* definition of the creative act:

> Ordinary language ought to be like the gray inaudible wife who services the great man: an ideal engine, utterly self-effacing, devoted without reminder to its task . . . it demands to be treated as a thing, inert and voiceless. (Gass, 1973, p. 93)

As this shows, criticism seems to have to come to terms with women writers in every new age, treating each fresh generation of women as if they were the first of their sex to pick up the pen. It is not the least interesting aspect of women's writing that its very existence has constantly to be explained (away?). As Patricia Meyer Spacks observed in *Contemporary Women Novelists*:

> Critical discussion of women writers seems even now at a primitive stage, though women have written a large proportion of published novels ever since the genre first developed in the eighteenth century. . . . Conceivably the relative invisibility of women writers reflects the special difficulty in dealing with them. (Spacks, 1976, p. 153)

How this feels from the point of view of one on the receiving end was deftly satirized by Alison Lurie in *Real People*:

> I suppose I was irritated by Nick because he interrupted a conversation about my book. . . . And even more because of the way he did it.
> NICK: You a writer? Hey, Baxter, pass the salt. Yeah, I thought you looked like a lady writer.
> That looks harmless written down, but it wasn't; it was coarse and dismissive.
> Of course it's been said before, but not in that tone of voice. What's occasionally meant (and sometimes also said) is that I look a little like pictures of Virginia Woolf—a less fine drawn, less neurasthenic, middle-class American version. . . . Somebody asked once if that was why I decided to become a writer. "Not at all," I replied indignantly. "Long before I had even *heard* of VW, I wanted to be a writer." Quite true, but so do a lot of young girls. And who can say it

didn't influence me when I found out? . . . A lady writer. And why should I mind that anyway? Do I mind being a writer? Or being a lady? (Lurie, 1969, pp. 30–31)

Both critical and authorial comment, then, have repeatedly wrestled with the question, "Why do women write novels?" Fortunately, the majority of women writers have simply picked up the task from generation to generation, and gone on writing. In itself, that has not always been easy. Given the routine denial to women of everythng that does not fall within the restrictive paradigm of "femininity" or "womanhood," it is hardly surprising that women writers in the past have not been able either confidently to create new traditions, nor even to hang on to what had been achieved. As Elaine Showalter stresses in her magisterial study *A Literature of Their Own: British Women Novelists from Bronte to Lessing* (1977), "each generation of women writers has found itself . . . without a history, forced to rediscover the past anew, forging again the consciousness of their sex" (pp. 11–12). It is this silence of annihilation, unwilled and all too often enforced, that women's writing has always sought to combat. Recovering the lost tradition while finding the individual voice has involved rediscovering in every generation the terms of confrontation with the dominant masculine world. Yet in no sense is the writing that these women produced in response to their subordination to be seen as reactive or second-class. On the contrary, from their inferior position, women novelists succeeded in capturing the heights. Singly and in numbers they have established the novel as the female form. As writers, they have repeatedly demonstrated their outstanding mastery of it; as readers, they have continuously turned and returned to it for the vital task of making sense of their experience as women, and harmonizing the often unbearably painful conflicts of their lives. And all this they have achieved in the face of long-standing, deep-rooted hostility and denial.

And the achievement has been stupendous. It is the continuing paradox of women's writing that from its very inception, while female writers were continually having to deny, disguise, justify, or apologize for their existence, they have also quietly got on with the job of mastering the novel form and making it their own. On any criteria of "greatness"—enduring quality, human relevance, mythic resonance, capacity to delight—women have undoubtedly captured the heights with everything from *Evelina* (1778) to *The Color Purple* (1983). They have also explored all the highways and byways they thought attractive and appropriate, and while the numerous signs declaring the novel territory for "Men Only: No Trespassers Allowed" have undoubtedly deterred many women, it has never been possible for the border guards to keep all women writers at bay.

Now as the twentieth century draws towards its close, it seems likely that women writers are at last not simply making ground, but holding on to their gains and the ground that has been won. The battle, predictably, is not over.

Whatever the authority of women's writing, its individual practitioners cannot always shake off the sense of strangeness with which their productions are likely to be greeted. It is as if there is some irreconcilable tension between the two realities of being a writer and being a woman. Alison Lurie's writer-heroine finds that only another woman is aware of and understands this:

> . . . I met H.H. Waters in the vegetable garden. . . . One of the best conversations about writing I've ever had. Maybe because HHW . . . knows what it is to be a "lady writer". . . .
>
> Really most people don't like the idea of a serious woman writer, or find it incongruous. They prefer to forget either that you're a writer or that you're a woman. . . . (Lurie, 1969, pp. 82–83)

In a sense, then, the hard work is only just beginning. The struggle to abandon the restrictive categories of "masculine" and "feminine" together with the pejorative associations of the label "woman writer," has yet to be seriously engaged. Further, taken simply as individual females rather than in relation to men and to society, women have not easily freed themselves from long centuries of fictional exploitation. The stress upon women's sexuality has become a means of obscuring or denying their full humanity. While their rational, creative, or administrative skills go largely unremarked, their bodies prove a goldmine for others, mainly men; both individuals and corporations have been making huge sums of money out of the partial and degraded representations of women as sexual creatures and sex objects, in a series of developments not as far removed from the protected calm of the "lady novelist's" study as many would like to think. This degradation of women is further accomplished in the contemporary cult of brutalism, with its vaunting of masculine aggression, hostility, and violence. When women writers acquiesce in this disparagement of their sex or lend themselves to lowering it still further, then the result is particularly depressing.

Accordingly, there is now much to be done that only women can do, in the recognition and weeding out of some continuing notions, in the readjustment, where possible, of the historical bias against women. As long as the accepted mode of society remains masculine in its orientation, then the general consciousness will continue to be influenced by attitudes inherited from the pursuit of two world wars and the virtually unchanged possession by males of all property, authority, and power. In this situation, the position of women both as subjects and authors of fiction will need to avoid remaining "special," anomalous, and disadvantaged. It is significant that even in the most futuristic avenues of the so-called "apocalyptic" novel in America or in that odd sport of fiction, the sci-fi novel, there are few real advances posited for the female of the species. Writers who are capable of dreaming up horrendous changes affecting total environment, technology, and personality, still see change as affecting every area of human experience other than this.

With a few notable exceptions, very markedly in the work of "sci-fi" writers

like Suzette Hagen Elgin, Ursula Le Guin, and Joanna Russ, female characters continue to mainly meander through the unimaginative timescapes of
the future, still "emotional," still in need of masculine domination, and still
unable to understand the workings of the internal combustion engine, or even
how to use a screwdriver.

To work against this is still the major task for writers as women (see Nicki
Gerard, 1989, for further discussion). As creative artists, they must widen their
field of vision: it is only by developing a sense of others and of the ways in
which individuals interact within society, that women writers will free themselves and their sisters from the constrictions of sex-typing and of the sex-
based stereotype. To make the particular the general: to assert the power of
the female's full and compelling humanity; to go outward with a sense of community; to look to the moral rather than the purely emotional dimension; to
make the right choice and to make it work; that is the task and the obligation.
Writers need to be constantly on the alert for the dangerous encroachments
of these belittling assumptions, must resist the temptation of the creeping sug-
gestive generalization. Twentieth-century fiction must make an effort to shake
off the rags and tatters of nineteenth-century fiction that still hang about it.
It should seek to develop the growth of psychological and sociological knowledge in discovering ways for men and women to live together, free and equal.
Then, and only then, will we have the novels that will make "woman's novel"
a fatuous and superannuated phrase.

As to the women themselves, they see different scenarios for the future
of the novel and the freedom of the women writing within it. Bertha Harris,
author of the experimental lesbian novel *Lover* (1976), envisaged a future free
of the sex war, free of man-the-enemy because free of man:

> There is not a literature that is not based on the pervasive sexuality of its time;
> and as that which is male disappears (sinks slowly in the west) and as the origi-
> nal all-female world reasserts itself by making love to itself, the primary gesture
> leading to the making at last of a decent literature out of a decent world might
> simply be a woman like Djuna Barnes [author of the lesbian novel *Nightwood*]
> and all she might represent down a single street on a particular afternoon. (Harris,
> 1976, p. 137)

Yet other women writers feel strongly about the work that still has to be done
in the world of men, much of it because men are unable or unwilling to confront it themselves. As the black woman writer Alexis de Veaux expressed
it to Claudia Tate in Tate's anthology, *Black Women Writers at Work* (1985):

> Men are more afraid because of the way they are taught to experience them-
> selves, and because they have such a heavy burden to live up to in terms of
> what they think manhood is. . . . Women have a certain primary sense of things
> like blood, which is life. . . . Men also seem more conservative in their treat-
> ment of "taboo" themes. Women tend to explore subjects that are not taken seri-
> ously by male writers, or that are far less concerned with bravado and being

number one, and some other mythologies created by their male experience. . . . male writers are less inclined to want to explore new themes, new images of themselves. (Tate, 1985, p. 54)

"New themes, new images," women's versions of the world where men and women will live together, free and equal—these have the gleam of tremendous promise. So too does the idea of a female culture acting as an intellectual center and emotional base for all women writers to draw on and come home to at need. The female culture will only be fostered and allowed to grow by a renewed and sustained attention to women's experience in its every manifestation. Yet this is not without its problems and traps. The radical separatist, feminist demand that would tie women to writing only of the world of women would not seem to be a wholly fulfilling direction for either women writers or the novel to take. On the other hand, any denial of the validity of women's lives and experience— any denial—is inescapably the same old misogyny rising up from the prime-val swamp, whether expressed by a man or, as frequently happens, a woman. This denial can take many forms, can even come on in the guise of "encourage-ment" to women writers to "realize their potential." Something of this sort seems to be at work in the often-expressed desire for women writers to transcend their sexual identity and become "writers only," dealing with "the real busi-ness of the world." Has anyone ever expected Tolstoy, Dickens, Hardy, Lawrence, Scott Fitzgerald, or Hemingway to make this transcendence? Al-though espoused by a number of writers and critics, of whom the most dis-tinguished remains Virginia Woolf, this theory of the woman writer aspiring to an androgynous nirvana where she would be neither male nor female was, is, and always will be inescapably derogatory to the individual woman, to the work she has produced, and the whole of the female tradition that lies behind her.

How strong that tradition is may be illustrated by the treatment of just one theme, picked at random from a cluster of books by women, old and new: the experience of abortion. An early account of Colette's in *The Pure and the Impure* (1932) hints at the psychic pain of a woman involved in this most lonely of actions:

Married to man she hated, my narrator had not dared to confess her despair when she fancied she was pregnant, except to an old footman, an ancient cor-rupter of princelings, a valet she feared.
    He brought me a concoction to drink," she said, touched at the recollection, "He and he alone in the world pitied me. . . . What he gave me was pretty hor-rible. . . . I remember I wept. . . ."
    "With grief?"
    "No, I cried because, while I swallowed that horror, the old fellow tried to hearten me by calling me *nina* and *porbrecita,* just as he had when I was a child." (Colette, 1932, p. 79)

Later, Marge Piercy was able to use the abortion itself as a metaphor for her heroine's condition: "she was caught, she was stalled. She floated like an embryo in alcohol, that awful thing the Right to Life people had in that van on the street" (1976, p. 20). Yet the woman trapped in an unwanted pregnancy is not always simply a victim:

> "I'm going into hospital on Monday." Dolly fluffed her hair. "I persuaded him not to use that butcher on me. It cost a lot, but it will be a real hospital operation. Not with that butcher who does it on the whores cheap." Dolly spoke with pride. (Piercy, 1976, p. 20)

The opposite experience, of the woman who has to carry out these abortions, is the focus of Fay Weldon's concern in *Praxis* (1978):

> I expect you're right [Mary writes to Praxis on the question of a woman's right to choose] but I feel you're wrong. I spent most of a year on a gynae ward. I was the one who got blood on my surgical gloves, remember, actually doing abortions. I'd do it happily for the older women who at least knew what was going on and were as distressed as I was, but I resented having to do it for the girls who used me as a last-ditch contraceptive because they didn't want their holidays interfered with. (Weldon, 1978, p. 255)

Provocatively, the "right to life" argument is juxtaposed with an account straight from the heart of what it is to have to care for a newborn baby:

> The household was under considerable strain. Serena's baby had infantile eczema, and cried and cried, and scratched and scratched, and had to be fed on goat's milk, and dressed in muslin, and receive Serena's full attention. Philip could not sleep. Work dried up again. Serena and the baby spent most of their nights in the spare room. The royal child, confused by the ups and downs in his life, wet his bed and soiled his pants. Serena, her eyes wide with strain and dismay, did her breathing exercises, started each day with a glassful of wine vinegar and honey, and achieved the lotus position, but little else. (Weldon, 1978, p. 256)

Now women could not only discover for themselves what such moments and episodes might mean, but with the freedom to publish came the even greater freedoms: to share and compare these quintessentially female experiences with other writers and readers, and, through their characters, to create different and opposing versions of the same event, to construct and contain contrarieties. Now, at last, women are producing the narrative voice, and the quantity and quality of work that will overthrow the long-established assumption that women writers are somehow "not there" yet—that they still have journeys to make, distances to travel, changes to undergo, before they "arrive" as novelists. George Eliot (1856) while considering that women had the potential to write great novels—"we have only to pour in the right elements: genuine observation, humour and passion"—seems to have been sublimely unaware that she herself had raised the novel to heights previously unattained and not subsequently exceeded. Virginia Woolf also pinned her hopes on the future;

on the famous "five hundred a year, and a room of one's own," on "the habit of freedom and the courage to write exactly what we think" (p. 123):

> Then the opportunity will come and the dead poet who was Shakespeare's sister will put on the body she has so often laid down. (Woolf, 1929, p. 142)

Even Elaine Showalter, in her impressive study of women writers, A Literature of Their Own, strikes at last the part-visionary, part-hopeless note of "next year in Jerusalem":

> If contact with a female tradition and a female culture is a center; if women take strength in their independence to act in the world, then Shakespeare's sister, whose coming Woolf asked us to await in patience and humility, may appear at last. Beyond fantasy, beyond androgyny, beyond assimilation, the female tradition holds the promise of an art that may yet fulfil the hopes of Eliot and Woolf. (Showalter, 1977, p. 319)

"May yet?" Along with the "patience and humility" recommended above, this apologetic timidity is exactly what has prevented women novelists and critics from laying claim to the multiple greatnesses women have achieved. Always the expectation of women fulfilling the promise of the novel is set somewhere in the future—yet, from the moment when women first picked up the pen, the target has mysteriously and steadily receded before them. Even the women who, by any standards, were conquering the heights, were still led to believe that they were merely toiling away in the foothills—that somewhere in the future lay the woman writer, the woman's novel, that would justify the efforts and existence of all.

In the past, carrying the countless chains and scars of their subordination which they struggled with mixed success to cast off, women writers had a double task. They had both to write the novels and continuously to negotiate their right and space to do so. Small wonder then that they could take nothing for granted, not even their own individual success, as the bench mark of their worth. Criticism can now right the centuries-old wrong that has been done to generations of women writers and, in asserting the triumph of the form, insist without contradiction that from its foundation the novel has been and remains the female form.

## REFERENCES

Barthes, Roland. (1972). Mythologies. Paris: Editions du Seuil.

Burney, Fanny. (1778). Evelina. London: Thomas Lowndes.

Colette. (1932). The Pure and the impure. [Originally Ces Plaisirs, title changed to Le Pur et L'Impur, 1941. English edition, London: Secker and Warburg, 1968].

Eliot, George. (1856). Silly novels by lady novelists. The Westminster Review 66, 442–461. In Thomas Pinney (Ed.), Essays of George Eliot. London: Routledge and Kegan Paul.

Eliot, George. (1858). Scenes of clerical life (2 Vols.). Edinburgh: Blackwood.

Ellmann, Mary. (1968). Thinking about women. New York: Harcourt Brace.

Gass, William. (1971). *Fiction and the figures of life.* London: Carcanet Press.

Gerrard, Nicci. (1989). *Into the mainstream: How feminism has changed women's writing.* London: Pandora Press.

Harris, Bertha. (1976). *Lover.* New York: Harcourt Brace Jovanovitch.

Lodge, David. (1966). *The language of fiction.* London: Routledge and Kegan Paul.

Lurie, Alison. (1969). *Real people.* London: Heinemann.

Mailer, Norman. (1967). *Cannibals and christians.* London: Andre Deutsch.

Mailer, Norman. (1971). *The prisoner of sex.* London: Allen and Unwin.

Mainiero, Lisa (Ed.) (1979–1981). *American women writers: A critical reference guide from colonial times to the present* (4 Vols.). New York: Frederick Ungar.

Piercy, Marge. (1976). *Woman on the edge of time.* London: Penguin.

Seymour-Smith, Martin. (1980). *A reader's guide to fifty European novels.* London: Heinemann.

Showalter, Elaine. (1977). *A literature of their own: British women novelists from Brontë to Lessing.* Princeton, NJ: Princeton University Press.

Spacks, Patricia Meyer. (1976). *Contemporary women novelists: A collection of critical essays.* Englewood Cliffs, NJ: Prentice Hall.

Spender, Dale. (1986). *Mothers of the novel: 100 good women writers before Jane Austen.* London: Pandora Press.

Spender, Dale. (1989). *The writing or the sex? or why you don't have to read women's writing to know it's no good.* Elmsford, NY: Pergamon Press.

Tate, Claudia (Ed.). (1985). *Black women writers at work.* Harpenden: Oldcastle Books.

Todd, Janet (Ed.) 1984). *A dictionary of British and American women writers 1660–1800.* London: Methuen.

Walker, Alice. (1983). *The color purple.* New York: Harcourt Brace Jovanovitch.

Weldon, Fay. (1978). *Praxis.* London: Hodder and Stoughton.

Wilson, Colin. (1975). *The craft of the novel.* London: Victor Gollancz.

Woolf, Virginia. (1929). *A room of one's own.* London: Hogarth Press.

# Afterword:

## The Wages of Writing

=== Dale Spender ===

From the contributions to this volume it is clear that in the eighteenth century, women made their entry to the British world of letters and began the process of "living by the pen." Some of the reasons for their success, (and some of the rates of pay they received) are the substance of this "afterword," which seeks to summarize the gains that were made by the professional woman writer of this period.

It has been suggested that one of the main reasons for the rise of the woman writer—particularly the woman fiction writer—was that this was a time when more people became literate; as Jane Spencer (1986) has commented, the "expansion of the reading public to include the urban middle classes— tradesmen, shopkeepers, clerks and their families—and also to some extent, servants, has long been seen as the underlying social condition of the novel's rise" (p. 6). But if the extension of literacy made possible the emergence of the novel, it could also be said that the advent of the novel served as an impetus for the growth of literacy. Then—as now— the need *to be able to read* novels *in order to read* novels, could be quite a compelling one indeed.

But the growth of a reading public, on its own, was not sufficient to account for the expansion in professional opportunities for women; other social, political, and economic structures also had to change before women could find themselves published, and paid. One such system that required modification was that of *patronage*.

While engagement in the world of letters had been primarily an aristocratic pursuit, where the wealthy had acted as patrons for the few talented artists, women had effectively been excluded from production. But as reading (and writing) became more popular activities, the old forms of control were eroded and tradespeople, such as publishers and booksellers, rather than the privileged class, could "finance" authors; and this meant that the possibilities of a literary career were opened up to a new a breed of writers. This, of course, was precisely Pope's objection; that with the arrival of these scribblers, many of whom were women, the standards of literature had been lowered. And

237

he was not the only one to deplore the decline from art to trade, and the way in which women were bringing literature into disrepute.

> The debasement of literature in the market place was made even worse when women were successful sellers, and this "branch of the literary *trade*", sniffed one reviewer (meaning novel writing) "appears now to be almost entirely engrossed by the Ladies." (Jane Spencer, 1986; p. 4 quoting from *Monthly Review*, 1773; 48; p. 154)

The new tradespeople, however, did not always have the capital to completely support the new class of writers. Nor did they always have the inclination to risk their capital on the future success of a particular publication. In this context the method of publication by subscription developed as a convenient arrangement.

*Subscription* was something of a halfway house between individual patrons and mass sales; it is a practice which is documented by Cheryl Turner in her excellent thesis, *The Growth of Published and Professional Fiction Written by Women Before Jane Austen* (1985). A method of publication which became widely used during the eighteenth century, subscription was the means whereby a group of people—sometimes friends of the author—were persuaded to put up the money for publication. This ensured that the cost, and the risks, were shared. The process did involve:

> . . . securing an adequate list of investors for a projected work, whose contributions were paid partly in advance and partly on receipt of the book. Various devices were employed to attract support, such as advertisements in newspapers, selling subscription tickets in parks or resorts, or by inserting the proposal into a previous publication as Mrs. Brooke did for her projected translation of *Il Pastor Fido*. (Cheryl Turner, 1985, p. 280)

In these circumstances to have a wide circle of willing friends, particularly those who were solvent, could certainly help. Which is one reason that Fanny Burney made the most money from this form of sponsorship, for her novel *Camilla* (1796). According to Cheryl Turner, Fanny Burney allegedly cleared 3,000 guineas from the sale; "as the third novel of a fêted and successful author it was eagerly awaited" (p. 281) but it was also because Fanny Burney had spent time at court, and had wealthy and influential friends prepared to subscribe, that *Camilla* was so financially successful.

Another positive factor about subscription was that it gave women readers as well as women writers a role in literary production. While few women would have had the means to individually support a writer, an increasing number were able to subscribe, to become an important source of funding, and a "consulted" audience, for the emerging professional woman writer.

Not that women were allowed to declare an interest in financial matters; it was not done for women writers to reveal that they were ambitious, or that they wanted to make money. Indeed it could be argued that the more visible women became in the profession, the more pressure there was on them to deny that they were motivated by fortune or fame. Nowhere is this more apparent than in their prefaces where women felt obliged to excuse and explain their presence in the marketplace. Janet Todd has commented that throughout the eighteenth century:

> . . . as the sentimental, passive stance grew essential for women, in their prefaces they pleaded circumstances to prevent criticism and apologize[d] for the act of writing. Many (including Charlotte Smith, Eliza Fenwick and Charlotte Lennox) gave children as the excuse while others blamed a "sick husband" or "ancient" relative. (1984, p. 8)

Called on to account for her entry to the profession, the woman writer frequently was forced to maintain that it wasn't really her choice, and that therefore it wasn't her fault; it was *necessity* that had pushed her to trespass on men's territory. And many were the women writers who went on to insist that their professional status had not been achieved at the expense of their womanliness; they were still women before they were authors. Even Fanny Burney was adamant that she would sacrifice her authorship for her womanly image.

> Jane West declared that domestic duties always preceded writing, while Samuel Johnson said admiringly of the immensely scholarly Elizabeth Carter that she "could make a pudding as well as translate Epictetus." (Janet Todd, 1984, p. 8)

Women writers were prepared to go to considerable lengths to appease men, to assure them that they didn't want to be on the literary scene, that they weren't being ruined by such exposure, and that the little that they did make was not for luxuries, but necessities. In the preface to *Memoirs of the Miss Holmsbys*, (1788), Sarah Emma Spencer justified her authorship with the testimony that the manuscript had been "written by the bedside of a sick husband who has no other support than what my writing will produce" (quoted in *Monthly Review*, 1789, p. 169).

No doubt some women did resent having the role of breadwinner thrust upon them, and genuinely did protest that they wrote only because they needed the money. As Janet Todd points out, even some of the best writers of the period registered their reluctance to sell their literary labor.

> Elizabeth Inchbald complained of being forced to authorship, Charlotte Smith bitterly resented her dependence on her pen, and Sarah Fielding claimed she wrote because of "Distress" in her circumstances. (Janet Todd, 1984, p. 8)

To this day there are women writers who can feel that literature is a vocation, that writers have "a gift," and that to treat the creative task of authorship as a trade or business is crass and crude. So it is understandable that in Fanny Burney's era, for example, it was seen as undignified, even as vulgar, for an author to be interested in profit. But even authors need food and shelter, and to be able to provide for their progeny if they are to write, as Fanny Burney explained in a letter written just before the publication of *Camilla:*

> Should it succeed, like "Evelina" and "Cecilia," it may be a little portion to our Bambino. We wish, therefore, to print it for ourselves in this hope; but the expenses of the press are so enormous, so raised by these late Acts, that it is out of all question for us to afford it. We have, therefore, been led by degrees to listen to counsel of some friends, and to print it by subscription. This is in many-many ways unpleasant and unpalatable to us both; but the real chance of real use and benefit to our little darling overcomes all scruples, and therefore, to work we go! (Fanny Burney, p. 45)

But if Fanny Burney could afford to overcome her objections to touting her wares (and her friends could afford to subscribe) there were other women writers who were not so fortunate; with neither patrons, nor subscribers, they were required to convince publishers and booksellers that their manuscripts would be a big success, and then to sell them outright.

> Although there were distinct advantages to direct sale of copyright for women authors, the prices paid for novel manuscripts were generally low. Overall, there seems to have been a slight upward trend in payments for unexceptional material concurrent with the rise in retail prices, from a span of between two and five guineas in the earlier eighteenth century, to between five and ten guineas towards the end of the period. Thus the bulk of the popular novels, including those by women, were probably sold to the publishers for around the five guineas received by Phoebe Gibbes from T. Lowndes on 14th April 1763, "for the novel called The Life of Mr. Francis Clive."
>
> A number of authors managed to secure more for their material. Booksellers were occasionally induced to pay over twice the normal price for a better quality manuscript, or for one by a well-known author. Lowndes paid £20 for Burney's *Evelina* (1778), which in the event was well under its market value, and he paid a similar but more appropriate sum of twenty guineas for Sophia Briscoe's *Fine Lady* (1772). Anne Dawe obtained the same price for her *Younger Sister* (1770). A few authors were the recipients of considerably higher sums. After the success of *Evelina* (1778), Fanny Burney was able to extract £250 from Payne and Cadell for her second novel, whilst Ann Yearsley, then famous as Hannah More's "Milkmaid," received £200 for her *The Royal Captives* (1795). Such prices were rarely paid for any copyright, particularly for novels, but they were exceeded by the remarkable £500 and £600 paid by Robinson for Ann Radcliffe's *The Mysteries of Udolpho* (1794) and *The Italian* (1797), respectively. (Cheryl Turner, 1985, pp. 288–299)

The majority of women writers received payments in the between-two-and-ten-guineas-category and as the average copyright fee was roughly equivalent to the annual wages of a laundry, scullery, or dairy maid, they had to write many novels if they were to earn "respectable incomes" (of about fifty pounds per annum). "A novelist would have to write and publish as many as ten novels a year (which even the prolific Eliza Haywood only achieved in 1725) or like most other professionals she had to diversify into as many types of literature as possible" (Turner, 1985, p. 291).

Hence the number of women novelists who also wrote plays and poems, as well as providing translations, and who ventured into the equally new area of journalism and women's magazines. And of course there were the associated literary activities which developed with the expansion of the literary market; editing, reviewing, cataloguing—all of these were employment for the professional woman.

But again, Fanny Burney was fortunate, even when she sold one manuscript outright; she gives some idea of the difference in payment between women authors in the letter that she wrote to her father just before the publication of her last novel, *The Wanderer*, (1814):

> I am indescribably occupied, and have been so ever since my return from Ramsgate, in giving more and more last touches to my work, about which I begin to grow very anxious. I am to receive merely £500 upon delivery of the M.S.; the two following £500 by installments from nine months to nine months, that is, in a year and a half from the day of *publication*.
>
> If all goes well, the whole will be £3,000, but only at the end of the sale of eight thousand copies. (Fanny Burney, 1813, pp. 14–15)

In contrast most professional women writers expected to survive by selling many works at low prices; for Delarivière Manley, Eliza Haywood, Charlotte Lennox, Ann Skinn, Elizabeth Griffith, Frances Brooke, and Sarah Fielding, for example, life was "a continual struggle against poverty, and they required opportunism, assiduity, luck and talent in order to survive" (Cheryl Turner, 1985, p. 290).

The living that the various women writers made by their pen provides a fascinating study; while many of the records have been lost and much can only be speculation there is still sufficient material available to provide a few profiles. Mary Davys, for example, made five guineas from her first novel (1705) "but the coffee shop she set up in Cambridge seems to have provided a more regular support" (Jane Spencer, 1986, p. 11):

> Later in the century Sarah Scott, of very good family and with enough to live on after separating from her husband, wrote novels to add to her income. She remarked that though she received very little for *Millenium Hall* (1762) she had taken less than a month to write it and so had been paid about a guinea a day for her efforts.

Sarah Fielding had a few literary "patrons" (she was given some support by Elizabeth Montagu), but a couple of her novels were also profitable, including *Familiar Letters Between the Principal Characters in David Simple* (1747) which had 500 subscribers and sold at ten shillings a copy.

And of course, by the beginning of the 19th century "Jane Austen, as an unknown, got 10 guineas for *Sense and Sensibility*" (Jane Spencer, 1986, p. 8).

Charlotte Smith's domestic circumstances have been documented in earlier chapters, and the fact that it was widely known that she was "obliged to purchase her freedom from a vile husband" by writing, (Charlotte Smith, 1817, p. 295) helped to justify her literary pursuit, and payment.

If she had to write, Charlotte Smith would have preferred to pen poetry (which was her first publication, and a self-financed one), and she would have preferred even greater payments than the more lucrative novel provided. The author of nine novels, all of which went to three, four or five volumes, Charlotte Smith was paid approximately £50 per volume; they were then sold at between three and four shillings a copy. But with twelve children, Charlotte Smith complained that even this remuneration was not enough to support the family.

> My situation is extremely terrible—for I have no means whatever of supporting my Children during the Holidays, nor of paying their Bills when they return to School; & I am so harassed with Duns, that I cannot write with any hope of getting anything done by that time—I know not where I find resolution to go on from day to day—Especially under the idea of Mr Smith's being in London, liable every hour to imprisonment. (Charlotte Smith, 28 Dec 1791; Bod. MS Eng.Lett.c. 365, fol 60.)

One of the most steadily successful professional women writers was Elizabeth Inchbald. She began her career as an actress, and in the early stages she certainly endured periods of poverty (at one time being reduced to eating raw turnips taken from a field as her only form of nourishment). As an established actress she was paid £3 per week and in 1782 she received £20 for a play that she had written. Because her work proved to be so popular she went on to have eleven of her plays accepted and she received £600 for one of them; a hundred guineas was the price paid for *The Mogul Tale, or the Descent of the Balloon,* which was produced at the Haymarket in 1784, and she was offered £1,000 for her memoirs! As a novelist she also earned quite a living from her pen:

> Elizabeth Inchbald received initial payments of £200 and £150 respectively, for her novels, *A Simple Story* (1791) and *Nature and Art* (1796). These were high fees, but not unprecedented for a celebrated writer. The novels were a publishing success, and as second edition of *A Simple Story* was ordered less than three months after the first. On the basis of this Robinson was prepared to pay £600 for their extended copyright and they were sold again in 1810 to Longman. In total she earned over £1,000 from the two novels. (Cheryl Turner, 1985, pp. 289–290)

Elizabeth Inchbald was not an average woman writer, but the fact that by the end of the eighteenth century she could earn such a substantial living by her pen, is an indication of the extent to which women writers had become professionals. They might still apologize for their achievements, plead dire necessity and take pains to prove that they had not lost their womanliness, but this did not really disguise the gains they had made. The authors of more than two thirds of the novels (F.G. Black, 1940) and the authors who enjoyed the greater commercial sales, the women might have been accused of lowering the standard by their entry, but they were also clearly seen as a threat; which is why Cheryl Turner concludes her chapter, "Professional Women Writers and the Novel" with the comment:

> Perhaps the most dramatic indicator of their commercial status as popular novelists is the behaviour of these male authors who reversed the procedure and adopted female pseudonyms in order to facilitate the sale of their material. (Turner, 1985, p. 307)

## REFERENCES

Black, F. G. (1940). *The epistolary novel in the late eighteenth century.* Eugene: University of Oregon Press.

Burney, Fanny. (1813). Letter to Dr. Burney, 12 Oct 1813. In Edward A. Bloom & Lillian D. Bloom (Eds.), *The journals and letters of Madam D'Arblay, VII.* Oxford: Oxford University Press.

Burney, Fanny. (1795). Letter to Mrs. —. 15 June 1795. In Joyce Hemlow et al. (Eds.), *The journals and letters of Madame D'Arblay, VI.* Oxford: Oxford University Press.

Figes, Eve. (1990). *Sex and subterfuge: Women writers to 1850.* London: Pandora.

Smith, Charlotte. (1817). *Letters from Mrs Elizabeth Carter to Mrs. Montagu,* Vol III. London: FC & J Rivington.

Spencer, Jane. (1986). *The rise of the woman novelist: From Aphra Behn to Jane Austen.* Oxford: Basil Blackwell.

Todd, Janet. (1984). *A dictionary of British and American women writers, 1660–1800.* London: Methuen.

Turner, Cheryl. (1985). The growth of published and professional fiction written by women before Jane Austen. Ph.D. Thesis, University of Nottingham.

# Author Index

# Subject Index

# About the Editors
and Contributors

## ABOUT THE EDITOR

Dale Spender is the author/editor of thirty books and with Cheris Kramarae is currently editing the *International Encyclopedia of Women's Studies* (WISE, Pergamon Press). Her publications include *Man Made Language; Women of Ideas—and what men have done to them; Mothers of the Novel; The Pandora Anthology of British Women Writers* (with Janet Todd); *The Writing or the Sex? or why you don't have to read women's writing to know it's no good; The Diary of Elizabeth Pepys;* and *The Knowledge Explosion; Generations of Feminist Scholarship* (with Cheris Kramarae). She has also written about Australian women writers and is the editor of the Penguin Australian Women's Library and other series. She is currently working on *Talking Comfort; Women's Language;* is researching and writing in the area of the relationship between computers and the literary tradition; and is concerned with the nature of knowledge requirements for the twenty-first century. She would like to live in one place but with her constant companion, her Toshiba laptop.

## ABOUT THE CONTRIBUTORS

**Katherine Anne Ackley** is professor of English, assistant to the dean of graduate studies and is in her ninth year as coordinator of the Women's Studies Program at the University of Wisconsin—Stevens Point. Her book *The Novels of Barbara Pym* was published in 1989, and *Women and Violence in Literature: An Essay Collection* (edited) has also been published. *Essays from Contemporary Culture* is forthcoming in 1992. She has been a participant in the National Endowment for the Humanities Summer School and has been the recipient of scholarly awards and grants.

**Ros Ballaster** was educated at Oxford (St. Hilda's College and St. Cross College) and has been a visiting fellow in the Department of English and Ameri-

257

can Literature at Harvard University (1988–89). She has written articles on women and romance reading, and eighteenth-century women writers. She is interested in critical theory, popular fiction, and women's writing in the period of 1650–1850.

**Pat Elliott** is writing director and nineteenth-century specialist at Regis College, Weston, Massachusetts.

**Heidi Hutner** teaches English at Hunter College of the City University of New York. A Ph.D. candidate in English at the Graduate Center of the City University of New York, she is currently at work on the problems of gender, race, and class in the late-seventeenth and eighteenth centuries. She is presently editing a volume of essays on the plays, novels, and poetry of Aphra Behn.

**Mary McKerrow** was born in Warwickshire and educated in North Wales and at Liverpool University, where she graduated in classics and English literature. She has collaborated in the translation from Latin of the Historiae Scotorum for Caroline Bingham's *The Stewart Kingdom of Scotland 1371–1603,* and she has written a variety of articles on Scottish authors. In 1982, her biography of *The Faeds* was published, and *A Biography of Mary Brunton* is forthcoming.

**Rosalind Miles** is the founder of the center for Women's Studies at Coventry Polytechnic and author of *Danger! Men at Work, Women and Power* and *The Female Form; Women Writers and the Conquest of the Novel.* She was educated at St. Hilda's College, Oxford, and subsequently studied at the Shakespeare Institute, University of Birmingham, where she completed her Ph.D. Her most recent book is *The Women's History of the World,* which is to be made into a documentary film series. She now works as a writer, lecturer, broadcaster in Europe, America, and Australia and lives in Warwickshire, where she was born.

**Mitzi Myers** currently teaches writing and literature at the University of California, Los Angeles, where she is also a research associate of the Center for the Study of Women. She has published numerous essays on early women writers, including Mary Wollstonecraft, Hannah More, and Maria Edgeworth and is currently working on a book-length study of Edgeworth's family romances and children's stories. She has won awards and grants from the Children's Literary Association, the American Philosophical Association, and the National Endowment for the Humanities.

**Katharine M. Rogers,** research professor of literature at the American University, is the author of *Feminism in Eighteenth Century England* and coeditor of *The Meridian Anthology of Early Women Writers; British Literary Women from Aphra Behn to Maria Edgeworth.* She is currently at work on a companion volume of early American women writers.

**Mary Anne Schofield,** a professor of English, is the author of *Masking and Unmasking the Female Mind; Disguise Romances in Feminine Fiction, 1713–1799* (University of Delaware Press, 1989); *Eliza Haywood* (G.K. Hall, 1985); and *Quiet Rebellion; The Fictional Heroines of Eliza Haywood* (University Press of America, 1981). She has edited many reprints of eighteenth-century women's novels for Scholars' Facsimiles and Reprints and has co-edited two first-of-a-kind collections of critical essays about eighteenth-century women; *Fetter'd or Free? British Women Novelists, 1690–1815* and *Curtain Calls; British and American Women in the Theatre, 1660–1810.* She has edited *Cooking by the Book; Food in Literature and Culture* and has published widely in professional journals. She is currently working on a book about the women writers of World War II.

**Judy Simons** is senior lecturer in English at Sheffield City Polytechnic, where she specializes in the teaching of fiction and of women's writing. She is author of *Fanny Burney* in Macmillan's "Women Writers" series (1987) and has written a critical introduction to Virago's reissue of Fanny Burney's *Cecilia* (1986). She has also published *Masterguides* to Jane Austen's *Sense and Sensibility* and *Persuasion.* In addition to numerous articles, she has also written regular reviews of feminist criticism. Currently she is working on a study of the journals and diaries of literary women, from Fanny Burney to Virginia Woolf.

**Jane Spencer** is a lecturer in English literature at the University of Exeter. She is the author of *The Rise of the Woman Novelist; from Aphra Behn to Jane Austen* (1986) and a forthcoming volume on Elizabeth Gaskell.

**Helen Thomson** is a senior lecturer in the English Department at Monash University, Victoria, Australia. She combines her interest in the written word with a commitment to the performing arts and has been a theater and dance critic for Australian periodicals for several years. She has lived in England, Germany, and the United States, and her primary academic interests are eighteenth-century women writers and Australian literature; she lectures in the area of contemporary drama, publishes in the area of women's writing, and is consulting editor for the Penguin Australian Women's Library.

**Carolyn Woodward** is an assistant professor of English at the University of New Mexico, Albuquerque, where she teaches feminist theory and eighteenth-century British literature. She has edited *Changing Our Power:*

*An Introduction to Women's Studies* (forthcoming 1990). Her current projects include a critical study of the work of Sarah Fielding and an investigation into the relationship between the development of feminist theory in eighteenth-century Britain and experiments in narrative form in fiction written by eighteenth-century British women.